PHOTO-ATTRACTIONS

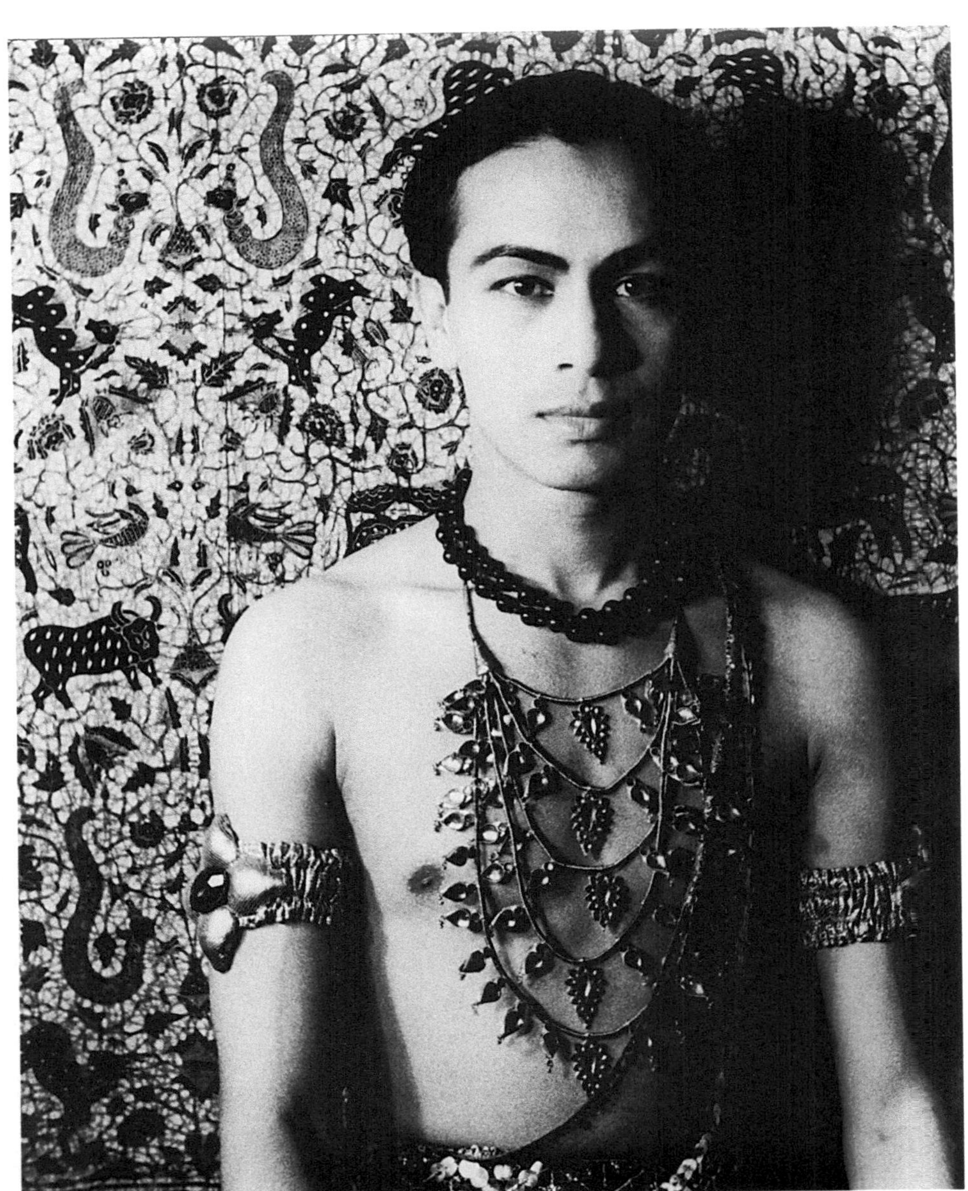

PHOTO-ATTRACTIONS

An Indian Dancer, an American Photographer, and a German Camera

AJAY J. SINHA

Rutgers University Press | New Brunswick, Camden and Newark, New Jersey, and London

Library of Congress Cataloging-in-Publication Data
Names: Sinha, Ajay J., 1956– author.
Title: Photo-attractions : an Indian dancer, an American photographer, and a German camera / Ajay Sinha.
Description: New Brunswick, New Jersey : Rutgers University Press, [2023] | Commentary on and selections from black and white photographs by Carl Van Vechten from the Beinecke Rare Book and Manuscript Library. | Includes bibliographical references and index.
Identifiers: LCCN 2022007401 |
ISBN 9781978830486 (paperback) |
ISBN 9781978830493 (hardcover) |
ISBN 9781978830509 (epub) |
ISBN 9781978830523 (pdf)
Subjects: LCSH: Ram Gopal, 1917– —Portraits. | Dancers—India—Portraits. | Portrait photography. | Van Vechten, Carl, 1880–1964. | Photographers—United States. | Harlem Renaissance. | Beinecke Rare Book and Manuscript Library—Photograph collections.
Classification: LCC GV1785.R3 S56 2023 |
DDC 792.802/8092—dc23/eng/20220422
LC record available at https://lccn.loc.gov/2022007401

A British Cataloging-in-Publication record for this book is available from the British Library.

∞ The paper used in this publication meets the requirements of the American National Standard for Information Sciences—Permanence of Paper for Printed Library Materials, ANSI Z39.48–1992.

www.rutgersuniversitypress.org

Manufactured in the United States of America

FOR ELDERS

CONTENTS

PHOTO-ATTRACTIONS

PRELUDE

This is the story of a discovery that lingered like a puzzle and grew into a book. In spring 2015, I participated in a semester-long conference of scholars and practitioners of photography that gathered monthly at Yale University to reflect on global photography and assess the collection of South Asian photography at the Beinecke Rare Book and Manuscript Library. Our public presentations were followed by closed sessions at the library, where we were mostly shown images of picturesque places, royal processions, political rallies, and vignettes of village life, along with leisurely afternoons at luxury hotels, taken by American tourists in India in the early twentieth century. In between these structured sessions, I wandered in the library on my own, and struck a cache of 111 black and white photographs that stopped me in my tracks. In front of my eyes, a beautiful young man wearing fantastical costumes and gold ornaments took a variety of dance poses against fabric backgrounds and careful arrangement of lighting. The images, each an enlargement of approximately eight by ten inches, were meticulously framed on cardboard mounts. The back included a personal stamp of a photographer named Carl Van Vechten and a negative number and a date in

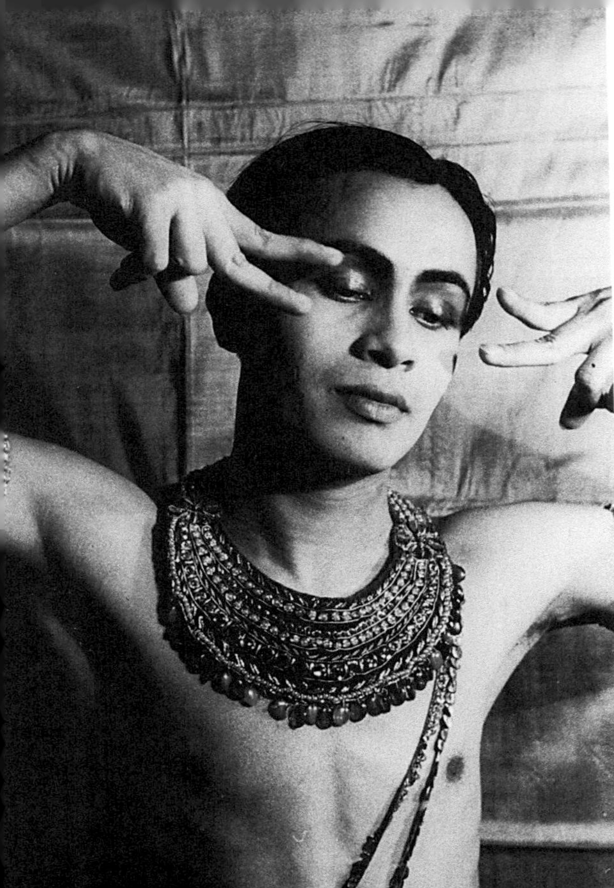

Figures P.1 and P.2. Carl Van Vechten, *Ram Gopal*, May 11, 1938, XX M0, front and back. (Beinecke Rare Book and Manuscript Library, Yale University; © The Van Vechten Trust)

April and May 1938 written in pencil and sometimes green ink. The dancer was named Ram Gopal (figs. P.1 and P.2).

No one in the conference knew about the existence of the set, the photographer, or the subject. Given that the conference focused mostly on photographs taken in South Asia, I assumed that Van Vechten might have traveled to India in search of his subject. It turns out that, in the spring of 1938, Gopal, a trained classical dancer, traveled for a concert in New York, where he came in contact with the writer-photographer. The two collaborated in a three-day photo shoot in Van Vechten's studio apartment on the Upper West Side in Manhattan. The images are a small part of Van Vechten's over seventeen thousand photographs of celebrities and people in the arts at the Beinecke. The photographs are unknown to scholars of South Asian photography in part because they belong to the Van Vechten Papers and are catalogued under the Yale Collection of American Literature, with which Van Vechten is associated. The Beinecke images are overlooked also because of the disciplinary boundaries separating American literature, and photography for that matter, and Indian visual and performing arts. My book grows in the blind spot between the disciplines and finds in these photographs a compelling record of an underrepresented history of cross-cultural artistic and medial encounters in the interwar years of early twentieth century, made briefly visible through photography.

The Beinecke images are by no means a complete set. In 1965, 179 photographs of the Indian dancer were given by Van Vechten's studio assistant in the 1930s, Mark Lutz, to the Philadelphia Museum of Art (PMA), making it the largest single collection available to us today. The PMA images have the museum's accession numbers. By contrast, the Beinecke set carries Van Vechten's stamp, negative numbers, and occasional comments that help us reconstruct the photo shoot in the sequence in which it unfolded and help us imagine a cross-cultural conversation evolving between the photographer and the dancer in the New York studio over the period of three days on April 21, May 5, and May 11, 1938. Van Vechten's negative strips at the Beinecke also give us a glimpse of images the photographer took of other subjects just prior to, in between, and after his sessions with Gopal.

Why should we bother with these photographs? For one, they give us a rare view of a rich interaction between two major cultural practitioners of their time. Ram Gopal (1912–2003) is a recognized pioneer of Indian classical dance. Of this "Nijinsky of India," the dance critic Ashish Khokar writes, "It would be accurate to call him India's first international classical dancer, for it was indeed Ram Gopal who was the first one to present the variety of Indian classical dance styles and their rich vocabulary to a Western audience."[1] The Van Vechten photographs provide the earliest visual document of this major dancer and advocate from the founding moments of India's classical dance. When Gopal met the American photographer, he was on his first tour outside India. The meeting could not have been more timely for him. By the 1930s, Van Vechten (1880–1964) had earned a considerable reputation as a writer and critic in New York for advocating for diversity in literature and the performing arts. In the first two decades of the twentieth century, he distinguished himself as among the first to introduce European ballet and modern dance to what he considered a staid and parochial cultural scene of the city. He was also among the first to advocate for the African American performers of the Jazz Age and promote the writers of an artistic culture known as the Harlem Renaissance. His connections with the African American literary figures, as well as the controversies over his provocative novels, along with his interracial homoerotic relations with Black men, dominate the scholarly literature on his work. Gopal's absence in that literature has an unexpected consequence; Van Vechten's practice is exclusively pressed into the service of American studies.

This book is not an effort to restore the place of either Gopal or Van Vechten within their admittedly separate domains of practice. Nor is it an attempt to fulfill a lacuna in the history of Indian dance or American photography. In the 1950s, Gopal's autobiography fully assured his place in the history of classical Indian dance, and in recent decades a body of literature has grown around his importance to that history.[2] Scholarship on Van Vechten is a flourishing industry.[3] It is surprising, however, that neither Van Vechten nor Gopal mentions their extensive collaboration on the photo shoot, nor do we see the results of the photo shoot published anywhere in the literature on these two major practitioners.

The photographs of Gopal from 1938, thus, represent what Michel-Rolph Trouillot calls a resounding "silence" that echoes through the archives and historical accounts.[4] Trouillot reminds us that the archives are not simply built from a "passive act of collecting. Rather it is an active act of production that prepares facts for historical intelligibility."[5] The production and curation of archival memory begins first with the historical participants themselves. In the 1950s, Gopal curated his presence as a founding figure of Indian classical dance. In addition to his autobiography, he published one of the first books on the classical forms of India, tracing them from their mythological origins to the twentieth century and illustrated with his photographs. In this curatorial mode of writing history, the transnational circuits of Indian dance that we see in the Van Vechten photographs disappear.[6]

Trouillot's axiom is true also for Van Vechten, who built two substantial collections at the Beinecke. The James Weldon Johnson Collection was established by Van Vechten in 1941 to commemorate the African American writer, activist, and dear friend of Van Vechten's who died in a car accident in 1938. Its mission was, and is, to celebrate eminent African Americans who contributed to the cultural diversity and political life of the country. Separately, the Beinecke's collection of Van Vechten's papers include his correspondence, writings, photographs, artworks, scrapbooks, photo albums, and other ephemera gathered until his death in 1964. My chance discovery of Gopal among the Van Vechten Papers resonates as a "silence" only because the Indian dancer's presence disappears into Van Vechten's overall interracial interests as represented by the two collections at the Beinecke. The Johnson Collection perfectly fits Trouillot's definition of the "active act" of shaping "historical intelligibility" in the archives. It is fully used in Van Vechten scholarship and has achieved a greater visibility also in recent decades with the rise of African American studies and critical race studies. By contrast, the Van Vechten Papers lurk in the shadows. When the Beinecke closed for renovation in 2015, reopening briefly in 2020 before closing again because of COVID-19, the Johnson Collection was the first to become available, and the well-intentioned staff frequently redirected my requests for studying the Van Vechten Papers toward that collection, as if the two could serve my purpose equally. In the Johnson Collection, Gopal appears accidentally, in six small photographs by Eslanda Goode Robeson tacked on a page torn from a photo album (fig. 2.2).

Van Vechten's photo shoot with Gopal complicates the archival memory and cultural presence of both practitioners. In particular, it highlights a uniquely transnational aspect of the photographer's as well as the dancer's practice that has remained largely overlooked in scholarship. As a first step to address the silence of the dancer's photographs in the Van Vechten archives, I pull away from those individual practitioners and develop a "site-based" investigation of the photo shoot that took place in New York in 1938. The primary referent of these photographs is the photo shoot. By giving primacy to the evidence of conversations and exchanges during the New York photo shoot in these images, the book pushes the various separate fields of Indian dance, American photography, and American literature beyond what Allan Sekula calls "the limits of national identity" imposed on cultural practice.[7]

A fundamentally transnational view of the photo shoot helps us address one major silence in the archives and history writing, namely, that of the historical subjects of photography. The history of photography is typically written from the point of view of the photographers. Their control of the camera and their vision as represented in their photographic oeuvre are emphasized in part because of the way archives are built and catalogued. Van Vechten gave his extensive photographic collection to the Beinecke complete with meticulous documentation, including negative numbers for each image he took over a career of thirty years. Gopal's images are a small part of this collection, and their provenance is defined by the photographer's legacy in the archives. The PMA set shows even more vividly the role of archival legacies in shaping the provenance of a historical document. The photographs do not have Van Vechten's negative numbers, only the museum's accession number and the year of the gift, 1965, attributed to the photographer's assistant, Mark Lutz. In documenting the acquisition, the PMA's ordering system gives consistency to the gift and the photographer's presence in it. Gopal recedes into the "past," as Trouillot means it, locked in this system by a date that holds meaning only within a chronology of practice attributed to the photographer. Gopal's "presence" in the archives will need to be recovered through interpretative strategies that work around and against the coherence of the photographer's oeuvre. A guiding question for the book is, What is the provenance of the dancer's presence and participation in these images? Arranging the photographs according to the negative numbers available at the Beinecke is one of the strategies I have used to find out how Gopal brings himself into existence in the photographic archives. We will find that his presence in the Van Vechten archives is a "silence" in yet one more way; it is at variance with Gopal's own curated presence in the history of Indian classical dance.

My story is, first and foremost, guided by the photographs. Contained in them is a microhistory of a moment when photography created a space for border crossing and self-fashioning for both the American photographer and the Indian dancer. I closely read the images and re-create the photo shoot that took place in New York in April and May 1938. I describe the material conditions of the makeshift studio in Van Vechten's private living quarters. As I locate the photo shoot in the moment of the 1930s, an uneven terrain of cultural interactions opens up within the space of the photo studio. The interplay of cultural and personal interests is framed by the interracial, erotic dynamics of New York's underground counterculture, with which Van Vechten was associated. I explore Van Vechten's homoerotic interests in Black men, to which scholarly literature has drawn substantial attention, but in order to further ask, What happens when his racial fascination turns on the Indian dancer? I explore how Gopal eroticizes himself in front of the photographer's lens and describe in his bodily representations a history of dance reform taking place in India in the 1930s. Gopal also displays in his body a residue of his world journeys, starting with a concert tour to Southeast and East Asia with the American Orientalist dancer La Meri and including his interactions with Hollywood celebrities when he arrived at the port of Los Angeles from Tokyo. In particular, I discover in these images Gopal's own fascination with photography and film and a distinct interest in posing for the camera. I describe his self-presentation during the New York photo shoot as "photo-dance" to distinguish his deliberate and self-aware manipulation of the photographic medium from his live performance. Last but not least, I highlight the important role of the German camera during the photo shoot, arguing that Van Vechten's Leica is key in creating a space for mutual attraction and fantasy-making between the dancer and the photographer. Van Vechten's photographs provide an unusual case of photographic intimacy and self-fashioning alongside the violent collision of diverse life worlds during the interwar years of the 1930s. By slowly untying the various cultural and medial knots that bind this visual record of 1938, the book reveals a small part of the layered interactions of world cultures in that period.

"Photo-attractions" describes in a granular way a space opened up by photography for a series of affective exchanges between the American photographer, the Indian dancer, and the German Leica placed between them. In other words, it is about global flows, a topic of broad interest in the history of photography and other cultural and artistic practices at least since the 1990s.[8] My primary interlocutors are the scholars of South Asia's visual culture who have recently shown the global dimensions of South Asian art by digging deeper into the existing archives.[9] Their project, however, is largely historiographical and revisionist, whereas my interest is to shed light on a material history of cross-cultural and intermedial exchanges in the New York photographs. The difference is important. The book is not aimed simply to refine our understanding of South Asian art history. In my account, the New York studio is treated as a historical (even an archaeological) site of investigation, where the Indian dancer as well as the American photographer engaged in cultural border crossing in 1938. The presence of the camera complicates their interpersonal exchanges. "Photo-attractions" in the book's title is intended not only to describe the exchanges between two widely separated cultural figures but also to materially describe the lure of the camera and the gelatinous surface of the photographic print in transcultural desires.[10] Global flows across bodies and media require conceptual tools drawn from various areas of cultural study beyond the studies of the arts in South Asia.

The book brings together South Asian visual and performing arts as well as American cultural practices into a close conversation using a mix of perspectives on global interactions, including postcolonial theories, studies of Orientalism, critical race and ethnic studies, queer and sexuality studies, and studies of global media and affect. I discuss those perspectives separately shortly but wish to draw a major distinction here. While most approaches give historians and cultural practitioners tools to reveal the unequal distribution of cultural capital across the world, this book highlights an equalizing negotiation of cultural difference that proves to be counterintuitive to the existing understanding of global flows. Scholars and students who investigate the power relations dividing the Eastern from the Western world in different humanities and social sciences disciplines might find in the details of my story surprising evidence of photographic intimacy and collaboration belonging to the same period of global modernity that produced representations of colonial exploitation, racial inequality, and cultural prejudice across distant world cultures. The book describes the material, ideational, and social worlds that poured into the spatial and temporal sequence of the New York photo shoot of 1938 itself. In this way, it shows why it matters not only to critique the larger structures of power embedded in the motives of photographers and their subjects but also to interrogate the technical structure and visual composition of photographs.

Written as an art historian, the book is positioned at the intersection of multiple areas of cultural inquiry. In drawing out the global exchanges in these photographs, my research interacts with two major perspectives on the history of global flows in photography: postcolonial studies and studies of Orientalism. My case, however, does not fit the basic assumption informing both perspectives, namely, that it is the (Western, Euro-American) photographers who travel with their camera to distant, non-Western countries driven by a desire to control and capture the exotic. The spatial relationships between the mobile photographer and the stationary subjects continue in the imaginings of revisionist thinking in both areas. I too had assumed that Van Vechten's photographs were taken in India, only to be surprised by my findings. The shocking revelation became a point of departure for my book, and I turn to capture the pulse of multiple histories that might have coursed, perhaps arhythmically, through the images themselves.

Nevertheless, my book is inspired by postcolonial approaches to what Christopher Pinney and Nicholas Peterson have called "photography's other histories" in non-Western countries.[11] Such histories have drawn from the "visual turn" in numerous humanities and social science disciplines since the 1990s and brought attention to the rich archives of photographic practices beyond the canons of photography in the British, French, German, and American colonies in Asia, Africa, and North and South America since the beginnings of photography in the nineteenth century. Postcolonial scholars interrogated, and "provincialized," the broad, geopolitical foundations on which the Eurocentric canon of photography rests.[12] They also documented vernacular practices that showed how the colonized subjects resisted the colonizer's gaze and appropriated the colonial technology.[13] My book may appear as one more, potentially late and limited example of those "other histories." But it deviates significantly from the investment in this discourse of resistance posed by the regional and national vernaculars in world photography. Instead, it invites postcolonial studies to consider a more integrated loop of exchanges across the East and West divide.

For that purpose, I draw on studies of Orientalism, the fantasy of the East in Western imagination and knowledge production. Orientalism dominates the study of global flows in image practices. My book benefits from a recent revisionist scholarship that challenges the uneven, subject-object relations of Orientalism, shown originally in literary studies, by turning to art and architecture for a two-way mimetic interaction between the East and the West.[14] But while the revisionist scholarship continues to locate the fantasy of the East in Turkey and Java, it is important for my study to acknowledge New York City as the primary site of Orientalist fantasy. Exploring in Gopal what happens when the East travels to the West, I maintain a steady focus on Orientalism's fundamental interest in the space of both enchantment and estrangement in which a desire for alterity unfolds. In this way, I avoid a slippage into the cultural accounts of diasporic desires and immigrant assimilation in Euro-American cities, represented by a growing literature on Indian dance in the diaspora as well as on Gopal after he settled in the United Kingdom in the 1950s.[15] Instead of this "diasporic" turn, I deepen my investigation into the visual technology used in Orientalist fantasy-making and demonstrate how Van Vechten's Leica maintains a productive blind spot of Orientalist translations and refractions throughout the interpersonal exchanges between the Indian dancer and the American photographer. As their mutual fantasy-making incorporates the German camera, my story breaks away from the Orientalist binary of East and West altogether and makes Van Vechten's New York studio a radically "transcultural" site of global exchanges.[16]

In the New York photo shoot, I explore the contact zones not only between world cultures but also the arts in India and the United States. The story of interactions between the visual and performing arts leads to some surprising discoveries. For instance, the interweaving of photography and choreography leads to what I have called "photo-dance." I develop the idea as a distinct aspect of global performance history, drawing partly from the discussions on "Screendance."[17] I hope historians who base their stories of Indian performing arts exclusively on biographical accounts of dancers and stage performances might at least consider the idea useful to think with.

My book is also inspired by critical race and ethnic studies as well as Black feminism, whose rich and varied literature reveals the logic of racism and the power structures of whiteness in everyday economies, social technologies, and cultural practices in Europe and the United States. But the details of the numerous interracial, intercultural, and intermedial networks in my account might surprise advocates who narrate the history of racial inequality and violence. The New York photo shoot is framed by racism. But here is the difference. Critical race studies considers both photography and race as the evil and interrelated historical twins that, by design, reduce the humanity of the racial subject.[18] In such accounts, it is in the nature of photography to produce racial and ethnic stereotypes out of individuals. Consequently, the project of critical race and ethnic studies is to resist the systemic structuring of photographic abjection and relocate human communities and individual identities against the (photographic, white, capitalist) representation of their race and ethnicity. The resistance is achieved partly by building archives and collecting stories that humanize the racial subjects and highlight their robust lives prior to their alienating representation and partly by narrating the abject individual's own social self-fashioning.[19] My case study differs from such a sociopolitical self-fashioning only in its conceptual framework. The scholarly desire to "remember" (that is, both recall and put together once again) the human body through "ornate" and "resonant" metaphors of "wounds and scars" do not apply to my project. For Black feminist scholars, the locus of racial violence is also gendered female, whereas my subject includes men.[20]

To be sure, a major topic of the book is the Indian dancer's bodily entanglement with the alienating mechanism of photography. But Gopal refuses the photographic framing of abjection seen in race studies and takes the alienating logic of photography in an altogether different direction. Instead of abjection, he pursues what Walter Benjamin calls the "innervation" of the human sensorium through modern visual media.[21] He speaks of "becoming god," a reference I describe as a case of "photo-erotic" self-fashioning, drawing on recent scholarship on modern media and self-fashioning.[22] Van Vechten's Leica provides the alienating logic for organizing the dancer's body as a "radiance of form."[23]

In *Photo-Attractions*, we see the Indian dancer and the American photographer arriving in the New York studio in 1938 from two widely separated countries and negotiating their cultural difference. To elaborate on the uneven registers of desire at play in their negotiations, I have organized the chapters in a recursive and iterative way, always returning to the photo studio and picking up a trace of their interactions from the grainy, slate-colored surface of these amazing photographs. Chapter 1 locates us in Van Vechten's apartment-studio in New York, where the dancer and the photographer expose themselves to mutual estrangement, wonder, and fantasy-making. The New York studio remains a constant in each chapter, and returning to that material site helps in separating out, day by day and perspective by perspective, the shifting layers of interactions documented in these photographs. Chapter 2 explores how the Indian dancer arrives in New York and steps in front of Van Vechten's camera. Gopal's interests are rooted in the early history of "classical" Indian dance in the 1930s, his training in Kathakali and other "male forms" of dance in his home town of Bangalore, and his international journey, including a brush with Hollywood celebrities that brings him to Van Vechten's studio. Chapter 3 attends to Van Vechten's enchantment with photography and the hospitality of his photographic practice that invited the Indian dancer to his studio. I address Van Vechten's interracial interests from his early career as a writer for the arts, his participation in New York's cultural underworld, and his attraction for glamour that shapes his fascination with the German camera and his view of his subjects. In chapters 4 and 5, Van Vechten's Leica appears as a major participant during the photo shoot. The Leica enchants the studio and shapes the homoerotic desires and interactions of the human participants into what I call a photo-erotic threesome. Chapter 4 explores how the intimacy of this triangulation affects Van Vechten's image practice. Chapter 5 returns to the studio to highlight in Gopal's enamored self-presentation a long history of entanglement between photography and Indian classical dance.[24] First, let us enter Van Vechten's apartment studio in New York City with Gopal and witness the photo shoot as it unfolded that spring of 1938.

CHAPTER 1.
THE PHOTO STUDIO

They get right to it. Ram Gopal had just arrived at Van Vechten's apartment studio on 101 Central Park West in a double-breasted jacket. He quickly changes into a dance costume. Van Vechten had been photographing around his sprawling apartment. He finished in the grand foyer. The negative number M20 on roll XI shows an oil portrait from his younger days painted by Martha Baker in 1906 prominently displayed against the star-shaped floor pattern of a gorgeously designed Art Deco space (fig. 1.1).[1] Then followed M21, the first shot of the dancer. Gopal takes a standing pose against a fabric curtain. He is wearing a tall, conical cap and a short skirt with pleated panels in front and a longer drop of flat, embroidered panel that hangs down to his feet. Armbands with puffy, diamond-shaped flowers, a choker, and a set of necklaces of different lengths made of beads and shiny metal discs cover his naked chest. In a little pocket

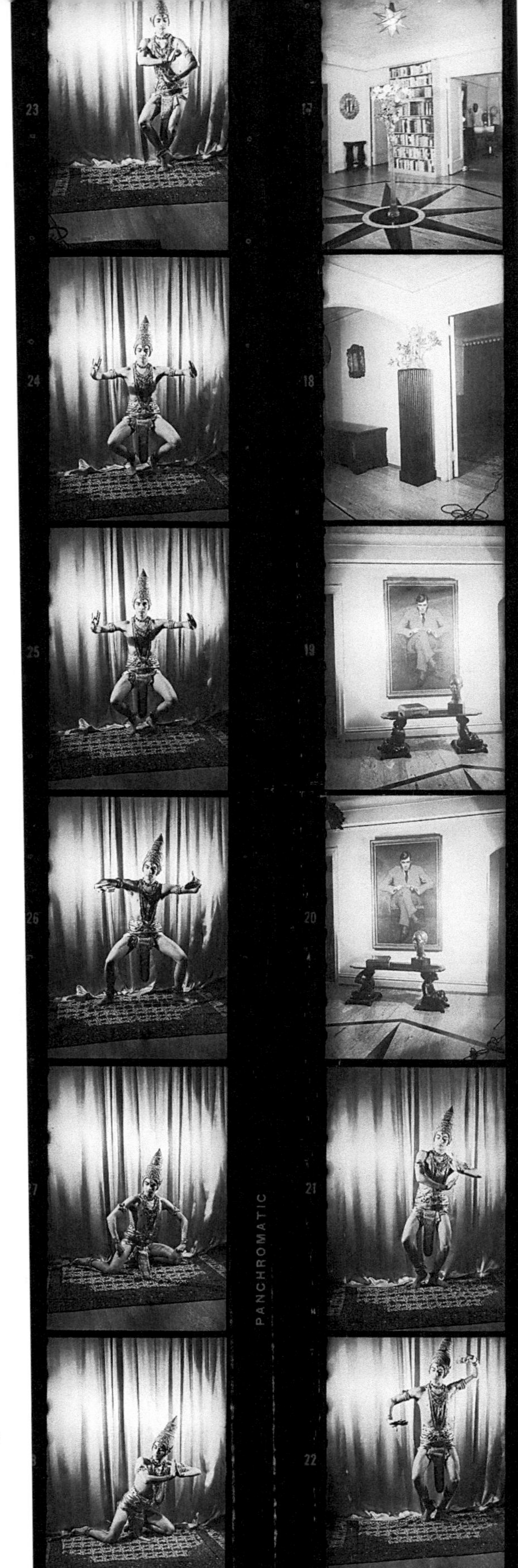

Figure 1.1. Carl Van Vechten, negative roll XI, April 21, 1938, two strips, M17–28. (Beinecke Rare Book and Manuscript Library, Yale University; © The Van Vechten Trust)

book Van Vechten carried with him for quick notes during his photo shoots, he briefly wrote, "in gold costumes."[2] The phrase vividly captures what struck him the most when the Indian dancer transformed in front of his camera on the first day of the photo shoot on April 21, 1938.

Gopal starts with the standing positions from his training in India, then kneels and spreads out on his knees. Van Vechten holds the figure in full length using a Leica camera mounted on a tripod. The unusual figure and unpredictable movements are challenging. In order to accommodate the height of Gopal's crown, as well as the many variables in the dancer's poses, Van Vechten places the camera a little farther from the figure than what he would have usually preferred for a tight, full-length image. As a result, more of the background curtain comes into the view behind the dancer. Van Vechten aims the two studio lights on the figure, one from the left side and one from the right. Backlit in this way, the body becomes silhouetted against the tall, glowing folds of the background. Because of the small size of the lighting cans, an orb is inevitably included in the image. When the dancer sits on his knees, as in M27, the key light hits his crown while the rest of his body recedes into darkness.

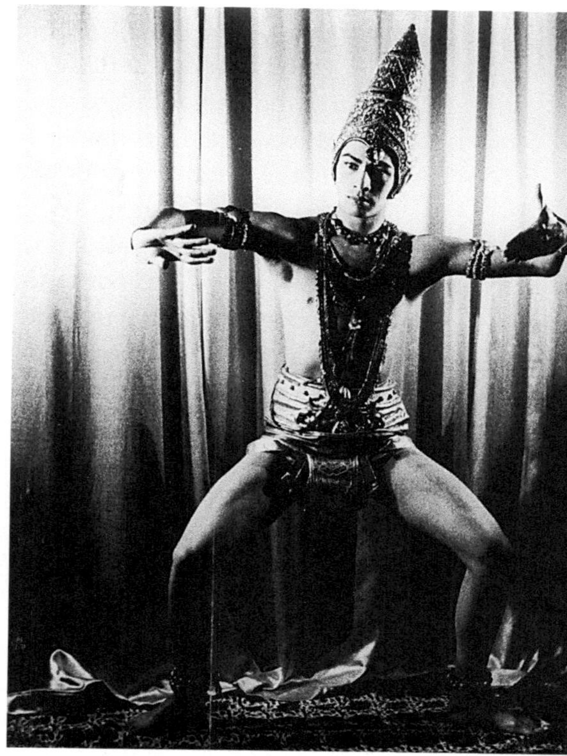

Figure 1.2. Carl Van Vechten, *Ram Gopal*, April 21, 1938, XI M26. (Beinecke Rare Book and Manuscript Library, Yale University; © The Van Vechten Trust)

Something shifts in M24, M25, and M26, however. The swaying and sprawling figure snaps into a geometrical shape, and the photographer catches on. Van Vechten centers the figure in his viewfinder. Later, he makes enlargements in the darkroom, trimming the images to contain the dancer's body as tightly as possible within the frame (fig. 1.2). He also elaborates on the geometry of the composition (fig. 4.15).

For M26, Gopal takes on a basic stance from his training in Kathakali. It is an upright position, a *mandala sthana*, standing on sturdy, outstretched legs, knees bent and feet turned outward and flat on the ground. Derived from martial arts, Kathakali thrives on such virile poses. Arms extend out to the sides, and the figure makes a firm, square geometry in space. Each hand makes a specific, mimetic gesture (*hastamudra*). With the upright thumb held apart and all other fingers held together straight, the left hand assumes the *hamsapaksha* (swan's wing). With outstretched fingers but the thumb folded into the palm, the right hand becomes the *pallavam* (sprout). Combined, the gestures could narrate an auspicious beginning or growth.[3]

The dancer moves to other positions but holds each posture steady for a brief moment, giving the photographer enough time to click. Nevertheless, the oddity of framing and lighting, not to mention the problem of legibility of Gopal's exotic representations, remains. Van Vechten takes the camera closer to the dancer's body for half-length images before the roll finishes. These last images bring greater attention to the dancer's decorated body, stylized hand gestures, and facial expressions, as if expressing the photographer's curiosity over the technicalities of Indian dance.

While Van Vechten changes the film in his camera, Gopal changes into a sarong and wears an ornate, metallic breast plate. The armband stays, the crown comes off, and a broad wristband and a beaded choker are added. The dancer steps back into the light. For the first two exposures, he also includes a metal pot (fig. 1.3).

Oddity persists in these full-length images. The dancer keeps moving to one side of the frame while the folds of the curtain take up the other side in almost equal measure. Lighting the figure is a perpetual limitation owing to the small size of the metal covers for the bulbs. Only a narrow band of light ripples across the top half of the image. When the photographer aims at the dancer's face and torso, the lower portion of the image is shrouded in darkness except for the wavy crest formed on the floor by the rumpled edges of the curtain caught in reflected light. One might even imagine Van Vechten picking up the camera on its tripod and taking it a little forward or back. Most negatives end up showing the lighting cans, which are barely left outside the frame by cropping the final image during enlargement. The excess fabric and uneven lighting slip into the image anyway. The columnar folds of the curtain distract from the figure's perfect pose. The backlit dancer almost dissolves into an alternating rhythm of bright glare and deep shadows across the overall image.

The photographs are a result of an uneasy negotiation between the American photographer and the Indian dancer's somewhat unpredictable moves and poses. All fourteen photographs of Gopal in this pose with the sarong carry the same oddity of the off-centered figure and the band of light across the image. But by the fifth shot in this group, one notices a significant shift in the approach to these limitations of the studio (see fig. 5.18). The collaboration achieves a breakthrough. As if to provide a reverse shot of the previous images, the dancer turns his back toward the camera. The light beaming from the left hits the side of his body to produce a clear silhouette. Gopal gives up the pot and raises his empty hands instead, both to imitate carrying a pot over his head only with hand gestures and to frame his face. He looks sideways, directly into the band of light, offering a profile to the camera. For the last two images in this group, he also centers his body and stretches his arms across that luminous band, as if to measure it. By now, in other words, what started out as a struggle with the limitations of

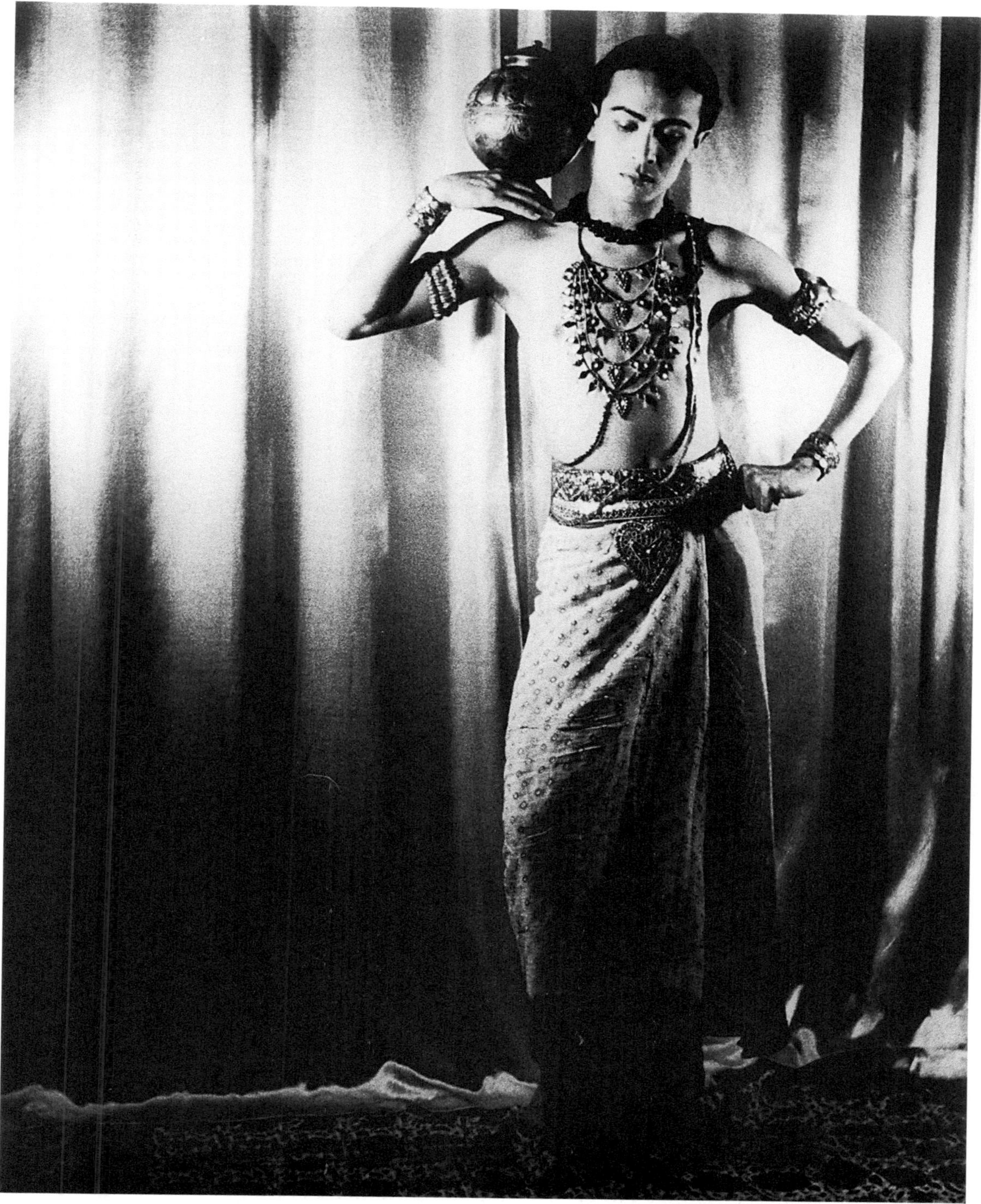

Figure 1.3. Carl Van Vechten, *Ram Gopal*, April 21, 1938, XII M2. (Beinecke Rare Book and Manuscript Library, Yale University; © The Van Vechten Trust)

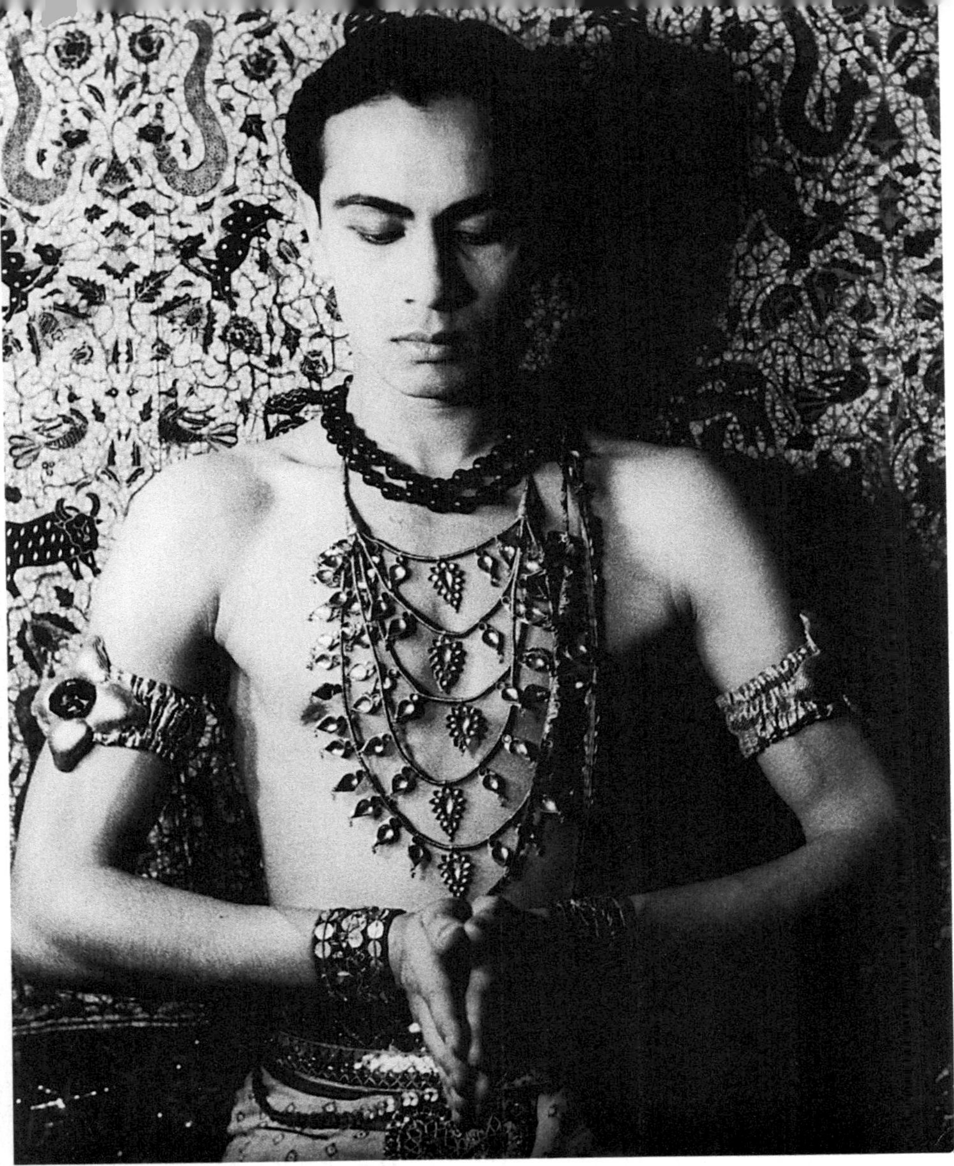

Figure 1.4. Carl Van Vechten, *Ram Gopal*, April 21, 1938, XII M15. (Beinecke Rare Book and Manuscript Library, Yale University; © The Van Vechten Trust)

the studio and the oddities of the image becomes an intentional part of the overall design.

Both the dancer and the photographer seem to hit their stride by the second roll, numbered XII, on the first day of the photo shoot. They get playful in their collaboration and start to "narrate" the messiness of the studio as part of the image. The oddness of lighting and the asymmetrical composition become part of their conversation, and the two discover what the studio can contribute to the dancing figure. The conversation between photography and dance becomes inspiring. Van Vechten pulls out more fabric for backdrops and indulges in picture-making. For the fifteenth image in the second roll, he places the dancer against a printed batik backdrop and moves the camera close to capture a tight, half-length portrait (fig. 1.4). Gopal stands upright, eyes lowered to his folded hands in a gesture of reverence (*anjali*) that contributes to the symmetry of the photographer's composition. His ornamented body glows from the left. The leaves and flower pendants on his wiry breast plate and the beaded choker, as well as the sharply delineated eyebrows, echo with the pointed, holly-like leaves, beaded flowers, and vines and tendrils, as well as outlines of peacock feathers, the curling snakes, and dotted tigers and cows, seen through the fibrous web of traces from the wax-dye in the background fabric. For a brief second, the shadows on the right also become a figural double of the dancer's body.

Other images in this group build on the visual echo between the foreground figure and the web of natural motifs represented in the background fabric. For M16, Gopal brings the two hands together in a composite hand gesture that represents the unfolding of a lotus blossom (see fig. 1.19). For yet another image, M18, he swings his torso to the left, head tilted to the right and glancing sideways at his raised arms. Hands come close to each other, with the index fingers curled against the thumb in the *mudrakhyam* (eyes of a doe), as if to represent the doe-eyed Krishna or to depict butterflies fluttering against the background's pastoral scene (fig. 1.5).

Before the end of the roll, Gopal changes into at least two more costumes. For XII M26–28, he wears beaded necklaces and a golden cap with square floral patterns, and Van Vechten pulls out a chintz fabric with a

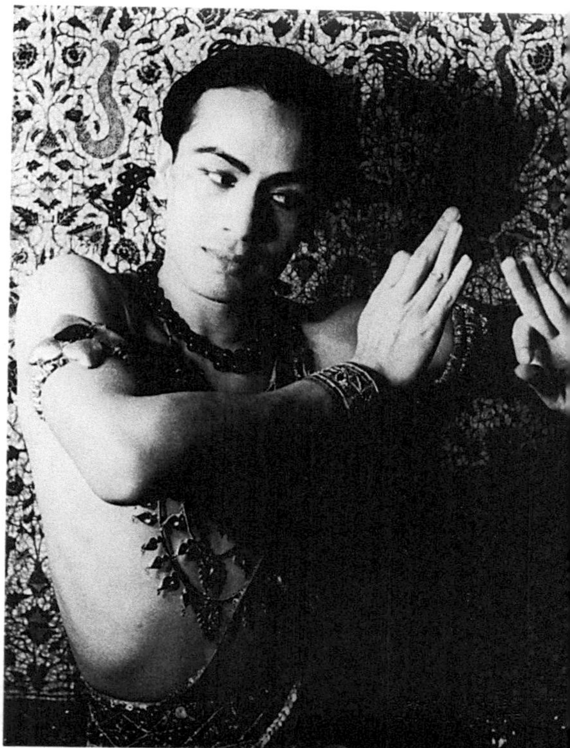

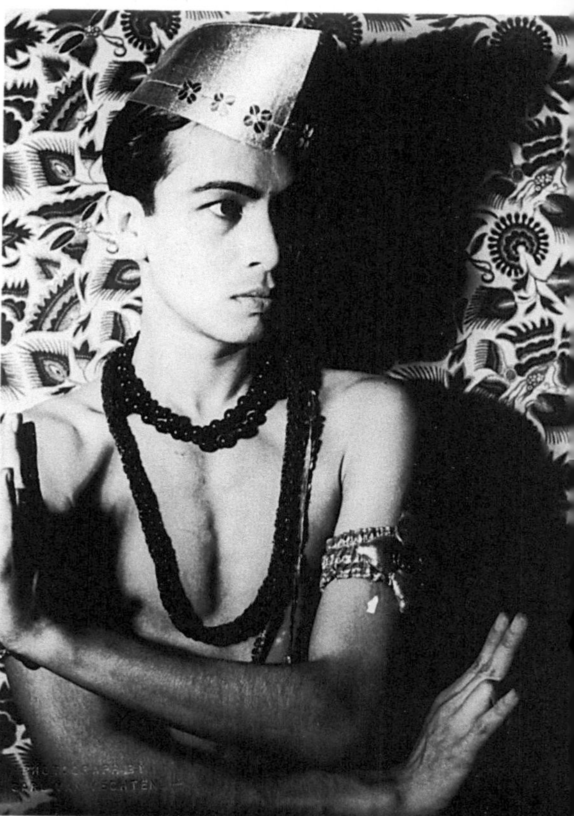

Figures 1.5 and 1.6. *Top*, Carl Van Vechten, *Ram Gopal*, April 21, 1938, XII M18. *Bottom*, Carl Van Vechten, *Ram Gopal*, April 21, 1938, XII M27. (Beinecke Rare Book and Manuscript Library, Yale University; © The Van Vechten Trust)

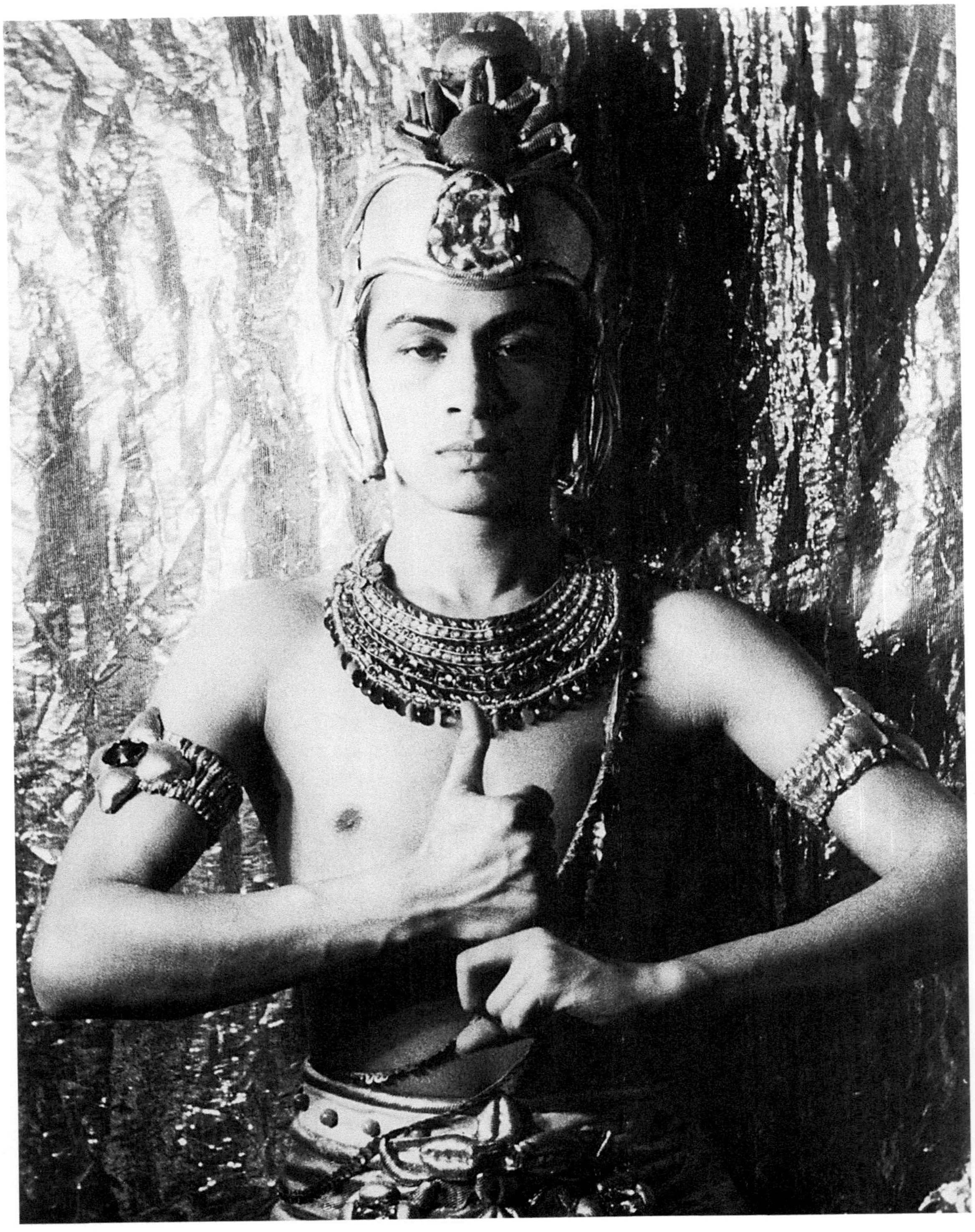

Figure 1.7. Carl Van Vechten, *Ram Gopal*, April 21, 1938, XIII M3. (Beinecke Rare Book and Manuscript Library, Yale University; © The Van Vechten Trust)

densely printed pattern of geometrical flowers and leaves overlapping with angular peacock feathers (fig. 1.6). By the end of the roll, Gopal wears his dazzle again. The short skirt with fan-shaped pleats returns but without the long sash. He complements the bold, beaded flowers on the belt with equally bold floral pattern on the ornament across the chest, held by a neck band and a strap across the rib cage. A wiry tiara extends into tendrils beyond the skull and curls around his ears. For one image, now in the Museum of the City of New York, Gopal poses as the Lord of Dance, Shiva Nataraja (fig. 5.4).[4] For another image, Gopal holds a white lotus in his raised hand, taking the iconography of the Buddhist deity of Compassion, or what the program for his New York concert calls "The Picture of Bodhisattava" (fig. 2.9). Van Vechten seems enamored by this group. He lingers on it, pursues it in his darkroom experiments, and uses at least one image as a picture postcard to send to the dancer, calling it "my favorite" photograph (fig. 4.3).

When Van Vechten changes to a new film roll, XIII, Gopal wears yet another costume. The short skirt remains, but he wears a broad, beaded choker and a golden helmet with an earflap and a crest that appears to be like a multihooded snake framing a large gem stone. Some poses represent what the New York program calls the "Cobra Dance," taken from the Kathakali repertoire. Van Vechten is captivated. The headgear and the broad choker appear more like Roman helmets and Egyptian necklaces seen in Hollywood films of Cecil B. DeMille than anything Indian. Van Vechten uses a shiny, crinkled fabric to raise the dazzle with a familiar trope of "cinematic" sparkle of the silvery screen (fig. 1.7).

At the end of the first day of the photo shoot, Gopal puts back on his double-breasted suit and poses for a few formal portraits that we will discuss in chapter 2. The dancer sits against a backdrop showing an Art Deco chain-link pattern that Van Vechten reserved for portraits of celebrities.[5] Surprisingly, we also see Van Vechten posing with Gopal. Clearly a third person is present in the studio taking these pictures. On the back of the photograph, Van Vechten writes in green ink, "The lights were arranged, the camera set and focused by CVV, snapped by Aleksander Janta" (figs. 1.8 and 1.9).

Alexander Janta, a Polish writer and journalist, accompanied Gopal to the United States and is in the New York studio during the photo shoot. We will have much to say about Janta in the book. For now, the three men taking turns in front of the camera indicate a mood of relaxed and playful sociality within the privacy of Van Vechten's studio. Standing behind the camera, Janta catches an intimacy between the dancer and the photographer. Van Vechten's face is animated. His body leans slightly toward the dancer, looking down and exposing an enormous forehead, under which, through somewhat-pinched eyebrows, he sends out a knowing, hungry stare at the dancer. Gopal holds himself upright in the narrow space given him in the frame, setting up a distance from which to scope out his partner. He looks straight at the photographer, tilting his head ever so slightly, wearing a bit guarded but unhesitant smile.

The unexpected appearance of the photographer in the image reflects the amateurism of Van Vechten's photographic practice. The distinction between the photographer, standing invisible behind the lens, and the subject, caught and made visible by the camera, is an established covenant of "realistic" practice in the canons of photography. The covenant also informs the histories of photography in faraway world cultures where the camera first arrived through European colonial incursions.[6] In this book, by contrast, we will often see Van Vechten performing in front of the camera as if to try out a backdrop or a prop on himself before using it on his subjects. For Edward White, Van Vechten's visual presence is part of his self-fashioning. White writes that Van Vechten cultivated a conscious "demeanor of aloofness" to compensate for his sense of social oddness but enjoyed being in front of the camera as much as behind it. A hint of the colonial power dynamic is encoded in the exchange of looks in the photograph of the two men. White notices a "predatory" relationship in Van Vechten's look and expression: "The pose that he re-created hundreds of times over the decades, the one he used to communicate the mythology he wove around him: his mouth gripped shut, teeth hidden from view; his anvil of a jawbone jutting out defiantly; his stare fixed and predatory, like a tiger waiting to pounce."[7]

Van Vechten also takes several shots of Janta posing with the dancer (fig. 1.10). The three individuals communicate physical closeness and eroticize their

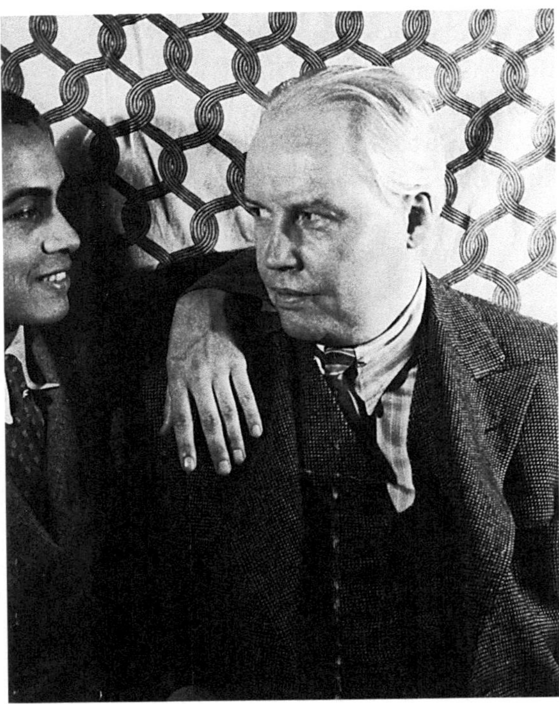

Figures 1.8. and 1.9. Carl Van Vechten, *Ram Gopal*, April 21, 1938, XIII 22, front and back. (Beinecke Rare Book and Manuscript Library, Yale University; © The Van Vechten Trust)

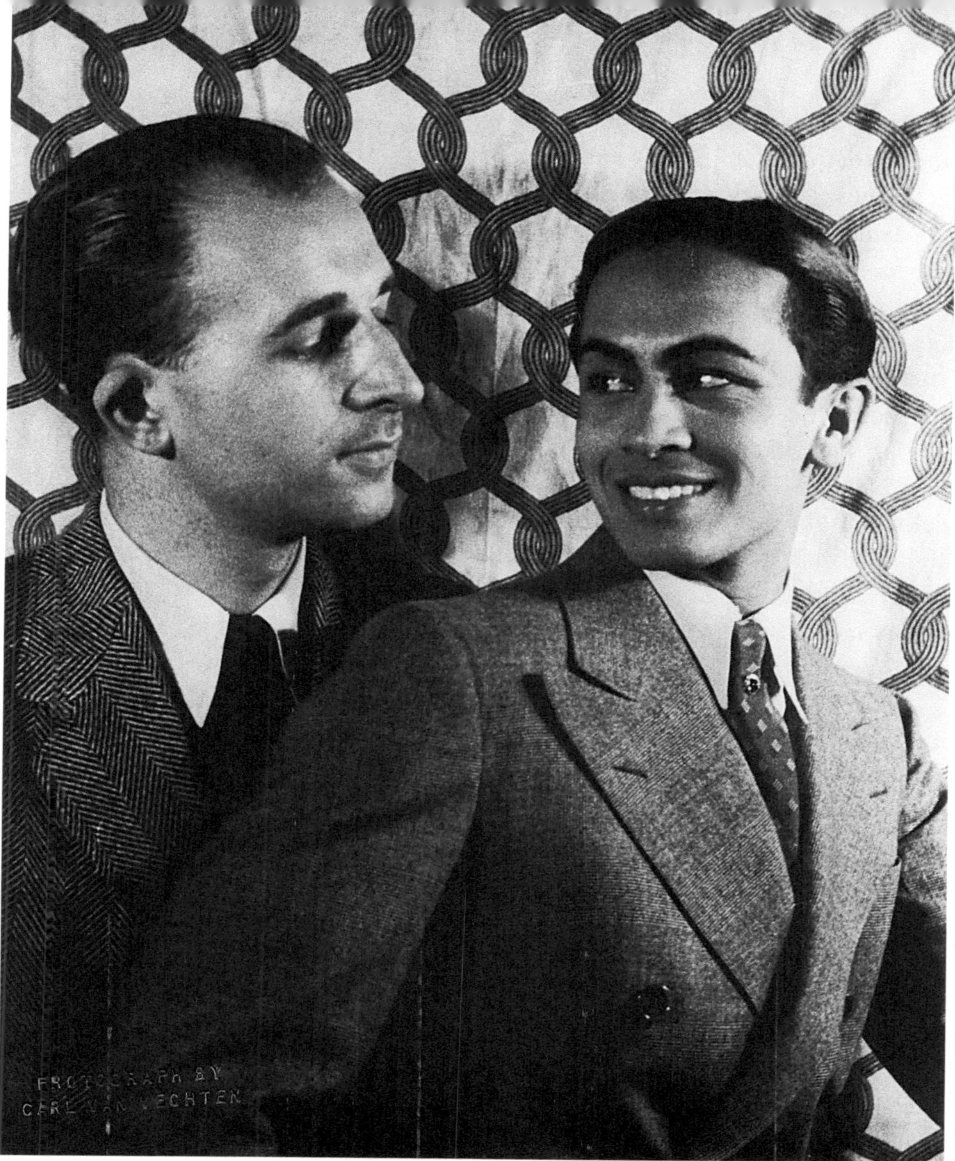

Figure 1.10. Carl Van Vechten, *Ram Gopal and Aleksander Janta*, April 21, 1938, XIII M19. (Beinecke Rare Book and Manuscript Library, Yale University; © The Van Vechten Trust)

appearance. Gopal holds the same blank smile for both men, who look intently at him. What is the play in this group of photographs? Is the dancer sitting or getting up from the journalist's lap? Is the elegant hand between him and the photographer a barrier or an invitation? The images help us imagine the photo shoot as a lighthearted, collaborative foolery around the Leica camera standing on its tripod. Historians of Indian dance had known Janta's name and his long relationship with Gopal, but we see him in person for the first time when he takes turns with Van Vechten behind the camera and in front. Gopal becomes the object of their gaze.

Material Site of Performance

In September 1936, Van Vechten and his wife, the Russian American theater actress Fania Marinoff, moved from their 150 West Fifty-Fifth Street apartment in Manhattan to 101 Central Park West. A photograph that Van Vechten took of the moving van is dated September 11, 1936.[8] The van must have carried furniture, partition screens, beds, and trunks full of ceramic cats, prints, sculpture heads, and other objects displayed all around the new apartment that sooner or later made their way in his photographs. Van Vechten's biographer Bruce Kellner notes that the apartment was cramped. "The entrance hall was lined with part of Carl's staggering collection of books; the overflow spilled into his bedroom, which functioned also as a library. The Victorian room was nearly duplicated, but the drawing room's appointments were somewhat more conventional than the pink and purple and emerald green Chinese combination at West Fifty-fifth Street. The new photographic studio, for all its improvements, did not necessarily relax the subjects who came—still by invitation only—to sit before Carl's camera eye."[9]

Van Vechten confesses, "As was often my wont, I used various parts of my apartment as backgrounds."[10] A photograph of the apartment indicates how he might have converted a living room into a studio space. The photograph, now in the New York Public Library, is part of a set produced by Emelie Danielson, a professional photographer of designed interiors in New York who was hired in 1942 to take a photographic inventory of each room of the apartment of Van Vechten and Fania Marinoff at 101 Central Park West (fig. 1.11). Let us use the photograph to imagine how Van Vechten staged his photo shoots.

Notice the heavy curtain between the sofa and the Victorian cupboard on the right. Hanging from a rod suspended from the ceiling just a few feet away from the window in the back, it could be drawn to block out the daylight. For the many images we have seen so far from the first day of the photo shoot, Gopal would have simply stood in front of that curtain and on the raised floorboard on which the sofa rests. On December 6, 1938, a few months after the dancer's visit, the Broadway singer and actress Ethel Waters posed sitting on the sofa. The tiger skin seen in the Danielson photograph was removed, and the two carpets were rearranged to cover the floorboard (fig. 1.12). In this makeshift arrangement, Van Vechten could also use the painted door panels of the Victorian cabinet on the right of the Danielson photograph as an ornate background, as he did in 1953 for the film actor Hurd Hatfield's dramatic photograph as Lord Byron in Tennessee William's play *Camino Real* (fig. 1.13).

For a photograph from 1935 of the New York writer and Hollywood socialite Mercedes de Acosta, he repurposed the tiger skin on the sofa as a dramatic design feature (fig. 1.14). The tight frame brings the figure and the backdrop into a visual synergy. De Acosta's body is swept up to a crest picked up in the wavy pattern of the tiger skin hung behind her. We will have much to say about Mercedes de Acosta in chapter 2. She met Gopal in Hollywood when the dancer

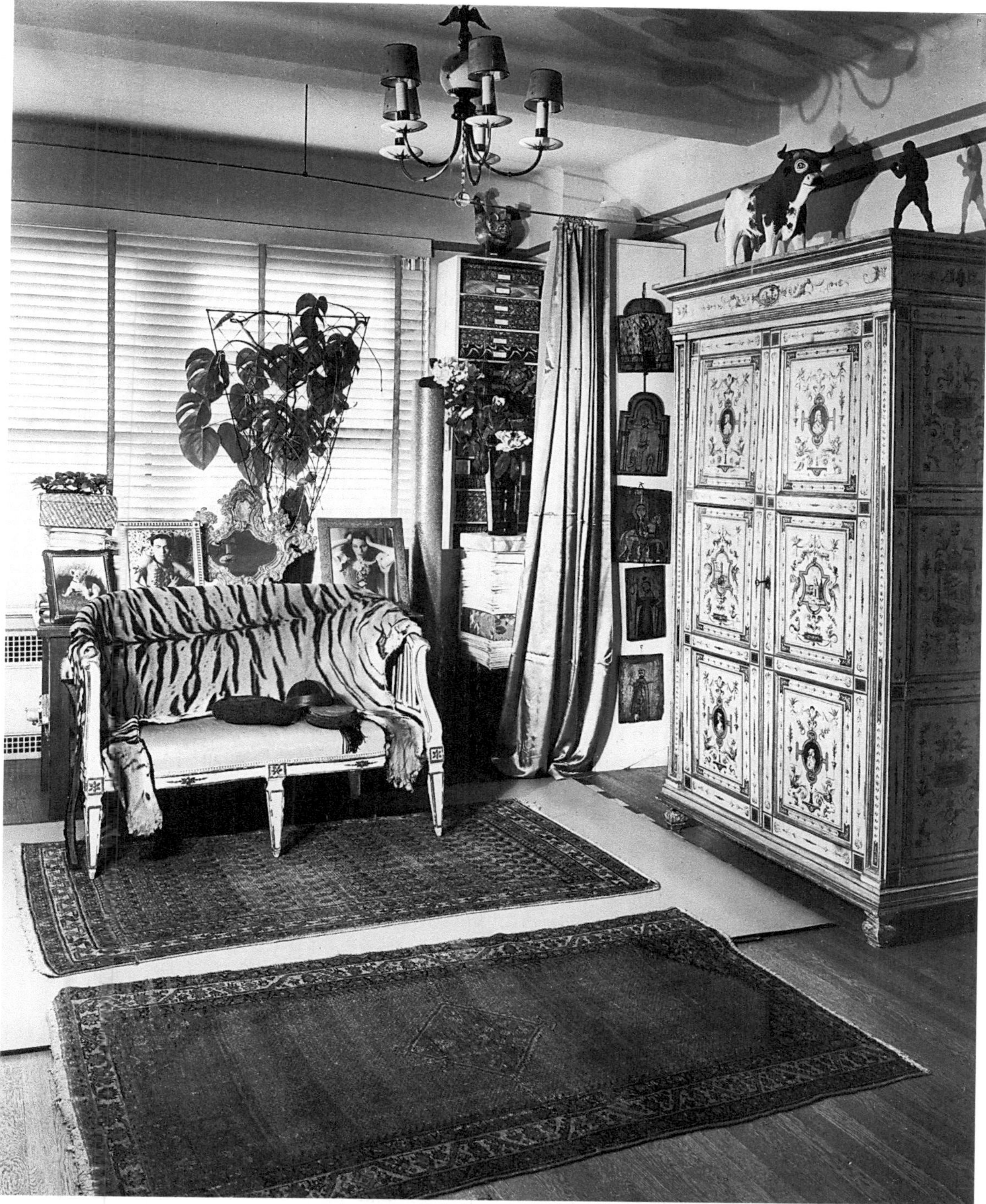

Figure 1.11. Emelie Danielson, *Living Room, Apartment of Carl Van Vechten and Fania Marinoff, 101 Central Park West*, 1942. (Courtesy of Manuscripts Division, New York Public Library)

arrived at the port of Los Angeles in the winter of 1938 and became a long-term friend and promoter. De Acosta accompanied him to New York for his debut concert and is probably the person who introduced him to Van Vechten.

The use of available props and backgrounds became important in Van Vechten's photography as artistic framing and picture-making. He wanted his photographs "to be simple and clear and sharp, but all these are artistic as well as documentary values." He wrote, "Soon the matter of backgrounds began to obsess me and almost before I was aware of it I began to reflect the personality of the sitter in his surroundings. Sometimes this is an extremely subtle reflection and sometimes it is downright, but almost always it is to be discovered in my photographs."[11] The comments suggest an interest in building a personalized narrative for the sitter in the image, to be discovered by friends and family as an inside joke. One of the first color slides that Van Vechten made when Kodachrome film became available in 1939 was that of Benny Garland Jr. sitting on the tiger skin spread back on the sofa (fig. 1.15).[12] Garland was a child of the niece of Van Vechten's housekeeper, Pearl Shower. The pearl necklace we see in the image is probably a playful and "downright" reference to his as well as his grandaunt's name.

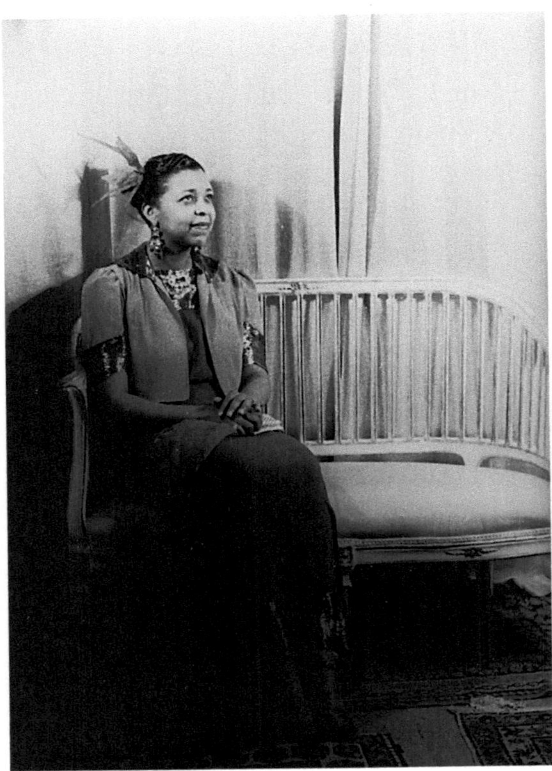

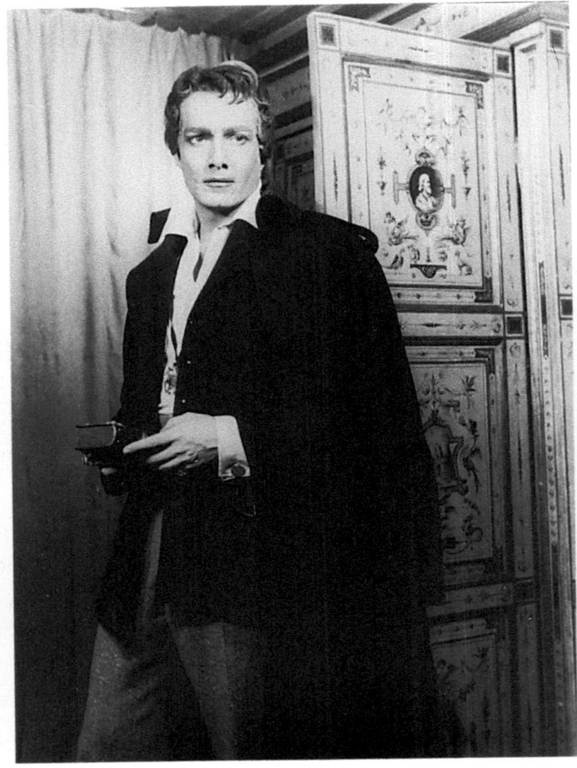

Figures 1.12 and 1.13. *Left*, Carl Van Vechten, *Ethel Waters*, December 6, 1938, XIX N. *Right*, Carl Van Vechten, *Hurd Hatfield as Lord Byron, Camino Real*, April 21, 1953, XV KK.16. (Beinecke Rare Book and Manuscript Library, Yale University; © The Van Vechten Trust)

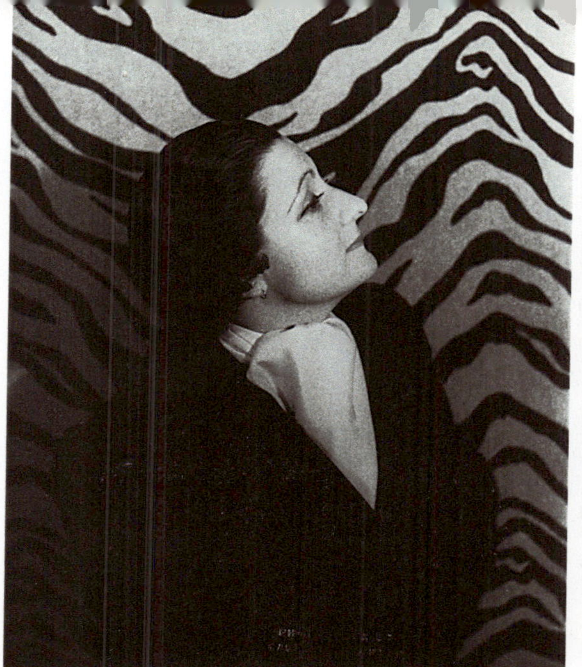

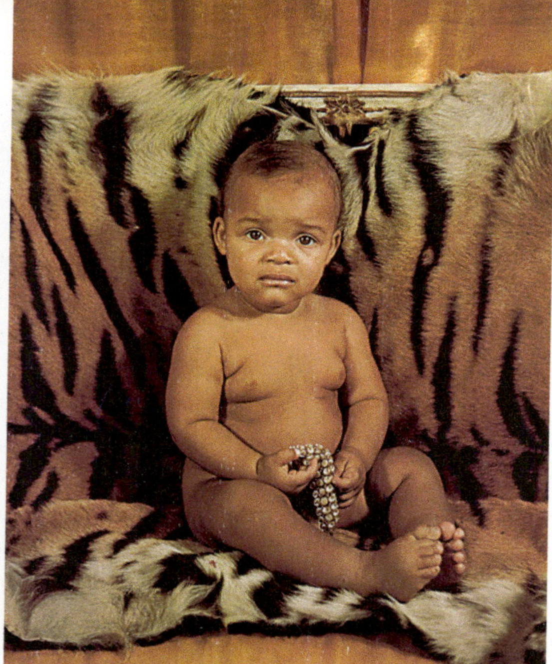

Figures 1.14 and 1.15. *Left*, Carl Van Vechten, *Mercedes de Acosta*, March 8, 1935, XLI G:4. *Right*, Carl Van Vechten, *Benny Garland Jr.*, October 15, 1939, image set XLII, Kodachrome slide 2. (Beinecke Rare Book and Manuscript Library, Yale University; © The Van Vechten Trust)

The bric-a-brac of Van Vechten's cluttered apartment, including Victorian cupboards and sideboards, posters, ceramic cats, and antique sculptures, all entered his pictures. In a striking image of himself, Van Vechten juxtaposes his head in profile with the official poster of the 1936 Berlin Olympics that was displayed in his library (fig. 1.16). The background informs the foreground, but the juxtaposition inverts the distinction between a two-dimensional poster and the three-dimensional head. Van Vechten places the camera somewhere at the level of his chin so that his profile head is flattened against the picture plane. By contrast, the idealized, wreathed head of the athlete-hero, which is in gold in the original poster, appears monumental in a low-angle view. The visual exchange conveys in Van Vechten's head the geometrical structure of the classical head and raises his profile to a mythic level.

Figures posing against a variety of backgrounds bring to the makeshift domestic space of the apartment the atmosphere of a commercial photo studio, where subjects are invited to pose and role-play against backdrops and props for the camera. Soon after the invention of photography in the nineteenth century, commercial photo studios cropped up in small towns and cities in Europe and America. They developed a clientele for the new technology by framing the sitters posed as if for a painted portrait, thus also conferring on them a social status resembling aristocracy.[13] The orchestration of pose, costume, and background became, for the photographers, an "artisanal practice," and they advertised their artistry in *cartes de visite* that included painting equipment along

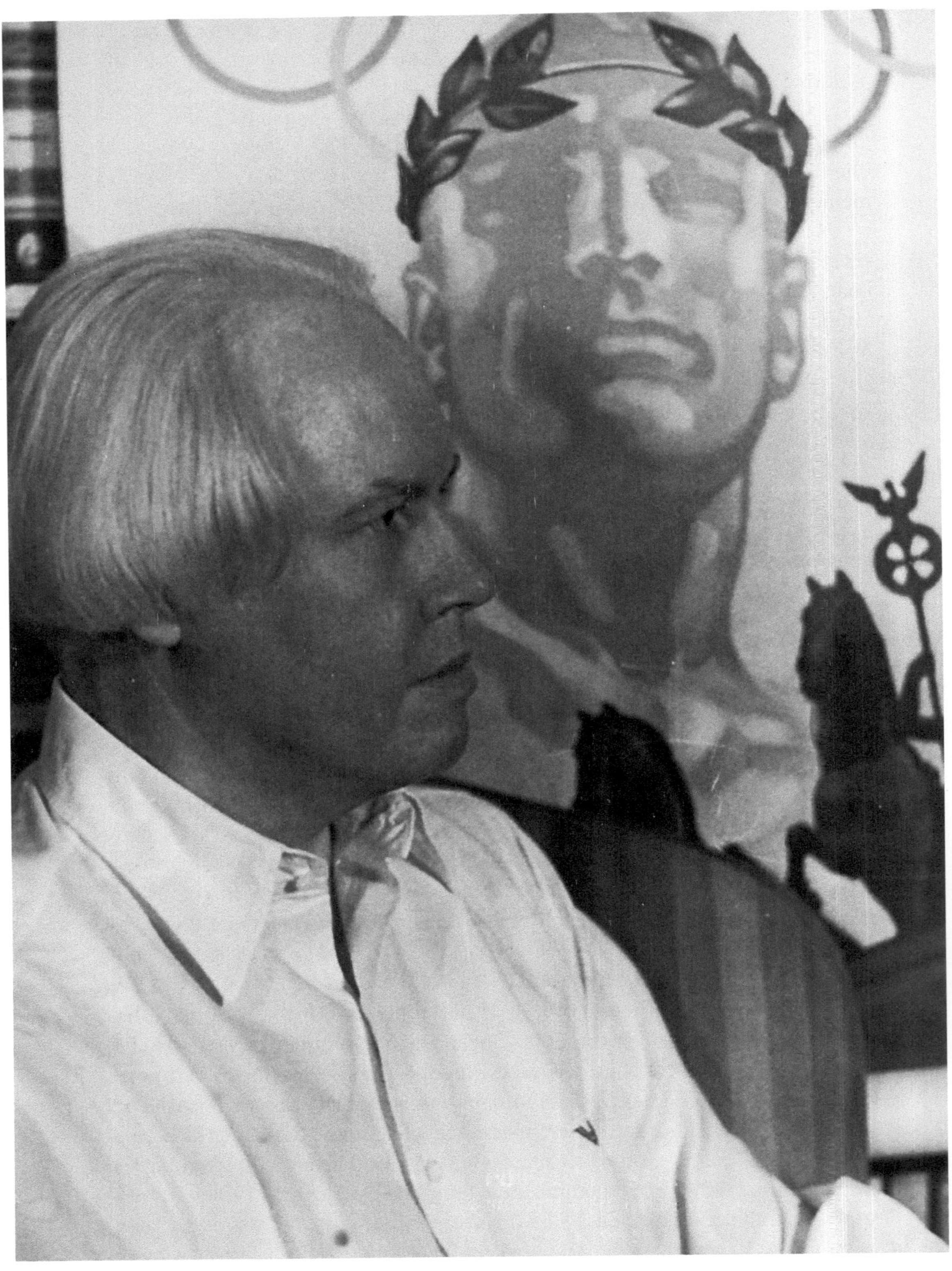

Figures 1.16. Carl Van Vechten, *Carl Van Vechten*, September 1, 1935, XXII i:8. (Beinecke Rare Book and Manuscript Library, Yale University; © The Van Vechten Trust

with cameras.[14] Painting and tinting the black and white photographs added to the cheap chemical image on paper the social value of an expensive, one-of-a-kind oil portrait or miniature painting. In a reversal of equal flourish, artists associated with aristocratic courts painted miniature portraits to include the gray tones of a black and white photograph. Thus painted to look like painted photographs, these courtly images constructed the allure of the modern visual medium and lent paintings what we could call a modernity value.[15]

While the clients of commercial photography may have been migrant workers or people belonging to different social, class, race, and religious backgrounds, images displayed what Anthony Lee calls "the camera's capacity to level social difference and fictionalize status."[16] The sitters came into the studio wearing formal party clothes as a mark of a respectable social position. The photographers may have framed their aspirations further by guiding their poses against appropriately chosen printed and painted backdrops as well as props including a mahogany table with a flower vase or a motorcycle. An iconography of an urban middle class emerges in these aspirational images through a sameness and repetition of look designed by the commercial studios.

Studios normalized social self-fashioning.[17] In images of well-dressed Chinese immigrants in the shoe-factory town of North Adams, Massachusetts, in the late nineteenth century, Lee analyzes their middle-class aspirations, and David and Judith MacDougall document the practices of commercial studios in the hill station of Mussourie in late twentieth-century India, where vacationers would dress up to become bandits and village belles from Bollywood movies and convey a desire to be in an imaginative space of "elsewhere."[18] Whether showing clients in their Sunday best for social respectability or in outlandish dresses for a flight of fancy, these studios launched a vernacular practice that harnessed photography for the local marketplace of small towns, cities, and tourist sites all over the world.

Van Vechten's practice imitates the commercial practice in many ways. Whether fanciful images or straight photographs of well-dressed people, all commercial images exceed mere documentation of the subject (as if there was such a thing) and bring photographic image closer to the subject's own "self-image."[19] In this sense, all images are in some measure fanciful. James Van Der Zee (1886–1993), who owned a commercial establishment in the Harlem district of New York in the 1920s and 1930s, explained his studio practice in this way: "I tried to see that every picture was better looking than the person—if it wasn't better looking than the person I was taking, then I wasn't satisfied with it—I would retouch the pictures and take out some unnecessary lines and shadows and then, before taking them, I would figure out the best angle to try to get as much light and expression and character into the picture as possible. I tried to pose each person in such a way as to tell a story."[20]

Unlike the anxious clients of commercial studios, however, Van Vechten's subjects were practiced performers and other people in the arts: ballet dancers, stage actors, Hollywood celebrities, and fashionable, literary personalities of Harlem. He invited them into his studio as friends to a party. By nature, then, glamour and theatrical skills dominated the performance that evolved around the camera within the privacy of his Upper West Side apartment. Van Vechten's photographs convey a close collaboration between the photographer and the subject. Together, they create a *tableau vivant* akin to Victorian theatricality and expressivity. Julia Margaret Cameron's staged photography, for example, contained a literary or biblical allusion and suggested something of the inner mood of the sitter.[21] If the commercial photographers provided comfort to their clients by promising them a chance to be somebody else or to be "better looking than the person," as Van Der Zee said, the dictum in Van Vechten's studio might be to "be yourself" in an expressive way.

Van Vechten's practice hardly related to the social ethics of photographers such as James Van Der Zee, which came to fruition in aspirational images of younger African American photographers such as Roy DeCarava (1919–2009). Similar to Van Der Zee but not within the framework of commercial photography, DeCarava's sometimes staged and sometimes candid images pursued urban middle-class life of African Americans in New York. They were all taken in the thrall of the civil rights movement and provided a corrective to the racial stereotypes of the Jim Crow–era segregation. Glamorized, backlit portraits of musicians of the Jazz Age in performance highlighted their urban lifestyle and normalized and politicized them in a contest over the American dream. By contrast, Van Vechten highlighted artificiality.[22]

Van Vechten's images suggest a deliberate riff on the commercial studio practice. Skirting the boundary between documenting his subjects and complimenting his sitters in posed images, as Van Der Zee did, he wrote, "I am certain that my first interest in making photographs was documentary and probably my latest interest in making them is documentary too. Nevertheless, even documents may have an artistic value and I saw no reason to make bad photographs or ugly photographs merely because they were intended to be documents."[23]

Van Vechten's photographs typically carry the look of the artisanal images of commercial studios, with sitters in careful poses, in theatrical costumes, and against a range of backgrounds. But the more tightly he closed the frame around his subject, the more activated his backgrounds became, distracting us from the subjects. Our attention is distributed evenly across the image, as we saw in case of Mercedes de Acosta or Van Vechten's self-portrait against the poster of the 1936 Olympic Games. His "formalist" experiments skew the balance toward his artistry. Van Vechten also often literally placed himself in front of the camera, trying out new props, backgrounds, and ways of framing a figure before trying his artistry on his subjects. In short, his hospitality complicates the commercial studio's investment in its subject's self-image and social identity. Instead, photographs turn social identities into an artful presentation contained within the tableau and process of image making.

Van Vechten brought other pretentions to his studio practice. "Carl always puttered a little," writes Kellner, giving us a feel for the nervous energy of the studio:

> An assistant set up the lights. Carl adjusted his camera on a wooden easel; the assistant supplied stools, chairs—indeed, chaise longues or beds—against the draped or otherwise decorated fourth wall. Then the subject sat. The lights were excruciatingly hot, and the room was stuffy. Carl stood behind his camera, staring like a mad scientist in the movies, waiting for the "right moment," in which he always believed. Then the shutter began to snap, sometimes quickly, sometimes with syncopated hesitations, always with Carl's embalmed stare above. Occasionally, there were stops while the composition was improved or complicated with props: robes, costumes, banshee hat, Easter eggs, masks, feathers, cats, marionettes.[24]

The waiting for the "right moment" recalls Henri Cartier-Bresson's photography. Cartier-Bresson's readiness to capture a "decisive moment" out of the nervous flow of everyday life is indicated in a well-known image of the photographer in the outdoors cradling the small German Leica hanging on a strap around his neck.[25] The Leica's promise of capturing the bustle around the photographer as perfectly as an artwork became a motto for the users thereafter. Cartier-Bresson and other photographers took the handheld camera with its famously fast shutter speed to the streets. Its thirty-six-exposure film roll allowed them to select a singular, representative "moment" from the humdrum of busy streets and marketplaces all around the world. In that context, however, it is odd that Van Vechten mounted his Leica on a tripod (or wooden easel, as Kellner notes) and used it largely in his studio. The energy of the studio betrays his amateurism, expressing a pride in the new technological machine that Van Vechten rushed to own in 1932 when his friend, the cartoonist Miguel Covarrubias, brought a Leica from a trip to Germany and boasted about it. Kellner's reference to a "mad scientist in the movies" makes us imagine his studio also as a lab where the photographer became absorbed in an instrument of observation and experimentation.

Bricolage

The difference between a commercial studio and Van Vechten's apartment can be marked in one more way when we ask, What might Van Vechten's sitters be looking at? While a commercial studio might have a storefront opening to a commercial street, Van Vechten's subject would see into the rest of apartment beyond the camera. While the commercial space might have glass cabinets displaying *cartes de visite*, images of other sitters, advertisements, and storage boxes of unused photographic equipment, the clutter was kept separate from the space of fantasy-making. By contrast, Van Vechten's crammed living space included the coffee table with Van Vechten's ceramic cats, a piano in the corner, and the glass cabinet displaying expensive china, with everything up for offer. You could get a glimpse of the adjacent library with bookshelves or the bedroom. Kellner writes,

> A session in the Van Vechten studio was never the easiest thing to survive with savoir-faire. Sometimes, the background was already chosen; sometimes, one had to be dragged out of the catalogued rolls of materials and papers stacked on shelves against one wall of the studio. Another wall bore a fantastic collection of posters, paintings, and sketches; gimcracks and gewgaws perched on every available ledge or edge. A third wall, heavily hung with two or three sets of draperies, contained a casement window through which the subject might see, while waiting for the lenses to be focused, a lovely view of Central Park, just across the street.[26]

Van Vechten added to the ever-changing bricolage of the studio a large selection of fabric curtains, and he asked his models to bring along costumes they might like to wear, matching their appearance with an appropriate prop or backdrop. The broad range of changing backgrounds differed from the generic look of commercial, vernacular photography and became part of Van Vechten's signature style. His meticulous collection of fabrics benefited from a growing demand for internationally made textile in the fashion and furnishing industries of New York in the 1920s. Inspired by the Arts and Crafts movement of the nineteenth century, there was a sudden popularity of Asian textiles, such as Indian Kalamkari and chintz and Indonesian batik. Immigrant artists from Europe who exhibited in the Armory Show of 1913, such as Marguerite Zorach and Pieter Mijer, also explored batik as a medium for painting and sold works through such bookstores as the Sunwise Turn, which Van Vechten must have frequented. Mijer's influential publication *Batiks and How to Make Them* (1919) made batik famous among the modern artists of the Greenwich Village bohemian culture.[27] By the 1930s, interest in "Oriental" textiles pervaded New York in part because of publications such as *Batik in Java*, written for the Needle and Bobbin Club of New York by Tassilo Adam, soon to become a curator at the Brooklyn Museum, as well as the exhibition of Indonesian textiles at the Metropolitan Museum of Art in 1932.[28] Museum collections provided limited historical evidence for motif and techniques, while modern "American Batik" included modernist interpretations inspired by Art Deco.[29] Abby Lillethun also points out that American batik exaggerated flowing lines and an excess of "cracks" using *canting* as a tool for applying wax on the cloth, simply as evidence that the cloth was hand-printed as opposed to industrially produced. These artisanal affects added to the overall look of Van Vechten's images, seen in an example of American batik that Van Vechten may have just acquired in 1937 and used for many images from then onward (figs. 1.17–1.19).

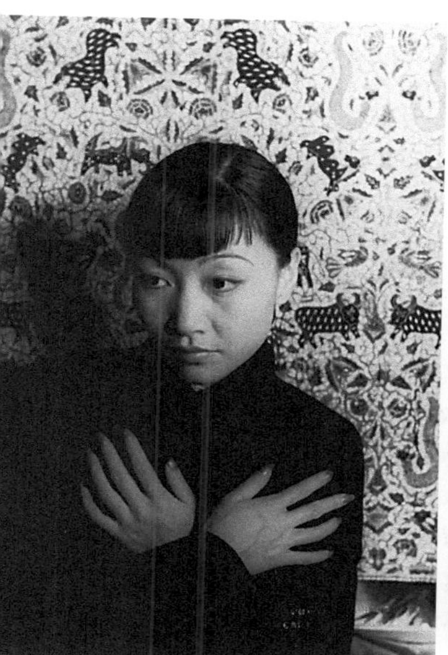
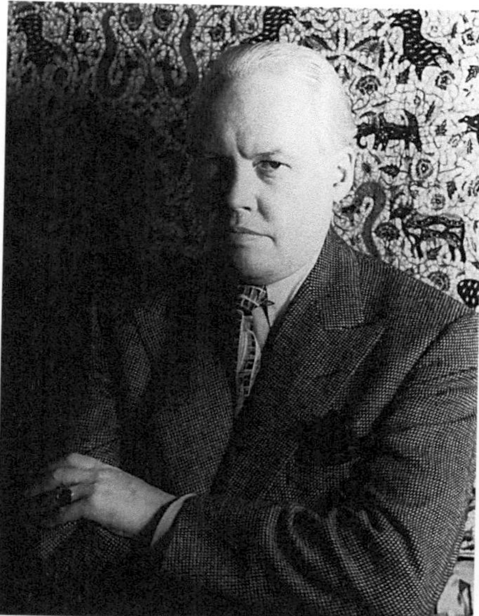
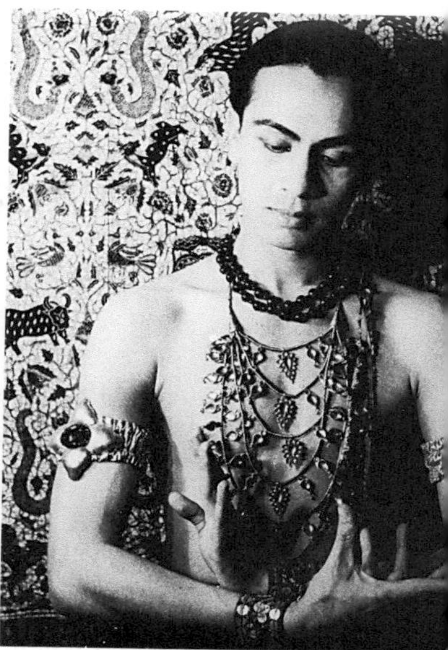

Figures 1.17–1.19. *Left to right*, Carl Van Vechten, *Anna May Wong*, April 29, 1937, XXVI K:20; Mark Lutz, *Carl Van Vechten*, April 25, 1937, XV K36; Carl Van Vechten, *Ram Gopal*, April 21, 1938, XII M16. (Beinecke Rare Book and Manuscript Library, Yale University; © The Van Vechten Trust)

Framing Ram Gopal

How can we glean the nature of the conversation that might have taken place between Gopal and Van Vechten from the photographs? From Kellner's description of the studio, we can imagine Gopal becoming intrigued by the unavoidable sense of the "gimcracks and gewgaws" around the apartment. When the dancer stands in costume in front of the Leica, the photographer takes his position behind the lens. The dancer shows off his training and wonders how the host might respond. The photographer is dazzled but unsure of how close or far from the dancer he should place his camera. We saw Van Vechten's struggle with judging the right distance in the first few photographs from the first day.

As the dancer responds to the conditions of the studio, we can imagine the conversation turning to one important aspect, at least from Van Vechten's side, namely, the camera and the process of image-making. In an interview for the Columbia Oral History Project, Van Vechten claims that, for him, "photography is a very personal thing, even a magical act."[30] We can imagine Van Vechten praising the new German camera and inviting Gopal to appreciate the "magic" of photography. Van Vechten kept a small diary as a record of his daily photo sessions. The diary included the name of his subjects and the date and negative numbers. A key in red ink (a little square, U, a dash, O, etc.) identified the subjects according to the following categories:

Negroes
Authors

Actors
Painters
Photographers
Musicians
Dancers
Athletes
Chinese

The categories are idiosyncratic and troubling. They indicate an impersonal objectification of the sitters and, worse, a white, American photographer's gaze on his racialized subjects. The entry for Ram Gopal ("U" for dancers) says, "Gopal, Ram. April 21, 38, XI M–XII M. XIII M—in gold costumes, jodhpurs and with CCV—May 5, 38, XVII M—in costumes—May 11—XVIII M (with Janta as god) XIX M–XX M . . . moves to another subject."[31] We will soon see what he meant by "Janta as god" on the last day of the photo shoot, on May 11. The comment about "gold costumes" and "jodhpurs" suggests Van Vechten's response to the exotic appeal of the dancer's costumes. Van Vechten may have shared with Gopal images of other performers and the way he constructed their exotic and erotic appeal with matched fabric acquired from the boutique shops in the bohemian districts of the city.

The printed fabric seems to have stabilized the conversation between the two men. Van Vechten had just tried the batik with the pastoral scene on himself and the Chinese American Hollywood star Anna May Wong (figs. 1.17 and 1.18). A tight midshot brought out an interplay between the background motifs and the lively face and expressive hands of the performers in front. Wong spreads her hands like the open wings of a bird against her black turtleneck sweater. Gopal catches the drift and brings his two hands together, his left in the *pallava* (leaf or petal) and the right in *alapadma* (open flower) gestures, combined to show the gradual opening of lotus blossoms (fig. 1.19).

Meanwhile, what personal interests does the dancer bring to the conversation? We have no evidence except for what the images themselves offer. In chapter 2, we will explore in them traces of his life and training in India as well as the long, eventful journey that got him to New York and in touch with Van Vechten. In the studio, he opened the two suitcases full of dance costumes he was carrying with him, enough to excite the photographer's taste for exoticism and to inspire his choice for an appropriate fabric backdrop.

Van Vechten's studio notebook records two more sessions following Gopal's concert at the 46th Street Theatre on May 1, 1938. On May 5, Van Vechten photographs the dancer "in costume." Gopal wears a princely dress including a shiny, embroidered kurta and a pair of tight white pants that Van Vechten calls "jodhpurs," and the photographer catches the seated dancer against a batik fabric with circular disks printed on it. In one such image, he also unusually wears a fez cap (fig. 1.20). Then, on May 11, he wears a long black jacket (a sherwani) and wraps a turban around his head (fig. 1.21). Van Vechten complements the elegant silhouette with a delicately embroidered fabric background. In this group of portraits, the dancer may be displaying Indian ethnic types and reflecting possibly the attire of the members of various groups participating in the nationalistic political struggles of the time in India.[32] For the turban, Gopal could have simply used the cotton sash he wore around his waist in other photographs. But it is unlikely that Gopal would have carried a fez cap among his dance costumes. It is more likely that the fez is Van Vechten's contribution, and the dancer may have simply been playing out the photographer's fantasy of the Orient.

Vivek Bald describes the emergence of a taste for "the Orient" in white middle-class culture of US cities such as New York and Chicago since the 1890s. An overall lifestyle, reflected in interior design, dress, and food, was inspired by "the sensual and exotic East." Themed rooms for men's leisure activities included "smoking rooms with plush Oriental rugs, hookahs, tiger skins, elephant tusks, daggers, scimitars, and images of 'eroticized Eastern women.'"[33] The fez cap became a part of the dressing code for a "smoking-room culture." Significantly, Bald adds two interracial twists to the fez that Americanize the cap in the early twentieth century and bring it close to Van Vechten's tastes. First, Bald documents a traffic of peddlers from India, especially Muslim men from Bengal, who plied embroidered silk and cotton fabric handkerchiefs and other exotic trinkets in New York, at seashore getaways in New Jersey such as

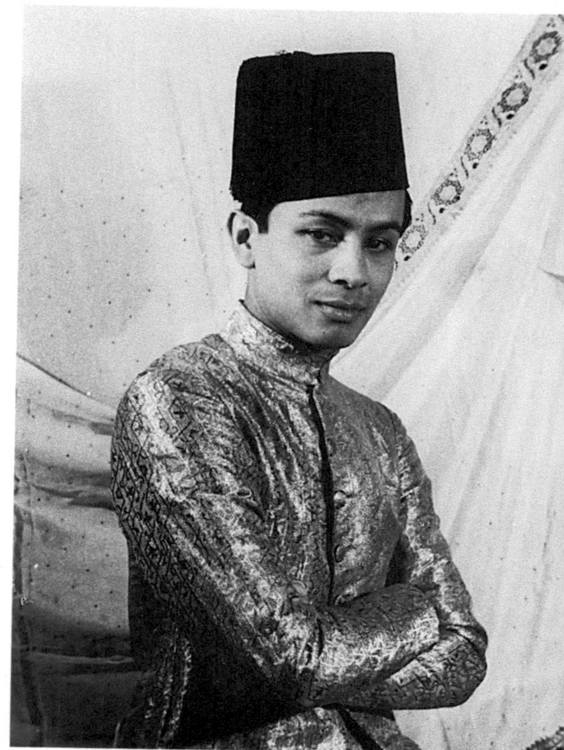

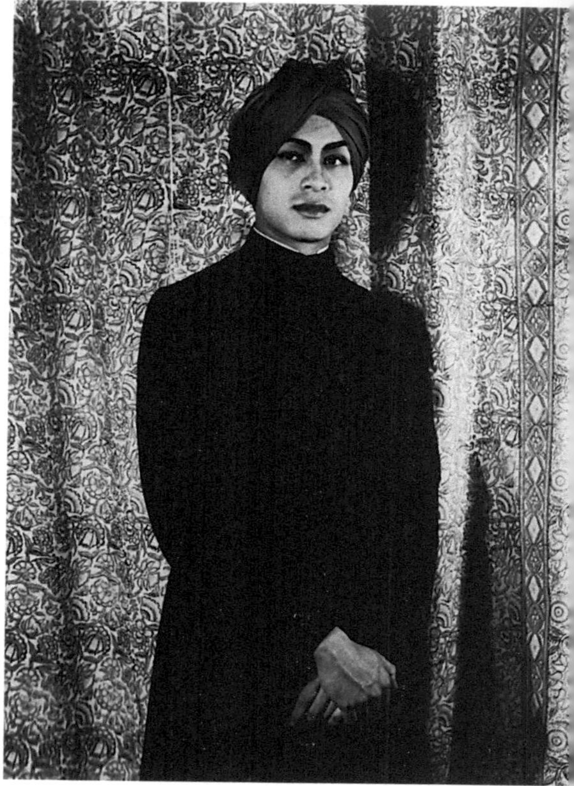

Figures 1.20 and 1.21. *Top*, Carl Van Vechten, *Ram Gopal*, May 5, 1938, XVII M8. *Bottom*, Carl Van Vechten, *Ram Gopal*, May 11, 1938, XVIII M4. (Beinecke Rare Book and Manuscript Library, Yale University; © The Van Vechten Trust)

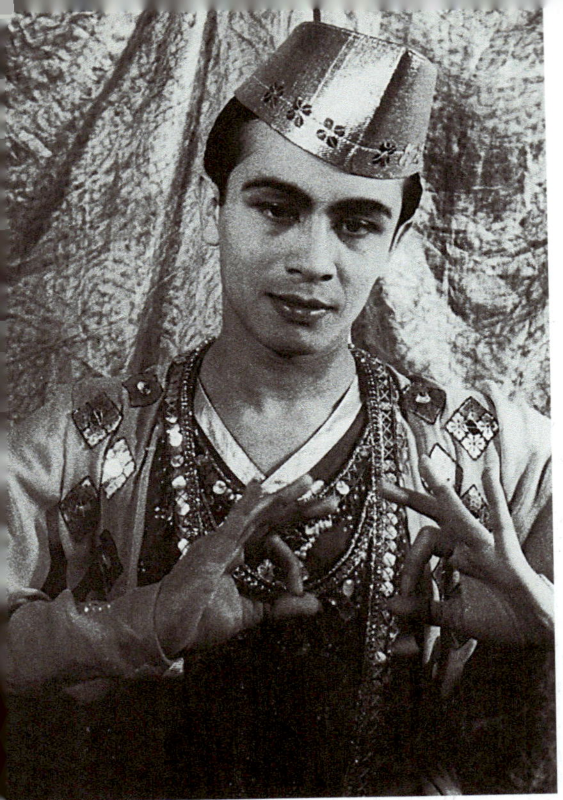

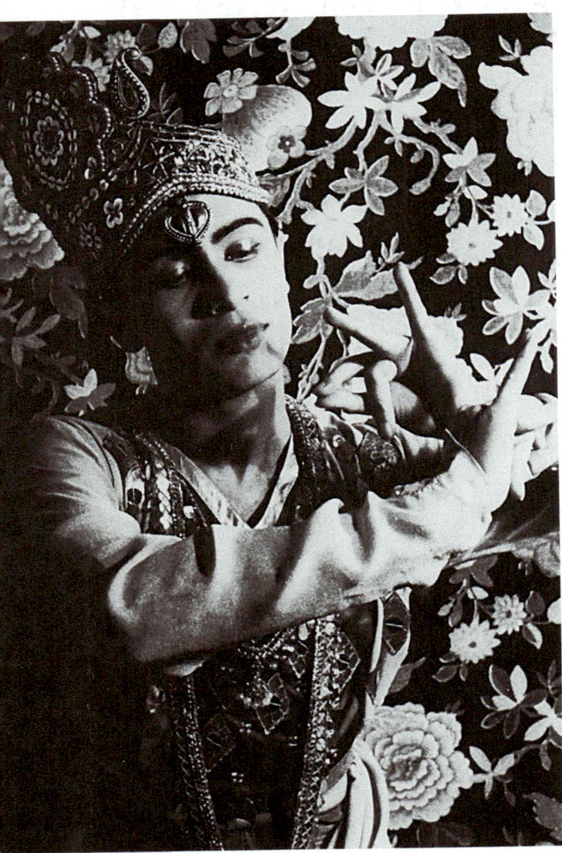

Atlantic City and Asbury Park, and in southern cities such as Charleston, Atlanta, and New Orleans. In order to claim the authenticity of their products, the men played up their own exotic "Hindoo" identity, becoming "peddlers of notions" by wearing "'fezes,' 'frock coats,' and 'interesting blouses.'" And here is the second twist in Bald's story. By the 1920s, when Asians were legally barred from becoming naturalized citizens, these South Asian men ended up living in African American neighborhoods of a racially segregated United States and occasionally "passed" as whites. Intriguingly, just as these men disappeared into the segregated communities of the Jim Crow era, African American men wore turbans, fezes, and gowns in order to escape racial violence by pretending to be spiritualists and magicians from the exotic East. A Black community magazine thus noted that "some of the race's best folk tales are tied up in turbans and a half dozen other ways dark negroes 'pass' down south."[34] Gopal's turban and fez cap are not simply representations of Oriental types but also representations of a promiscuous, interracial passing in the eyes of the photographer. In chapter 3, we will discuss a painting by Florine Stettheimer that places Van Vechten in the segregated beach of Asbury Park, where he is shown on a terrace with a turbaned "Eastern" figure in front of a gold urn (fig. 3.6).

Probably the most elaborate session follows on May 11, 1938, taking more than two film rolls and producing the bulk of the images. After turban and sherwani, Gopal returns to dance. He takes on the costume

Figures 1.22 and 1.23. *Top*, Carl Van Vechten, *Ram Gopal*, May 11, 1938, XVIII M23. *Bottom*, Carl Van Vechten, *Ram Gopal*, May 11, 1938, XVIII M33. (Beinecke Rare Book and Manuscript Library, Yale University; © The Van Vechten Trust)

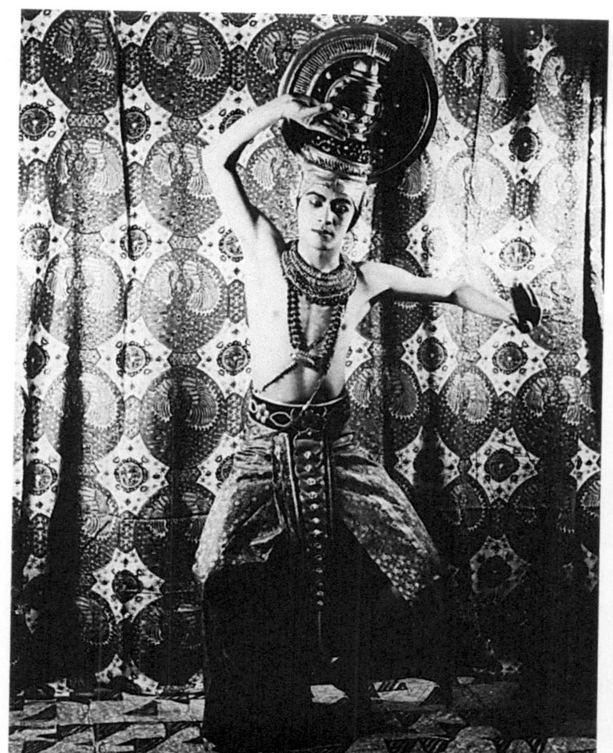

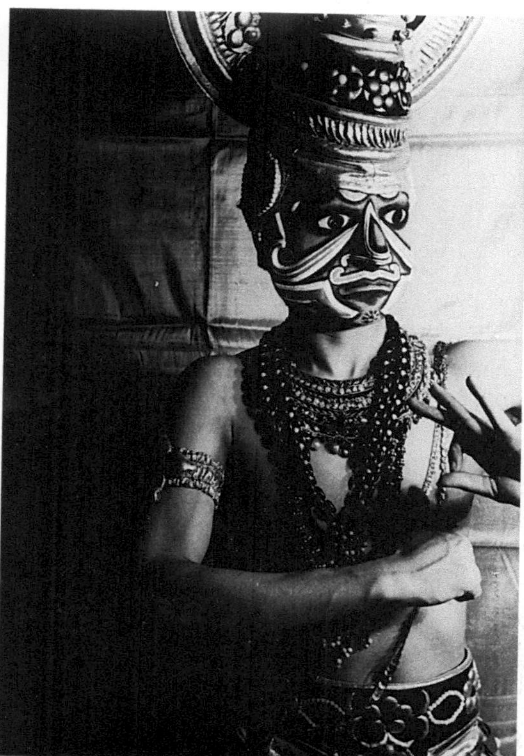

Figures 1.24 and 1.25. *Left*, Carl Van Vechten, *Ram Gopal*, May 11, 1938, XIX M10. *Right*, (Beinecke Rare Book and Manuscript Library, Yale University; © The Van Vechten Trust)

of the North Indian Kathak, wearing a long, gold-trimmed *achkan*, a dress with a flowing skirt and cap that derived from the courtly cultures of Mughal India. He demonstrates the Kathak's hand positions, and in one photograph, he performs a typical pirouette that blurs the skirt and hands (figs. 1.22 and 5.3). Gopal also wears a sumptuous, gem-studded gold crown, hands lifted to the side in a *kataka mukha* (as if opening a chain link) to depict a flower garland or portray Krishna playing the flute, which Van Vechten complements with a bold, floral background (fig. 1.23).

We can clearly see Gopal's participation in the photo shoot and hear his voice as an expert in classical Indian dance. He demonstrates the postures and hand gestures that make up the narrative motifs in various traditions. From Kathak, he continues into the South Indian form of Kathakali, in which he was primarily trained (figs. 24 and 25). He starts in an informal costume worn by Kathakali dancers during practice sessions. He then puts on the bulbous crown with a circular halo and then, oddly, a mask intended to mimic the usual face paint of a traditional Kathakali dancer.

As Gopal gets into the technical weeds of Indian dance, the conversation guides Van Vechten's camera. A series of half-length photographs appear like

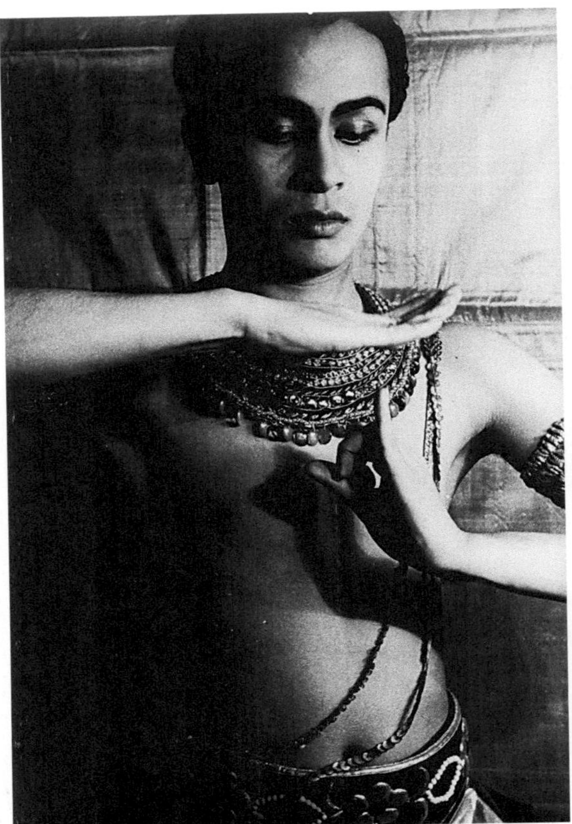

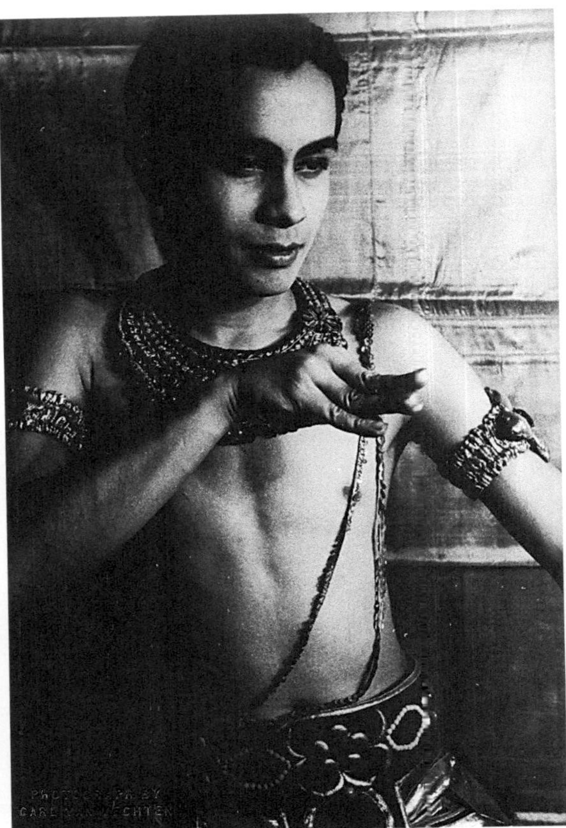

Figures 1.26 and 1.27. *Left*, Carl Van Vechten, *Ram Gopal*, May 11, 1938, XIX M27. *Right*, Carl Van Vechten, *Ram Gopal*, May 11, 1938, XIX M36. (Beinecke Rare Book and Manuscript Library, Yale University; © The Van Vechten Trust)

study images that focus on the hand gestures (*hastamudras*) against a plain background. In one, Gopal brings his left hand to his heart in a *simha mukha* (lion face), with the right creating a shelter over it using a *tripataka* (three flag), suggesting in combination a *mudra* for a wise sage (fig. 1.26). In another, he pinches and points his fingers forward to show the attack of a Garuda eagle or the dart of a cobra snake (fig. 1.27). For an image at the New York Public Library, the dancer holds up his hands to frame his eyes with his two fingers, and Van Vechten writes on the back, "Ram Gopal: The gesture means: I have beautiful eyes" (fig. 5.13). Van Vechten asks the dancer to stand on a stool for a set of extreme close-ups, and Gopal demonstrates the foot positions from his foundational training in the South Indian Kathakali, characterized by the raised large toe (fig. 1.28).

The images from the last day of the photo shoot indicate a two-way exchange between the dancer and the photographer. Several close-ups and half-length views taken that day show the dancer feeding the photographer's curiosity about Indian dance. The images also show how the photographer arranged for quickly changing to backgrounds that suit the dancer's figurations. He piled up several fabric curtains on top of each other, ready to use, suspending them from the same rod from which the basic heavy curtain hung in his living room, as we saw in the Danielson photograph. In many images, we see the different fabrics layered behind each other, ready to be pulled forward or pushed aside on short notice, as needed. In the Kathak pirouette image, for example, we see the base curtain on the right and a block-printed fabric with black, red, and yellow disks draped over it (fig. 5.3).[35] When Gopal wears the Kathakali crown, Van Vechten matches the circular halo with decorative rondels containing dancing peacocks (fig. 1.24).[36] In a series of close-ups, a sundial echoes the Kathakali halo (fig. 1.29).

Toward the end of the last day's photo session, the photographer and the dancer give free rein to their fantasies. Gopal goes beyond his training. For one group of images, he wraps himself in a transparent veil, in essence feminizing his body (figs. 2.22 and 3.1). I explore these images of a veiled, half-naked, dancer in chapter 3 and propose them as the photographer's fantasy that Gopal entertains. Also, before finishing the roll on that day, Van Vechten photographed Janta as a four-armed Indian god (fig. 1.30). For that purpose, Gopal gave the Polish journalist a quick lesson in Kathakali. He also provided Janta with the additional pair of hands. Referring back to the Danielson image, we can imagine Gopal standing hidden in the narrow space between the window of the living room and the curtain, draping

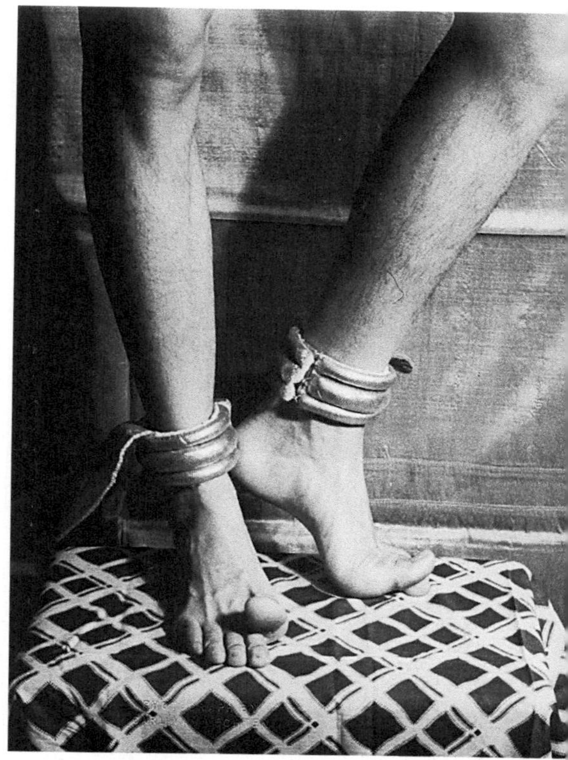

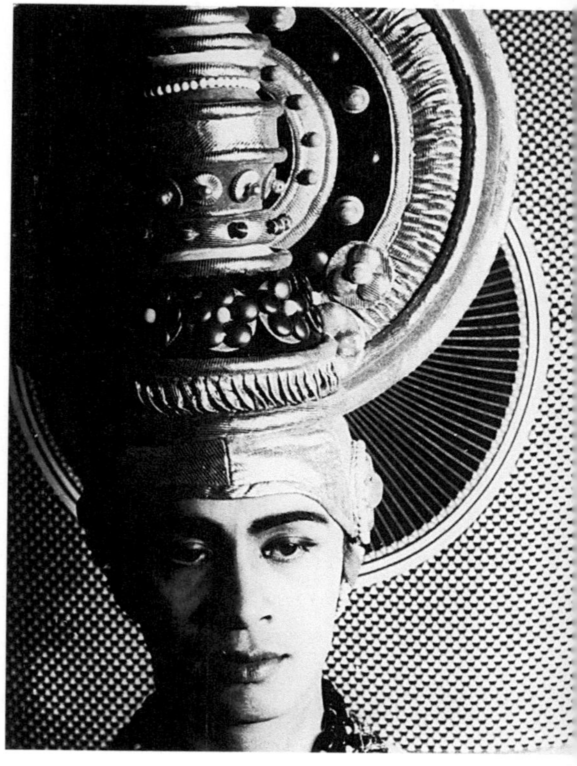

Figures 1.28 and 1.29. *Top*, Carl Van Vechten, *Ram Gopal*, May 11, 1938, XIX MI4. *Bottom*, Carl Van Vechten, *Ram Gopal*, May 11, 1938, XIX M23. (Beinecke Rare Book and Manuscript Library, Yale University; © The Van Vechten Trust)

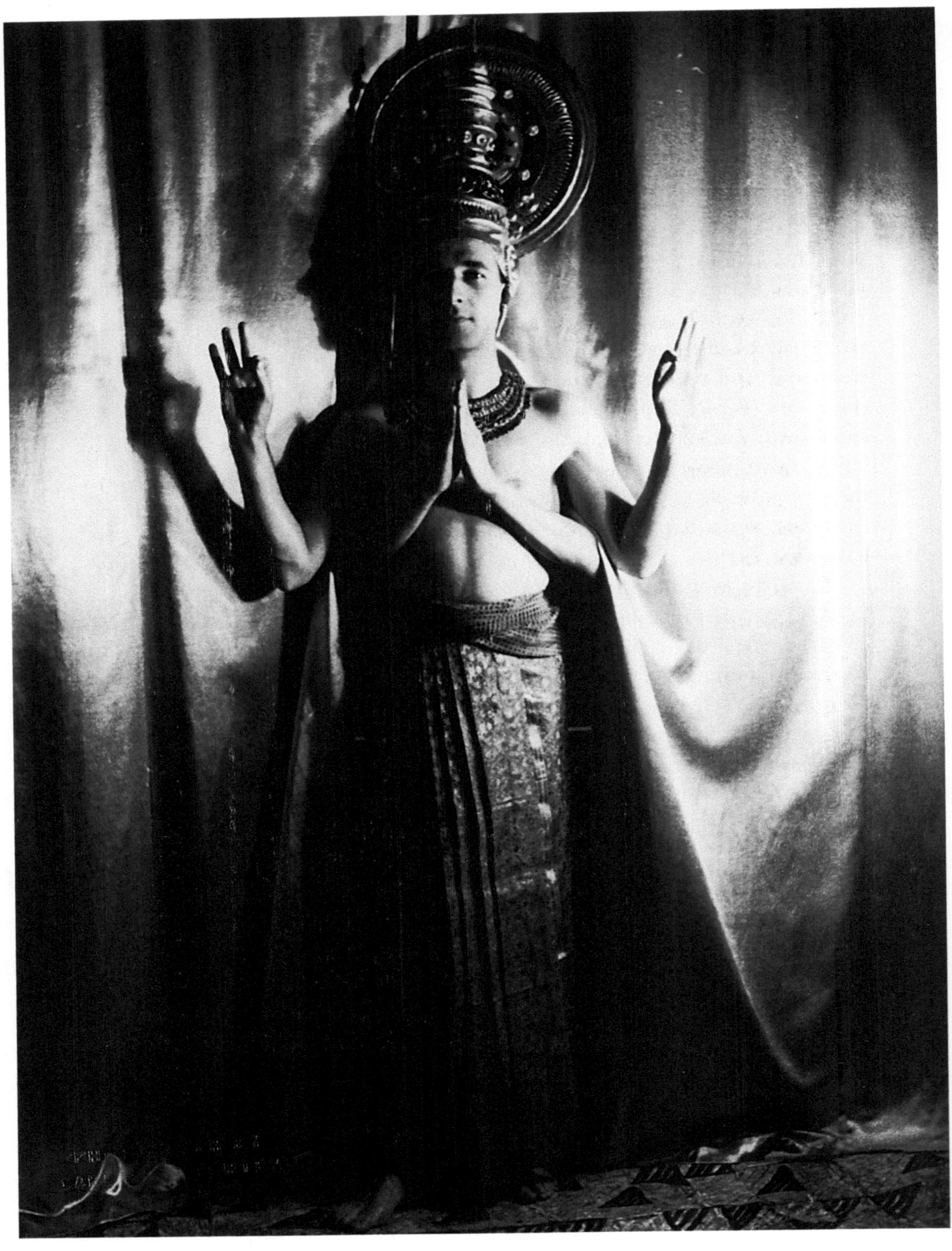

Figure 1.30. Carl Van Vechten, *Ram Gopal and Aleksander Janta*, May 11, 1938, XX M28. (Beinecke Rare Book and Manuscript Library, Yale University; © The Van Vechten Trust)

the fabric around his arm to keep the outside light out of the picture. The four arms make different gestures for four different photographs. The curtain folds are also manipulated for different effects, sometimes looking like a cape and sometimes wings behind Janta's body. Van Vechten places a single, strong floodlight a little to the right of the figure. The light throws a profile shadow of Janta's face on the left so as to evoke a second head attached to this multiplying deity. The spotlight also creates a circular orb around the figure similar to the ring of fire surrounding Shiva Nataraja in the ancient South Indian bronze sculpture. In a letter to Van Vechten on August 8, 1938, Janta quipped, "even I like myself in Kathakali poses, which I seldom do, believe me."[37]

The more or less shot-by-shot inventory of photographs helps us imagine Van Vechten's apartment studio as a space in which a slowly evolving conversation takes place between the Indian dancer and the American photographer in the spring of 1938. The conversation is intimate and private, but it depends on their capacity for indulging each other's fantasies instead of an easy familiarity with each other. The dancer not only represents his training but also mirrors the desires of his somewhat-enamored, exoticizing viewer. The Polish journalist participates in this cross-cultural fantasy, energized by the material possibilities of the studio.

The sequential arrangement helps us discover an uneven negotiation of cultural expectations, as well as a flow of interests and desires over the span of three days. The first session on April 21 was probably led by Van Vechten, while Gopal responded with the splendor of his dance as well as costumes that go beyond his dance training. By the end of the session, with Janta's participation, the three form a bond around playful, homoerotic configurations. The second session on May 5 was brief and possibly unplanned, as if Gopal showed up wearing his "jodhpurs" for a social evening and Van Vechten grabbed the chance of the dancer's presence in the studio, taking portrait-like images without putting too many demands on him and even lending him a fez cap to wear over his princely attire.[38] The third and final session, on May 11, was animated by Van Vechten's appreciation of Indian dance and the knowledge he may have gained after seeing Gopal's stage performance. The dancer may have led the conversation that day and addressed the curiosity of the photographer about India's dance traditions. Images illustrate the technical details. Costumes raise the "authenticity" effect of forms such as Kathakali and Kathak. Janta's representation of Shiva from Kathakali may have been Gopal's idea, but the three collaborate equally, putting the Polish body, the Indian arms, and the American lighting cans together to produce the Orientalized image of a multiarmed, multiheaded Indian god. Finally, Gopal's poses with the veil indicate a moment when the dancer let his hair loose, so to speak, and allowed Van Vechten to play out a fantasy of a feminized figure from modern dance on his body.

After the Photo Shoot

For everyone involved, the first day of the photo shoot carried a unique sense of newness and adventure in the studio. Standing in front of the camera, Gopal stepped out of his tradition. Van Vechten faced the challenges of lighting and framing a dazzlingly exotic figure that he had never seen except in Hollywood films. Both the dancer and the photographer notched up the dazzle in the studio in their own separate ways.

On May 6, 1938, a few days after Van Vechten had a chance to see Gopal's concert at the 46th Street Theatre on May 1, he sent Gopal a picture postcard of one of his images from the first day. On the back, he wrote in green ink, "Dear Ram, as a photograph I think *this* is my favorite!" (fig. 4.3). We will discuss the postcard in detail in chapter 4 and speculate on why Van Vechten considered the oddly skewed image of the dancer his favorite. For now, the postcard helps us understand that the conversation between the two men in the studio was not only about dance but also about photography. On May 11, after the postcard was delivered, a long photo session followed that was their most adventuresome by far, leading us to wonder what the intent of the postcard might have been. Was it simply a photographer's boast of his image practice or an invitation to the dancer to collaborate one more time and explore together what the Leica could do?

Van Vechten returned obsessively to that first day of the photo shoot to experiment with the dancer's figurations in the darkroom. We will discuss those experiments in detail in chapter 4. For now, it is useful to emphasize that, for Van Vechten, the darkroom and the studio were interlinked spaces where a single creative process evolved, except under different conditions. "When you're taking pictures, you depend somewhat on the subject, and if you have an assistant, which I have, he does the lighting. But developing and printing are fascinating, are far the most interesting part of photography. And without being tricky—I never have photographs retouched, or never do tricks of any kind . . . like trimming down bodies, printing with distortions and what-not."[39]

The quotation suggests that the darkroom was for Van Vechten not a separate space for manipulating and transforming a photograph taken in the studio. Rather, it was where the conversations taking place around the Leica were completed. We will complicate Van Vechten's disclaimer about "tricks of any kind" in chapter 4. But we will also take his claim seriously and treat the darkroom as a space in which a thought process from the studio gained focus and intensity away from the studio's noise and commotion. "Developing and printing are much the most fascinating part of photography, because you don't have anybody around but yourself and you have to do things in a very skillful way and depend entirely on yourself."[40] Before we turn to how Van Vechten took the studio's cross-cultural conversation into the quietness of his darkroom, let us return to the studio to hear the dancer's voice in that conversation more clearly.

CHAPTER 2.
THE DANCER

It is one thing to consider the photographer to be the master of the camera, the studio, the darkroom, the image. A photographer's control over the photograph's subject has been a founding premise in the history of photography since its inception in the nineteenth century anyway, and it continued to be so when photography became a part of the colonial domination of regions around the world. It is quite another matter to imagine the way the subjects being photographed write themselves into that history. In chapter 1, we saw Ram Gopal engaging the American photographer in a conversation in the New York studio. But given the controlling presence of the photographer and the imperialism of the camera at work in history writing and the photo archives, this chapter asks, How does the Indian dancer control his presence in the Van Vechten archives? Gopal's presence is not authored in the same way as Van Vechten's. It is an ephemeral presence, in two ways. First, in the archives, Gopal briefly occupies a moment indicated by a date in the photographer's oeuvre. The full-bodied representations we see in the 1938 photographs also remain ephemeral in another way. They disappear under a robust identity and presence that Gopal created for himself in the history and living memory of Indian dance. This chapter explores the dancer's spectral presence in Van Vechten's archives as what Trouillot calls "the silence of the past," a silence produced by the historical participants at the moment of history making as well as the archives and histories built around that silence.[1] To break through that silence, the question guiding the chapter is, How does Gopal control the camera in New York and bring his body into existence in the Van Vechten archives?

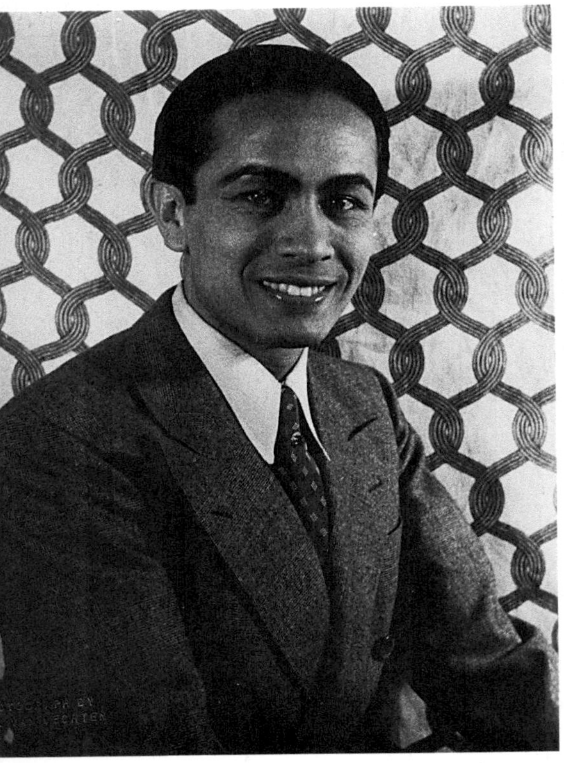

Figure 2.1. Carl Van Vechten, *Ram Gopal*, April 21, 1938, XII M12. (Beinecke Rare Book and Manuscript Library, Yale University; © The Van Vechten Trust)

To identify Gopal's role in image-making, I can of course do no better than lead the story with the images themselves. In them, I gather traces of a journey that brought the dancer to New York City in the spring of 1938. When we locate him in the moment when he appeared in Van Vechten's studio, his manipulation of the camera becomes apparent, and his archival presence comes to the surface of the image.

Toward the end of the first day of the photo shoot on April 21, 1938, Gopal sat for a series of portraits (fig. 2.1). He is well dressed in a double-breasted jacket he wore aboard the ocean liner that brought him to the United States.[2] He looks assured, if somewhat reserved, staring at the camera with a slightly guarded smile. The carefully composed figure recalls the everyday normalcy of a passport photo. The image is unusual only because we know that Gopal started the photo session with his costumed dance poses. We can still see traces of the eyeliner and the gloss on his face. Are we then to see the image simply as a portrait, separate from his dance photographs, or as yet another performance in front of the camera?

Gopal was included in Van Vechten's social circle immediately upon his arrival in New York City. We get a hint of his welcome from six photographs, mounted on a single black, velvety page from a household photo album (fig. 2.2).[3] The dancer stands against a brick and stone frame of a street-level entrance to an apartment. The double-breasted suit in which we see him in the Van Vechten

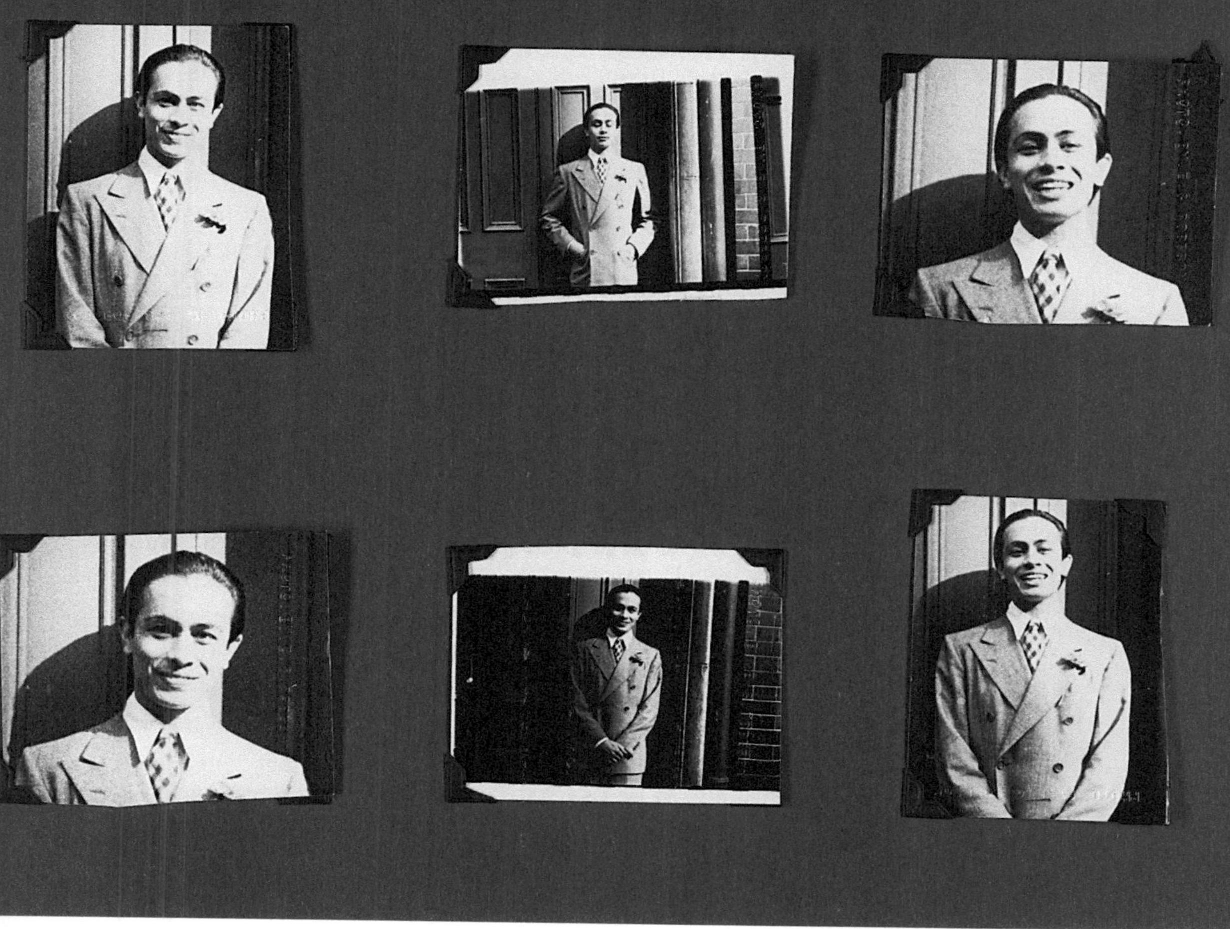

Figure 2.2. Eslanda Goode Robeson, *Ram Gopal*, September 1939, London. (James Weldon Johnson Collection in the Yale Collection of American Literature, Beinecke Rare Book and Manuscript Library)

portrait seems overexposed in the outdoors, and the tie is checkered. It must be a different day and a different photographer. The name of the photographer, "E. G. Robeson," embossed on each image, refers to Eslanda Goode Robeson, the anthropologist-photographer wife of the African American stage actor and activist Paul Robeson. The Robesons were close family friends of the Van Vechtens, as attested by Van Vechten's many photographs of them taken over a long period of time.[4] Gopal's album pictures were taken in London in September 1939 during the dancer's return to Europe for a concert tour (he did not go to New York City at that time). The images are cut from picture postcards Robeson may have sent to Van Vechten. The album page indicates the Robesons' shared friendship with Gopal that continued at least for a year after the dancer's 1938 visit to New York.

In the Robeson album pictures, Gopal shuffles between folding his hands in front of his body and tucking them in his jacket pocket. As the camera pulls close to him, a beaming smile appears on his face, conveying good-humored sociality on his part. By contrast, in Van Vechten's studio, Gopal's appearance is guided by the photographer. We imagine Van Vechten asking him to look away from the camera and fix his eyes at a point in the distance so as to steady the face. We almost hear Van Vechten saying, "Turn a little to the left. No, a little more to the right. Perfect."[5] At that angle, the tip of the young man's nose and the pouting lips touch the curve of his farther cheek without breaking its smooth, linear sweep. Gopal wraps his arms around his belly, showing containment and distance. There is no smile. The image captures formality. The dancer holds back all signs of interiority and objectifies himself as a distinguished gentleman in front of the camera. The expression feels performed (fig. 2.3).

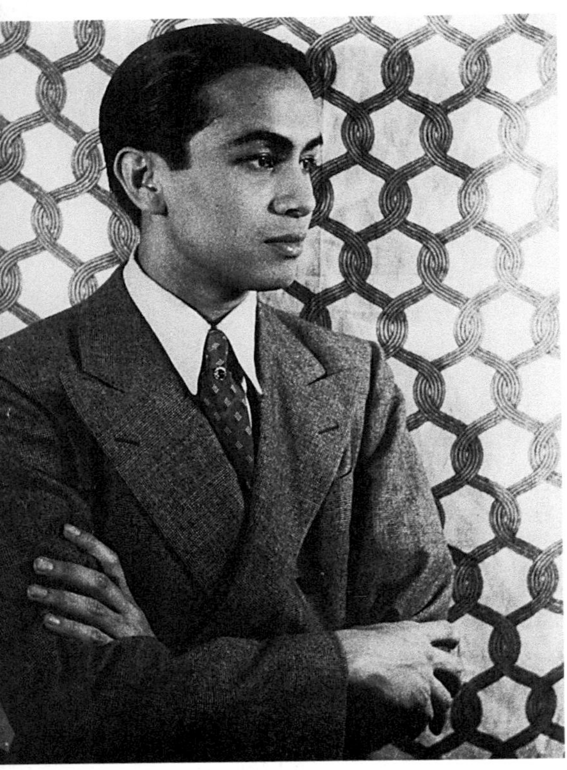

Figure 2.3. Carl Van Vechten, *Ram Gopal*, April 21, 1938, XIII M15. (Beinecke Rare Book and Manuscript Library, Yale University; © The Van Vechten Trust)

Van Vechten's portraits clearly refer to the practices of a commercial photo studio, where sitters came to pose, lit against a plain or painted background, for images that complemented and normalized their social ambitions. For Gopal, Van Vechten chose a fabric showing geometrically arranged chain links of intertwined chords, which he reserved for formal portraits of friends dressed in their fine social attire.[6] Stretched like wallpaper, the Art Deco print conveys the offstage stylishness of a celebrity. The sameness of these images differs from those of performers in theatrical costumes and roles, which he regularly matched with cellophane glitter and a wide variety of printed fabrics.

Van Vechten's reference to the commercial practice is playful. After all, his is not a commercial enterprise. Photography was a private sport for him. He took pride in being an amateur. He exposed many more rolls than might be economically viable for a commercial establishment. While a commercial photographer might select a single negative to make multiple prints in different sizes, Van Vechten extravagantly printed all his negatives, frequently in large-format prints and picture postcards to send to friends. If commercial photography normalized the social status of clients through a steady repetition of frame as well as looks and appearances, Van Vechten's multiple negatives and differently composed figures highlighted the artificiality of pose and picture-making during the photo shoot. In negative strips or Van Vechten's enlargements arranged in sequence, we detect bodily movement in Gopal's

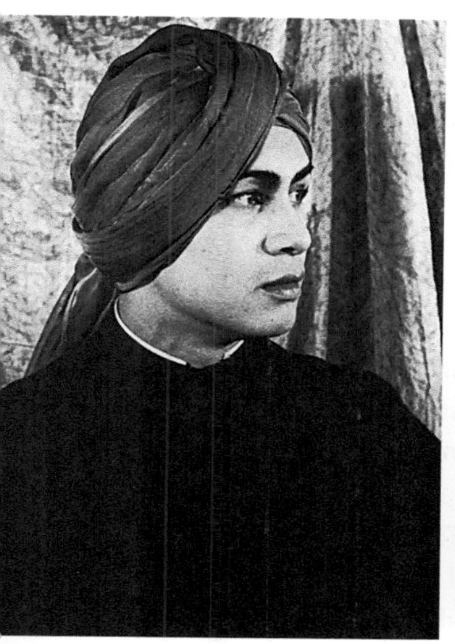
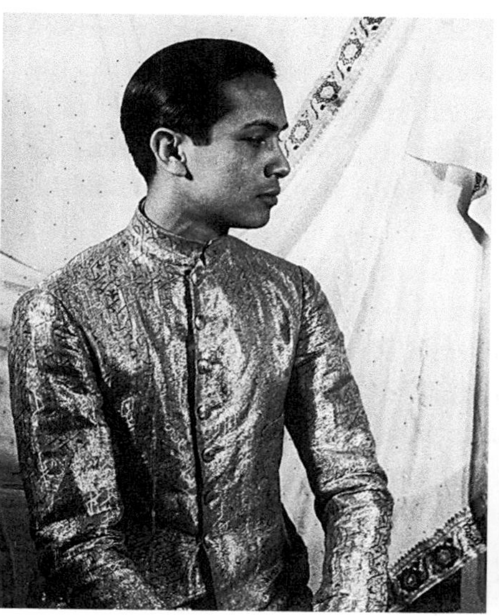
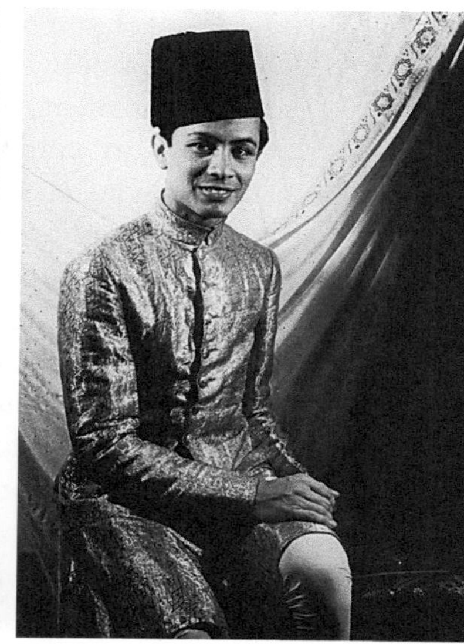

Figures 2.4–2.6. *Left to right*, Carl Van Vechten, *Ram Gopal*, May 11, 1938, XVIII M8; Carl Van Vechten, *Ram Gopal*, May 5, 1938, XVII M7; Carl Van Vechten, *Ram Gopal*, May 5, 1938, XVII M14.

appearing and disappearing smile and his various costumed poses as in a flip book or motion picture (fig. 1.1).

Gopal participates in Van Vechten's playful riff on commercial photography. As the photographer brings Gopal's body within the convention of formal portraits, the dancer generates a proliferation of distinct identities in front of the camera. The theme of the second day of the photo shoot, on May 5, 1938, is indeed the multiplicity of social identities. Gopal switches costumes, wearing ethnically marked dresses of different urban social types in India. He wears a black Sherwani and a turban to suggest a religious reformer or a nationalist leader. Then again, wearing an embroidered, buttoned-up kurta and hair combed back, he sits upright like a prince to be photographed in profile. He then relaxes and switches to a smile and looks at the camera, wearing a fez cap (figs. 2.4–2.6). Most of Gopal's costumes may have come from India, but the fez cap is unusual and, as discussed in chapter 1, may have been furnished by the photographer.[7] The dancer's body seems to have become an instrument of play for both the dancer and the photographer.

The representation of various social identities brings Gopal's photographs close to the portraits of Parisian gentlemen by the French nineteenth-century photographer Félix Nadar as well as the photographic portraits of prominent gentlemen in the princely state of Indore in India, which Christopher Pinney has documented.[8] The Indore portraits were displayed in a gallery in the maharaja's palace to showcase the cosmopolitan culture of the state under the British colonial rule. Gopal might have been exposed to a similar display of colonial elites in the princely state of Mysore in South India.

Gopal grew up in Bangalore, a major cosmopolitan hub within the South Indian princely state. At a distance from Mysore, the official palace city of the Wodeyar rulers, Bangalore was first established as a base for the British army in 1799, when it defeated the formidable Muslim ruler of the region, Tipu Sultan, and installed the Hindu clan of Wodeyars as the custodians of the region. The city was designed to house the princely bureaucracy and serve the interests of the military officials and soldiers. The relationship between the British and the local administrative sectors was clearly built into the fabric of the colonial city. The Cubbon Park, built in 1864, separated the British enclave from the old city, which came under the jurisdiction of the princely state and centered on the fort and Tipu Sultan's palace. The military cantonment evolved around a parade ground under the British administration. By the 1900s, residential neighborhoods called Richmond Town, Benson Town, Cleveland Town, and Frazer Town developed around manicured, gated parks and included bungalows belonging to both British residents and Indians serving in the British civil service. Around Artillery, Brigade, Infantry, and Cavalry Roads grew a mix of clubs, churches, shops, polo grounds, gymnasia, breweries, and tobacco factories. A resident official of the maharaja was stationed within the cantonment on what became the Residency Road. By the 1930s, Dewan Mirza Ismail, the visionary prime minister of Maharaja Krishnaraja Wodeyar IV, commissioned major public buildings including the Bangalore Town Hall and initiated the construction of industrial sectors, workers' housing, commercial streets, and theater and cinema halls that brought the two parts of the city into a close interaction.[9] A diversity of architectural styles by British and European architects distinguished palaces, civic buildings, and industrial and housing complexes of a new urban topography. Dewan Mirza Ismail also promoted the idea of Bangalore as a beautiful city through a picturesque mix of vineyards, orchards, and an array of large water tanks (or lakes) available for strolls and boat rides.

The city carried an air of leisure and came to be known as a place to retire after a successful career in the British civil service. Here, the Mysorean elites, British soldiers, and an international community of professionals, scholars, musicians, and artists commingled in commercial districts, in palace gatherings, at tennis courts, and in the Theosophical Society compound. Ram Gopal's father settled in Benson Town after a successful law practice in Burma and became an amateur scholar of Shakespeare. Ram Gopal grew up in a sprawling bungalow, grandly called the Torquay Castle. The cantonment culture, with its mixed, mostly English-speaking crowd, suited Gopal's half-Burmese and half-Rajput background. In a letter to Mercedes de Acosta, Gopal recalls the leisurely lifestyle of his youthful days, sunbathing on a boat on a lake outside the city along with oiled, naked bodies of friends. On the edge of the lake was a Russian farmer who raised chickens and pigs and fed them fruits and vodka.[10] In the 1940s, when Gopal established a dance school in the Torquay Castle, a student at that time, the great Bharatanatyam dancer Mrinalini Sarabhai, remembered Gopal frequently missing lessons to be with friends and play tennis at one of the British clubs.[11]

Gopal brings the urban lifestyle of the princely city to Van Vechten's studio. His myriad images in regional and ethnic costumes are no different than the portrait gallery of progressive elites in Indore or Nadar's Parisian portraits, except that Gopal absorbs the typology of social elites in his own, singular body. Thus, in stark contrast to the normalizing function of portraiture in commercial photography, Gopal generates a diverse multiplicity of social types through what may be called *autoethnology* or voguing in Van Vechten's studio.[12] The social performance belonged to the everyday practices of worldliness in a progressive state. In Bangalore, a variety of fashion protocols were followed for different social occasions. A formal *darbar* (court) or a ceremonial gathering at the palace may require a dress code different from a concert or a ball at the Opera House. Voguing, in other words, was part of being worldly in the cosmopolitan culture of the princely state. Even his double-breasted suit may be regarded as yet one more costumed appearance in this context.

In Van Vechten's studio, the dancer blurs the line between his stage and social performance. In two images from the third and final day of the photo shoot, May 11, 1938, Gopal wears an ornate silk cap and a collarless shirt with mirrored beads and an embroidered diamond pattern (fig. 2.7).[13] The close-up is not different from other portraits we have examined. It is only when the camera pulls back to show the dancer in full view that we recognize the costume from the North Indian Kathak—a single, long garment with an embroidered breast panel separating the torso from a flared skirt (fig. 2.8). Kathak

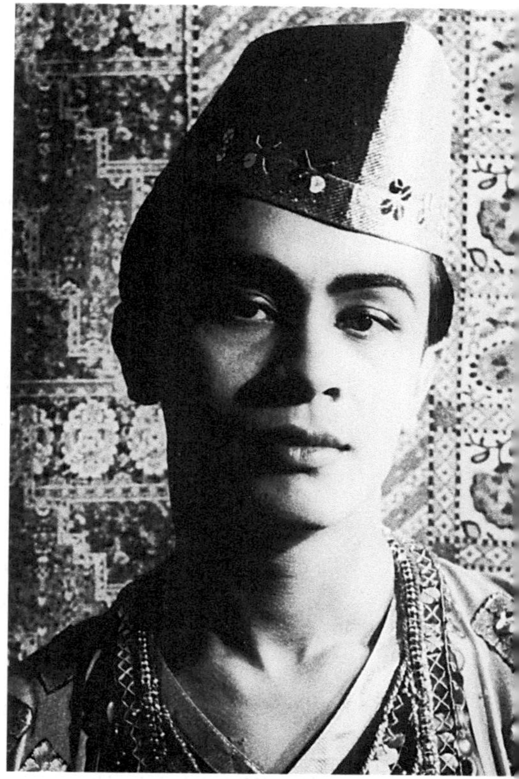

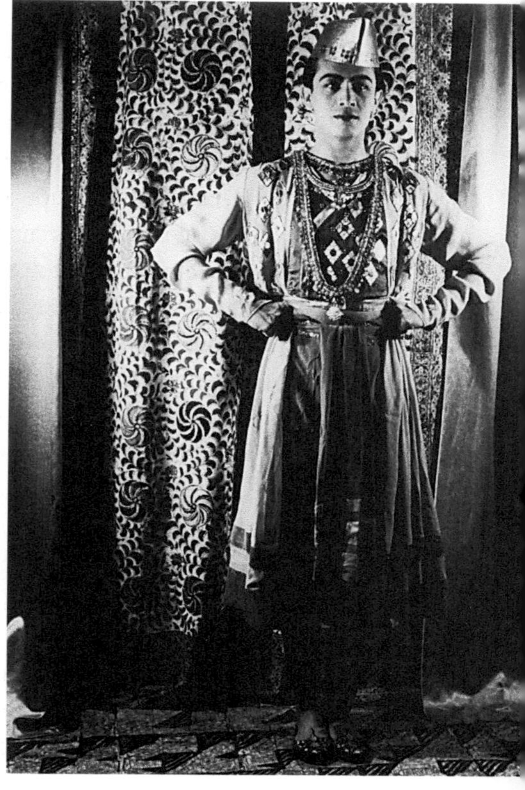

Figures 2.7 and 2.8. *Top*, Carl Van Vechten, *Ram Gopal*, May 11, 1938, XVIII M (cropped from XVIII M30 on neg. strip?). *Right*, Carl Van Vechten, *Ram Gopal*, May 11, 1938, XVIII M12. (Beinecke Rare Book and Manuscript Library, Yale University; © The Van Vechten Trust)

is one among many Indian dance forms that Gopal displays in Van Vechten's studio.

When I showed the Van Vechten photographs to the celebrated Bharatanatyam dancer Geeta Chandran in New Delhi in 2017, she was not impressed. I wanted Chandran to identify for me the various styles Gopal was demonstrating and explain the narrative meaning of his poses. Almost all the images, however, came down in the end to what she called "portraits." By this term, she meant to point at images in which Gopal's poses do not clearly represent a known and recognized repertory of narrative *mudras*.[14] Portraits signified images that were unreadable within her practice. Chandran might be using the term simply to dismiss Gopal's eclectic representations, but I want to take it seriously. A portrait as understood by the dancer is counterintuitive to an art historian's understanding of a visual representation that makes a living person recognizable.[15] And here is my breakthrough. Chandran's definition derives from her experience and expertise in live performance. A narrative meaning that unfolds in real-time choreography could become illegible in a single, still image of the performing body. A "portrait" is thus caught in a paradox between movement and stasis. It dwells in a temporal zone where choreography has come in contact with photography. In this chapter, I want to propose that Gopal explores this expanded, "intermedial" notion of portraiture during his New York photo shoot.[16]

In merging dance with social performance, the Van Vechten photographs are consistent with Gopal's account of his life. In his autobiography, *Rhythm in the Heavens*, published in the United Kingdom in 1957, Gopal considers his growing up as a young man to be the same thing as becoming a dancer. When and how he became a dancer cannot be known. He claims to have had an innate sense of rhythm and "some talent as a dancer" when he was "barely a boy." His public appearance got a jump-start on a day in 1936 when the maharaja of Mysore invited him to perform at the Lalita Mahal Palace in the capital city of Mysore. The event was put together at the last minute; the viceroy of India was flying in from Delhi that night. Since there was no time for Gopal to bring his costumes from Bangalore, the palace flung open its "treasure room," and the dancer picked up what he wanted for his performance: "jewels, pearls, emeralds and rubies," as well as "golden head-dresses that are placed on the Palace gods on festival days."[17]

The spontaneous performance at the Mysore palace is clearly exaggerated. The coincidences are extraordinary. The young Bangalorean happened to be in Mysore with a friend who happened to be a senior staff member at the royal house of Mysore. The "intimate" crowd at the palace comprised "a thousand people." The precious jewels from the palace treasury glamorize the evening and blur the distinction between a dancer's performance and the lifestyles and rituals of the royalties. Gopal describes a glorious view of Mysore from his car window on his way to the palace. It may be an ordinary day, but the city unfolds in Cinemascope. In the distance, the Chamundi Hill is laced with electric lighting.

The approach to the palace is "beautifully . . . laid out with flowered gardens," and concealed lights illuminated water fountains.[18]

In other words, on that wonderful day of Gopal's debut concert, he saw through his car window not a bustling urban landscape but a vision of what Manu Bhagavan calls "princely modernity."[19] Bhagavan explains that the enlightened, cosmopolitan culture of princely states such as Mysore and Baroda finely balanced their intimacy with the British colonial rule with a defiance of colonial expectations. By the 1930s, Mysore became a spectacular city dotted with lakeside palaces and grounds connected by wide avenues and shimmering in electric lights.[20] The "modernity" of Mysore and other such states resulted from the politics of colonial India. Formed as a reward for assistance in British warfare as well as placed under surveillance by colonial administrators, the princely states negotiated their autonomy over their princedom by collaborating on public projects that were mutually beneficial. Railroads, dams, palaces, and other institutional buildings were funded by the royal coffers and designed by British architects and engineers, while British-trained archaeologists engaged in the conservation of ancient monuments within princely territories. Sunila Kale puts a finer point on these colonial negotiations and argues that, while railroads and canals crisscrossed and benefited both the princely states and British territories, the electric grid was local and came to represent "the ambiguous freedoms of indirect colonial rule" in these decentralized, semiautonomous princely states.[21] Under Maharaja Krishnaraja Wodeyar IV, Mysore boasted of being one of the first states in India to have its own hydroelectricity. The maharaja saw in it a symbol of his state's independence and progress. By the 1930s, the Mysore power grid included not only Mysore and Bangalore but also the rural parts of the state. The maharaja ritualized the celebration of his industrial achievements through a bedazzling spectacle of electric lights in the capital, especially during the annual Dasara festival, when the entire city was lit and the outlines of palace buildings sparkled against the night sky.

The dazzle of the progressive state carried into Gopal's performance that evening. Adorned in royal ornaments, he felt a wave of energy coursing through his body. Helped by some champagne offered in a delightful mistake, he felt like a "winged eagle" and found himself "wildly dancing like Siva, God of the Stars and the Moon."[22] It is noteworthy that Gopal makes no reference to his dance training at this point, and only later does he start a serious regime in the narrative form of Kathakali. It is as if his palace performance was a result of the excitement of the evening itself. It is particularly remarkable that Gopal makes no mention of the hereditary dancers and teachers who were regularly patronized by the Mysore court and who could have been easily summoned to fulfill the maharaja's last-minute wishes.[23] From the reference he makes to the British viceroy, we might only speculate that the traditional dancers may not have served the purpose of the evening. Their practices were regarded unfavorably by the colonial authorities since the nineteenth century. By contrast, Gopal's spontaneous appearance represented the glow and splendor of princely modernity in an embodied form.

After the concert, the Mysore maharaja declared Gopal a "genius." The "brother of Royal Highness, the Yuvaraja," became his "first patron" and invited him to lead a dance troupe to Europe and the UK. Gopal earned a royal fellowship of two thousand rupees to study and revive "what has been lost in the Mysore state, in fact most of South India," and to make dance costumes for the European tour as he wished. A research project led him to the "big library in the park," where he studied stylized hand gestures in books and traced jewelry patterns.[24] In the bazaars of Bangalore, he commissioned craftspeople to design costumes and ornaments based on his research.

Gopal criticizes the traditional dancers he saw performing in Bangalore and Mysore. He complains that the ungainly costumes covering the women dancers from head to toe were thoroughly compromised by Victorian missionary morals.[25] The books he pulled out of the library shelves were probably not related to live performances but to the visual arts. Gopal mentions one author as "Gangoly," most probably the art historian O. C. Gangoly, whose well-known publication on South Indian bronze sculpture (1915) is most certainly the "big book" that guided him in the choice of his first costumes.[26] Gopal also traveled to the ancient temple sites within the princely state and visited other parts of South India, where ritual performances took place at sacred temples away from the corrupt practices of colonial cities. He saw the hereditary Kathakali dancers in the Malabar district of Kerala and the Bhagavata Mela Natakam, a dance drama similar to Kathakali in its use of masks and makeup, in the village of Soolamangalam in the Tanjore district of Tamilnadu. In Tanjore, he sought out "Meenakshisundaram Pillai and Ponniah Pillai of 1880 West Main Street" as teachers, who also showed him "Dasi Attam—the female courtesan dance of Tanjore," which their ancestors had developed from the Bhagavata Mela Natakam. In Kumbhakonam, he witnessed the Dasi Attam performed by the two great dancer sisters Varalakshmi and Bhanumati.[27] In the end, however, ancient Indian sacred sculpture remained for him a fundamental bedrock for all dance traditions.

Classical Dance and Sculpture

In front of Van Vechten's camera, Gopal imagines himself not as a stage performer but as a sculpture. Wearing a short, stiffly pleated skirt and bold metal ornaments, he aspires to "be as naked as the bronze images allowed."[28] He trains his posture into a relaxed, upright *abhanga* stance of human figures in those sculptures. He brings their measured elegance into his lowered eyelids and the curl of his fingers. The emulation re-creates in his body the androgyny of ornate metal and stone figures. The photographic emulsion even gives the body a metallic glint (fig. 2.9).

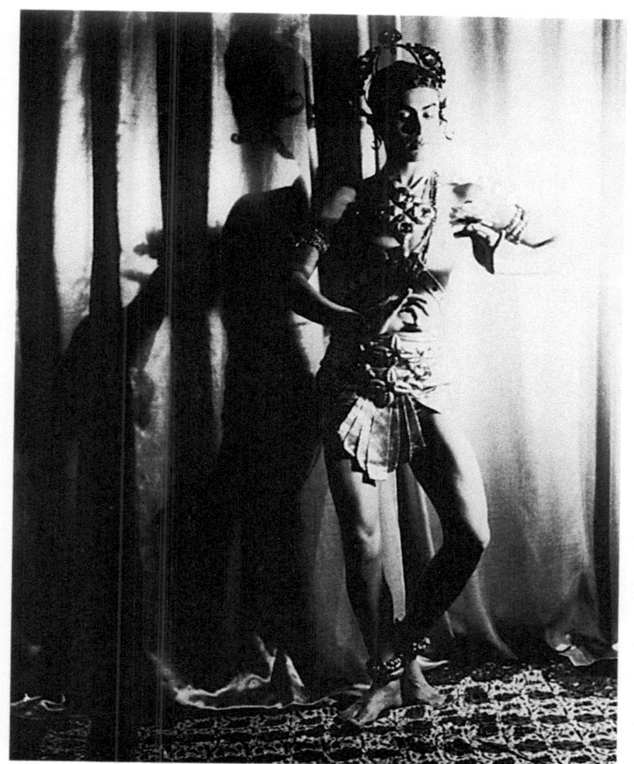

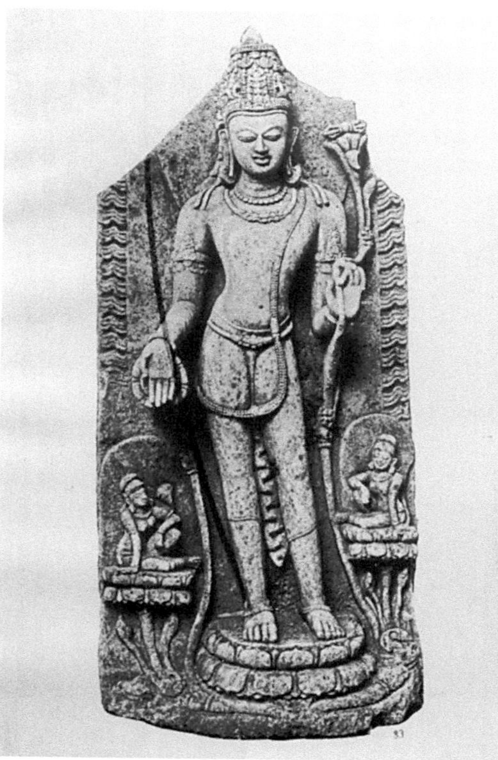

Figures 2.9 and 2.10. *Left*, Carl Van Vechten, *Ram Gopal*, April 21, 1938, XII M22 (M29 on negative strip?) (Beinecke Rare Book and Manuscript Library, Yale University; © The Van Vechten Trust). *Right*, Bodhisattava Vajrapani from Kendrapara, originally from Nalatigiri, early eighth century, Indian Museum, Calcutta, plate 33, in Stella Kramrisch, *Indian Sculpture* (Calcutta: YMCA, 1933).

In ancient sculpture, Gopal found a shared heritage of the living traditions he studied. Unlike hereditary court dancers, who might learn dance within a lineage of performance transmitted through a *guru-shishya* (teacher-apprentice) tradition, Gopal emulated sculpture by visiting monuments within the Mysore state. In the 1930s, the maharaja funded the restoration of twelfth-century Hoysala Dynasty ruins at archaeological sites such as Belur, Somnathpur, and Halebid. Gopal's research trip at this time may have been inspired by the tourist industry that grew around those monuments and their highly decorated stone walls known for figures of dancers and musicians. In 1946, Gopal returned to Belur to perform in the precincts of the Chennakesava temple, and his fame by that time may have contributed further to the publicity of the site.

Although we have no visual evidence of Gopal in Belur in the 1930s, he took photographs in 1946 and included them in two publications: his book *Indian Dancing*, published in collaboration with the dance critic Serozh Dadachanji in 1951, and the autobiography published in 1957. *Indian Dancing* was one of the first publications in India to introduce the various classical forms to a literate, urban readership. The cover shows Gopal taking a pose from Bharatanatyam

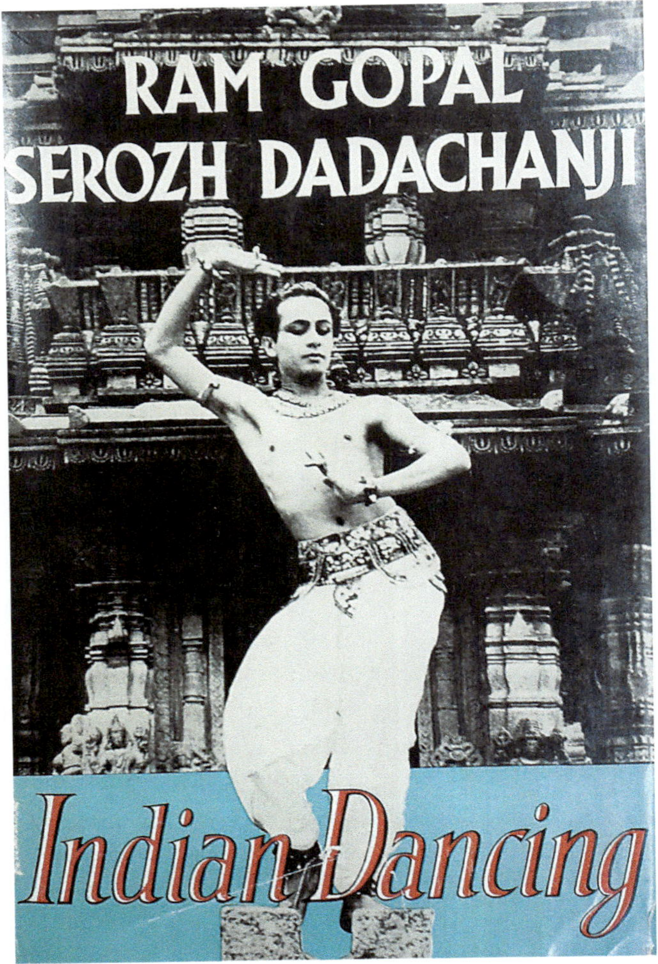

Figure 2.11. Ram Gopal and Serozh Dadachanji, *Indian Dancing* (London: Phoenix House, 1951), cover. (Downloaded from Amazon.uk, https://www.amazon.co.uk/Indian-dancing-Ram-Gopal/dp/B0000CHX1W)

against a stone balcony of the Chennakeshava temple in Belur (fig. 2.11). In the 1940s, Gopal had begun a regime of Bharatanatyam under Guru Muthukumaran Pillai, whom he invited to teach in his newly established dance school in the Torquay Castle along with teachers and practitioners of Kathakali and Kathak.[29] *Indian Dancing* includes a chapter on Bharatanatyam, but the cover is not designed to represent any single dance form per se. It is rather to frame the dancer's body against the stone carvings of the sacred shrine. The juxtaposition nominated the various living, regional practices represented in the book as classically "Indian."[30]

In distinguishing his practice from existing performance traditions and framing classical dance in the image of ancient sacred sculpture, Gopal aligned his research with a powerful movement that emerged in Madras in the 1930s to reform and refine Indian dance for a new urban public. The Madras movement is the subject of brilliant scholarship since the 1980s, and I summarize it briefly here.[31] The movement was designed to counteract a nineteenth-century practice, derogatively called "nautch" or "sadir kacheri," patronized by the royal courts of South India and performed at living temples by women called *devadasis*, or slaves to the god. In the British records, these women were called "temple dancers" or "temple prostitutes," whose scandal circulated across the British Empire as part of India's decadent practices through picture postcards and written accounts. The Madras reform evolved partly in reaction to those accounts and intersected with a number of sociopolitical movements in the 1930s: feminist activism against the exploitation of young girls who were "married to the temple" at the age of fourteen and trained to perform erotic dances; the nationalist struggles against the British colonial rule, in which new ethical standards were being imagined for a progressive citizenry of a sovereign nation; and an urban middle-class view of dance as a cultural inheritance to be protected from degeneracy and conserved by reaching back to ancient texts and Hindu temple sculpture. The refined dance was named Bharatanatyam after the sixth-century Sanskrit treatise on the arts known as *Natyasastra* by sage Bharata.

Bharatanatyam is inherently a product of the cosmopolitan culture of colonial cities. The Madras Academy of Music, founded in 1927 by nationalist reformers, became a prime venue for showcasing dancers.[32] Meanwhile, the dance gained an anticolonial ideology at the Theosophical Society. Founded in New York in 1875 by the Russian occultist Madame Helena Petrovna Blavatsky and the American spiritualist Henry Steel Olcott, the Theosophical Society established centers in India and aligned its ideas and practices with Vedic and Buddhist mysticism drawn from nineteenth-century Indologists such as Max Müller.[33] The society's mission was to form an alternative community of universal brotherhood against the industrialized societies of Europe and the United States, and it fueled anti-British sentiments among the colonial elite in India. The society's branches in cities such as Madras, Calcutta, and Bangalore gathered nationalist activists struggling for sovereignty in the first decades of the twentieth century. By the 1930s, the political edge of the Theosophical Society softened, but its compounds became hubs for a reform-minded citizens to gather around performances and lectures on Indian spirituality and world order.[34] Dance gained spiritualist overtones in this milieu. The Kalakshetra, founded by the theosophist Rukmini Devi at the Theosophical Society of Madras in 1936, became a major school for training young dancers. A syllabus was designed using translation of ancient texts, including the *Natyasastra*. A major reference for hand gestures and facial expressions was the *Abhinaya Darpana* of Nandikesvara, translated as "The Mirror of Gesture" by the Boston-based art historian Ananda Coomaraswamy in 1917. A rigorous regime of daily practice transformed the human dancer into what Uttara Asha Coorlawala calls a "Sanskritized body," a body shaped by dance reform and aligned with India's past artistic traditions as conceived within the nationalist movement.[35] When Gopal stood in front of Van Vechten's camera, he thus represented a "Sanskritized" body, one that was inscribed by dance reform.

Gopal, however, was not directly related to the Madras movement, and in important ways, he distinguished his version of Sanskritization from Bharatanatyam. While ancient Hindu temples remained a shared preoccupation, in Madras the connection was made on ideological grounds. Bharatanatyam detached itself from the "decadent" practices of royalty and living temples of its time by turning to ancient sculpture and religious rituals. The ideological break from functioning temples was achieved by leaning on the translation and interpretation of ancient ritual and dramaturgical texts. In addition to the "textual turn" to India's past, the modern proscenium stage was also reconstructed to include the sacred aura of religious shrines. Rukmini Devi, to whom the redesigning of the proscenium is attributed, installed a metal image of Shiva as the cosmic dancer, Nataraja, at one end of the stage. Fabric backdrops depicted temple halls, and plain black curtains reproduced the mystery of a dark sanctum onstage. The first dance number of an evening concert was usually the lighting of an oil lamp in front of the sacred image, in imitation of a religious ritual.[36] Away from actual temples, the virtual temple allowed women performers to display their sacred dances for the pleasure of urban connoisseurs. By contrast, Gopal responded to the ideological shifts and transformations in the traditional practice by taking his dance to real archaeological sites, as if to restore ancient stone with his living body.

To my knowledge, Gopal's 1946 photographs in Belur are the first to show an Indian dancer posing in an actual Hindu temple. In them, the dancer forges a visual affinity between dance and stone sculpture. Under a photograph published in *Indian Dancing*, a long caption says, "Ram Gopal dancing in the temple of Belur, Mysore State. He was the first dancer to perform there for centuries, thus reviving a custom inaugurated by the great Hoysala king and patron of the dance, Vishnuvardhana, and his queen, who built the temple a thousand years ago" (fig. 2.12).[37] The caption links the stone monument to an ongoing history of Indian dance, while the photographic image literally turns the dancer's body into monumental sculpture. Instead of simply posing next to a temple, Gopal becomes a caryatid-like human pillar upholding the ceiling of the temple interior, thus integrating his body with the stone fabric. Right under our eyes, the photograph and its caption transform the living dancer into a concrete part of the archaeological reconstruction of the sacred site.

In the mid-twentieth century, when Gopal's Belur photographs circulated through books, publicity materials, newspaper articles, and performance reviews, they pioneered a genre of dance photography in India. From then onward, it became common for classical dancers to take their publicity photographs against newly restored archaeological sites and religious monuments. Gopal's photographs of 1946 also provide a visual foundation for a nationalistic discourse of

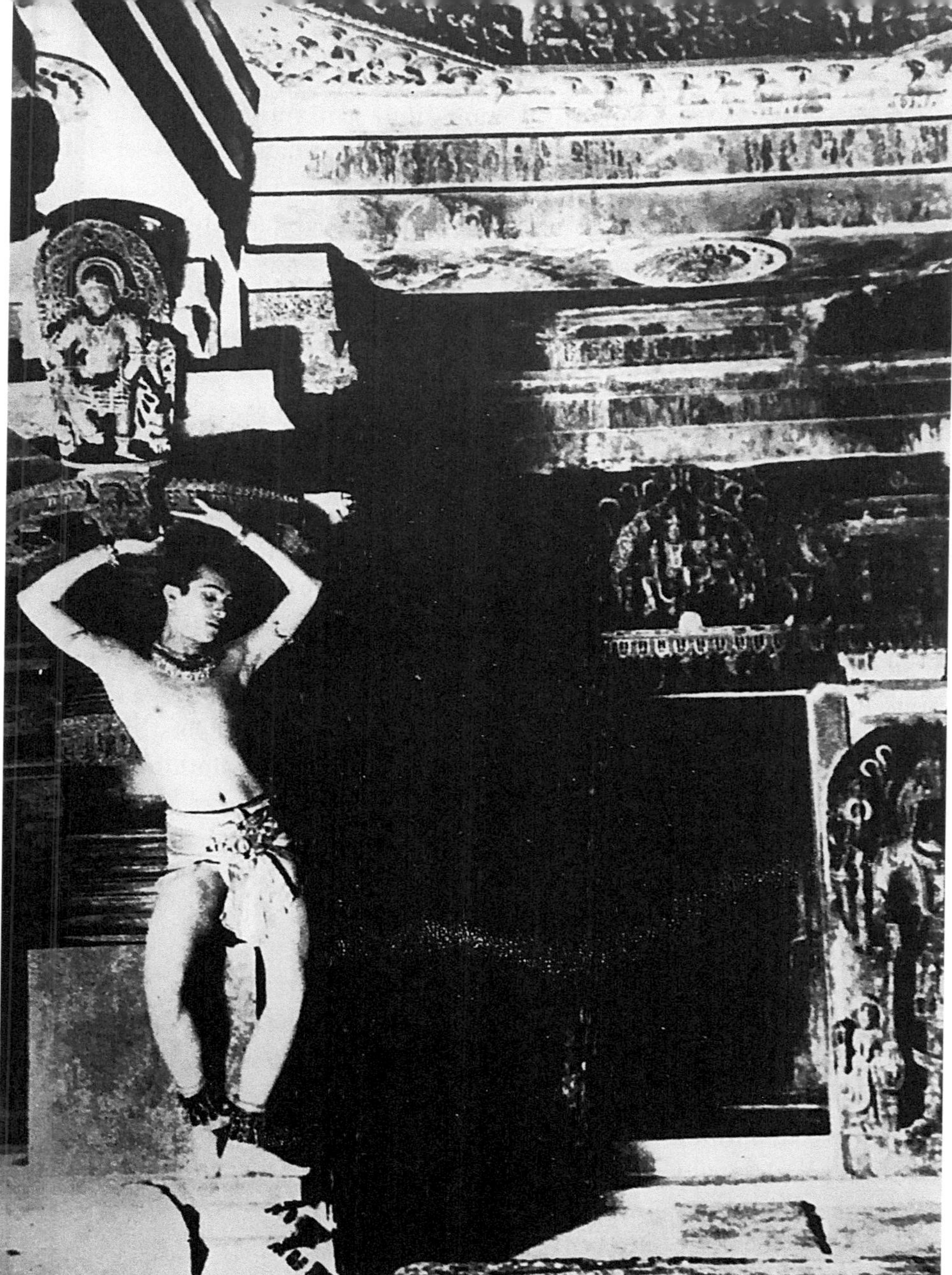

Figure 2.12. Ram Gopal and Serozh Dadachanji, *Indian Dancing* (London: Phoenix House, 1951), 33.

Indian dance in post-Independence India, when living practices in different regions were being nominated as India's classical dance by the newly formed national agency the Sangeet Natak Akademi (the National Performing Arts Academy) in the capital, New Delhi. While Bharatanatyam was grandfathered (or grandmothered) as the first classical dance of India, the practitioners from other regions of India offered arguments for granting a "classical" status to their regional styles by demonstrating their connection to ancient temple sculpture.[38]

The relationship between Indian dance and stone sculpture also became a major research topic for performers and PhD students at Indian universities. Finally, as temple ruins such as those at Konarak in Orissa and Khajuraho in central India became national heritage sites, restored for local and international tourism, they provided venues also for staging dance festivals in a way that Gopal initiated in the princely state of Mysore. Gopal's *Indian Dancing* was published in this moment of euphoria over dance as a cultural heritage and participated in the formation of a national canon for dance in India. More important for my purpose, in this period, he wrote himself into that canon as a pioneer of Indian classical dance.

This curated presence of the dancer in the history of Indian dance silences the global circuits of Indian classical dance that form a major part of his representations in Van Vechten archives, a point I want to develop now. Here is a twist in the restorative history of Indian dance and of Gopal's place in it as a pioneer. While in 1946 Gopal may have been the first Indian classical dancer to pose at an ancient stone temple, he was not the first performer to do so and photograph himself. That credit goes to the American dancer Ted Shawn two decades prior.

In 1926, Shawn took a series of photographs posing against the eighth-century Shiva temple on the shores of Mamallapuram in Tamilnadu during a visit to India with his wife, the American Orientalist dancer Ruth St. Denis (fig. 2.13). For his photo shoot, he commissioned props and costumes, which he brought back to the United States to use in his "Asian dances." They included a large wooden ring for his choreography of the "Cosmic Dance of Shiva," which he performed in 1928 at the Ziegfeld Follies in New York.

Seen alongside Shawn's photographs, Gopal's juxtapositions relate less to the local tradition of arts developing organically from the ancient to the modern times and more to the global circuits of Indian dance forming in the early twentieth century. The interest in relating the dancer's body to ancient Hindu temples first emerged within the framework of Orientalism, a fascination of "the East" in the Western imagination. Ruth St. Denis performed Orientalist fantasies of Hindu dance against painted fabric backdrops showing temple halls, a practice Rukmini Devi continued in her proscenium stage design in Madras. By turning from theatrical backdrops to real stone monuments, Ted Shawn and Ram Gopal introduced one significant shift in the historical associations between ancient and modern practices. They produced a physical and material analogy between the human performer and ancient stone sculpture. The exchange of human flesh and sacred stone was then fixed for eternity through the reality effect of a photograph, beyond the distant, metaphorical references to the sacredness of Hindu shrines on the Madras stage.

In focusing specifically on the figure of Nataraja probably for the first time in dance history, Shawn also showed an early familiarity with a key text of the dance reform movement, *The Dance of Shiva*, a volume of essays published in 1918 by the art historian Ananda Coomaraswamy. A short essay by the same

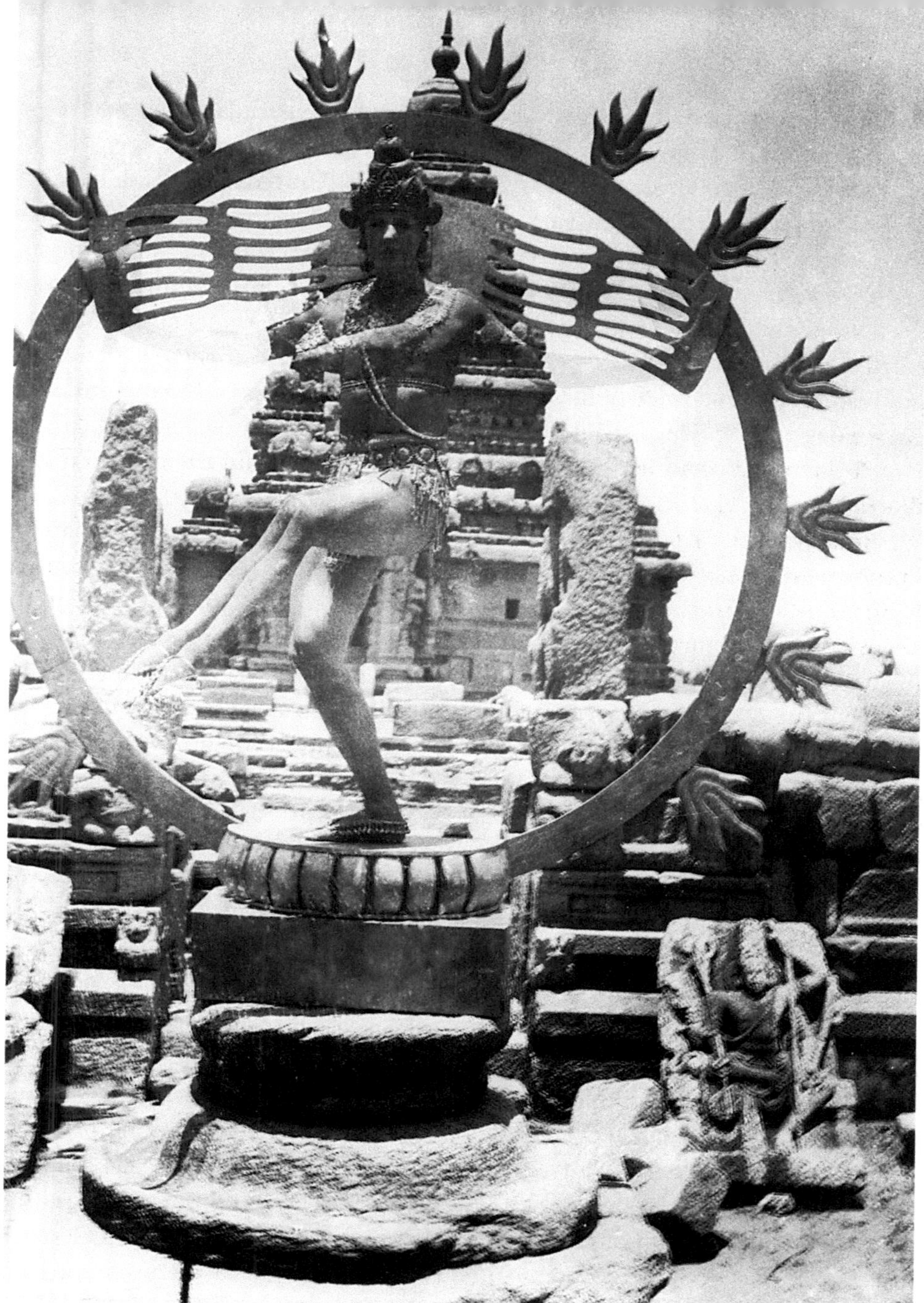

Figure 2.13. Ted Shawn, *Cosmic Dance of Siva*, Shiva temple, Mamallapuram, 1926. (Jacob's Pillow Archives)

title described the iconography of Shiva as a cosmic dancer, Nataraja. Using ancient Sanskrit texts, Coomaraswamy explained the celebrated dancing figure at the Shiva temple in Chidambaram in Tamilnadu and elaborated on the meaning of the various standardized symbols seen in the bronze sculptures from the Chola Dynasty of the tenth to eleventh centuries. Shawn's choreography literally followed the bronze sculptures, while Shiva's iconography and symbolism served as an ideational framework for Bharatanatyam in Madras.

Coomaraswamy's volume was widely read in the United States and in India. It was published by Sunwise Turn, a short-lived publishing house and bookshop founded by two women entrepreneurs, Madge Jenison and Mary Horgan Mowbray-Clark, at 2 East Thirty-First Street in New York City. The shop also showcased paintings and textiles by local and immigrant artists and held a literary salon for the modernist writers, including many in Van Vechten's circle in the bohemian Greenwich Village.[39] Coomaraswamy's volume became influential among both modernist intellectuals and the European dealers and collectors of Indian art who had migrated to the United States in the decades after World War I.

In spite of the title, the volume is not particularly concerned with dance. The Nataraja essay stands out as the only one devoted to the dancing figure. A series of speculative reflections on Indian philosophies and artistic forms addresses a world torn apart by the Great War. In the Nataraja essay, Coomaraswamy explains Shiva's cosmic dance of destruction using a long footnote quoting from the French writer Marcel Schwob's *Le livre de Monelle*: "This is the teaching: Destroy, destroy, destroy. Destroy within yourself, destroy all around you. Make room for your soul and for other souls. Destroy, for all Creation proceeds from destruction. . . . For building up is done with debris, and nothing in the world is new but shapes. But shapes must be perpetually destroyed. . . . Break every cup from which you drink."[40] At the Ziegfeld Follies, Ted Shawn's "Cosmic Dance of Shiva" brought home the Indian oracle of destruction and creation to the same New York audience that read Coomaraswamy's volume between the two world wars.

Coomaraswamy's readers were primarily international. For them, Brinda Kumar writes, Coomaraswamy "elevated the position of the Siva Nataraja form from one tied to specific practices to an ultimate universal object of aesthetic contemplation. As a consequence, his opinion on the subject became primary among American collectors, buyers and museums."[41] And indeed Saskia Kersenboom argues that Coomaraswamy's "Dance of Shiva" essay is not based on the actual performances in Chidambaram or any other religious place in South India. Instead, Coomaraswamy assimilated the various local performative traditions within a unifying ideology of physical and metaphysical destruction, a resonant theme in the interwar years. Relying largely on the cosmic mythology of Shiva as a "male" dancer of destruction, Kersenboom points out, Coomaraswamy overlooked the particular ways in which that mythology was distributed into different dance forms, separated according to seasons, and displayed within a highly differentiated performances of both men and women across South India. Further disconnecting the essay from performance altogether, Elisa Ganser argues that Coomaraswamy did not write the essay for dancers at all. He aimed it as an intervention in art history. A short version of the essay, published

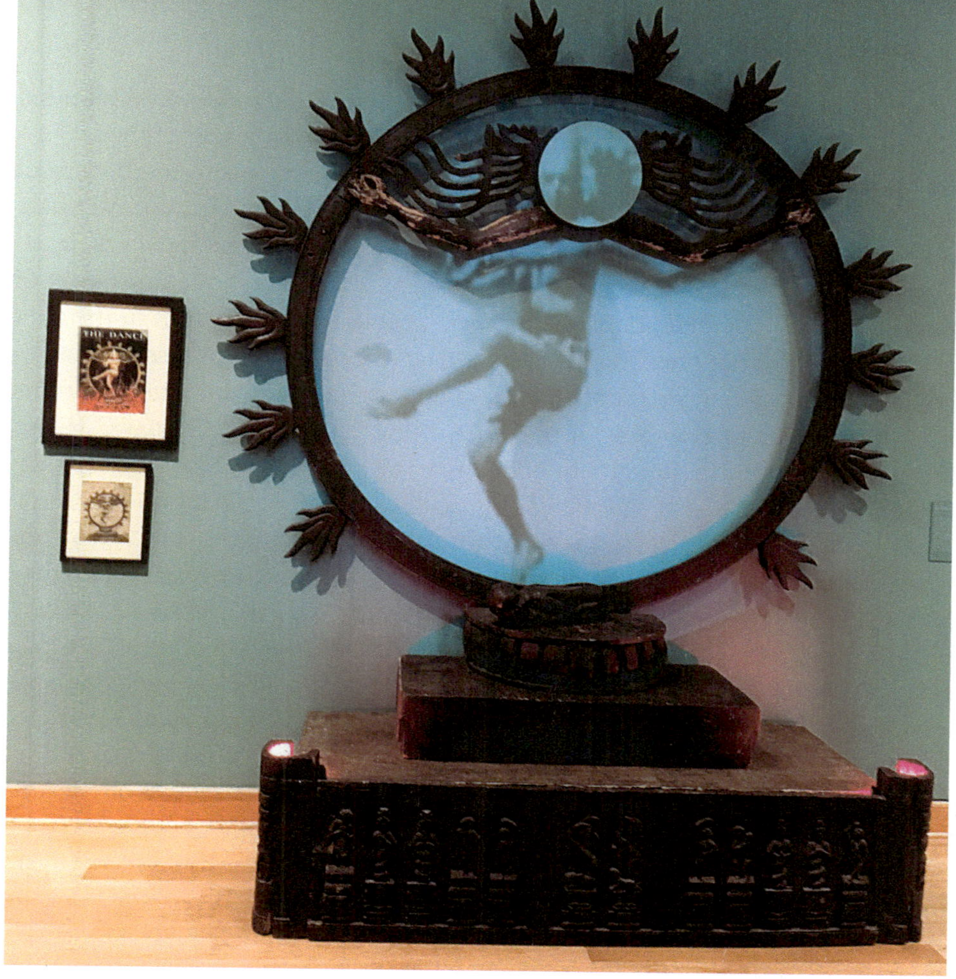

Figure 2.14. Ted Shawn, film projection on the wooden ring. (Exhibition display, Williams College Art Museum, seen August 11, 2018; photograph by the author)

in 1908 and 1912, gave ammunition to British Orientalist scholars and artists in Calcutta in their rallying cry against a deeply entrenched colonial view of Indian art as a degenerate, decorative tradition.[42]

Coomaraswamy's forceful plea to evaluate Indian art in its own terms rested on an arsenal of ancient Sanskrit texts and a command of the iconography of Nataraja in the bronze sculptures of South India. His plea resonated differently among his diverse readers. His authority as an art historian legitimized Indian sculpture among art historians. The weight of ancient ritual texts made the essay foundational to the legitimacy of Indian classical dance in Madras. Ted Shawn developed a choreography from the Nataraja sculptures seen in museums and photographic reproductions including the frontispiece of Coomaraswamy's volume. A video recording shows him literally framed inside the circular ring, reproducing the bronze statue in a frontal view like a photograph. His choreography follows the flat image faithfully. He steps on a narrow platform in front of the ring for limited, lateral movements before stepping back into the ring (fig. 2.14).

In these global entanglements of art history with Indian dance represented by Coomaraswamy, Gopal turns out to have been a serious reader of the art historian. His New York performance on May 1, 1938, started with the "Dance of Siva," for which the program note quotes a passage from Coomaraswamy's essay. Gopal, however, is less interested in reproducing the iconography of the dancing figure and more in reaching for the fiery dancer as a dynamic expression of the order of the universe. Beyond the stage performance, he bathes in the aura of the cosmic dancer, recalling his father's friend, a Sanskrit professor, saying to him as a child, "When you see the lightening flash and hear the thunder drums up in the clouds and it rains, it is the God Siva dancing his Tandava." When the boy splashes in the muddy rain water in the backyard of the Torquay Castle in Bangalore, the monsoon rain becomes a "wild primordial dance of Nature, of Siva, of God himself": "in the wake of this rain and thunder and wind I am transfigured."[43] Coomaraswamy's divine dancer shapes a consistent worldview for Gopal. In a chapter of his autobiography titled "War: A Pilgrim's Progress," he quotes the same passage of Marcel Schwob from Coomaraswamy ("destroy, destroy, destroy . . .") to describe his second visit to Paris in 1939 and compares the cloud of Nazi violence across Europe to Shiva's dance of destruction.[44]

In absorbing Shiva's cosmic dance as a series of bodily affects, Gopal distinguished himself from both the literal representation of Nataraja, as in Shawn, and the idealization of Shiva among the Madras dancers. Coomaraswamy's description launched in Gopal an affinity with Indian sculpture in all its materiality. In addition to the archaeological sites, he indicates an interest in museum displays. In 1948, Gopal's troupe was invited to the inaugural exhibition of the South Asian section of the Victoria and Albert Museum, London. A documentary film shows the dancer performing in the South Asian gallery.[45] The sculptures on display were on loan from the collection of Stella Kramrisch, the author of *Indian Sculpture* discussed earlier, and are now at the Philadelphia Museum of Art, where Kramrisch became a curator in the 1950s. For the publicity posters, Gopal stood in front of a display in the South Asian Gallery (fig. 2.15). Entering the gallery space, the dancer struck the pose of the Nataraja sculpture for a fraction of a second. In front of a bronze sculpture, he and his female partner, Shevanti, posed as if they were the divine consort Shiva and Parvati. Gopal's representations at the Victoria and Albert Museum sealed the institutionalized relationship between dance and India's sacred sculpture.

Gender of Dance and Sculpture

Ram Gopal's turn to art history distinguished his version of "Sanskritization" from Madras in one significant way. He used sculpture to reimagine the gender of the dancer's body. In Madras, Sanskritization was fundamentally a feminist project, aimed at rethinking the female dancer. Amrit Srinivasan argues that Bharatanatyam's transformation of a regional and local tradition into

THE DANCING TIMES

INDIAN CULTURE

The illustrated lecture on "Romance and Religion in Indian Painting and Dancing," given at the Victoria and Albert Museum on

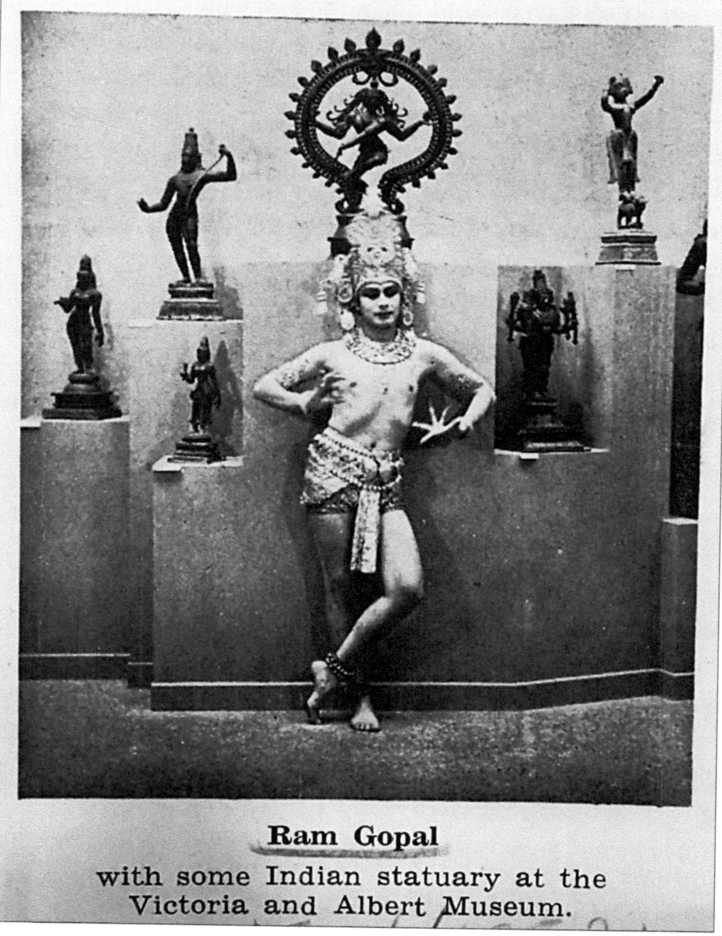

Ram Gopal
with some Indian statuary at the Victoria and Albert Museum.

Figure 2.15. Ram Gopal, lecture announcement at the Victoria and Albert Museum, London, *The Dancing Times*, February 20, 1952 (Jerome Robbins Dance Division, The New York Public Library of the Performing Arts; courtesy of *The Dancing Times*)

a pan-Indian nationalistic cultural form resulted in "a very different kind of performer—feminine, educated, English speaking and middle class—as against the local devadasi of temple bhakti Hinduism."[46] While both men and women joined dance schools such as the Kalakshetra in Madras, their performance was distinguished in form, content, and costume along gender lines. The female dancer became the target of dance reform. In reaction to the sexual exploitation of court dancers and their representations as temple prostitutes, the Madras reformers avoided the seductive use of flowy veils, scarfs, and skirts and removed the sexual content of the erotic *padam* in courtly literature from their choreographies. While men continued to represent the dance teachers and temple officials in their naturalistic costumes, wearing a silk *dhoti* (lower wrapped garment) and dancing with bare chest except for the sacred thread of a Brahmin priest or a sash tied across, women assumed a more streamlined look, using linear patterns of brocade on colored silk fabric that wound tightly around the legs, leaving a pleated sash that fanned out with outstretched leg movements.[47] The costume deeroticized the female dancer and organized her body as a dazzling, geometrical silhouette. Stylized movements and angular gestures drawn from sculpture, puppetry, mime, and other sources, as well as the introduction of the purely rhythmic *nritta*, denaturalized the performance altogether. The abstractions of Bharatanatyam interested Gopal but not the gendered distinctions for which they were used within the sexual economy of Madras.

Gopal showed a sharp awareness of the gendered discourse in Madras. After his impressive performance at the Lalita Mahal Palace in Mysore, he zealously pursued a mission "to revive the male forms of temple dancing."[48] Against Bharatanatyam's female form, the edge of his reference to the gender of his dance forms cannot be missed. It is particularly startling that Gopal never once mentions Bharatanatyam in his autobiography. Instead, he explains that the four main schools of classical Indian dance are "the Kathakali dance dramas of Malabar performed by an entire troupe of dancers and musicians [that] are all male. The Kathak dancing of Delhi and Jaipur which is mostly a solo dance; the Manipuri dance of Assam, lyrical and graceful in character; and the Bhagavata Mela Nataka Tanjore, all-male temple dance drama."[49] The omission is significant. While he devotes a section to Bharatanatyam in his 1951 publication on the classical Indian dances, he refers to Bharatanatyam in his autobiography simply as the female solo Dasi Attam performed by the courtesans and prostitutes of Tanjore.

The "male forms" encapsulate for Gopal an altogether different lineage from the Madras Bharatanatyam. For the Bangalorean dancer, the classical dance of India is gendered male. It evolves from "Nataraja, God of the Dance." The four schools of dance (Kathakali, Bhagavata Melam, Manipuri, and Kathak) are grounded in the ancient Indian textual traditions traced back to the Bharata Natyashastra, as in Madras. But in Gopal's view, the Natyashastra systematizes three performance "styles" for those schools: *natya*, *nritta*, and *nritya*. The dancer learns to perform those styles in two distinct ways, the "tandava" or "masculine" way and the "lasya" or "feminine" way by modulating his body appropriately. The practice is "preserved for centuries down to this day" in India's villages by being "handed down from father to son, both written and unwritten."[50] For Gopal, then, the classical dance of India is fundamentally a homo-mythic form, emerging from Nataraja and transmitted through a continuous, homosocial tradition of practice from the ancient to the modern period.

Gopal's "masculine" genealogy is partly acknowledged in Madras. Hari Krishnan points out that Bharatanatyam's original carriers were primarily men employed by the courts of Thanjavur and Mysore. Traditionally, men served as teachers for both men and women and continued to serve as gurus through the twentieth century. Men also played women's roles in Bhagavata Mela Natakam and other forms, while women were limited to dancing the solo Dasi Attam. The male teachers taught women to perform their femininity onstage based on poetic descriptions drawn from erotic *padam* as well as social conventions. To demonstrate their virtuosity in "gynemimesis," they also performed for their royal patrons occasionally.

Krishnan argues that the reformed Bharatanatyam changed the gender relations of traditional practice in Madras. Dancers divided the choreographies strictly according to their gender. Men played male mythological heroes, such as the majestic Garuda bird, and performed only the virile dance of Shiva (Gopal's "tandava"), while women danced the feminine roles and only occasionally included a choreographed reference to Nataraja in the abstract, rhythmic, *nritta* part. For Krishnan, Bharatanatyam's gender norms were largely shaped by a "hypermasculine" visions of nation and nation-building that permeated the Indian dance culture by midcentury. Backstage, the male teachers continued to train male and female dancers along with a few other women gurus.[51]

Gynemimesis is the main organizing principle for Gopal's "male forms" of classical dance. He claimed that the male dancers he witnessed during his research were extremely good at playing women's roles, while the reverse was not true. In the Madras circle, only his friend E. Krishna Iyer, a major figure in the reform movement, played female roles, as was the practice in the Bhagavata Mela Natakam. Gopal traveled with Iyer to study that form in Thanjavur.[52] Back in Bangalore, he learned one more "male" form, the North Indian Kathak, under gurus Jailal and Sohanlal.

Significantly, gynemimesis helped Gopal modulate his bodily practice toward the visual and conceptual logic of Indian sculpture. As we saw earlier, Gopal was exposed to sculpture by "Gangoly" and other art historians as well as his visits to temple sites. In the first decades of the twentieth century, the art historical discourse on Indian sculpture drew from a colonial politics of gender and participated in a broad nationalistic reaction to the Victorian notions of masculinity. The Victorian notion was defined by a "manly Englishman" imagined in British sports and military exercises, against which the "effeminacy" of the Indian man represented the physical and moral weaknesses of a colonized subject.[53] We have two documented responses to the colonial imagination. In a rich body of nationalistic texts in nineteenth-century India, Mrinalini Sinha has found a discursive formation of an indigenous social body in a contrapuntal and equally "hypermasculinist" representation of virility, chivalry, militancy, and celibacy in India, while Sugata Ray has analyzed the role of Indian art history in valorizing the "demasculinized male body" itself. Ray points out that, while the Victorian body was modeled after the muscular athletes in ancient Roman sculpture, Indian art historians found a visual and conceptual counterpoint to that ideal in the fifth-century figures of the Buddha. Eyes downturned, seated upright in meditation and gently swaying while standing, the smoothened body of the Buddha might look "effeminate" to the British eye, but it represented for the art historians the movements of a "subtle body" underneath the musculature, comparable to the smooth, harmonized circulation of life breath (*prana*) in yogic practice.[54] Gopal's autobiography is replete with references to yoga but not to sculpture per se.

Let us turn one more time to Gopal's emulation of Indian sculpture in Van Vechten's studio (fig. 2.9). The poised, stylized body we see in the photograph represents what his New York program calls "The Picture of Bodhisattva."[55] True to the iconography of the Buddhist figure of Compassion, the dancer balances a white lotus lily in his raised left hand and uses the mimetic gesture of his right hand to pluck the long, swaying stalk of the imaginary water plant. The dancer's body also reproduces the gentle sway of the invisible stalk in a relaxed contrapposto, coming close to a contemporary art historical view of Indian sculpture. The art historian Stella Kramrisch, describing an early eighth-century Bodhisattava sculpture in her classic publication *Indian Sculpture* (1933), writes, "The lotus stalk leads the compositional rhythm. Its movement is not only taken up by the main figure, but also by the Devis, and especially by their arms" (fig. 2.10).[56] The mimetic play between the human figure and vegetation regulates the "surging linear rhythm" of the sculpture that Kramrisch defines as the overall "plastic quality" of Indian sculpture.[57]

The gender-fluidity of Gopal's dance develops into what Kramrisch calls the essential "naturalism" of Indian sculpture. As distinct from the Western art historical understanding of naturalism as an imitation of nature seen by the human eye, in Indian sculpture, Kramrisch notices "the tree, the animal and the human figure by the side of one another, or else interpenetrating each other." In the fifth-century figures of the Buddha, a high point is achieved when the vitality of animals and the flowing rhythm of vegetation mutate into the human frame and "nature as a whole is taken into and expressed by a transfigured body."[58] In 1938, in Van Vechten's studio, Gopal stretches his gynemimetic training toward the expanded naturalism of Indian sculpture. He systematically incorporates animal and vegetal life into his gender-fluid human frame and represents a more integrated view of nonhuman nature in his body image as a cosmic dancer. This "complexity" in Gopal's response to sculpture in 1938 was silenced (in Trouillot's sense) by the mid-twentieth century, when India's sacred temple art became a means to claim a cultural heritage for Indian classical dance.

In the 1930s, Gopal anchored his dance training not in Bharatanatyam but in a narrative form called Kathakali. He enrolled at the Kerala Kalamandalam, a school for Kathakali established in 1933 in the town of Cheruthurutty in the Thrissur district of Kerala by the reform poet Vallathol Narayana Menon (1878–1958). There, under Guru Kunju Kurup and Guru Ruvunni Menon, he began a serious regime, which he describes in detail.[59] The Van Vechten photographs show his footing firmly in Kathakali, and the few images we discussed in chapter 1 show his free assimilation of various other traditions into his Kathakali training (figs. 1.2, 1.24, and 1.28).

At the Kalamandalam, Gopal admired Guru Ruvunni Menon, "noted for teaching his men to dance like men." We should know by now that this does not mean a training only in the virile, masculine movements but rather a training in gynemimesis. After a full day's strenuous practice of muscle and eye movements, his principal teacher, Guru Kunju Kurup, might summon him to perform epic stories with him, saying, "You shall be the beautiful maiden Damyanti [*sic*] and I shall be your handsome prince Nala, and I want you to convince [me] by every look, gesture and expression that you are truly, deeply in love with me." Beyond role-playing, Gopal calls this a training in "bewitching and enchanting himself."[60] It is a bodily practice of going beyond his own gender and subjectivity to become an androgynous object of desire for his viewers.

So, when Gopal holds a translucent veil against his ornamented body in a Van Vechten photograph, he is fully using gynemimesis from his Kathakali training (fig. 2.16). The representation is unusual, and his particular stance and costume are unrecognizable in that tradition. The veil stretches into a misty curtain helped by the glare of flood lights. Gopal wears the same short lower garment we see in his "Picture of Bodhisattva" and a wing-shaped leather crown designed possibly for his dance of the mythic bird Garuda. But instead of Kathakali's female characters, the feminine form viewed through an atmospheric haze is reminiscent of the American modern dancer Isadora Duncan, known for her nearly naked body wrapped in a sheer, flowing, Grecian robe. We may also be reminded of the Orientalist re-creation of dancers such as Ruth St. Denis and her student Martha Graham and Ballets Russes' stage re-creations of the Oriental themes.[61] These references form a constellation closer to Van Vechten from his days as a dance critic in New York, far away from Kathakali. In chapter 3, we will discuss one specific reference in detail, the dance of the seven veils in Oscar Wilde's 1896 play *Salomé*, which obsessed Van Vechten since he saw its interpretation in the Richard Strauss opera at the Metropolitan Opera in New York in 1907.

It is unclear whether Gopal was familiar with Van Vechten's references. Scattered hints in his autobiography suggest he may have known some of them prior to his arrival in New York. He was an avid watcher of "Metro films" in Bangalore and may have seen the Hollywood adaptation of Wilde's *Salomé* in the 1923 silent film by Charles Bryant and Alla Nazimova. A program of his concert in Los Angeles on March 11, 1938, includes a list of Hollywood celebrity sponsors including Nazimova and others. Gopal's connection with Van Vechten's world

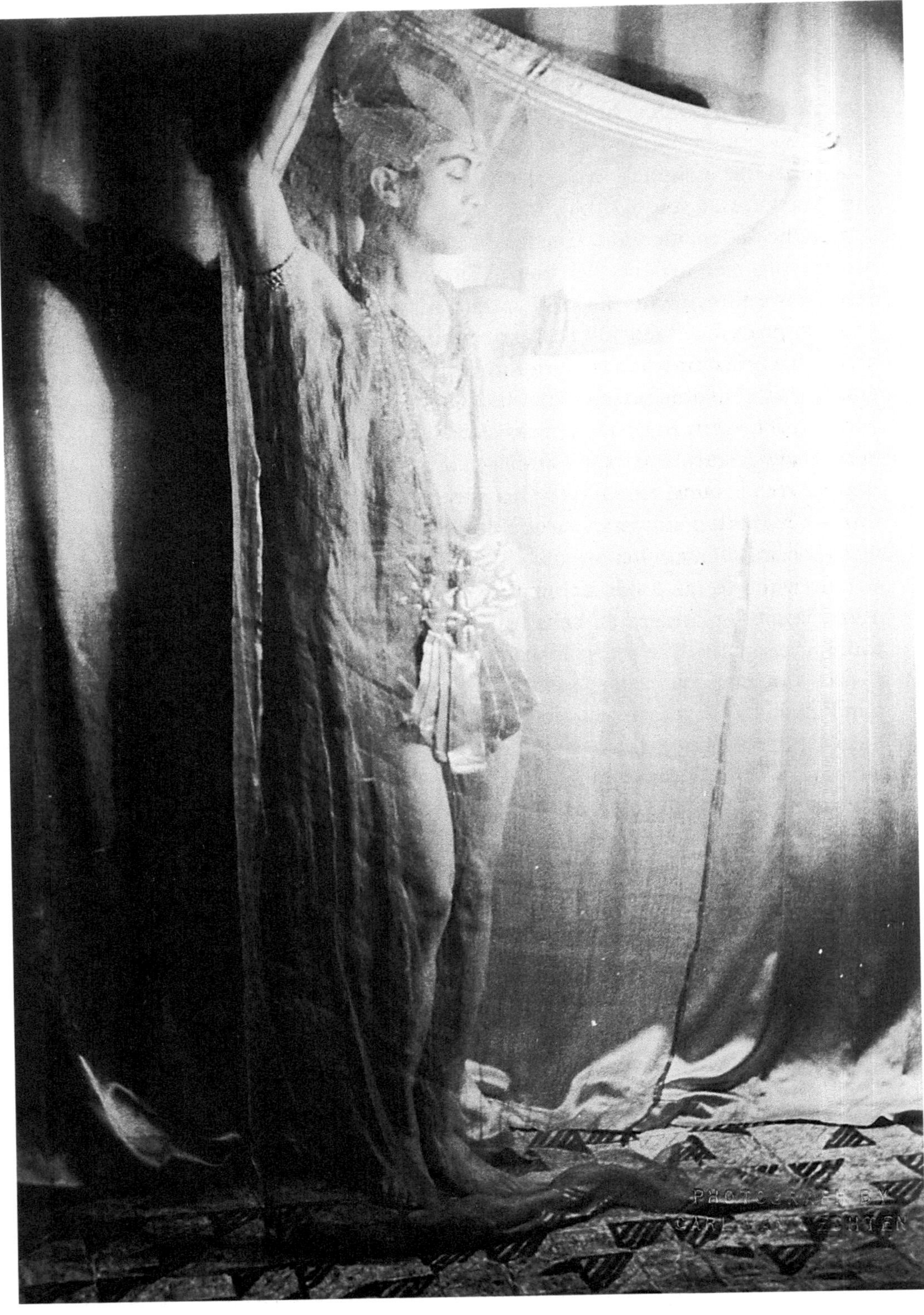

Figure 2.16. Carl Van Vechten, *Ram Gopal*, May 11, 1938, XX M23. (Beinecke Rare Book and Manuscript Library, Yale University; © The Van Vechten Trust)

was, however, indirect at least at this point in time, and we will approach it using his images and his growing international exposure.

From Gopal's veiled image, one thing could be said for certain. In New York, Gopal modulates his Kathakali training to reflect the cultural world of the American photographer. The cross-dressed dancer may even have extended Kathakali's gynemimesis to appeal to Van Vechten's interracial, homoerotic fantasies. In the early twentieth century, Gopal's training in female impersonation related to a pervasive feature of India's popular theater, in which male actors became star celebrities for playing women's roles onstage, complete with elegant costumes, makeup, and bodily demeanor that often set a trend for feminine social appearance.[62] Gopal might have called this gender authenticity a technique of "enchanting and bewitching" his performance and fully transforming himself into that other gender. But in the audience response to the stage appearance of these stars, Kathryn Hansen also documents a "male-to-male dynamic." For instance, when star Bal Gandharva appeared onstage surrounded by "her companions," young men in the audience gave out a "lusty applause," while a supporting male actor felt a "unique thrill" standing close to him.[63] For Hansen, these instances indicated that it was not only the authenticity of the female character that excited the audience (at least not always) but also the awareness of the cross-dressed star underneath the role that appealed to a knowing, adoring male's gaze. In comparing the Indian example to a similar tradition of cross-dressing in the *onnagata* (woman role) of Kabuki theater in Japan, Purnima Shah highlights a major difference. She points out that, in the North Indian Kathak, the dancer typically performs solo, thus playing without a change in costume "a series of roles or [impersonating] the female with the audience's absolute awareness and full view of his natural male appearance."[64] For Gopal, who also performed solo in 1938, addressing the American photographer's homoerotic desires through the transparency of the gauze would simply mean taking the performative traditions of India into a global context.

Dance and Global Flows

The Mysore maharaja's plans for Gopal's European tour never materialized. By the winter of 1937, Gopal found himself dancing not only for the royalty but also at the Opera House in the Bangalore cantonment. It was here that the theater's manager, one of many Parsi entrepreneurs, whom Gopal calls "Mr. Cooper," introduced him to an American "Ethnic" dancer named La Meri (Russell Meriweather Hughes, 1898–1988).[65] It was a chance meeting at the Cantonment train station where Mr. Cooper was receiving La Meri for a performance season at his theater, and Gopal was dropping off a friend on his way to Madras. La Meri tells a slightly different story of their meeting. She recalls a young man who came to meet her and asked to join her troupe: "He impressed me most, even if he did perform a dance of India to the music of Ravel's *Bolero*."[66] She mentions that Gopal's parents allowed him to join her troupe only after making sure she was not traveling alone, and she assured them that she was with her husband and the company's manager, the Italian impresario Guido Carreras, who had earned his reputation managing the ballet dancers Anna Pavlova and Vaslav Nijinsky.[67]

Whatever the truth of the particular meeting, it speaks to the international networks of the Bangalore cantonment. As in other colonial cities, Indians and British citizens typically came together in Bangalore at parade grounds, tennis courts, recreational parks, the Theosophical Society, and entertainment venues such as the Opera House to enjoy a full calendar of Indian and Western dances along with Hollywood films, jazz music, and Parsi theater.[68]

Located at the junction of Brigade and Residency Road, the Opera House was built in the 1930s as a destination for entertainment in colonial India similar to the Victoria Hall that La Meri describes in Madras and the Jubilee Hall that Hansen describes in Rangoon, Burma.[69] It was a venue for visiting performers of world music and dance passing through Bangalore. Performances included the ballet and the opera, and Gopal also describes it as a "large local theatre" that showed "Metro films."[70] Hari Krishnan explores such "intermedial cultural flows" in the performance halls of Madras, where "cinema screenings were supplemented by live performances in a range of musical and dance styles, including courtesan dances, Western dance, and eventually the reinvented Bharatanatyam."[71]

The Bangalore Opera House appears much like the military barracks built in the cantonment by the British Public Works Department. Even while Gopal saw "Metro films" there, it was not exactly like the famed Metro Cinema in Bombay, built in 1938 in the grand Art Deco style by the Metro-Goldwyn-Mayer (MGM) Studios to exclusively screen Hollywood films. By contrast, a photograph from 1945–1946 by a cadet in the British Army, Anthony Loach, shows a modest brick, cement, and plaster structure with red tiled roof.[72] A projection booth was added and raised on stilts on the narrow side on the left. A flight of stairs led up to an open verandah lined by a row of columns and a railing of hourglass-shaped balusters. The main entrance to the compound opened at an angle on the traffic intersection. Inside, a raised stage at one end could convert the cavernous ballroom dance floor into a formal performance space, and a screen above it could be used for screening films. The open hall could be filled with movable furniture or cleared of it, depending on the event. On the lower level, the hall opened to a pavilion covered by an awning, where people mingled and refreshments could be served. The multipurpose space became a cultural hub where an international population gathered during an evening of variety entertainment.

It was here that La Meri was invited to perform her "Ethnic Dances." Starting out as a variety entertainer in Texas and a ballet dancer, La Meri traveled widely. She started in Latin America, picking up dance numbers from different world traditions, which she performed in the United States and elsewhere to great acclaim.[73] Funded by the Australian impresario A. D. M. Longden, La Meri set out with Carreras on a tour of Asia and the Pacific islands, starting in Australia and New Zealand in the summer of 1936 and arriving in Madras in January 1937. Her stay in Madras was formative. She was introduced to the film producer and impresario G. K. Sheshagiri, who managed a venue similar to Bangalore's Opera House, called the Renaissance Theatre. E. Krishna Iyer, a member of the Madras Academy of Music, invited La Meri to a performance of Bharatanatyam by the famous sisters Varalakshmi and Bhanumati from the devadasi community in Kumbhakonam. La Meri soon took lessons in Bharatanatyam from the teacher of the young sisters, Papanasam Vadevelu Pillai, and performed a short *varnam* in a concert she shared with the sisters at the Victoria Public Hall under the aegis of the Renaissance Theatre.[74] La Meri stayed in Madras until early February, except for a short, two-day stint in Bangalore on January 13 and 14, 1937, when she came in contact with Gopal.

In Gopal's autobiography, he mentions the same cast of characters from Madras, including the sisters and their teacher. But he does not mention Madras. He saw the sisters Varalakshmi and Bhanumati perform in their hometown of Kumbhakonam. E. Krishna Iyer was a friend with whom he traveled to Thanjavur. When La Meri returned to Madras after her brief stint in Bangalore, Gopal did not join her. Being invested in Kathakali by this time, it is possible that he saw the Madras circle only from a distance. Gopal joined La Meri's troupe in Bombay on February 25, 1937, traveling thereafter to "all the big cities in India and then from Calcutta . . . to Rangoon, Malaya, Java, the Philippines, China and finally Japan."[75]

La Meri learned from Gopal "all she [knew] about Kathakali," while her "Ethnic Dances" brushed off on him. La Meri's brief reference to Gopal's use of Ravel's *Bolero* hints at his interest in adapting his Kathakali training to a global culture of dance. Photographs with La Meri show Gopal wearing a white suit, cradling a sombrero in a duo of "Mexican dance."[76] Spending more than a month in Java in May–June 1937, the duo performed, gave lecture demonstrations, observed classes and rehearsals, and took lessons in the classical Javanese dance and theater. In the first decades of the twentieth century, Java became a destination for an international traffic of visitors, in part due to the meteoric rise of Margaretha Zella, the Dutch wife of a military officer stationed in the Dutch colony who launched herself as the exotic Javanese dancer Mata Hari in Europe around 1900. In 1905, Mata Hari performed in front of the Shiva Nataraja in the Musée Guimet in Paris, and her dance soon came to be called "the Hindu Ballet."[77]

By the 1920s, the royal households of the semiautonomous princely states of Yogyakarta and Solokarta patronized local performance traditions to assert their cultural autonomy within the Dutch colony of Java. The palace of Mangkunegoro VII of Solokarta hosted visiting performers, scholars, and thinkers from the United States, Europe, and other parts of Asia to encourage international interest and cross-cultural exchanges. In 1922, Ananda Coomaraswamy visited

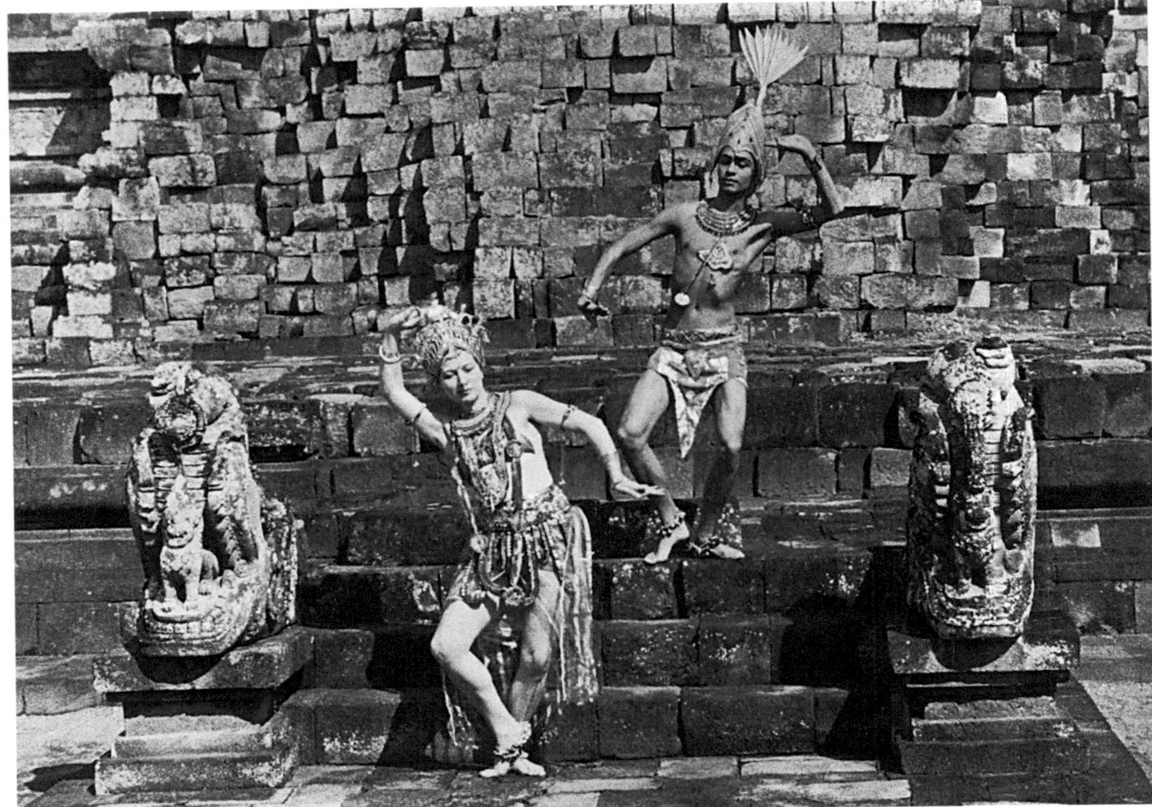

Figure 2.17. La Meri and Ram Gopal dancing in Java on Kalasan Temple, stairs, May 1937. (Jerome Robbins Dance Division, The New York Public Library of the Performing Arts)

Java with his third wife, the New York–based dancer Stella Bloch, who returned to the United States and performed the "Javanese dance" in the city. In 1927, the Indian poet laureate Rabindranath Tagore extensively toured Java, posing in front of the great Stupa in Borobudur. The poet saw in Java the vestiges of ancient Indian culture that were lost in his own time in India.[78]

So, when Gopal and La Meri posed against the ruins of a Javanese temple in May 1937, they were clearly following what Matthew Isaac Cohen calls "Javanese Orientalism," a global fascination with the ruins and the living arts of the region of Java (fig. 2.17).[79] On May 16, the dancers attended a lecture demonstration at the Yogyakarta palace and saw a professional rehearsal of "probably the *wayang wong*," a dance drama based on the Indian epics *Ramayana* and *Mahabharata*.[80] On May 18, the two participated in a large open class at the Solokarta palace. The photograph may have been taken soon thereafter. The two dancers pose as the romantic king Klana and his beloved, Candra Kirana, popular in the *wayang wong* performances.[81] La Meri wears an openwork crown and long necklaces and tassels that might have sparkled and jingled with her movements. Gopal wears a conical turban, behind which is attached a tall fan, posing as the king chasing a gazelle-like fairy. The photograph was taken in the ruins of the temple dedicated to the Buddhist goddess Tara, in Kalasan, about ten kilometers east of Yogyakarta. The temple was restored in 1927–1929 in the yard of the local Dutch resident of Java and became one among many temple sites for tourists to visit on their way from Yogyakarta to Solokarta, the residence of Mangekunegoro VII. An archaeological photograph taken during its reconstruction indicates that the fantastical, gaping mouths of the *makara* were not yet placed where we now see them framing the dancers.[82]

The costumes and ornaments designed for Gopal during this trip appear in Van Vechten photographs. They are partly drawn from *wayang wong*, but we do not see the more recognizable horn-shaped crown and shoulder pads that Gopal wears in a photograph from 1946.[83] The "traditional" representations are underplayed in 1938. Instead, he pulls out the bejeweled accordion turban we see in the Java photographs, but without its broom finial. The headgear cannot be called "traditional" and comes close to the Orientalist re-creations of Java in Hollywood films such as that of Greta Garbo's 1931 film *Mata Hari* (figs. 2.18–2.20). Garbo's costume for *Mata Hari* was designed by Adrian, whom Gopal and Janta met at a Hollywood party several months later, when they landed in Los Angeles prior to their arrival in New York. But Gopal already had the crown in his suitcase, indicating that its design came from La Meri's familiarity with Hollywood Orientalism or Gopal's memory of Garbo's film in Bangalore.

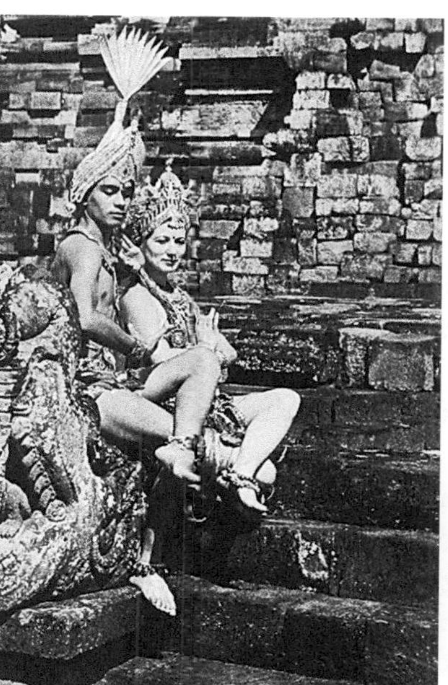

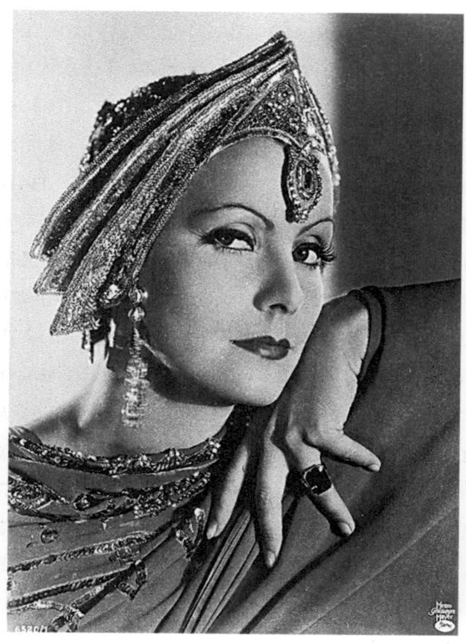

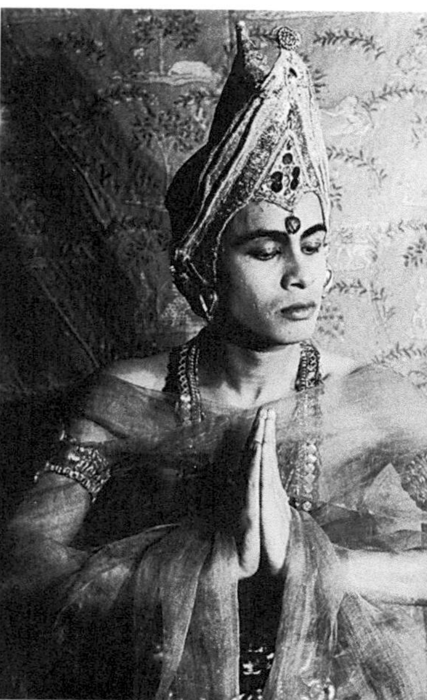

Figures 2.18–2.20. *Left to right*, La Meri and Ram Gopal in Java on Kalasan Temple, seated on *makara*, May 1937. (Jerome Robbins Dance Division, The New York Public Library of the Performing Arts); Greta Garbo, *Mata Hari* (1931), black-and-white photograph from the Rijksmuseum (Courtesy of GetArchive LLC, PICRYL; download September 30, 2021; © Creative Commons CCO 1.0 Universal Public Domain Dedication [CCO 1.0 Dedication]); Carl Van Vechten, *Ram Gopal*, May 11, 1938, XX, M16.

The American Gaze

Gopal parted company with La Meri in Tokyo. On September 14, 1937, La Meri sailed to Hawaii on the *Chichibu Mari* and then to Los Angeles in October, leaving behind the Indian dancer.[84] In his autobiography, Gopal mentions waking up one morning to find the entire troupe gone. It was a fallout between the two dancers.[85] They had just had three concerts at the Hibiya Hall, but something went wrong when a seemingly well-regarded English critic, I. J. Fischer, expressed an "unreserved admiration for Ram Gopal" in the Tokyo papers and complained that he was not given much stage time and was denied an encore even when the audience demanded it.[86] La Meri mentions the onset of the Sino-Japanese War as the reason for dropping her plans for the rest of the tour and returning to the United States. Gopal, who had also dreamed of going to America, remembers being told by La Meri, "you can dance your way back to India doing cabaret in some hotels, maybe you'll get engagements."[87] In 1937, the looming possibility of World War II may also have impinged on their concert tour.

In Tokyo, Gopal came in contact with the Polish writer and journalist Aleksander Janta, whom we met in chapter 1. Janta first traveled to Japan and China to cover the Sino-Japanese conflicts and soon became a travel writer visiting India, Africa, and the United States.[88] When he met Gopal in Tokyo, he was covering the cultural scene for the *Gazeta Polska* and was probably introduced to the dancer by his hotel-mate, the American artist and children's book illustrator Thomas Handforth.[89] Janta probably led the way to United States for the dancer, having taken the trip from Japan once before. The two traveled to Los Angeles via Hawaii on the same *Chichibu Mari* that La Meri had taken a few months prior, and a program booklet at the Dillingham Hall in Honolulu billed Gopal's concert on January 19, 1938, as his "first American appearance."[90] On February 10, 1938, the two men landed at the Los Angeles harbor. The *Herald Express* that day announced, "Indian Dancer Here. . . . Wearing a pearl as big as a marble, India's most distinguished dancer, protege of the Maharajah of Mysore, arrived at Los Angeles harbor today aboard the Matson liner Matsonia." The *Los Angeles Times*, on February 12, also announced Janta as "his Polish manager."[91]

Gopal's encounter with the customs officer at the port captures the excticizing gaze that Gopal would thoroughly enjoy in the United States. He describes the scene with a sense of drama: "'Say, is this the wardrobe of a man or a woman?' a casual, burly, tough-looking Customs officer demanded. 'What's this stuff?' drawing a Javanese *kris* or sword acquired there during my tour. 'And this, and this . . . and this,' and so he went right through my strange and exotic assortment of stage costumes."[92] The officer's bafflement might have been increased by Gopal's androgynous look and possibly his unlocatable complexion. Complicating matters further, the Polish journalist did not look like the dancer's brother, in spite of a hint of intimacy between them.

From the Los Angeles harbor, Gopal and Janta headed straight for Hollywood, armed with a letter of introduction from the US ambassador in Tokyo to the "great showman" Cecil B. DeMille. Gopal found the great director to be "a sage, a seer, a sort of *rishi* of the cinema world," whom he compared to Gandhi. Throughout March 1938, the dancer met many other Hollywood celebrities. He was enamored and started name-dropping. At the home of Bernadine Szold Fritz, a theater socialite, he met the Hollywood costume designer Adrian, "who had dreamed up Garbo's fantastic dresses in her pictures." Above all, he struck a friendship with Mercedes de Acosta, who was known as "that furious lesbian" in Hollywood circles for her tumultuous relationships with Greta Garbo and Marlene Dietrich.[93] Gopal's autobiography communicates his excitement about the glamorous possibilities associated with Hollywood: "And that was how Pandora's Box of the magic screen opened to me, . . . and many new threads, all gleaming and shining started off a chain reaction of influence in my life."[94] His concert in Los Angeles on March 11, 1938, contained a long list of Hollywood celebrities as sponsors.[95]

Janta and Gopal travel to New York. A letter from one of the Los Angeles sponsors, the influential Polish pianist Arthur Rubinstein, to the powerful impresario Sol Hurok gained the dancer a concert at the 46th Street Theatre in New York on May 1, 1938. The Hollywood network soon brought Gopal in contact with Van Vechten, who had photographed Rubinstein on November 30, 1937, and de Acosta a little earlier (see fig. 1.14). De Acosta, a New Yorker herself, may have introduced the dancer to the photographer. By this time, she had nominated herself as a promoter for the Indian dancer. When Gopal and Janta visited Europe after their New York stint, de Acosta also traveled and introduced them to the American exile poet in Paris Gertrude Stein, after a suggestion by Van Vechten, who was a close friend and promoter of the writer in the United States.

On the morning of May 1, 1938, Gopal's concert was announced in the *New York Times* as the "authentic temple dances from North and South India."[96] The announcement includes a photograph taken by George Hurrell, the photographer of Hollywood celebrities and a celebrity himself (fig. 2.21). Gopal wears a studded breast plate, a Kathakali crown, and a stiff sash over the same short, pleated skirt in which we saw him in his photographs with La Meri in Java. The pose is from his "Cobra Dance." The dancer sits on his knees, arms stretched on the side with elbows bent, palms in the open-palm *pataka* mudra, mimicking the outstretched hood of a sejant cobra ready for attack. He dilates his eyes, pulling the eyelids up while turning the pupils down, using his training from Kathakali.

In a *New York Times* review the following day, the dance critic John Martin writes about the performance, "The high point of the evening was [the] cobra dance, after the manner of the Kathakali school." The review is discerning and critical. Martin describes Gopal as "a slender, pictorial young man who does not look the twenty-two years accredited to him." The dancer does not rise up to the critic's taste and judgment: "Truth to tell, his dancing is at present equally

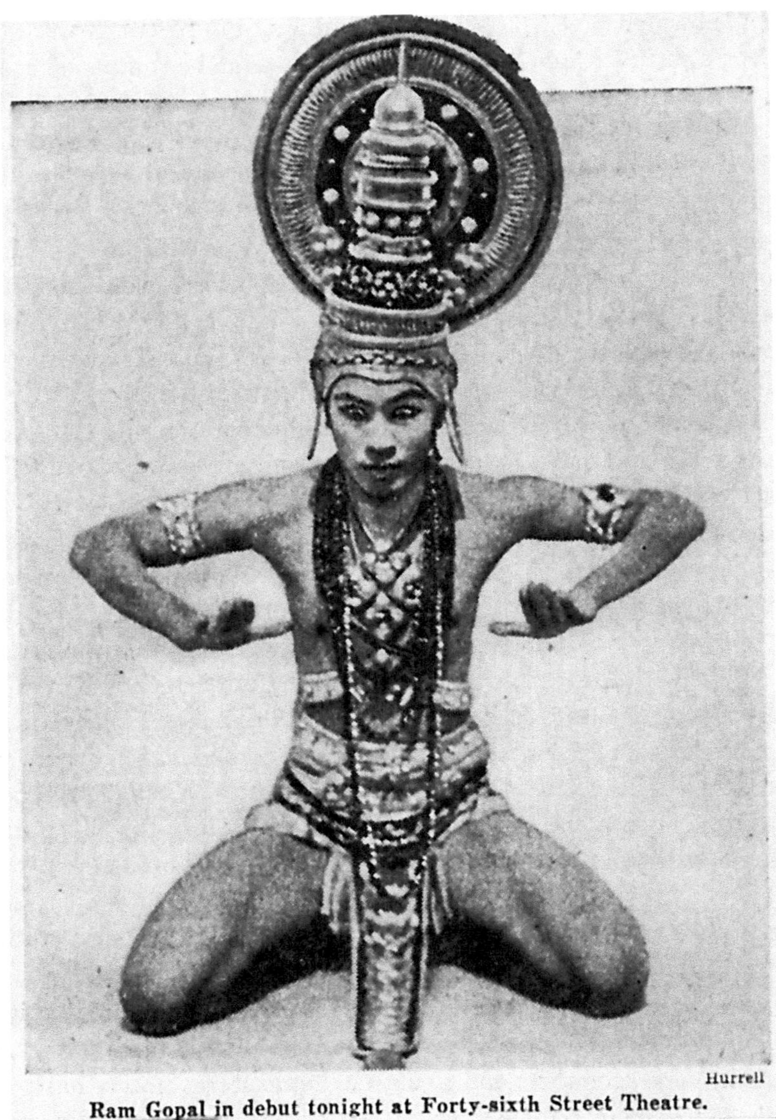

Figure 2.21. Announcement of concert on May 1, 1938, with photograph by George Hurrell, *New York Times* ("Ram Gopal, Clippings," MGZR, Jerome Robbins Dance Division, New York Public Library; courtesy of *New York Times* and George Hurrell Estate)

slender, equally young and equally pictorial." Martin finds Gopal's numbers only "effective as theatrical presentations" that were, to his chagrin, "applauded heartily" by a large audience. He concedes that the dancer has potential: "Gopal has a beautiful carriage and handles his body well," but he is hardly a "master of the great subtlety which lies in the technique of the Hindu dance." Even his Kathakali-based dances are "scarcely in a class with those of Madhavan of Shankar's company."[97]

The comparison with Uday Shankar is significant. A senior contemporary of Gopal, Shankar was the North Star of Indian dance for critics in Europe and the United States by the time of Gopal's visit.[98] In the 1920s, as an art student in London, Shankar collaborated with the ballerina Anna Pavlova on an Indian theme of "Radha and Krishna," and by the 1930s, he had formed a large troupe of dancers and musicians and gained international acclaim for his choreography of "Hindu Ballet."[99] In India, he established a dance school in 1939 called the Uday Shankar Indian Cultural Center (USICC) in Almora in the foothills of the Himalayas, sponsored enthusiastically by an international group of philanthropists, dancers, and critics including John Martin.[100] The American critic had championed Shankar's dance company since at least 1934, when his "Hindu Ballet" took New York by storm. He also defended Shankar from harsh criticism by the connoisseurs of classical dance in India, such as G. K. Sheshagiri, the same influential impresario of the Renaissance Theatre who had embraced La Meri during her visit to Madras. Sheshagiri commented that Shankar's dance was "tolerable" as a presentation, but "considered as Indian dance, either as Bharata Natya, or Nritya, or Nrtta, it was absolutely unconvincing except for the costumes, the décor and the music." Martin shot back with a rhetorical question: "Is the dance to be a specialty of the scholar and the aesthete or does it belong to the general ranks?"[101] Against Sheshagiri, Martin pitches an argument in the name of "artistic democracy." In relation to Gopal, however, the critic repositions himself as an expert. He finds Gopal's Kathakali training far inferior to Madhavan in Shankar's company, and his popular appeal in New York was nothing but a sellout compromise of Indian dance based more on "surface qualities than anything else."[102]

While Shankar was himself untrained as a dancer, he recruited dancers belonging to various Indian traditions and trained them to perform expressive movements interpreted from daily life, ethnographic documentation, and contemporary film.[103] Madhavan stood out for his Kathakali. Wearing the traditional costume with padded skirt, headgear, and sometimes a mask, he performed the virile dance numbers from the Kathakali repertory, such as Shiva's dance of destruction and the abduction of Sita by the demon king Ravana, along with "his own solos as a tribal or warrior."[104] In this context, Martin's comparison of Gopal with Madhavan, not Shankar, makes sense. Gopal too was a trained Kathakali dancer, but he danced solo to prerecorded music during the 1938 trip and did not keep to the traditional costumes.

Joan Erdman points out that Shankar primarily choreographed group dances and was the only male dancer in a troupe of women before Madhavan joined in 1935.[105] A printed program of "Shan-kar and His Hindu Ballet" at the Academy of Music in Philadelphia on December 11, 1937, gives us a glimpse of Shankar's troupe and the dances that Martin and Van Vechten might have seen in the 1930s. The concert was organized by the same Russian impresario, Sol Hurok of S. Hurok Attractions, 30 Rockefeller Plaza, New York, who arranged

Gopal's New York concert in 1938. The lead dancers were Shankar himself, Madhavan, and a host of women simply named "Simkie, Zohra and Uzra." The music was composed and directed by Vishnudass Shirali, and musicians included "Rabindra, Brijo Behari, Sisir Sovan, Nagen Dey," who also doubled as dancers for group numbers such as the tribal "Bhil dance." The dance numbers were largely based on Hindu mythology. Shankar performed the "Kama-Deva" in the story of this "god of love and passion." Madhavan danced the "Partha Kritharth," a story of the hero Arjuna in the epic *Mahabharata*. "Lanka Dahana" was a group dance involving the abduction of Sita by the demon Ravana and the subsequent burning of Ravana's palace in Lanka. The "tandava nritya" that Shankar performed was "a dance of archaic character" involving Shiva, "the god of creation and destruction," and "his divine wife, Sati."[106]

Shankar's cast of characters were distributed along clearly marked gender roles. Costumes based on Indian miniature paintings and colonial ethnographic photographs indicated their cultural authenticity. The cover of the Philadelphia program shows a tight huddle of the three women dancers wearing a saree over their head. Other archival photographs show Shankar commonly in a dhoti, with a naked upper body, possibly with a sacred thread of a brahmin across his chest. The basic masculine attire was modulated according to mythological characters, the gods Indra or Krishna, using ornaments and crowns inspired by popular Ajanta paintings, calendar prints, Parsi theater, and mythological films. Shankar occasionally posed as a "temple prostitute" for still photographs that recall British picture postcards of female dancers, but it is unlikely that he performed feminine characters onstage the way Gopal might have.[107]

Martin's critique of Gopal distinguishes the expert from the crowd and reveals his pursuit of cultural authenticity in Indian dance. Gopal was aware of his comparison with Shankar's dancers: "John Martin, Walter Terry and others were most kind and constructively critical of my performance, given so soon after Shankar, my countryman, had danced there only a short while ago." But he defended himself against Shankar: "Shankar gave them, in the words of one of my American admirers 'the works.' Translated, this meant sex, girls, instruments and himself, with a large company to carry him through the full two-hour programme. And I had danced alone!"[108] A newspaper review clinched the popular response to Gopal's solo performance that evening: "The gospel of Hindu dancing has been well preached by Uday Shan-kar [*sic*] and his cohorts, so that the gathering knew more or less what to expect in the nature of the choreographies. But the manner of Mr. Gopal's dancing, his remarkably fine muscular control, and his fascinating and exotic costumes must have won new converts to the cause."[109]

Martin was particularly troubled by Gopal's "Picture of Bodhisattva." If the dancer's appearance onstage was anything like the figure in Van Vechten's photograph, Martin would have had difficulty locating it within the known traditions of Indian dance (fig. 2.9). To make matters worse, he would have readily seen in the studded breast plate, the short skirt with fan-like pleats, the bold beaded waist band, and the tiara a reflection of ancient Egyptian and Roman costumes from Orientalist films of Cecil B. DeMille and the Oriental costumes of Ted Shawn and Ruth St. Denis from their "Siamese Dance" in the 1920s. Worst of all, unlike the vigorously masculine "Cobra Dance," which he admired, here the "slender pictorial man" appeared particularly androgynous in his ornaments worn over an almost naked body. Madhavan's performance had represented Kathakali to be a masculine dance form relating to the martial arts of South India. Gopal's version was shockingly different. It is one thing to have an androgynous body, for which dancers such as Shankar and Vaslav Nijinsky were also known. It is a quite another to perform androgyny deliberately. It was wrong all around.

The Scandal of Van Vechten Photographs

Martin would have been scandalized by Gopal's gynemimetic performance in Van Vechten's studio. Janta was surely worried, as is evidenced by a letter he wrote to Van Vechten on August 8, 1938, from his family estate in Poland, Mata Komorza. The letter responds to a stash of photographs from the photo shoot that he received from Van Vechten at his estate at Tuchola in Pomorza, where Gopal was spending a few leisurely days. Janta was "speechless" over the photographs, in which "Ram's being divine." Inspired by them, he pitches an idea for a book, "a better one than ordinary albums, a book of 24 studies—by Carl van Vechten. The title being Ram Gopal." He even selects images from the set he had received and identifies them using Van Vechten's negative number. He would have published the book himself, and it would have taken him no more than a few weeks; but the book really needed to be Van Vechten's. At the end of the letter, Janta expresses only one major concern: "By the way XX Mi 15, XX Mi 18, XX Mi 16, the ones I would call 'sitting veil poses' rather pathetic, isn't it? And of course not to be seen, as I doubt whether you do such things as destroying the negatives."[110] What was Janta's worry?

The "sitting veil poses" were all from May 11, 1938, the last day of the photo shoot (fig. 2.22). It is possible that Janta considered that session as nothing more than three friends horsing around within the privacy of the New York studio. To select images for publication from such a session, however, was a different matter. In his letter to Van Vechten, Janta found himself striding a thin line between a private sport and a public image of the dancer. By now, Janta was publicly recognized as Gopal's manager, a role he took seriously. Just prior to receiving Van Vechten's photographs that summer, Janta had arranged the dancer's concert at the Royal Opera House in Warsaw and designed posters for it, including quotations from Van Vechten. In his letter, he was making a hearty pitch for a book that could conceivably include an essay by Van Vechten but where a distinction needed to be made between publishable and unpublishable images. The "sitting

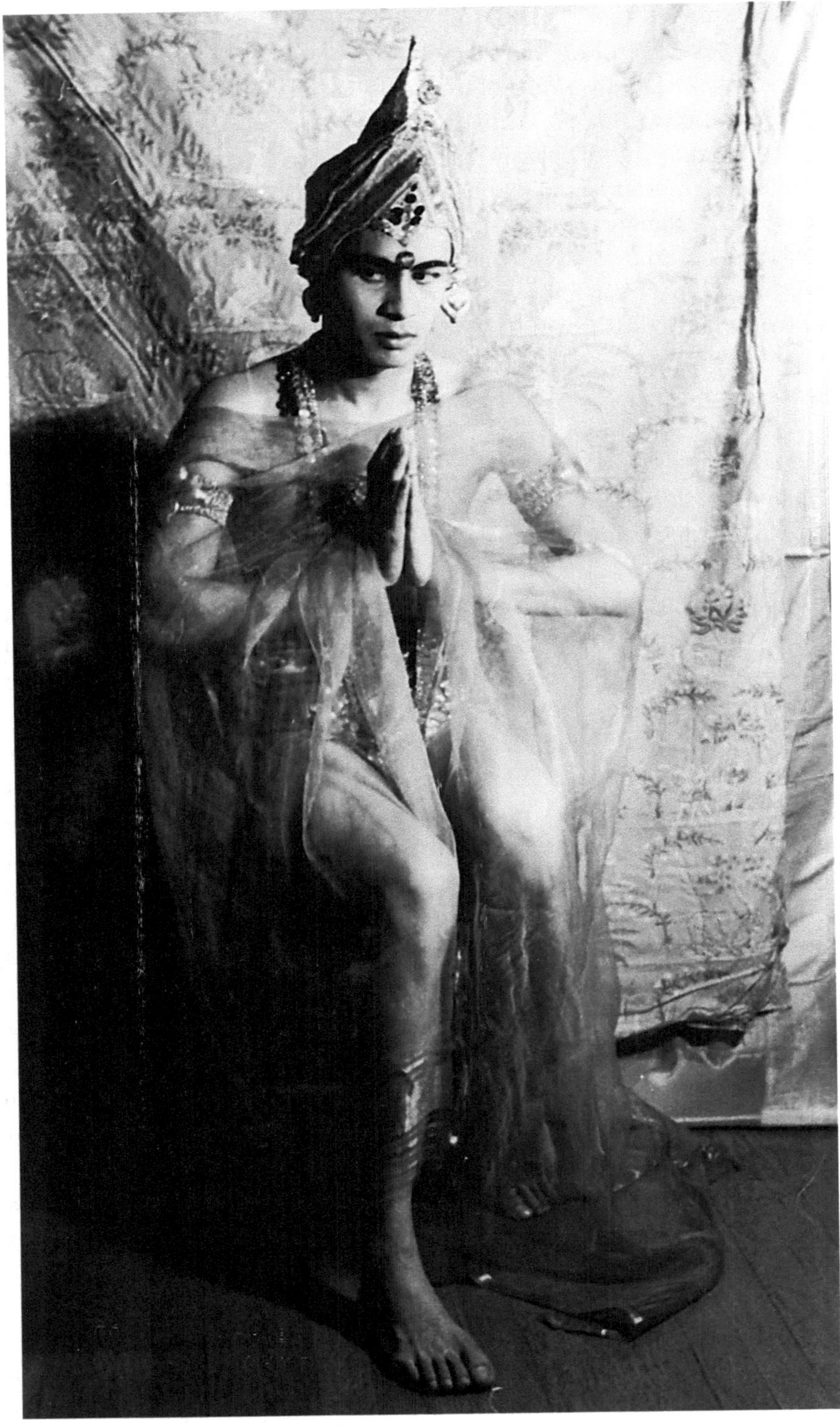

Figure 2.22. Carl Van Vechten, *Ram Gopal*, May 11, 1938, XX M18. (Jerome Robbins Dance Division, The New York Public Library of the Performing Arts; © The Van Vechten Trust)

veil poses" could not be seen in this promotional context. Just imagine John Martin getting hold of them!

Why did Gopal's gynemimetic performance in front of Van Vechten's camera go too far for Janta? He should have known by then about the dancer's Kathakali training. He could have persuaded Martin-like critics that gynemimesis was an integral part of a dancer's Kathakali training in Kerala. What was the line being crossed in the Van Vechten photographs? I suggest that Janta found the "feminine" representation in those photographs marked differently than the Kathakali conventions. They deviated from the recognizably "hyperfeminine" female stereotype represented by the mythological characters on the Indian stage and screen.[111] In other words, Gopal's gynemimesis crossed a "cultural" boundary. The sitting veil poses looked too much like Salomé and came too close to the representations of modern Western women dancers. The crown was too much like a Greta Garbo knockoff, which Janta could never have justified to critics such as Martin.

Janta, Martin, and Van Vechten would have all recognized the global circuits of Indian dance in Gopal's Kathakali, but they dealt with that recognition differently. Martin was disappointed. Janta was anxious, while Van Vechten indulged the dancer in a three-day photo shoot. It is remarkable that Van Vechten did not photograph Shankar, Madhavan, or any dancer from Shankar's troupe. He surely attended the concerts prior to meeting Gopal, as the program of Shankar's 1937 Philadelphia concert in the Van Vechten Papers at the Beinecke indicates. It is possible that Van Vechten simply did not feel the same affinity with Shankar as he felt with Gopal. It is also possible that the cultural authenticity of "Hindu Ballet" was not interesting enough for Van Vechten, as it was for Martin.

On January 6, 1933, when Van Vechten had the chance, he invited Shankar's musicians for a photo shoot in his studio. One image shows three musicians in a tight huddle (fig. 2.23). On the left, Vishnudass Shirali plays the tabla; in the center, Annada Charan Bhattacharya picks up the bow of his *esraj*; and on the right, Rajendra Shankar plays the flute, while the photographer stands over them with his camera possibly mounted on a tripod. The image has the indifferent look of an ethnographic diorama at world's fairs, and Van Vechten frames their cultural exoticism against a chintz background.[112] Van Vechten's curiosity may have been piqued by the colorful turbans, the beautiful instruments (notice the peacock head of the *esraj*), and the manner of playing them, which he, as a music critic, may have found to be different from the musicians he had known and photographed in New York.

In Gopal, by contrast, Van Vechten found a kindred spirit. The dazzling "surface qualities" of Gopal's solos, which irked Martin, were exactly what drew Van Vechten to the Indian dancer in 1938. In full views, midshots, and close-ups, Van Vechten matched Gopal's figurations and costumes with changing backdrops and lighting. The visual conversation between photography and choreography set up in the studio went beyond the concerns for cultural novelty or

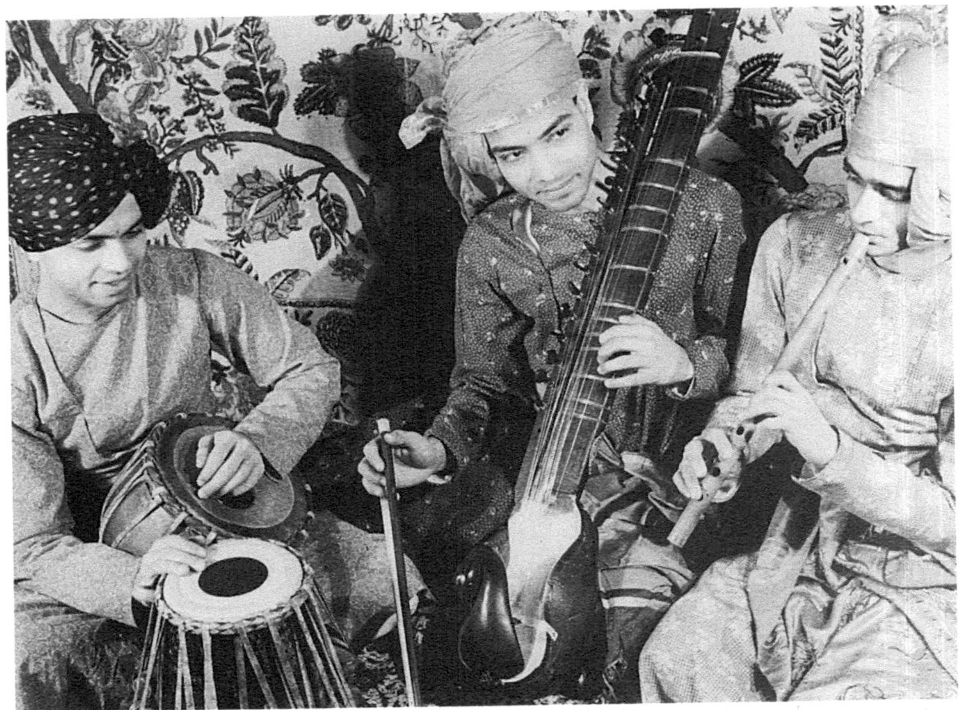

Figure 2.23. Carl Van Vechten, *Vishnudass Shirali, Annada Charan Bhattacharyya, Rajendra Shan-kar,* January 6, 1933, XV b:26. (Beinecke Rare Book and Manuscript Library, Yale University; © The Van Vechten Trust)

the authenticity of Hindu ballet. If not for cultural authenticity, what was Van Vechten pursuing?

Here is a thought. Van Vechten was enamored by the shape-shifting, androgynous body of the dancer that could not be located in any performance tradition, Eastern or Western. Let us explore this cultural instability in a final set of two images from the New York photo shoot. In one, Gopal wears a crumpled dhoti and a sash as if in a practice or rehearsal session of Kathakali, and he demonstrates his "Cobra Dance" (fig. 2.24). We can imagine the pose from a description in Gopal's New York program: "The spirit of an infuriated Cobra takes possession of the dancer. This is performed with the Kathakali costume and technique."[113] The beaded necklaces, including a long rosary, suggest a snake charmer or a sorcerer being possessed by the object of his attention.

The legibility of the Kathakali performance is complicated, however, by another photograph of Gopal in the same costume, hands folded, contemplative, and glowing against a fabric backdrop (fig. 2.25). This is what Geeta Chandran would have called a "portrait." The fabric, like many others, may have been purchased at one of the boutique shops of the bohemian Greenwich Village that Van Vechten frequented. But in this case, its imagery is legible. It shows a Persian miniature painting of the fifteenth century. Two panels of Islamic calligraphy can be seen on the left top, and the dancer's eyes lead to two figures in the lower left corner.

Julia Bailey identified the printed image for me as the central part of a painting "derived (with considerable adaptation), from folio 26v in the British Library's OR 2265 from a famous *Khamsa* of Nizami dated to 1539–43. The image in question, from Makhzan al-Asrar, depicts a contest between physicians, witnessed by a ruler and courtiers."[114] The original painting shows a garden party, and the inscription we see in the Van Vechten photograph is from the gate and the garden pavilion, with a cypress tree showing behind the fence. The configuration is block printed several times across the fabric.

I was thrilled to discover the original source of the fabric print, but its specificity is irrelevant to our reading of the photograph. The Indian dancer disconnects the background from its Persian reference, while the fabric print takes the dancer out of the framework of Indian classical dance altogether, displacing the figure from its geographical location in India and the Hindu dance tradition of Kathakali. The photograph repositions the foreground and the background in

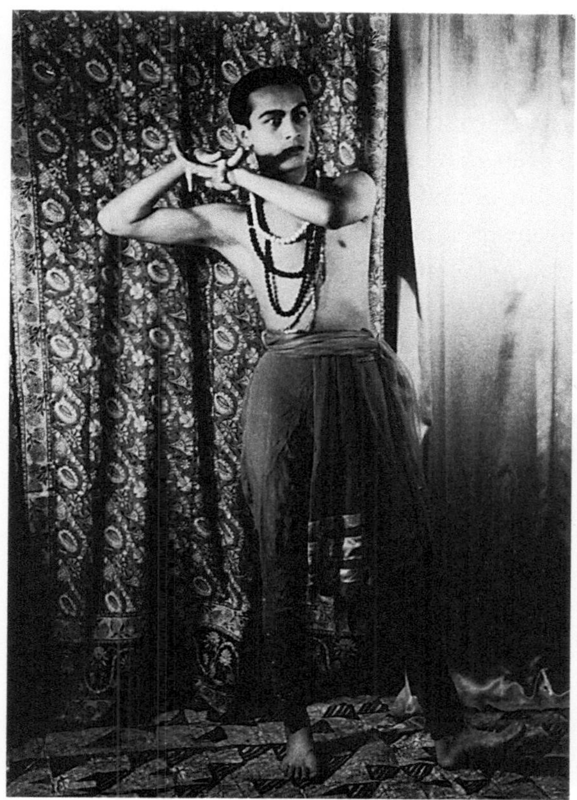

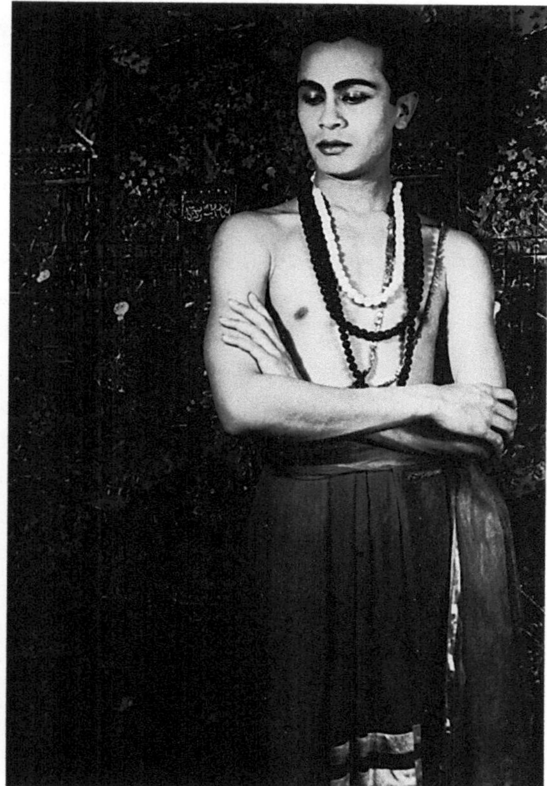

Figures 2.24 and 2.25. *Left*, Carl Van Vechten, *Ram Gopal*, May 11, 1938, XIX, M00. *Right*, Carl Van Vechten, *Ram Gopal*, May 11, 1938, XIX M4. (Beinecke Rare Book and Manuscript Library, Yale University; © The Van Vechten Trust)

an indeterminate world, constituted by global circulation in which the exotic fabric print of a Persian painting purchased by the American photographer in a New York boutique shop comes together in a visible constellation with the exotic dancer's body. In this way, the photograph is Orientalist by definition, producing an imaginary East out of a loose amalgam of Persian and Indian markers. But if Orientalism is, classically, a means to bring distant world regions within the reach of Western imagination through concrete cultural stereotypes, the Indian dancer's representations in New York are an example of what Anne Anlin Cheng calls "Ornamentalism." It is a way for the Oriental body of Western imagination to represent itself within a racialized image and media practice, as Cheng shows in relation to the star Anna May Wong as a "yellow woman" of Hollywood film of the 1930s and 1940s. By deliberately wearing the racial and gender stereotypes, Wong both inhabits the glamorous screen image and reveals the artifice of media representations.[115]

For the Indian dancer, then, Orientalism is not simply about stereotyping but also self-fashioning. If the dance reform reclaimed the authenticity of India's cultural traditions on the modern proscenium stage, Gopal's collaboration with Van Vechten's Orientalist fantasy-making indicates the instabilities in tradition-making. Sharply differing from Madras, as well as Shankar's reach for ethnographic certainties, the malleable genealogy of world cultures built into Gopal's shape-shifting representations included modern dance, Hollywood films, Euro-American Orientalism, and the global circuits of Indian art history. Gopal's cultural nomadism drew on, and even glamorized, the princely modern culture of the semiautonomous colonial state of Mysore.[116] In his stylized dance as well as self-ethnologized voguing in front of Van Vechten's camera, we discover Gopal's strategy of "Ornamentalism." By the mid-twentieth century, however, when the dancer participated in the discourse of cultural inheritance, these globalized strategies of princely modernity seemed anachronistic even to him, as I elaborate in chapter 6. For now, let us turn to the photographer and his Leica to explore how they host the dancer's nomadic self-presentation within the privacy and intimacy of the New York photo studio.

Photography is a very personal thing, . . . even a magical act.

—Carl Van Vechten

CHAPTER 3. THE PHOTOGRAPHER

The photograph in figure 3.1 is an unusual image, at least from the dancer's point of view. The transparent veil is not from his dance repertory. John Martin would have disapproved of the way it feminizes the male dancer. The negative number XX M16 suggests that it is from the last roll exposed on May 11, 1938. I propose that the gauze was Van Vechten's idea, and Ram Gopal humored him as the photo shoot was winding down on that last day. The dancer was already wearing the armband and the necklaces for other images, but only now does he pull out the gorgeous, bejeweled, Garbo-like turban made for him during his visit to Java. Clinching the "Oriental" feeling, Van Vechten complements the dancer's ornate body with a brocade fabric, probably the Indian *kalamkari* or what Pika Ghosh calls *colcha,* with scenes of an outdoor soirée stitched into cameos from Indian Deccani painting and Chinoiserie porcelain.[1] The sharp contours of the

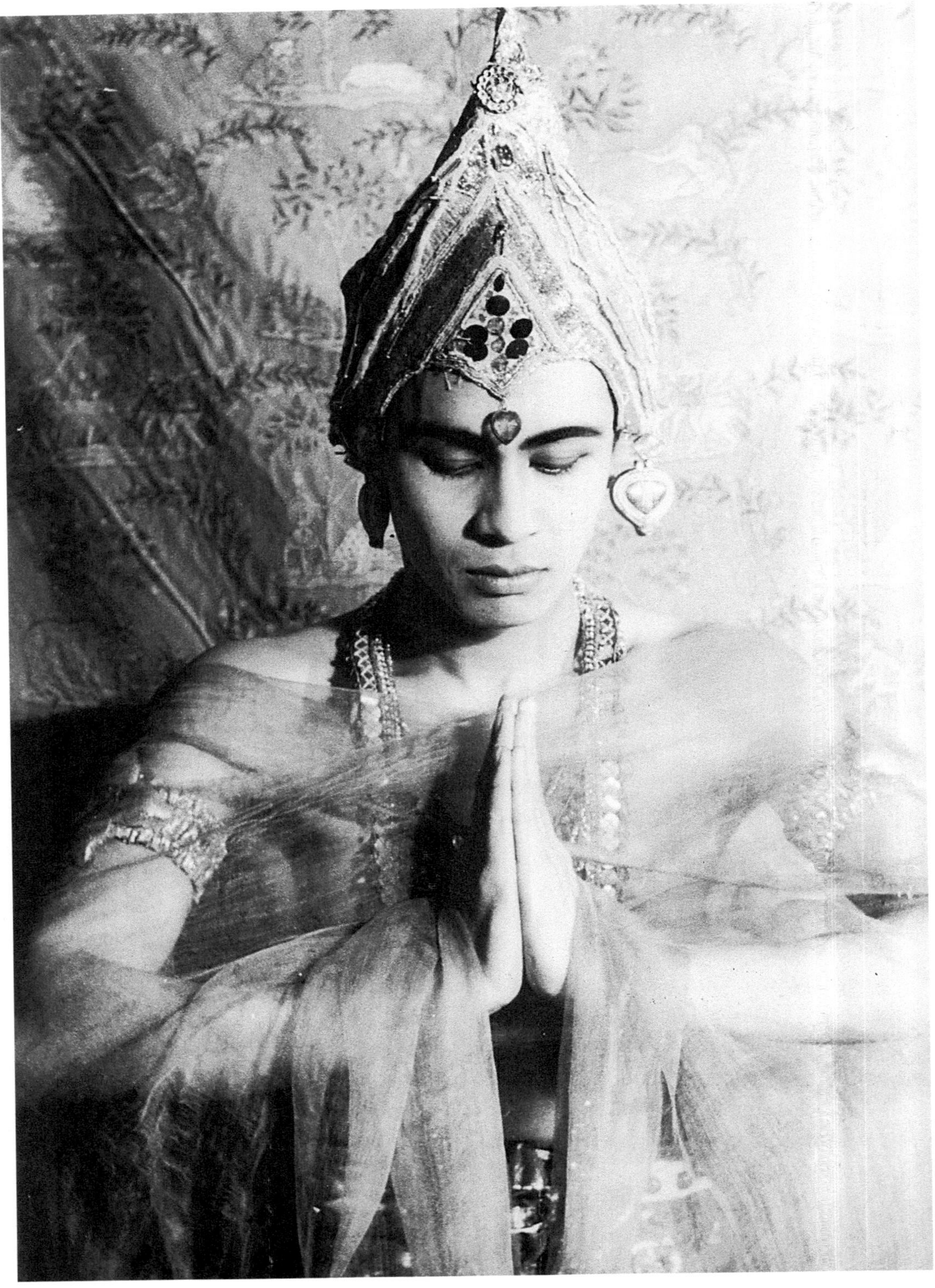

Figure 3.1. Carl Van Vechten, *Ram Gopal*, May 11, 1938, CVV, XX M15. (Beinecke Rare Book and Manuscript Library, Yale University; © The Van Vechten Trust)

headgear against the watery delicacy of the veil seem to have made the figure suddenly resonant for the photographer.

What did the photographer see in the image? This chapter explores Van Vechten's view of the Indian dancer when he looked through the viewfinder of his Leica camera. The cross-dressed dancer may have recalled for Van Vechten his younger days in Cedar Rapids, when he saw a local boy, Herbie Newell, dance a skirt dance. Since that time, as Edward White notes, Van Vechten pursued his interest in men in two ways, "performance of dance and female impersonation": "Both created brash and unapologetic visions of maleness transported beyond the gender norms of the early 1900s, and dance had the bonus of providing a socially acceptable means of publicly admiring the male body."[2] We will elaborate on Van Vechten's taste for gender bending so as to behold in a single image both maleness and its other (whatever that might be) and the place of dance in it.

The Indian dancer's richly decorated body added a glamorous sense of theatricality to Van Vechten's boyhood fantasies. His exotic appearance evoked other, distant times and places. As a dance and theater critic, Van Vechten would have immediately recognized in it a flicker of Salomé from Oscar Wilde's controversial 1893 play. The scandal of the play centered on Salomé's seductive dance of the seven veils at the climax of a biblical story about love, incest, and murder in which the niece and stepdaughter of the Roman emperor Herod won the head of Saint John the Baptist in revenge for his refusal of her sexual advances. When an opera by Richard Strauss based on the play opened at the Metropolitan Opera House in New York City in 1907, Van Vechten reviewed it for the *Broadway Magazine* and explained it as a "life-changing event."[3] What excited him the most was precisely its perverse eroticism, carried with great passion by the soprano, Olive Fremstad, whom Van Vechten later interviewed.

Peter Wollen points out that Wilde's play is a modern creation of an ancient story that becomes a key reference for the era of Decadence in fin de siècle Paris. The seductive image circulated in art, theater, and modern fashion, starting in the 1870s in Gustave Moreau's painting as well as Gustave Flaubert's tale in *Herodias* (1876), flourishing in the draped style of clothing promoted by the house of Paul Poiret in the first two decades of the twentieth century. Joris-Karl Huysmans's novel *A rebours* (Against the Grain, 1884) enshrined the Roman seductress in the Orientalist sizzle of "a scene heavy with perfume and a dance, which, though openly erotic in its bodily movements, was mainly characterized by the effects of light shimmering and glinting from bracelets, rings, necklaces, pearl embroidery, gold and silver cloth, which moved with the dancer as she danced."[4] Van Vechten developed the Orientalist fantasy of Decadent Paris in his collaboration with Gopal.

Persona

Edward White points out that Van Vechten's childhood interest in cross-dressed boys was only partly sexual. He was drawn more to their extravagant self-presentation. In the middle of his novel *Peter Whiffle* (1922), Van Vechten lingers on a vivid description of the protagonist as a flamboyant Decadent-style cross-dresser in his New York apartment.

> Peter was wearing green trousers, a white silk shirt, a tie of Chinese blue brocade, clasped with a black opal, and a most ornate black Chinese dressing-gown, around the skirt of which a silver dragon chased his tail. He was combed and brushed and there was a faint odour of toilet-water. His nails were manicured and on one of his little fingers I observed a ring which I had never seen him wear before. Later, when I examined it more closely, it proved to be an amethyst intaglio, with Leda and the Swan for its subject. It has been said, perhaps too often, that you cannot make a silk purse of a sow's ear. It is even more true that you cannot make a sow's ear out of a silk purse.[5]

Whiffle's extravagance comes close to the perfumed, ornate body of Huysmans's Salomé.

Cross-dressing has a lineage in the cultural politics of Salomé. Wollen elaborates on it against a Victorian belief in biological determinism in England and the United States that described sexual difference of men and women as "natural dichotomies." Using Thomas Laqueur, Wollen explains that both feminists and antifeminists of the nineteenth century believed that "men, by nature, were sexually active, women pure and passionless." By contrast, the Decadents celebrated Salomé because she rejected "any conventional ascription of sexual nature" and "portrayed a world of androgyny in which desire could run, against the grain, in the wrong direction and towards the wrong object." Salomé contradicted the cornerstone of heteronormative Victorian ideology and was thus deemed "the somnambulist and hysterical in her perverse desire to kiss the lips of Jokanaan's severed head." By the 1900s, Salomé offered visual artists, dancers, and fashion designers "a variety of different positions for the identification of both sexes." Wollen mentions at least one photograph of Oscar Wilde himself dressed as Salomé "in flowing skirt with bare stomach and jeweled brassiere, tresses running down the length of his back beneath the elaborate head dress," reaching out for the head of Saint John the Baptist on a platter. The image impinges "on masculinity quite as subversively as it did on femininity."[6] Van Vechten would have similarly glimpsed in Gopal that extravagantly ambisexual Wildean figure of Decadent Paris.

Lincoln Kirstein, a longtime friend of Van Vechten's and a dance critic, the cofounder of the School of American Ballet (1934), and the director of New York City Ballet (1948), saw in Van Vechten a "bubbly mixture" of Cedar Rapids and

Paris. He writes, "Carl was a dandy," in other words, characterized by a Wildean taste for gender transgressions through high fashion. Kirstein first met Van Vechten at the famous salonnière, Muriel Draper's house on East Fortieth Street in Manhattan in 1927, and recalled him as a "large, blond, faintly Churchillian baby [who] wore a red fireman's shirt." He was a part of "New York's High Bohemia." They became close friends around their mutual interests in dance, among other things. "Carl Van Vechten told me and taught me many things, the most important being a sense of the individual, idiosyncratic authority of elegance as style." It was a fiery pursuit of refinement and taste associated with the fashionable dandy Beau Brummell, "who introduced the daily bath to the British gentleman," and the Frenchman Jean Cocteau, who "once called the entire process of art 'the rehabilitation of the commonplace.'"[7]

Artfulness belonged to a dandy's alternative urban lifestyle in nineteenth-century London and early twentieth-century Paris, as well as in the world of Kirstein and Van Vechten. Through it, Van Vechten articulated a mode of rebellion against the Victorian gendered norms hardening since his childhood and youth in the American mainstream culture.[8] In the essay "A Defence of Bad Taste," Van Vechten rebelled against that America, "where men are supposed to know nothing about matters of taste and where women have their dresses planned for them." He protested the mainstream view that the exercise of taste and "self-expression" in clothing, in furnishing, in books, and in the arts was "a little *effiminé*, a trifle *declassé* for a business man (allowances are sometimes made for poets, musicians, actors, and people who live in Greenwich Village)."[9] Months after he came to New York, he began to wear colorful silk shirts and jewelry purchased at boutique stores on Fifth Avenue and in Greenwich Village.

Through the first two decades of the twentieth century, a deliberate outlook on public self-presentation through an exercise of taste in commercially designed products spread across Paris, Vienna, Berlin, London, and New York. Inspired by experiments in painting, clothing, theater, dance, and architecture and showcased in lifestyle and fashion magazines as well as shopping windows of department stores, these products generated an urban consumer for what Wollen calls "lifestyle modernism." For Wollen, the center of such modernist self-invention was Paris. Artists such as Henri Matisse, the costume designer of Ballets Russes Leon Bakst, and the fashion designer Paul Poiret, among many others, collaborated and brought about a change of taste and sensibility in Parisian high culture. Set designs for theater as well as clothing were helped by an international commerce that introduced Orientalist patterns and imagery in fabric and furnishing. Wollen writes, "A crucial dimension of early modernism involved . . . a parallel re-configuration of the human body, especially female body, in the name of emancipation and a new approach to sexuality."[10] This approach also meant a reversal of gender coding in fashion design. Thus, while Poiret brought a new taste for colorful Orientalist fabric patterns in men's fashion, Coco Chanel dressed women in masculinist black and white suits. While the

Russian constructivists as well as the cubist artist and fashion designer Sonia Delaunay introduced a lean, slick, if a little masculine, look for the modern woman, brightly colored silk shirts and gold chains defined a dandy, by definition a man such as the Van Vechten of Kirstein's description.

Romaine Brooks's portrait of Van Vechten from 1936 sums up Van Vechten's flamboyant lifestyle (fig. 3.2). We see Van Vechten in a fashionable cream-colored suit gleaming against dark and light panels dividing the canvas. On the left, a seascape with an ocean liner points to his frequent trips across the Atlantic that began with his first assignment to cover the arts in Paris for the *New York Times* in 1908 and became a regular part of his life after World War I. Van Vechten's clean, chiseled hairstyle and his face illuminated unnaturally from two sides and gathering a shadow line under the nose and chin lend the sitter the look and energy of that new industrial design aesthetic of "lifestyle modernism."

Sarah D. Coffin and Stephen Harrison have explored an international circulation of that aesthetic through tourism and consumer traffic across the Atlantic. Americans' presence in Paris increased in the 1920s, helped in no small measure by luxury liners that resumed business after a delay during the war. The liners were refitted, and their designs were changed from prewar "chateau" style to "moderne," inspired by the *International Exhibition of Modern Decorative and Industrial Arts* held in Paris in 1925. A conglomerate of cubism, constructivism, and other modernist styles showcased in the exhibition ushered a new "Art Deco" aesthetic in the design of ocean liners, as well as urban architecture, industrial products, advertisements, and covers of sports and fashion magazines, materially changing the taste, sensibility, and lifestyle of those consumers and travelers.[11] The cubistic zigzag of the seascape and the lit, vertical rows of apartment windows along a New York skyscraper at night on the right bring that "moderne" aesthetic into Brooks's canvas.

Both Van Vechten and Brooks participated in the community of American travelers, tourists, and consumers of European artistic and design ideas. When Van Vechten first came to New York to become a writer at the turn of the century, he lived close to Greenwich Village, one of a few settlements in Manhattan's south side crowded with European immigrants. In Greenwich Village, he gravitated toward the writers, artists, and social outcasts among these transatlantic bohemians and aligned his identity with their "bad taste" and risqué lifestyle ("a little *effiminé*, a trifle *declassé*"). He haunted cafés and bars resonant with discussions on sexuality, based on books by Sigmund Freud and Havelock Ellis. He visited bookstores that doubled as publishing houses, literary salons, art galleries, and boutiques for the sort of fabrics Van Vechten acquired and used in his photographs.[12] He became friends with the Pictorialist photographer Alfred Stieglitz, who had opened his Gallery 291 in Greenwich Village in 1905, where his collaborator, the photographer Edward Steichen, arranged shows of Parisian artists such as the fauvist Henri Matisse, whom Van Vechten photographed in the 1930s when he purchased his Leica. In 1908, when Van

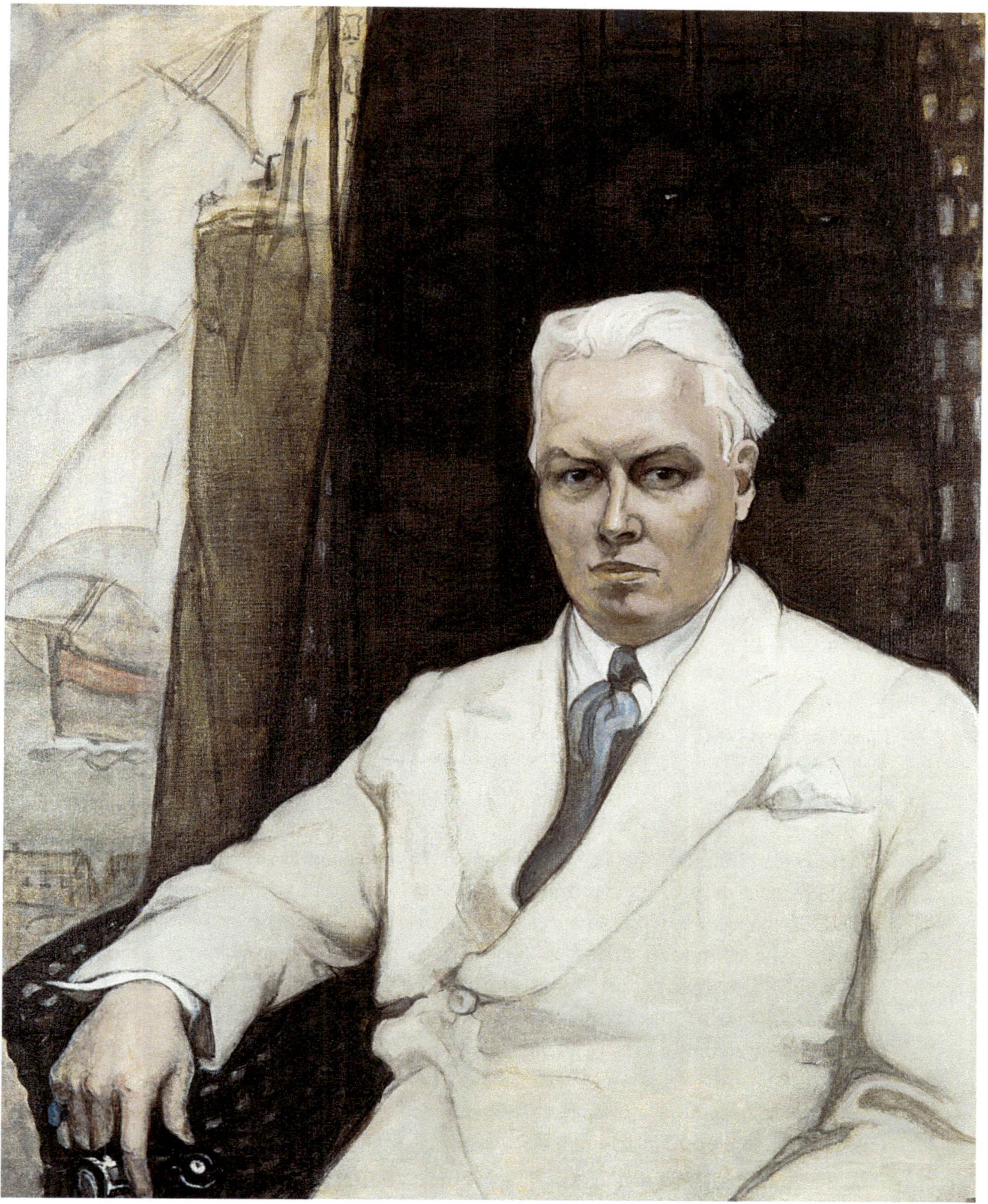

Figure 3.2. Romaine Brooks, *Portrait of Carl Van Vechten*, April 26, 1936, oil on canvas. (Yale Collection of American Literature, Beinecke Rare Book and Manuscript Library, Yale University; Art Storage 1980.323; Object ID 2064399)

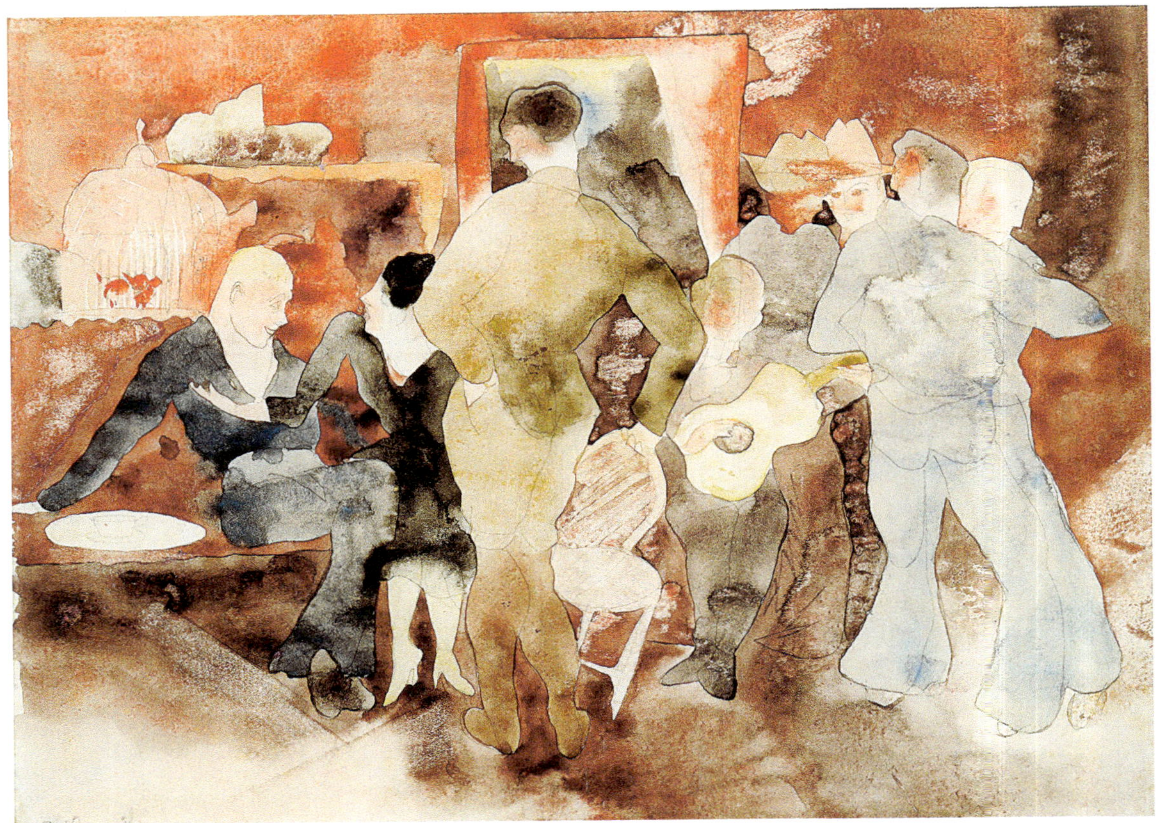

Figure 3.3. Charles Demuth, *Cabaret Interior with Carl Van Vechten*, watercolor, pen, and pencil on paper, 1917, 7¾ × 10¾ in. (Courtesy of Barbara B. Millhouse and Reynolda House Museum of American Art, affiliated with Wake Forest University, Winston-Salem, NC)

Vechten was commissioned by the *New York Times* to cover the arts in Paris, he swam effortlessly into its avant-garde scene, as if it were a seamless extension of Greenwich Village. Van Vechten's semiautobiographical novel *Peter Whiffle* describes the bohemian culture of New York and Paris through characters that are thinly veiled real people. Edith Dale, for instance, is the salonnière Mabel Dodge Luhan, who is recognized in the novel, as in real life, as a major patron of the first large exhibition of European artists in New York called the Armory Show of 1913.

In the bohemian areas similar to Greenwich Village that formed New York's cultural underground in the first decades of the twentieth century, Van Vechten was exposed to the arts as well as alternative fashion and sexual economies. Charles Demuth's watercolor *Cabaret Interior with Carl Van Vechten* (1917) locates Van Vechten in one such underground space along with migrants, sailors, artists, and literary figures (fig. 3.3).

A dapper-looking, yellow-haired Van Vechten lounges on a sofa on the left, engaged in a conversation with an elegant Parisian woman who could be his wife, the Russian American actress Fania Marinoff. The two had just married in 1914. Their body language communicates intimacy. A giant figure in a khaki marine suit, probably Demuth himself, according to Jonathan Katz, faces the couple.[13] With his back toward the viewer, arm in his pocket, he intrudes in their intimacy and listens into their conversation. The chair he has grabbed seems strangely humanoid, with its sharp, pointy legs echoing that of the elegant woman on the opposite side. Van Vechten's gaze seems aimed at his companion. But then again, it may as well skid across the room to a group of men carousing on the right edge of the painting.[14] The watery paint spreading across the paper in blotches captures the surreptitious mingling of people in the clandestine atmosphere of this underground space. Furtiveness is the mood, and Demuth shows Van Vechten leaning back from the jostle far enough to scope out the joint from a casual distance.

Interzones

Demuth's watercolor casts a dark basement light on such bohemian spaces that went underground during the controversies leading to Prohibition in 1920. The red birds in the cage on the left might be a little too literal as a reference to the restrictive conditions under which these cultural outcasts met. We will return to the painting's other features a little later. For now, let us note the appeal of its gritty underground feel and erotic charge that took Van Vechten to many such repurposed spaces at the fringes of the elite white residential areas of the Upper West Side. The hedonistic seeker was, for example, attracted to the Tenderloin District, an entertainment district between Twenty-Fourth and Forty-Second Streets and between Fifth and Seventh Avenues, at whose south end was the "Black Bohemia" inhabited by a large African American community. After the police brutality and social unrest in the Tenderloin, when many African American moved to the Dutch-Jewish settlement of Harlem in the northern extreme of Manhattan, Van Vechten followed them. By the 1920s, during the Great Migration to the North, Harlem also gathered a large influx of African American migrants escaping the injustices and brutalities of the racially segregated South.

New York's underground was formed around the cheap bars and nightclubs of these myriad areas. Kevin Mumford argues that the clubs and speakeasies, the music and theater, and the ballroom dance floors of Black Bohemia and Harlem served as "interzones" where individuals, Blacks and whites, mingled around entertainment, cruising, drinking, and slumming parties.[15] Here one listened and danced to ragtime music, and "in its most popular nightspots blacks and whites could carouse together in ways they never could on the street in the light of the day." Such places also afforded "non-heterosexual men and women, like Van Vechten, the chance to socialize, flirt, and even make pickups in relative safety."[16] Mumford goes as far as to say that these "public" establishments brought about a new sense of "the private" in New York (and Chicago and other cities) by providing a fluid space for people of all races both to pursue intimate encounters outside marriage and to form new marital alliances.

These interzones of New York were central to the emergence of a cultural efflorescence in New York called the Harlem Renaissance. Ann Douglas argues that the Harlem Renaissance was the result of a "militantly secular" culture of a "lost generation" of both whites and Blacks. While the "white moderns" rebelled against the norms of a staid Victorian culture by affiliating with alternative lifestyles and sexual economies, the "Black moderns" came out of a long history of slavery and segregation and the many injustices of the Jim Crow laws that made Blacks sadly "America's only truly orphaned group." While Black soldiers fought valiantly in World War I, they came home to the most brutal phase of "Ku Klux Klan lynchings, race riots and deportation" instead of a reward from a grateful nation.[17] The logic of Jim Crow was such that Blacks were legally free and equal but therefore also unprotected and exposed to a particularly blatant form of racism built into the legal and social structures of white America and exercised brutally in the deep South and elsewhere after the Civil War.[18] Many Black soldiers stayed back in Europe after the Great War to become performers in the nightclubs of Berlin and Paris, while other jazz and blues performers found in Europe a flourishing market away from a country torn apart by racism. In Harlem, meanwhile, Europe's artistic modernism fostered exchanges across the races and saw the emergence of the "New Negro Movement," also known as the Harlem Renaissance.

The bonds between Black and white moderns bordered on criminality. The interactions across the dividing lines of race as well as class existed just under the radar of the state's surveillance and the city's legal and political system shaped by segregation and Prohibition. The white patrons were economically necessary for the Black establishments of Harlem, and the "private" relationships also continued in mixed salon parties of white socialites on the Upper West Side. New York's interzones were spaces riddled with risk and rigged with cover-ups, legal actions, and revelations represented in Mumford's research through legal documents and essays of Black writers and activists in journals, as well as political debates at the National Association for the Advancement of Colored People (NAACP).[19]

In Brooks's portrait of Van Vechten, this furtiveness of interzones is represented in a black curtain behind the sitter. The heads of African American men and women form a dark halo framing Van Vechten's attraction to the African American community of Harlem. In many ways, Van Vechten came into his own as a social creature alongside the settlement of Harlem. He became a writer and photographer just when Harlem became a cultural and economic hub, ripe with a remarkable intellectual and cultural efflorescence. Bruce Kellner describes the economic emergence of Harlem, north of 125th Street and west of Fifth Avenue, as part of a large demographic shift around the turn of the twentieth century in what was until then just a small retreat town for affluent, white New Yorkers to escape to.[20] When the United States entered the war against Germany in 1917 and when the real estate market took a plunge, educated African American families were offered properties at lower prices, while others upgraded themselves from the real slums located around West 53rd Street. Harlem gained a new wave of migrants from the South when industrialists encouraged able-bodied people to move into the city for steady wages and upward mobility and to replace the labor force that had gone into the Great War. It was in Harlem that a Black literati culture grew. A theater with African American performers catered to an African American audience. The glitzy ballrooms, music halls, and theater halls around Broadway and 125th Street became places for gathering and entertainment for both Blacks and whites. Poets and novelists found an awakening of the New Negro Movement, and the leaders of the NAACP, such as W.E.B. Du Bois, Walter White, and James Weldon Johnson, established magazines such as the *Crisis* and *Fire* to raise the self-awareness of African American people in relation to the larger politics of a segregated country. By the 1930s, Van Vechten had already owned an apartment in a reclaimed slum at 150 West Fifty-Fifth Street, which he was to soon convert into a studio. In 1936, he moved his operation to 101 Central Park West.

Van Vechten wrote novels based on his close familiarity with the speakeasies and the club scene of Harlem and his affinity with Black men and women. His own sexual interests in Black men were well known by then. Van Vechten introduced Harlem to his friends as a place for commercial entertainment and erotic encounters. With tongue in cheek, Lincoln Kirstein called Van Vechten "my Dr. Livingstone," referring to the Scottish physician and Christian missionary in Africa David Livingstone, who was heroized in Victorian England for crusading against the African slave trade and leading expeditions to bring Africans into the fold of the legitimate economy under the queen during the abolitionist movement in the mid-nineteenth century. Van Vechten led Kirstein to "explore the marvelous dark continent where shone those magnificent palaces, the Savoy Dance Hall and the Apollo Theatre. It was a Harlem then oddly unresentful, open and welcoming to the Prince of Wales, to Miguel Covarrubias, to Muriel Draper, and to all writers and artists who recognized in its shadows the only authentic elegance in America." Van Vechten also introduced Kirstein to "a young Negro vaudeville dancer" who "was as odd, attractive, and exotic to [Kirstein] as a black unicorn."[21] The racist tones of this phrase is offensive in the same way as the Wildean imagery was to the Victorian tastes of the United States in the early twentieth century. In the composite creature, Kirstein captures the scandal of Salomé, the "beautiful and savage" feline whom Van Vechten relished and emulated in his own animal transgressions.

In 1965, Kirstein wrote about that moment in the United States, "we have the horrible conflicts of racism on our hands and shoulders," and he looked back at Harlem in an earlier moment in time: "It was not the tragic Harlem we know now. It was a Harlem far more parochial, private, remote, less dangerous. . . . It was the Harlem of Josephine Baker, of the *Blackbirds* of 1926, and of Ronald Firbank's *Prancing Nigger*."[22] The references are provocative. Firbank's 1924 novel is about the ambitions of a rural Black family in the Caribbean Republic—a mix of Cuba and Haiti—to assimilate into the high society of the city. Baker had made a name for herself by extravagantly performing Primitivist erotic dances in Paris and becoming a diva walking down the Parisian streets with her pet leopard, Chiquita, in its diamond collar.[23] Both Firbank's characters and Baker exemplify what Saidiya Hartman calls "wayward lives," lived glamorously. Summing up Van Vechten's enchantment with this Primitivist self-styling in Harlem, Kirstein writes, "Carl saw the surprising in the ordinary; he found, perhaps first in any articulate degree, the natural flair, the talent for rhythm and expressiveness, the joy, the fire, the murder, and the verbal accuracy in the vernacular in the day-to-day life of Harlem." Van Vechten's taste for artful expressions amid everyday violence made him "responsible for the early recognition and triumph of American jazz and jazz dancing in France, and throughout Europe and the world." Van Vechten used the international circuits of his writing career to also introduce Americans to other musical and performative traditions flourishing outside the United States and across the Atlantic. "His early studies of Stravinsky (whose interest in "ragtime" dates from before 1916), his expositions of Debussy's *Jeux* and Erik Satie's piano pieces gave American critics a courage to face new sounds, which although they heard them in their own doorsteps they did not recognize as art, but only as 'folk' or 'primitive' expression."[24] The recognition of modernity at "their own doorsteps" came into focus for Kirstein in Harlem.

Kirstein writes, "Carl made Harlem real to me."[25] What kind of Harlem did Van Vechten introduce Kirstein to? Van Vechten's Kodachrome slides from September and October 1940 show Harlem's everyday neighborhoods that transformed into Mumford's "interzones" by night. We see the bar called Rendezvous at a street corner on Lenox Avenue and the Savoy Ballroom, whose marquee impressively hangs over the entire sidewalk in front of the entrance. Van Vechten annotated a slide of the Lafayette Theatre on 132 Street and Seventh Avenue as "the first to seat African Americans in the orchestra [1912]" (fig. 3.4). By the 1940s, the Lafayette Theatre showcased theatrical productions such as Orson Welles and John Houseman's *Macbeth*, which opened in April 1936. The Shakespearean play was set not in Scotland but in Haiti. It employed an "all-Negro cast" and included "voodoo chants and dances" choreographed by the African dancer and choreographer Asadata Dafora. A year later, twenty-four African American dancers went onstage as part of the first Black ballet company in the United States, formed by the German immigrant dancer and choreographer Eugene Von Grona.[26] In these Kodachrome slides of ordinary-looking everyday places, then, Van Vechten was documenting the venues of interracial networks of transnational performers and performances.

While a number of white patrons supported Black writers and artists financially, Van Vechten "was always primarily a fan," Emily Barnard writes.[27] He was

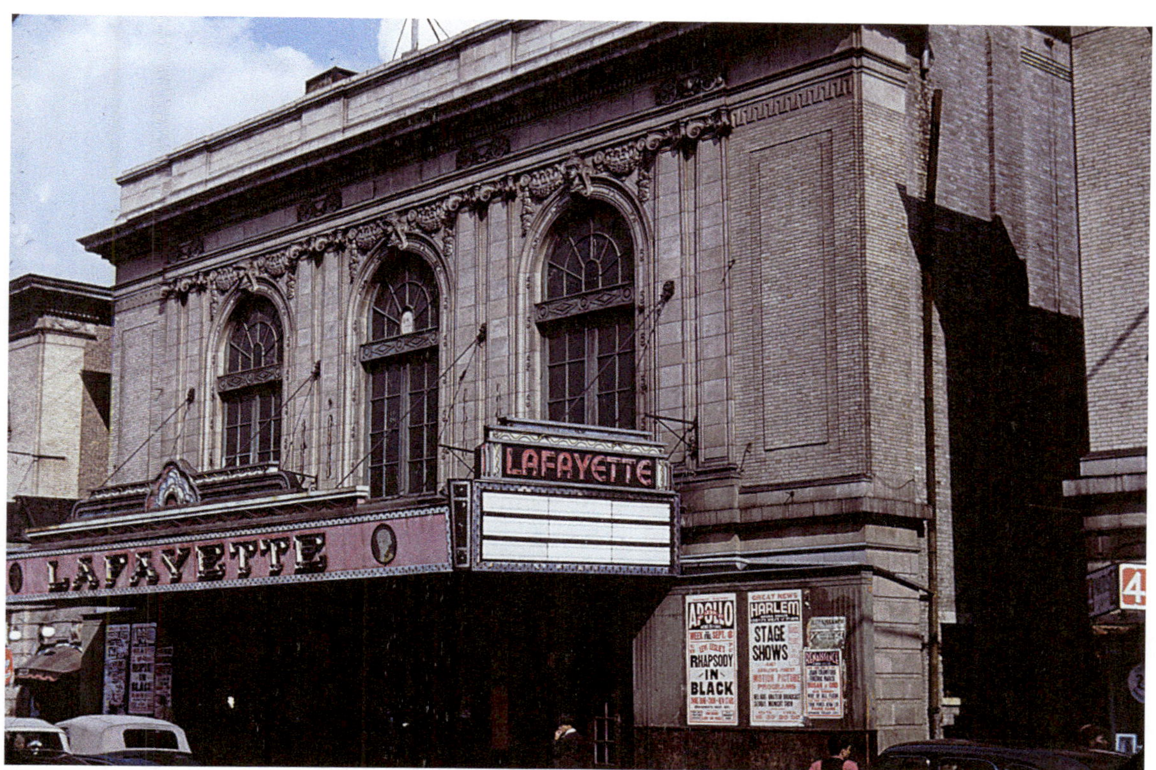

Figure 3.4. Carl Van Vechten, *Harlem, Lafayette Theatre*, September 4, 1940, Kodachrome slide. (Beinecke Rare Book and Manuscript Library, Yale University; © The Van Vechten Trust)

a witness to the New Negro Movement long before the Great War and the Black March of 1917 had ushered in the "Roaring Twenties," when that literary activism peaked in New York. He was among the first to review the blues, spirituals, and jazz, long before the "Jazz Age." His series of essays in 1925 in *Vogue* magazine brought African American music to the attention of the white thrill seekers of Harlem. Newly emerging African American poets and writers of the 1920s, such as Langston Hughes, gained their first major publications in white presses through Van Vechten's personal friendship with the publisher Alfred A. Knopf. Van Vechten's novel *Nigger Heaven* (1926) flared a controversy by foregrounding the participation of white, upper-class New Yorkers in both the "wayward lives" and the Harlem Renaissance in the African American community.

The caricaturist Miguel Covarrubias, Van Vechten's friend and colleague from his days as a writer at *Vanity Fair*, catches Van Vechten's place amid the literary elite of Harlem in his cartoon for the November 1, 1936, issue of *Vogue* (fig. 3.5). The image shows the mingling of "Negrotarians among the Niggeratti at the Lafayette Theater."[28] "Niggeratti" was Zora Neale Hurston's term for the New Negro writers of the 1920s. Hurston also "christened Van Vechten their king."[29] The caricature exaggerates, but without the searing critical edge of a Daumier.

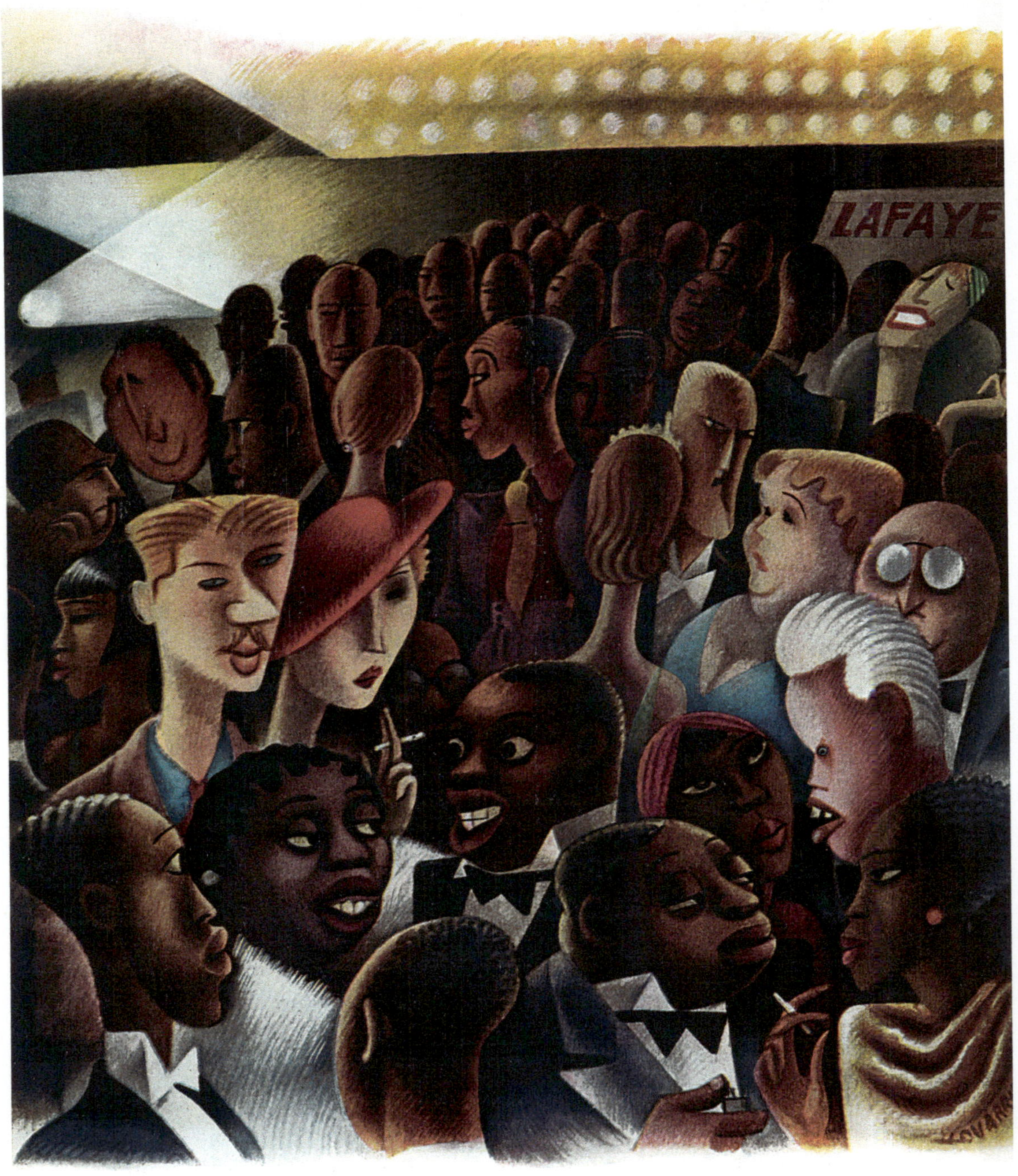

Figure 3.5. Miguel Covarrubias, *Negrotarians among the Niggeratti at the Lafayette Theatre*, color illustration, *Vogue*, November 1, 1936, 67. (© Condé Nast, Image Syndication)

The cubistic stylization of the beams of light in the back captures the excitement of a nighttime huddle of backlit heads as far as the eye can see. Well-dressed men and women glow in the foreground as if in a lifestyle magazine, their sharp noses, eyes, teeth, and hair randomly catching the myriad lights from the foyer's ceiling, side walls, and possibly a camera flashlight. On the lower right corner, Covarrubias picks out Van Vechten. In this tight jostle, his mop of white seashell hair over an oddly large forehead is lit from below, and the electrifying dress of a Black woman in front lends him a special dazzle.

The cartoon appears in color in the magazine opposite an article by Robert Littell titled "Every One Likes Chocolate." The article describes the opening night of Welles and Houseman's staging of *Macbeth* at the Lafayette Theatre on April 24, 1936. An estimated fifteen thousand people crowded the sidewalks and pressed against the stretched rope barricades set up for crowd control at the entrance of the theater. "The Negroes themselves came in droves." There were media people with their sound trucks, cameras, and floodlights. The play's sensational success owed as much to the playwright as to the buzz of Harlem, indicated in the article's racist reference to "chocolate." Even Shakespeare, feeling bored by "actors of his own pinkish pigmentation [who] play him with more reverence than zest, . . . steals away, ducks unobserved under a subway turnstile, boards an Eighth Avenue local, and emerges at One Hundred and Thirty-Fifth Street with the purpose of passing an hour or two in Harlem, among people whose skins are chocolate, whose souls are the many colours of their laughter." The article might as well be describing Van Vechten in the Covarrubias cartoon, who, with his own "pinkish pigmentation," must have similarly taken a subway train and equally "found it difficult to fight his way through the silk hats and ermine capes that jammed the lobby."[30]

The "Jazz" Subject

It should be clear by now that the spaces of the New York underground subculture carried for Van Vechten the aura of "modernism" distinct from the sordid basements seen from Demuth's point of view. In Van Vechten's mind, modernism—understood as an international circulation of urban lifestyles through the consumption and display of designed products, artistic ventures, and entertainment—is the glue that connected Greenwich Village to Harlem. Kirstein claims as much: "To us, Harlem was far more an arrondissement of Paris than a battleground of Greater New York."[31] Van Vechten's semiautobiographical novels are centered on characters that are immersed in what Van Vechten calls the "drunken twenties." *Peter Whiffle* absorbs the energies of the transatlantic artistic world of New York and Paris in the 1920s. Ambrose Deacon, the protagonist of *Spider Boy* (1928), is pulled accidentally into the glamorous lifestyle of Hollywood stars and achieves success without exercising ambition or will, when a series of events leads to a script that gets written for him by Hollywood's industrial system itself. Drawing heavily on his own experience as a journalist in Paris, New York, and Los Angeles, Van Vechten molds his characters into Baudelairean figures. Like sleepwalkers, they are swept up in a dream-world of dazzle and glitter in these cities and have an almost out-of-body experience of heightened stimulation in these landscapes of industrial capitalism.

Consider Peter Whiffle. The novel begins in the first-person voice of the narrator, named Carl Van Vechten, who is made the executor of the will of a recently deceased novelist, Peter Whiffle, and charged with completing his "literary work." The problem is that Whiffle has not put a single word on paper, and Van Vechten the narrator sets out to piece together an account of Whiffle's life based on the memories of his own sporadic encounters with Whiffle over the years. The novel is autobiographical in that its characters are thinly veiled real people from the artistic culture of New York, Paris, and Florence in the early twentieth century. Whiffle shows up everywhere, in the Parisian art scene, and among the Greenwich bohemians, in parties of fellow socialites such as Mabel Dodge Luhan (Edith Dale in the novel), who was inspired to arrange "the first great exhibition of the post-impressionist and cubist painters in New York," referring to the Armory Show of 1913.[32] The novel captures the buzz around that show. "Everybody went and everybody talked about it. Street-car conductors asked for your opinion of the Nude Descending the Staircase, as they asked you for your nickel. Elevator boys grinned about Matisse's Le Madras Rouge, Picabia's La Danse a la Source, and Brancusi's Mademoiselle Pogany, as they lifted you to the twenty-third floor. Ladies you met at dinner found Archipenko's sculpture very amusing, but was it Art? Alfred Stieglitz, whose 291 Gallery had nourished similar ideas for years, spouted like a geyser for three weeks and then, after a proper interval, like Old faithful, began again."[33]

How does Whiffle discover himself as a writer in this vibrant, transatlantic art scene? Early in the novel, Van Vechten the narrator asks Whiffle if he had started writing. "Well, you might say so, but I haven't written a line. I've collected the straws; the bricks will come later. You see those catalogues?" A long list follows that takes up six pages of the novel: "Perfumery catalogues . . . ; the Jewellery catalogues . . . ; Floral catalogues . . . ; Reaper's catalogues . . . ; Porcelain catalogues . . . ; Art dealer's catalogues . . . ; Furniture catalogues . . . ; Book-dealer's catalogues . . . ; Catalogues of curious varieties of cats . . . ; Catalogue of tinshops . . . ; Catalogue of toys . . . ; Cook-books . . . ; Catalogue of harness, bits, and saddles . . . ; Catalogue of cigarettes . . . ; Catalogues of liqueurs . . . ; Catalogues of paints . . . ; and Catalogues of hats." The list moves on to "dictionaries and lexicons" and "curious pamphlets" of medical treatments and finally "a pile of notebooks" in which Whiffle kept a daily list of all the places in Paris he walked. When asked if he is writing an encyclopedia, Whiffle replies, "No, my intention is not to define or describe, but to enumerate. Life is made up of a collection of objects, and the mere citation of them is sufficient to give the reader a sense of form and colour, atmosphere and *style*. And form, style, manner in literature is everything; subject is nothing. . . . All art is a matter of cataloguing life, summing it up in a list of objects. This is so true that the commercial catalogues themselves are almost works of art."[34]

Whiffle's philosophy of writing reads like the Borgesian story in which Michel Foucault finds an insight for his book on the order of things, but here is the rub: Whiffle's protean capacity for "enumerating" things develops from his deep absorption in the commodities of what Theodor Adorno calls the modern urban "culture industry." In each separate encounter, Van Vechten finds Whiffle shifting to an altogether different lifestyle that might be trending at the time, including bohemianism, spiritualism, Marxist activism around the Chinese migrants laboring in New York's Chinatown, and so on. Whiffle is sure to be the subject of Adorno's scorn. The bedazzled chameleon, changing color with each fashionable thing, lacks the critical apparatus needed to navigate the seductive environments of modern capitalism and claim one's subjectivity within its commodity structure. Whiffle's inability to exercise any sort of critical agency is the ironic result of his desire to write about a life-world in which he is fully absorbed. As he arranges his world into categories of words, he evacuates himself as a thinking subject.

Whiffle fits perfectly Adorno's definition of a "jazz subject," one who "achieves pleasure from the recognition of its own impotence in the presence of an omnipotent collective."[35] Adorno loved jazz but remained ambivalent about its cultural politics.[36] As a musical form, it was structured by the fragmentation and atomization of the individual musician, who improvised briefly on a given melody by drawing from the nervous energy of a performance. For Adorno, such music does not add up to the expression of human imagination that he celebrated in a symphony orchestra, in whose orchestration a composer gave expression to the regional and folk life and musical worlds of Europe, as in the opera of great individualists such as Richard Strauss. Adorno would have relished the electric shock and outrage experienced by Strauss's elite operagoers at the opening night of his *Salomé* in the industrial town of Dresden in 1905. Strauss's father found listening to its music equivalent to having "one's trousers full of maybugs."[37] In contrast to such defiant music, jazz imitates the exuberance of bourgeois industrial capitalism and reflects in its dispersed musical structure and syncopated rhythms the fragmented, dehumanizing conditions of modern industrial towns.

Adorno's position has been a topic of critique among media scholars and cultural theorists. Gary Zabel relates "Adorno's undifferentiated critique of jazz" to his European background and Eurocentric limitations that overlook jazz as an expression of African slaves in the New World, "braving the hostility of the surrounding white culture."[38] Adorno also does not distinguish between the longer African American musical tradition in the United States and American big-band music and its derivatives among Black as well as white musicians in Europe in the 1930s and '40s, which "tamed jazz in the interest of social conformity." Jazz also foregrounded for Adorno a largely European fear and anxiety regarding race when it arrived at European shores in the early twentieth century, according to Dina Gusejnova.[39]

Fumi Okiji defends Adorno's deep interest and continuing engagement with jazz by making a distinction between jazz as an industrial form, frozen in records and radio, and jazz as the collective music made by "communal individuals" such as Duke Ellington and Louis Armstrong, whom Adorno loved and idealized after coming to the United States.[40] At live performance venues, Adorno would have understood that jazz was produced not so much in the performance but in the listening, or more precisely, the way the performer(s) and the listeners form "a community" within the performance space. As a scholar-musician herself, Okiji explains what the jazz community may feel like on the ground. In the throaty voice of a singer such as Billie Holiday, Okiji listens for what Saidiya Hartman calls "the promiscuous coexistence of song and shackle" that seeped into the twentieth century from the painful history of slavery and collective experience of segregation.[41] Individual jazz musicians are thus not fetishized for their individualism, as in Adorno's culture industry, but rather admired because the violence and trauma of a shared, collective past saturate their voice and modulate their playing of even classical instruments such as the piano.

Okiji claims that Adorno walked a delicate line. Not seeing in jazz the bold experiments of a classical composer, he yearned for jazz to achieve a different kind of subjectivity that was not yet born, an African American kind, split by what W. E. B. Du Bois called "double-consciousness," which comes from inhabiting a skin that is subject to racialized surveillance. Okiji points out that the music critics of the 1930s overcame the stigma of race by picking out and celebrating individual performers of blues and jazz as stars. However, the genius of jazz is fundamentally based in its syncopated structure, in which the different parts of the composition, carried in an improvisational spirit by musicians jamming together in a live performance venue, come together in the ears of a listener as a richly textured whole beyond a single musician. The call and response of jazz also departs from the orchestration structure of a symphony. Thus, Adorno's limitation, according to Okiji, might be that he was first exposed to American jazz in its industrial form in European clubs, a form that existed alongside popular records and radio, in other words, the global technological media for circulating prefixed music far removed from the lived history of slavery that was made palpable in the distinctive "orality" of live performances in the United States.

Both Adorno and Van Vechten come to the same "problem of jazz" but from opposite sides. For Van Vechten as for Adorno, jazz occurred in a conflicted industrialized world, to which no ownership can be attached. Van Vechten also saw in jazz the fragmentation of the human body, as Adorno and many other early critics did. In *Black Manhattan* (1930), James Weldon Johnson claimed to have seen the "first modern jazz band ever heard on the New York stage" at Proctor's Twenty-Third Street Theatre in 1905. Johnson was astonished to note that everyone did everything including singing and dancing. Some musicians "played one part while singing another. That is, for example, some of them, while playing the lead, sang bass, and some, while playing an alto part, sang tenor, and so on, in accordance with the instrument each man played and his natural voice."[42] The performer of course operates with a single body, but as Ann Douglas glosses the point, "the body apparently doesn't know it."[43] The body is distributed into individual performing segments. Adorno would have mourned this segmentation of the body, but Zora Neale Hurston saw it as "the rhythm of segments," and Josephine Baker's biographer calls it "playing the various parts of the body as though they were instruments." The mechanization of the Black body in jazz exhilarated the architect Le Corbusier when he visited New York in 1935: "Negro music . . . is the melody of the soul joined with the rhythm of the machine. It is in two-part time; tears in the heart; movement of legs, torso, arms and head . . . [It is] the sound of modern times."[44] Adorno was reacting precisely against this objectification of the machine rhythms in the Black body.

In *Peter Whiffle*, Van Vechten refers precisely to that jazz subject, atomized by the global flow of industrial capitalism and thus incapable of world-making. Whiffle embodies the "impotence" of Adorno's scorn but is the subject of great affection for Van Vechten. The novel treats Adorno's sense of defiant individualism with a ludic sense of irreverence. By contrast, Whiffle exudes an almost orgiastic way of being in the modern world. His impotence is the source of his hedonistic pursuits. The impotence of Whiffle, both cultural and sexual, is indicated in the very name. "Whiffle," which described, along with "macaroni" and other slang words used since the eighteenth century and into Victorian England and America, a modern dandy, a man who "renders his sex dubious by the extravagance of his appearance."[45]

The one place where we get a good glimpse of how Van Vechten understood jazz is, curiously, not in the context of music but in the visual arts. Here, he was also not after the "jazz subject" but "jazz quality." Just around the time of the publication of *Peter Whiffle*, Van Vechten published an article titled, with a witty French riff, "Pastiches et Pistaches," in the February 1922 issue of *The Reviewer*. In it, he makes a striking observation of the paintings of his artist friend Florine Stettheimer: "This lady has got into her painting a very modern quality, the quality that ambitious American musicians will have to get into their compositions before anyone will listen to them. At the risk of being misunderstood, I must call this quality jazz." What does he mean, and what is the "risk"? At a time when the music of the Jazz Age was becoming known, Van Vechten seems to have been aware that he was treading in delicate territory. "Jazz, indubitably, is an art form in itself, but before a contemporary musician can triumph in the serious concert halls he must reproduce not the thing itself but its spirit in a more lasting form. This, Miss Stettheimer has abundantly succeeded in doing."[46] What did he see in Stettheimer? Van Vechten's remarks appear in the context of a comparison he sets up between Stettheimer's painting and Charles Demuth. And so, let us

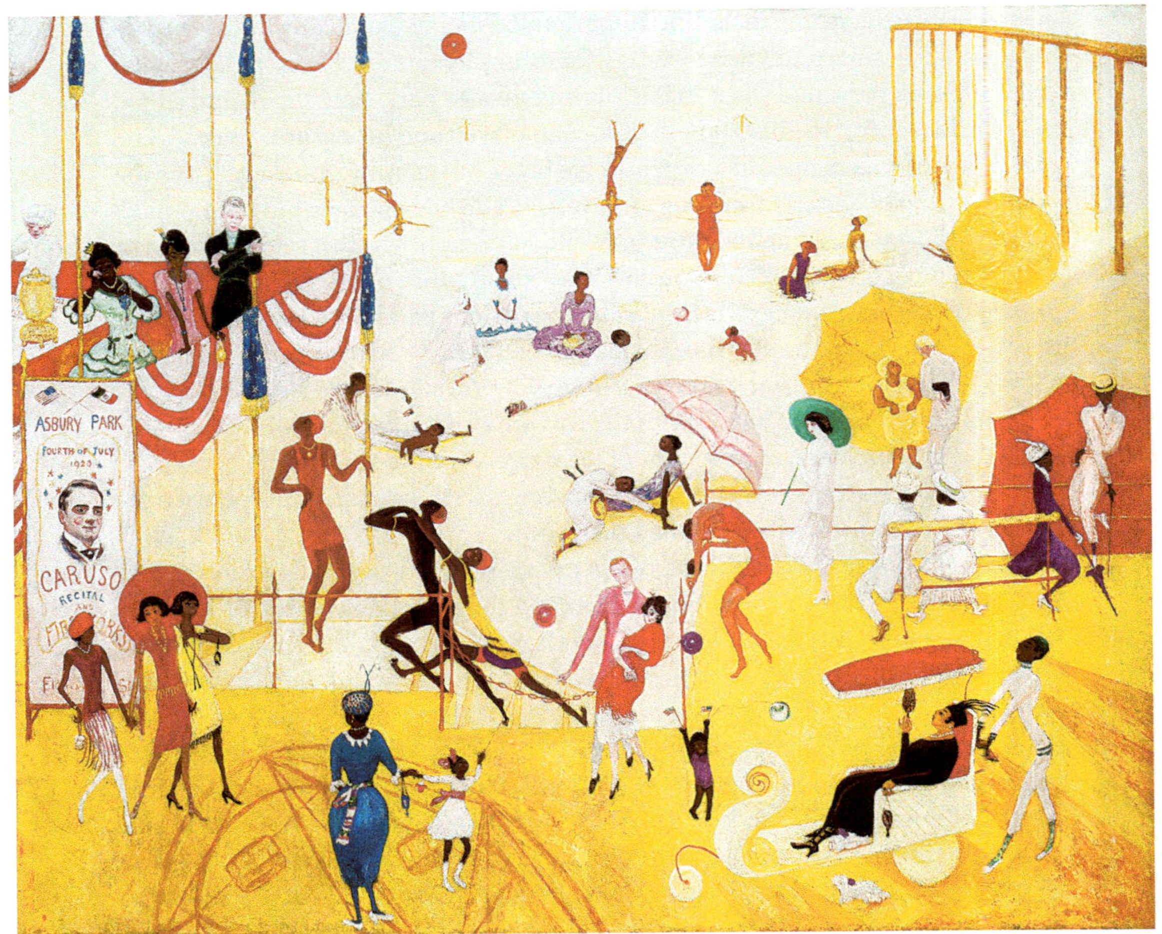

Figure 3.6. Florine Stettheimer (1871–1944), *Asbury Park South*, 1920, oil on canvas, 50 × 60 1/8 inches, signed. (Collection of halley k harrisburg and Michael Rosenfeld, New York; courtesy of Michael Rosenfeld Gallery LLC, New York, NY)

compare Demuth's watercolor discussed earlier with Stettheimer's oil painting titled *Asbury Park South* (1920), from nearly the same time (figs. 3.3 and 3.6).

Like Demuth, Stettheimer also captures an anonymous gathering place for entertainment and leisure. The view is of a beach on the Jersey shore, where the urban energy of New York is made as palpable as Demuth's underground. In this case, however, sunlight floods the canvas. Festivity is in the air. Stettheimer includes Black men, women, and children, who have appeared for the concert of the Italian opera singer Enrico Caruso on the Fourth of July 1920, as the poster on the left indicates. We see fashionable ladies in their elaborate hats, strollers with their parasols, children playing, and acrobats performing their acts to the amazement of viewers. Sprightly, elongated figures wearing pointed shoes skip across the space. As in Demuth's painting, Van Vechten also appears in Stettheimer's painting, up on a raised stage on the left, amid two bedecked African

American performers and an "Oriental" figure in a white turban in the back. As in Demuth's watercolor, here too Van Vechten is slightly removed from the bustle and only vicariously soaks in the energy of the place.[47]

Unlike Demuth's brooding dungeon and its secretive air, however, Stettheimer lets us pick and choose vignettes from a range of leisurely activities distributed across a panoramic view of the oceanfront. Strollers, picknickers, and gazers flutter across the space like colorful ribbons of confetti. The luminosity and saturation of paint builds up the sunny day on the canvas. Figures become silhouetted against the white glare of the sea and the golden sunlight piercing through umbrellas. Van Vechten found Stettheimer's "canvases as gay as the fête of Neuilly," in contrast to Demuth's dark eroticism.[48]

The visual and spectacular quality of Stettheimer's canvas is not without its conflict. Asbury Park was a segregated beach in the 1920s. In fact, the "gay" atmosphere is to be understood in relation to that era of segregation and the racial tensions of Jim Crow. Demuth would have surely painted such a scene darkly. By contrast, Stettheimer's urban panorama represents self-conscious, stylish display. The elongated and vigorous figures of African American dancers at the center left draw on figures in the Casino de Paris poster of Josephine Baker that we see in a photograph Van Vechten took of the equally charismatic jazz singer, dancer, and actor Cab Calloway in June 1933 (fig. 3.7).

In the 1920s, both Stettheimer and Demuth were part of the transatlantic traffic of performers, artists, and tourists who interacted closely with European modernist artists and intellectuals in the bohemian districts of New York. But in their work, Van Vechten saw the modernist culture taking two contrasting forms. He distinguished them along what he considered an American and a European sensibility. Demuth's is clearly European; his "perverse genius . . . would be recognized at once at full-value in Germany or France." His sketches for *The Turn of the Screw* by the great American novelist Henry James "are stranger than the tale itself. They do not reveal; they conceal. They keep the secret of the master in a decorative manner." His illustrations of *Nana* "elaborate in realistically fanciful arabesques the vicious horrors of Zola. How beautiful and how terrible the flowers: daisies with cabalistic secrets, cyclamens rosy with vice, orchids wet with the mystery of the Rosicrucians!" By contrast, Stettheimer's paintings seem more "honest" and lack the "perversity" of Demuth.[49]

Stettheimer's "honesty," however, cannot be taken literally. It is also an attitude, a turn of mind, a flourish, a "decorative manner" that is equally "ecstatic." Van Vechten explains: "Ecstasy is there but it is agathodemonic and not kakodemonic."[50] I had to look up those terms in *Wikipedia*, which explains the former as an angelic spirit of vineyards and fields that ensures good luck, health, and wisdom, while the latter is evil. The latter takes its tortured psychology seriously. The former takes nothing seriously, or at least not too seriously. If Demuth's brooding watercolors convey the sinister depths of racial and sexual economies, Stettheimer's pictorial surface shows racialized individuals performing their

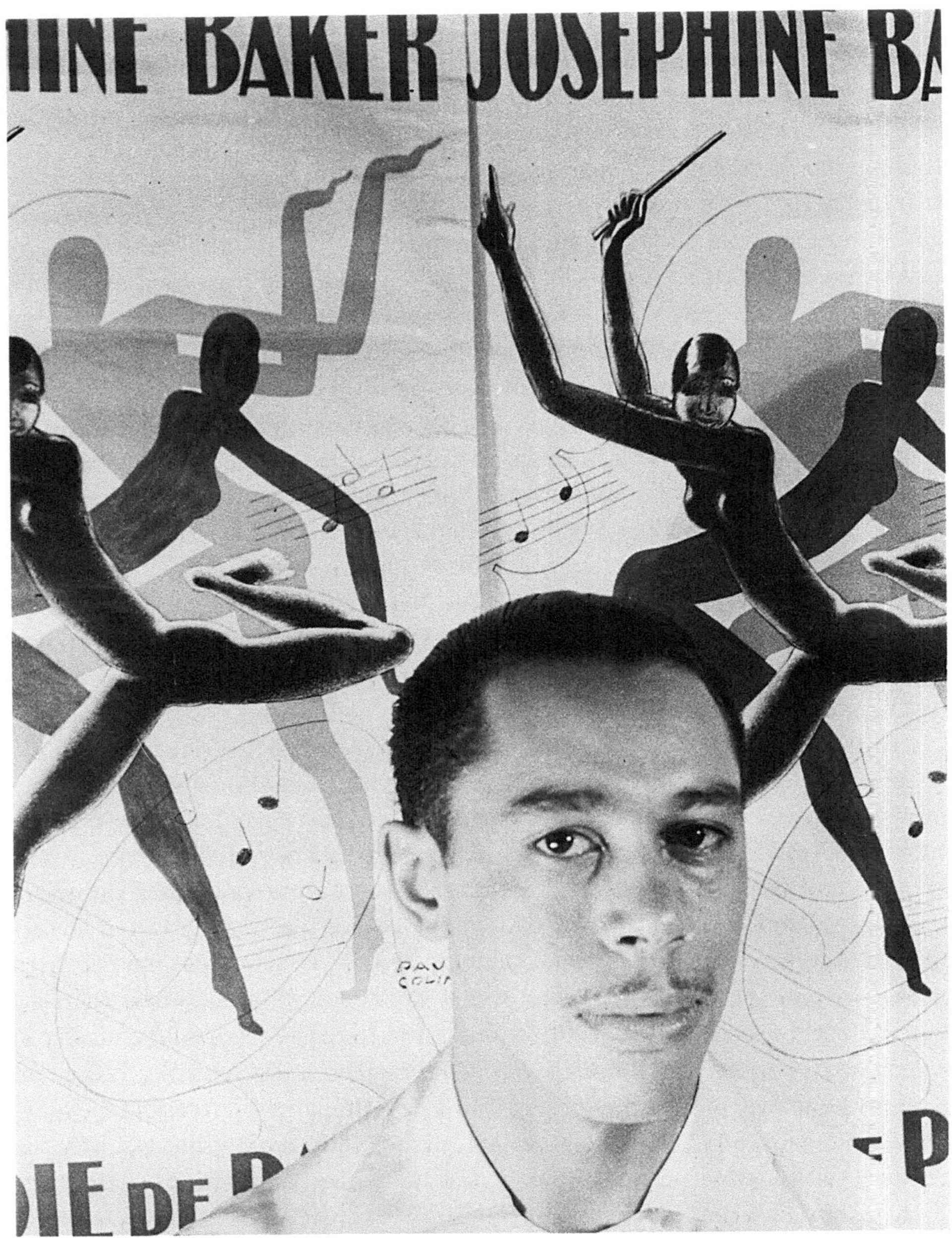

Figure 3.7. Carl Van Vechten, *Cab Calloway*, January 12, 1933, XX H:I. (Beinecke Rare Book and Manuscript Library, Yale University; © The Van Vechten Trust)

race with gusto, just as Josephine Baker had done in Paris. The "jazz quality" that Van Vechten perceived in Stettheimer's painting is comparable to Baker's brashly inventive production of her racialized skin as the "modern surface" onstage and in film.[51] In 1922, Van Vechten did not yet see American jazz music absorbing the modern world in quite the same way.

Van Vechten was broadening the use of the term "jazz" beyond music. In his time, the word was applied commonly to all sorts of things, usually in a derogatory way. It suggested street glitter as opposed to high art, and American popular club music as opposed to (the European legacy of) classical music. The "risk" of Van Vechten's "jazz quality" in his 1922 essay was, therefore, this. It related to the experience of urban modernity in Europe and the United States between the wars beyond the American experience of slavery. As part of a global culture industry, it blurred the distinction between high and low culture, only to sharply make visible the searing racist undertow of that distinction. Adorno's anxiety about jazz may also have related less to music per se and more to the musicians he may have heard against the flicker of neon lights in the cafés and nightclubs of Dresden and Berlin. The commercial districts of those cities assaulted the senses with a spectacular array of displays, including commodities in department-store windows, newspaper and media images, the click and whirr of projectors in movie theaters, the synchronized performances of the Tiller Girls on the large stage, and jazz music in small clubs—all objectifying the lure of a bourgeois, capitalist industry that was already hurtling toward a totalitarian state by the late 1920s. Jonathan Wipplinger calls the Weimar Republic the "Jazz Republic" to catch precisely the pulse of the consumerist environment of those cities against which American music was heard in the 1920s.[52] Van Vechten was an early witness to the Jazz Age and the consumer culture it created across the Atlantic during the "Roaring Twenties" and particularly after the Paris exposition of 1925.[53]

There is no reason to believe that Van Vechten was politically precocious, as Adorno was, in engaging with the rapidly changing world around him. His "jazz quality" merely identified a sensibility emerging from the global flow of modern lifestyles beyond the African American experience that Okiji underscores in the American music. In reaching for this "quality" in Stettheimer, Van Vechten bypasses the topic of subjectivity altogether and subverts both the American and the European understanding of jazz music. He dismisses both the tragic sense of individualism conveyed in Demuth and Adorno and the "double-consciousness" of the Blackness and jazz as perceived by Okiji and other recent scholars of African American studies, critical race studies, and Black feminism.

Keith Davis writes of Van Vechten's novels, "Van Vechten's urbane and sophisticated style had a distinctive mood. While deeply irreverent and sardonic, he never ventures into the darkly pessimistic terrain explored by others, more disillusioned, writers of his time." This was because "Van Vechten had not been traumatized by service in the world war. Most importantly, however, it reflected the coolly bemused stance of the true dandy."[54] The dandy's coolness might be a form of alienation but without the psychological weight. We see this extravagant form of alienation in the figure of Van Vechten as a distant, "bemused" observer in Stettheimer's painting, as well as the exuberant ways in which Peter Whiffle embodies his numerous identities in Van Vechten's novel.

"One of jazz's inner features is to be chameleon-like," Philip Bohlman and Goffredo Plastino point out.[55] Jazz incorporates into its form the industrial, capitalist structures in which it is implicated. For Adorno, the strategy of camouflage was not a sufficient resistance to what George E. Lewis calls "the bouncing and jostling that jazz experiences as it straddles the twin tigers of capitalism and imperialism."[56] In contrast to Adorno's longings, which Okiji locates in the communal "orality" of African American music, the "risk" of jazz for Van Vechten is precisely in its way of hiding in the capitalist world by wearing it. He pursues its strategy of camouflage as "style" both in his "Pastiches et Pistaches" essay and in the novel *Peter Whiffle*, both published in 1922.

Early on, thus, Van Vechten recognized jazz as a "global vernacular" accompanying the spread of US capitalism, as recent scholars also recognize: "Jazz is a music whose creation and development would be impossible without the metacultural ideas that undergird the capitalist formation in the United States for its practitioners rely on strategies of incorporation to create aural palimpsests that bear the traces of the materials they have encountered and transformed, if not erased: European harmonic procedures and song forms, to be sure but also ideas that emanate from more far-clung locales."[57] The revisionist scholarship resists the Americanization of jazz.[58] As Lewis suggests, the African American encounters in the United States are one, even the first, form that conveys through music "a fundamentally center-periphery relationship" with global capital. In addition to an African diasporic experience and slave stories in the United States, jazz allows "an African jazz musician of today . . . to speak of apartheid, or even contemporary forms of slavery itself, as in the Sudan. . . . The jazz stories of Dror Feiler (in Sweden) and Gilad Atzmon (in the UK) refer to Israeli-Palestinian politics, while Argentinian, Chilean, or Brazilian jazz stories refer to military rule and the unexplained disappearance of family and friends."[59] One way of thinking of jazz's chameleon-like spirit is that its musical identity is contingent on what it absorbs in the context of global capitalism. In other words, "jazz worlds" are created by music that endlessly "invades a pre-existing musical space, modifies it, and creates the conditions for fundamentally imitative performing activities, themselves later labeled as jazz."[60]

One of the most provocative representations of Van Vechten's own chameleon-like absorption of the interracial borderlines of the United States is given by Miguel Covarrubias's caricature, titled *Prediction*, which portrays Van Vechten disturbingly in blackface. The original caricature is in the National Portrait Gallery in Washington, DC, and it is often reproduced in the context of a controversy about the title and its intentions. Van Vechten regarded the original image as his "favorite portrait," but Emily Barnard claims that Van Vechten never wanted to "become black" in spite of Covarrubias's title.[61] To elaborate on that controversy, I reproduce another watercolor by Covarrubias, a Christmas greeting card that shows *Prediction* being carried as a gift by the Mexican cartoonist himself (fig. 3.8).[62]

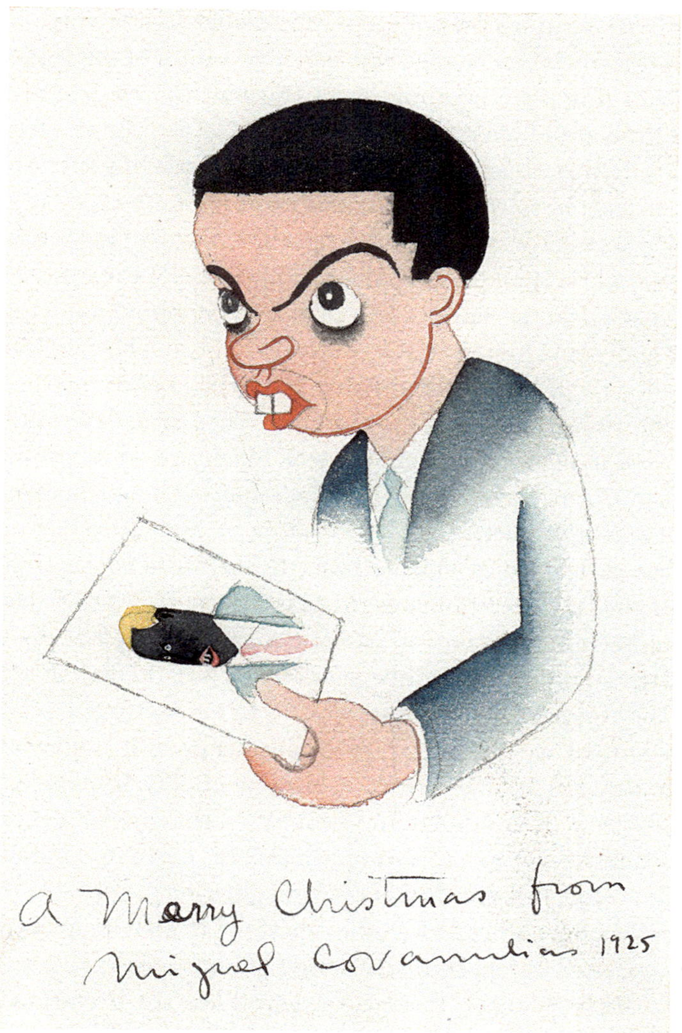

Figure 3.8. Miguel Covarrubias, *Christmas Greeting Card*, watercolor showing Covarrubias holding Carl Van Vechten caricature titled *Prediction*, 1925. (Yale Collection of American Literature, Beinecke Rare Book and Manuscript Library, Yale University, New Haven, CT; © Maria Elena Rico Covarrubias)

Covarrubias's Christmas card puts the limelight on *Prediction* as a jazz-like camouflage within the segregated, racialized discourse of the Jim Crow era. More importantly, the camouflage is relayed as a network of hyperbolic visual and performative practices, or burlesques, representing the landscape of hypervisible racial stereotypes of the Jazz Age. Covarrubias was fully aware of Van Vechten's Primitivist cross-dressing and border-crossing. After all, he was the set designer of Josephine Baker's *Banana Dance* at the Revue Nègre in Paris in 1925.[63] In the Christmas card, the blackface image appears as a nested part of a knowing, interracial relay, in which the Mexican cartoonist also participated.

Van Vechten's writings and photographs display a knowing, performative dimension of interracial exchanges between white elites of the Upper West Side and the African American community of Harlem. "At West 55th Street, Carl Van Vechten lived at the intersection of black and white," Emily Bernard writes. Harlem was the shiny object of his fascination and attachment. "He wanted to know it, experience it, to represent it, and most of all, to enjoy it."[64] The blues singer Ethel Waters credited Van Vechten for knowing "more about Harlem than any other white man except the captain of the Harlem police station."[65] When the singer Adelaide Hall signed a card with her photograph to send to Van Vechten, she addressed him as "the Moses who holds the key to Harlem."[66] Walter White dubbed Van Vechten and Fania Marinoff's apartment on West Fifty-Fifth Street the midtown office of the NAACP.[67] These are performative affinities of jazz expressed in hyperbolic terms by both Black and white people, as well as by the Mexican Covarrubias. These affinities may even be considered the self-fashioning of a "jazz subject."

In another caricature of Van Vechten, Covarrubias captures perfectly the corporeal imagination that animates the jazz subject (fig. 3.9).[68] The caricature describes Van Vechten's days on an assignment for *Vanity Fair* to cover Hollywood celebrities in 1928. In a tightly composed space, the hairstyle and Barbie-doll eyes of the women all look alike, while Van Vechten's open, toothy mouth and skewed, vertical eye communicate his obsession with Hollywood glitter. In Van Vechten, Edward White notices "a birdlike quality, a magpie's irresistible attraction to objects of ornament and beauty."[69] Covarrubias highlights a cinephile's bodily attachment to a screen image and his desire to animate the glamour of stardom into living creatures of his imagination.

Both Van Vechten and Peter Whiffle represent an absorbent corporeal imagination that indulges in fetishistic collecting of objects that glitter. Keith Davis describes Van Vechten's early fascination with itinerant performers of theater companies that passed through his childhood town of Cedar Rapids on their way from Chicago to Omaha: "Fascinated by the glamour and talent of these performers [Van Vechten] began an extensive collection of cigarette pictures and autographs of actresses. While this passion for cataloging stemmed naturally from his early interest in accumulating birds' nests, stamps and tobacco tags, it marked an abiding fascination with artistic celebrities."[70]

In Gopal's malleable representations discussed in chapter 2, Van Vechten would have recognized, probably for the first time, a choreographic counterpart to this absorbent spirit of jazz. In the 1940s, Vincent Warren called the choreographer Jack Cole's arrangements of various dance traditions "jazz dance." Cole, a dancer formerly of the Denishawn company and a student of La Meri in the 1940s, developed an experimental fusion of Bharatanatyam and American jazz music for the Broadway stage and the Hollywood screen. "Using the techniques of isolation and percussive footwork learned [in classes with La Meri and demonstrations of Uday Shankar] as well as rhythms of African American

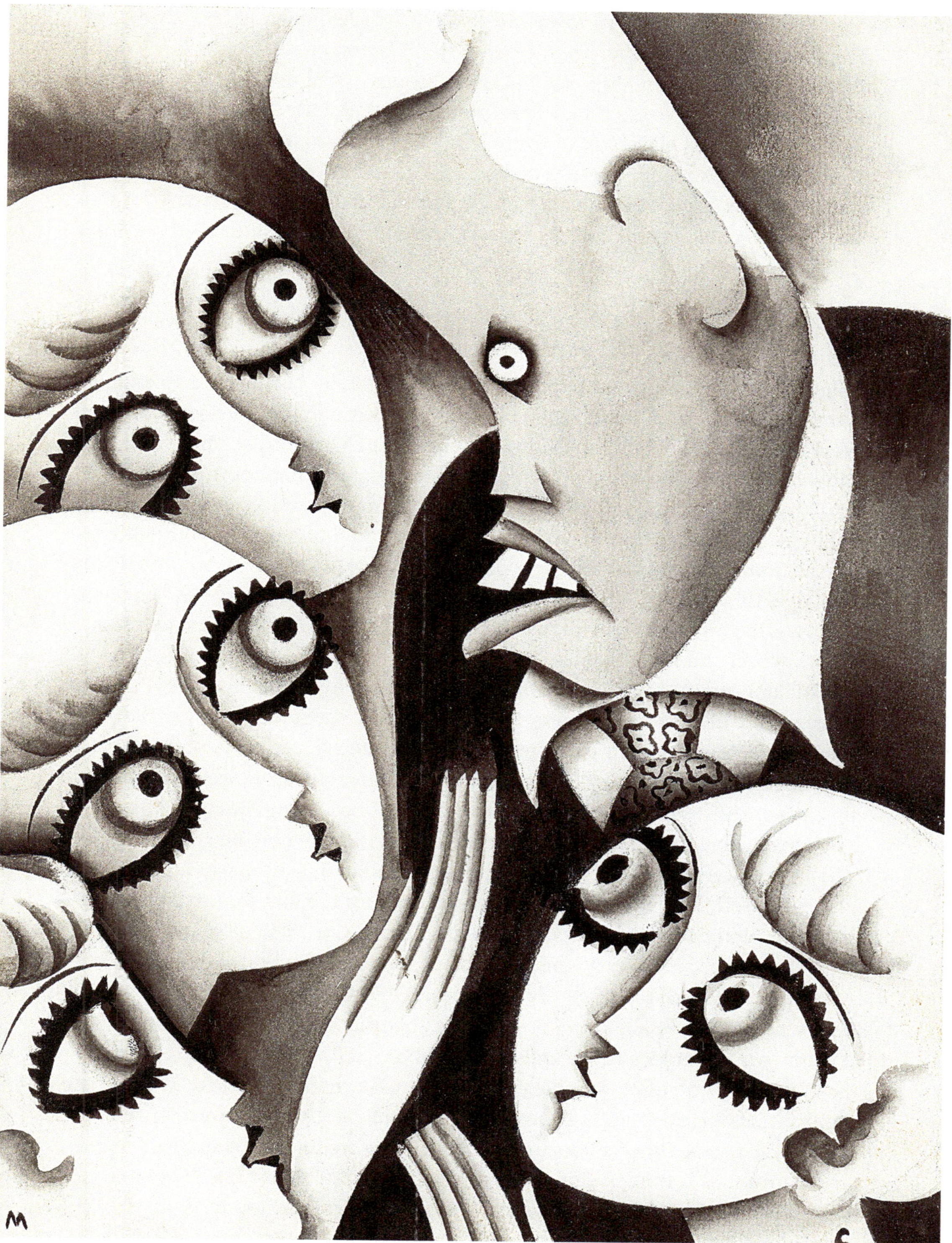

Figure 3.9. Miguel Covarrubias, *Van Vechten in Hollywood*, watercolor, 1928. (Manuscripts and Archives Division, The New York Public Library; © Maria Elena Rico Covarrubias)

dance, this new galvanized form hit the stages of Broadway, night clubs and Hollywood movies to emerge as jazz dance."[71] Warren cites Cole's choreography for the Hollywood film *Kismet* (1944) as a quintessential example of jazz dance. I suggest that Van Vechten may have perceived a similarly "galvanized form" of jazz in Gopal. His close-ups of Gopal's head or Kathakali's foot placement are similar to Cole's technique of isolation and reintegration of world dance and musical forms, except that, instead of a group choreography or a cinematic montage, Van Vechten was seeing those independent flourishes of dance in a single dancer's body.

Streets and Bodies

When Van Vechten turned to photography in 1932, he brought his roving, bedazzled eye for "jazz" in all kinds of subjects, starting with outdoor images of New York City, followed by friends and celebrities in his studio. At the Beinecke Library are four diaries in which Van Vechten pasted contact prints of his various sitters, accompanied by their written comments and signed names. The volumes are leather bound with metal clasps and embossed in gold with the photographer's name on the cover. On the first page of volume 3, accompanying Van Vechten's photograph with Gertrude Stein, the inscription reads, "The photographs in this book were all made by me with a Leica."[72] The German camera was thus recruited in his collection of glitter.

In January 1932, Miguel Covarrubias returned from Germany with a Leica camera and lit a fire for photography under Van Vechten's feet. Van Vechten wrote of his excitement when Covarrubias introduced him to the camera: "He explained in detail some of the advantages of this acquisition, a recent German invention, and another fan was born at once. So, I bought a Leica with an expensive lens during the course of the same day and immediately decided to regard photography seriously."[73] The small, elegant handheld camera was a glamorous object in itself that came with a shiny metal body for the first time in camera history. But along with the slick German machinery, Covarrubias also introduced Van Vechten to the energy and promise of photography and film he had witnessed in the media culture of the Weimar Republic and Europe. Soon, Van Vechten took the Leica to the bustling neighborhoods around him and invited friends to pose for him in his makeshift studio.

Van Vechten's photographic collection is idiosyncratic. At first, it indicates simply his fascination with the new camera. He took distant views of apartment buildings, a close-up of a doorway with cast-iron railing and stairway, the decorative front of a funeral home, the sign of West 134 Street from a low angle. On March 5, 1932, a month into his fascination, Van Vechten took an extreme close-up of a pushcart with pots and pans and "eggs and potatoes for sale at a market in Harlem," as if to simply capture the odd geometry of everyday things.[74] His images of a construction site, a demolished building, and squatters on the

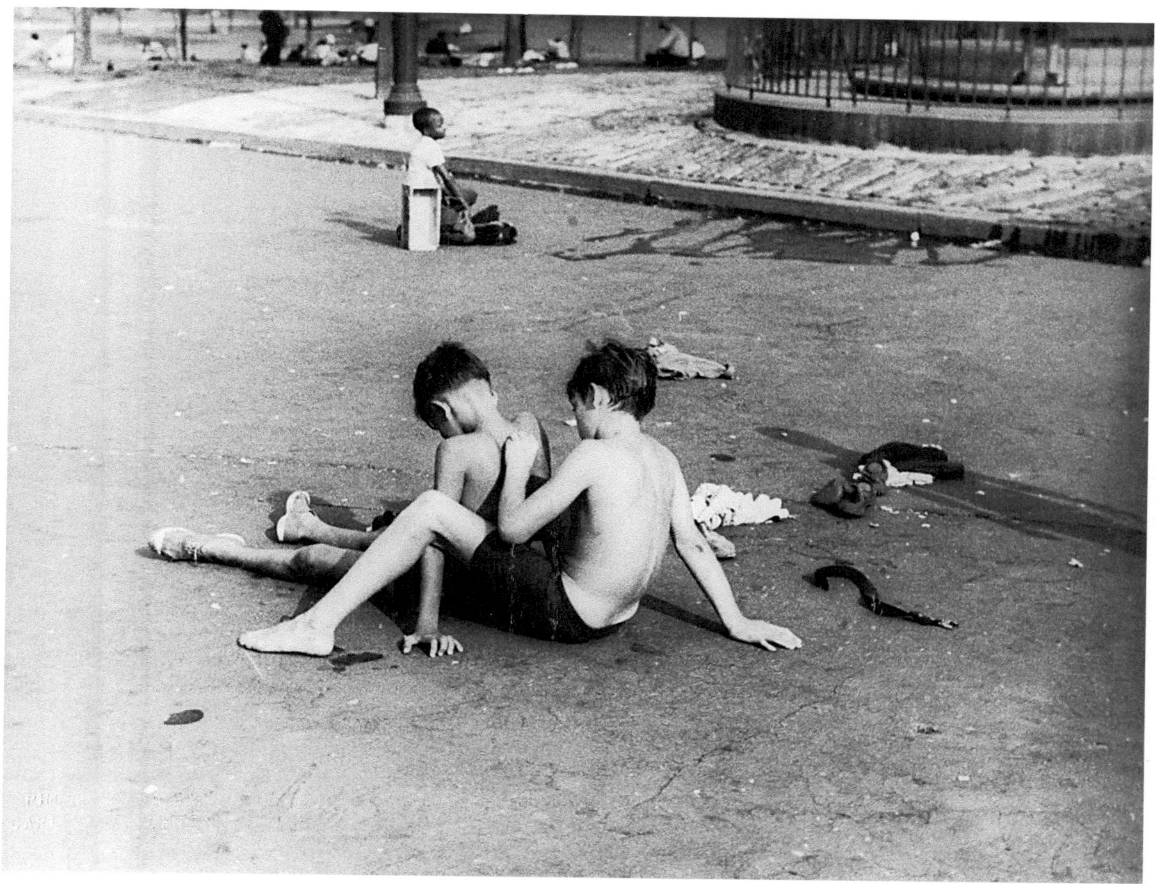

Figure 3.10. Carl Van Vechten, photograph of two boys sitting in the street close to Columbus Circle, September 3 1937. "This boy is writing on the other boy's back in white chalk: "F . . . the cops." Two boys, sitting in the street close to Columbus Circle. (Museum of the City of New York, X2010.8.149; © The Van Vechten Trust)

street recall the photography of the Photo League, a group that formed in New York in the 1940s and became known for candid images of a decaying city of immigrants. Many photographers were immigrants themselves, confronting a divide between the city's affluent and the dispossessed. But Van Vechten's images carry the wit and humor of his writings, while the Photo League images are bleak. A casual photograph of two half-naked boys on a hot summer day lounging around the Maine Monument at Columbus Circle becomes edgy when we read Van Vechten's caption: "This boy is writing on the other boy's back in white chalk: "F . . . the cops" (fig. 3.10). The image hides defiance, catching a traffic circle as a kind of habitation for the displaced, immigrant squatters who could be seen all around the city in the 1930s.

Lincoln Kirstein wrote in a tribute to Van Vechten at his death in 1964, "[Van Vechten] saw the surprising in the ordinary. . . . His scale was big, but it was domestic, to be assimilated; a transmuted domesticity, like the fire in a

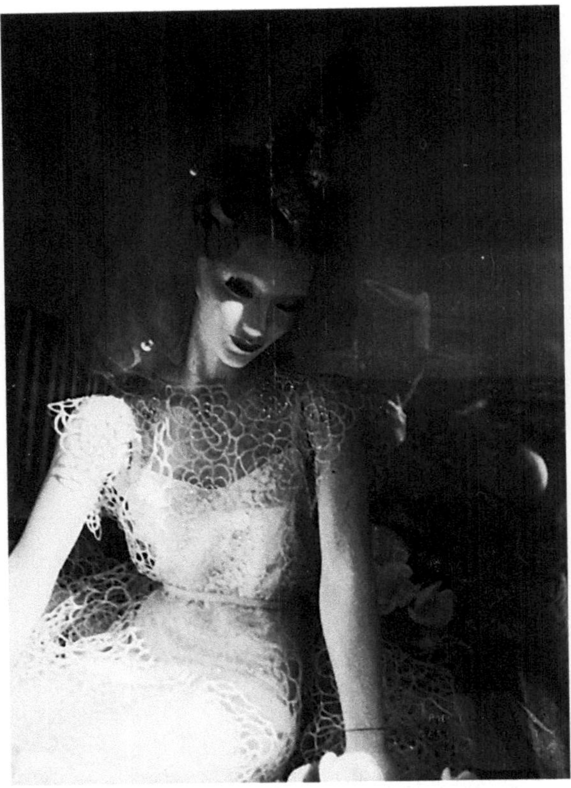
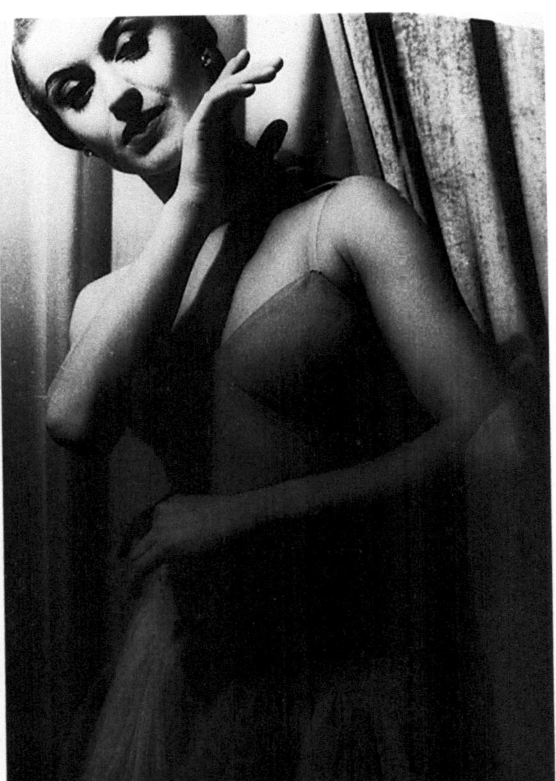

Figures 3.11 and 3.12. *Left*, Carl Van Vechten, *Lady in Bonwitt Teller's Window*, March 19, 1938. *Right*, Carl Van Vechten, *Violette Verdy in George Balanchine's "Serenade,"* December 4, 1961. (Museum of the City of New York, acc. nos. X2010.8.62 and 62.6.10; © The Van Vechten Trust)

hearth, the small proscenium where magic pictures glow."[75] The city comes alive as stage for a never-ending performance of people and automobile traffic as well as rising skyscrapers, architectural sculpture on Art Deco facades, public fountains, and decorative figures and vines on wrought-iron grills and doorknobs. A month prior to Van Vechten's photo shoot with Gopal, he took a picture of himself glued to the display windows of fashion stores on Fifth Avenue (fig. 3.11). The camera gets so close to the glass as to touch the figure's left hand. A soft light hits the figure's cheek, and its downcast eyes suddenly turn sideways toward the shadowy reflection of the photographer in the glass. The touch of his photography brings the mannequins to life.

Pose

Trained by such city images as the one in front of the display window, Van Vechten's animating gaze inspired his studio pictures. Compare his photograph of the mannequin in figure 3.11 to that of the ballerina Violette Verdy taken in his studio in 1961 (fig. 3.12). In a reversal of the Pygmalion effect, the cropped view of the ballerina turns her into an artwork displayed on a high pedestal, similar to the dressed plaster figure seen up close on a commercial street. In animating the sculpture while objectifying the human, Van Vechten draws out an uncanny aspect of his photographic realism.

For Van Vechten, photographic realism was a form of sorcery performed by the camera. He set up mimetic relationships between inanimate objects and human models in carefully built tableaux using props and backdrops. In one of his early experiments, dated June 1, 1933, he took a close-up of Paul Robeson against his sculpture bust by Jacob Epstein (fig. 3.13). Lit against a pitch-black background, the real head and sculpture echo each other. By making the models a part of the overall fiction of the photograph, Van Vechten flirts with the "realistic" paradigm of portraiture. Real people become artworks, as in his semi-realistic novels.

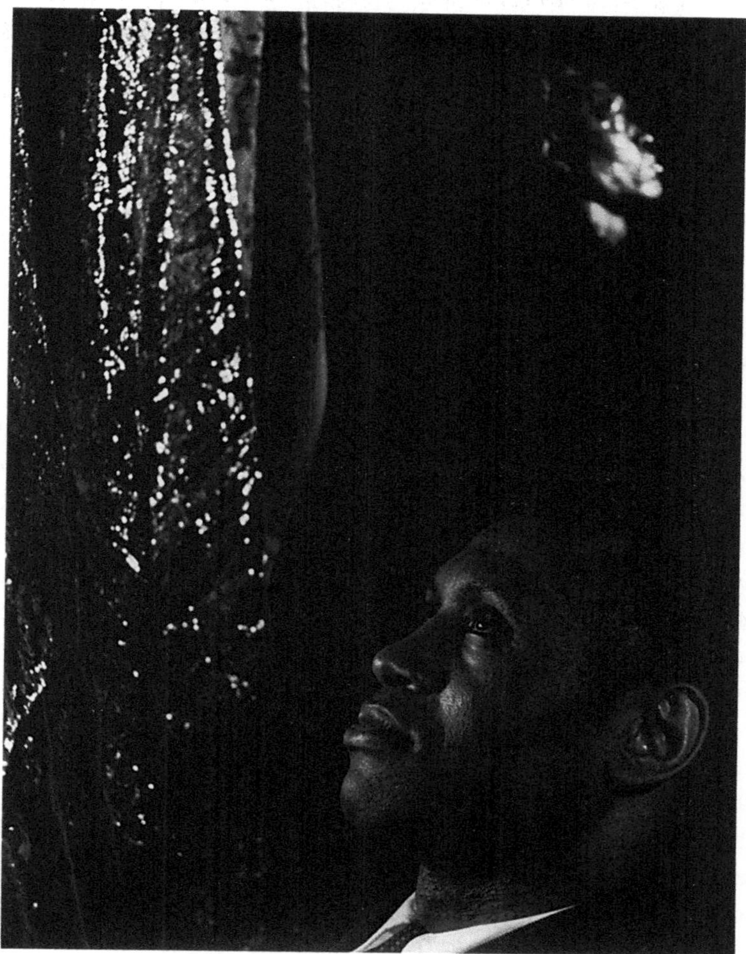

Figure 3.13. Carl Van Vechten, *Paul Robeson*, June 1, 1933, I d:13. (Beinecke Rare Book and Manuscript Library, Yale University; © The Van Vechten Trust)

In the era of photography with which Van Vechten engages, that is, Victorian America of the nineteenth and early twentieth centuries, a portrait was understood as a visual and literary strategy for singling out an individual against a social backdrop.[76] In Van Vechten's 1922 article "Pastiches et Pistaches," in which his Demuth/Stettheimer comparison appears, he radically inverts the Victorian idea of portraiture and realism. The article appeared in *The Reviewer*, one of the many short-lived literary magazines cropping up in different cities at that time; it was known for being "almost promiscuous in its wide array of topics and genres." According to Michael Kreyling, the magazine placed its tastes in a transition between the old and the new, occupying "an ambiguous, or conciliatory, middle ground between its Victorian predecessors and the emerging modernist insurgency."[77] Van Vechten articulates his "insurgency" in a series of disconnected thought bubbles on the pretensions of the Victorian world. He draws a contrast between what he calls "intelligence" and "pose." For him, both are artificial and untrue, but one of them is also clearly hypocritical. The section "The Intelligence of Cats" demonstrates the hypocrisy in the Victorian reasoning regarding cats, his favorite pet animal, about which he wrote a book. "No one, as far as I know, pretends to understand the cat. Let those who persist in asserting that this animal is unintelligent read the following dictum from Samuel Butler: 'Nothing, we say to ourselves, can have intelligence unless we understand all about it—as though intelligence in all except ourselves meant the power of being understood rather than of understanding.'" Van Vechten attacks the Victorian worldview on human knowledge as the exercise of the natural, God-given desire to know the unknown, as implied in the colonizing belief that the whole world is waiting to reveal itself to that human intelligence. Refuting that belief, the section "Concerning the Simplicity of the Great" gives a list of individuals known for giving up that (interior) sense of human intelligence by waging what the magazine might call "insurgencies" against norms of social respectability. "Beethoven striding through the tempest without coat or hat, ordering his dinner in a restaurant and then refusing to eat it, breaking the strings of his piano with his poundings, and insulting his friends, . . . James McNeill Whistler, whose life was so much of a pose that it almost became natural."[78] The list goes on, and the irreverence of "pose" becomes a politics in itself. In the privacy of his apartment-studio, Van Vechten invited friends and models to perform this irreverence extravagantly.

The Queer Politics of Irreverence

Van Vechten's studio became the perfect place for his subjects to perform real and imaginary identities. While subjects assumed their poses in front of his camera, images emphasized the artificiality of a staged tableau that blurred the line between a realistic portrait and deliberate performance. Van Vechten's fabric backdrops and props gave his images a look of sameness that we recognize as his signature style. In African American performers, the fictitious sameness also

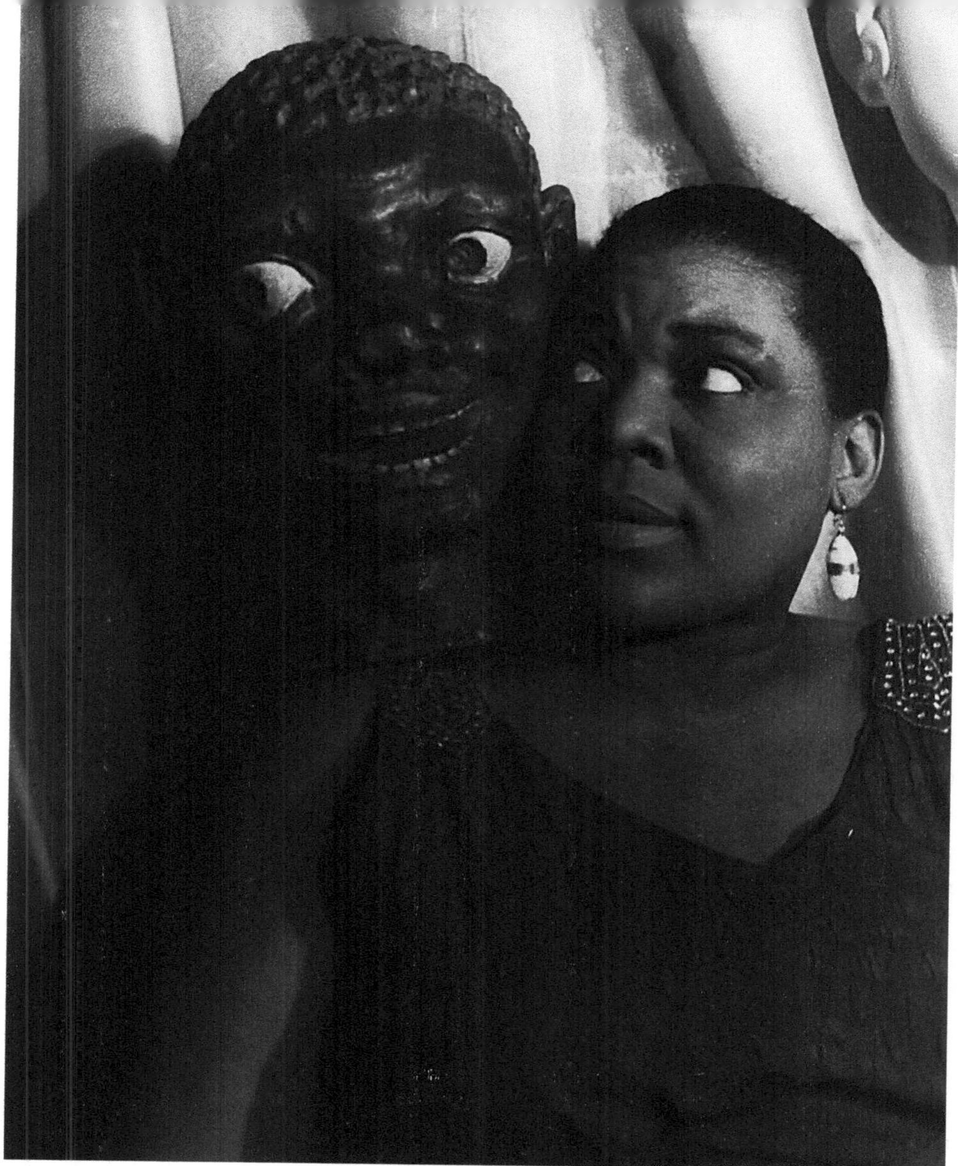

Figure 3.14. Carl Van Vechten, *Bessie Smith*, February 3, 1936, VJ:23. (Beinecke Rare Book and Manuscript Library, Yale University; © The Van Vechten Trust)

displayed a knowing awareness of the politics of segregation in the United States. If portraiture, as Sarah Blackwood defines it for the nineteenth-century United States, placed African American personalities against a realistic backdrop of US history, Van Vechten's stylized images make that historical place uncertain. On February 3, 1936, in a particularly salient example of fiction-making, the blues singer Bessie Smith posed for photographs in Van Vechten's studio. For a number of images, she showed herself as a stage performer in her glorious, white chiffon dress. But for one set of half-length portraits, her head is juxtaposed with a sculpture head representing blackface minstrelsy (fig. 3.14). The image is a disturbing evocation of the Jim Crow–era caricature of African Americans.

We must confront racism in Van Vechten's studio practice. One of the most disturbing comments is recorded in a 1960 interview with William Ingersoll:

> I remember once coming home almost jubilantly after a night in Harlem, and telling my wife in great glee that I hated a Negro, I'd found one I hated. And I felt I was completely emancipated, because now I could select my friends and not have to know them all. . . . Up to that time I had considered them all as one. Now, I feel about them exactly the way I feel about white people—I like some, am uninterested in others, and some of them I find very distasteful. But at that time, I hadn't got around to that.[79]

The glee in his voice cannot be excused on two counts: it is ridden with racist imaginings, and it fetishizes his emancipation from it in a racialized individual. In other words, it is riddled with Primitivism, a term describing a white Euro-American fascination with nonwhite people. In the 1960s, when the comment was made, it must have been particularly wrong sounding and offensive in the context of the emerging civil rights movement. Van Vechten has been described as a racist voyeur, and his inexcusable attitude toward race has made scholars of critical race studies ignore him altogether. But as Emily Bernard argues, he was not the only racist in New York City in the 1930s. She writes that racism has been and is an integral part of US history and culture; it is just that Van Vechten often made himself conspicuous.

Van Vechten's photo shoot was framed by racism. But where can we point to it? As his Black (and white) performers enjoyed the performance, as Bessie Smith clearly did, it raises some puzzling questions. For one, what made so many Black models willingly come to Van Vechten's apartment-studio and participate in his racist fantasies? It is especially remarkable that the models include such powerful and outspoken personalities as the blues singer. In an interracial party at Van Vechten's apartment, where Smith was invited not long before the photo shoot, she got drunk and left in a huff, knocking Van Vechten's wife, Fania Marinoff, to the floor when she approached the singer for a hug.[80] Does the photograph, then, represent Van Vechten's racist studio practice or a knowing wink between Van Vechten and his commanding, even brash, subjects?

Van Vechten's photographs make visible a looped circuit of racialized interactions that may have gone underground in the post-civil-rights discourse of racial divide. For Bernard, the interracial interactions we see in Van Vechten are more difficult to see in the twenty-first century, when the talk about race has hardened into such terms as "the Black community" or "the Black people," as well as Black Lives Matter, in both the political rhetoric of the country and academia. To speak of racial equality in these terms presumes, in Bernard's view, that "in their very state of being black or white, the two groups are fundamentally different." Van Vechten is by no means free of what Bernard calls "the [impossible] riddle of race."[81] It may therefore be more useful to ask how exactly Van Vechten distinguishes himself in that context, in other words, what is the "controversy" around Van Vechten?

Let us start that inquiry by asking a question of Bessie Smith's photograph: In whose imagination should we place the racialized scenario played out in the image, that of the photographer or the performer or both? Bernard helps rephrase the question in an important way: "Does race make a difference between the enjoyment taken by the black audience and the enjoyment taken by Van Vechten?" According to Bernard, "To black friends who shared his racial worldviews, it did not." I argue that there is some difference, relating to "self-perception," since the "black audience" is also the subject of the image, but Bernard's focus on "enjoyment" is important. The enjoyment of race was complicated for African American intellectuals of Harlem. To explore their pleasure in their own "race" and celebrate "blackness that extends across oceans and time, and reinforces a concept of black difference," many African American intellectuals traveled to Africa, only to find out that "Black difference" was elusive. Langston Hughes, for one, was disappointed by his trip. Nevertheless he advocated for that difference. As Bernard writes, "Hughes believed in black difference as a defense against the internalized racism he saw infecting the lives and imaginations of black people."[82] In other words, racial difference was an intellectual and poetic strategy of self-presentation within a segregated United States. While Bernard studied written texts as "the black and white of things"—letters, fiction, articles, and essays written by Van Vechten as well as by his African American friends, Van Vechten's black-and-white photographs give us the best opportunity to explore the strategy his subjects used for emancipation from the riddle of race. This is because, while literature brings us close to an author's thoughts on their subjects, photographs bear witness not only to the photographer behind the scene but also to the presence of the subjects in front of the lens. The images attest that Van Vechten's racialized models came into his studio with full recognition that a white photographer-spectator such as Van Vechten was a necessary part of their strategy.

What is that strategy of self-presentation? Ann Douglas gives us a name. She calls it "minstrelsy." "Black performers playing jazz, singing the blues, dancing, and doing comedy acts for white audiences at Harlem night spots had the long, rich and complex tradition of minstrelsy behind them." Starting as a popular entertainment for white audience in the 1830s, with white actors in blackface performing "a medley of purportedly Negro jokes, tall tales, song-and-dance routines, and spoofs of elite art and contemporary manners that had its roots in Southern Negro plantation culture," minstrelsy was picked up by Black performers, mostly men, who imitated the white performers instead of offering a corrective to their racial stereotypes, which could prove fatal. Within an evolving loop of popular entertainment, thus, it became "the essence of minstrelsy that whites played blacks and blacks played whites-playing-blacks, that men played women and performers enacted a range of materials that included and mimicked all classes." While minstrelsy was obviously "racism in action," and offensive at that, for Black performers, the "double mimicry . . . was also an art, and an especially American kind of art. Black minstrels not only imitated whites-playing-blacks but also burlesqued them; minstrelsy involved stereotype upon stereotype, opponents as look-alikes, mocking and criticizing each other." By the 1920s, as the demeaning representations were attacked by activists, minstrelsy was also being performed by "big names in the show business," including Black actors such as Bill "Bojangles" Robinson (whom Van Vechten photographed in 1933 and 1941) as well as movie stars such as Rudolph Valentino and Cary Grant.[83]

Let us return to Van Vechten's image of Bessie Smith to see the loop of minstrelsy at work in a visual image. The blackface sculpture makes a direct reference to that long and problematic tradition. The juxtaposition of a human face with sculpture refers here, as in Paul Robeson's photograph, also to an equally long and problematic tradition of Pictorialist photography exemplified by Robert Demachy's *Contrasts (A Study in Black and White)*, from 1904 (fig. 3.15). Wendy Grossman points out that Demachy's juxtaposition of a prepubescent girl with a white, classicized bust highlights in her body and skin tone an Orientalist fantasy of the East. The title of the image, however, brings the fantasy of racial and sexual difference into a formalist experiment of art photography.[84] This is the double move of modernist art, a gendered and racialized practice sublimated into the high art of white male artists, whose lineage Grossman traces from Demachy's Orientalism to the Primitivism of Man Ray's *Noire et Blanche* (1926). We will discuss Man Ray's airbrushed image of a white woman's disembodied head against an African sculpture in chapter 4, but for now, we might simply note high modernism's sublimation of heterosexual fantasies, on which Van Vechten's photography picks up.

As an artistic venture, Van Vechten's images are crude when compared to Demachy's artful framing. On the top right edge of the photograph of Bessie Smith and the minstrelsy sculpture, we see a part of a white plaster cast disrupting the frame and distracting our attention. The crudeness may be part of Van Vechten's amateurism. But here is the twist. For other images, Van Vechten pulls back the camera and reveals the cast as the sculpture head of Antinous, the favorite beloved of the Roman emperor Hadrian (fig. 3.16). The singer poses with both sculptures, as if to represent Van Vechten's own version of Demachy's *Study in Black and White*. When we view the Smith images as a series, that is, through Van Vechten's Whiffle-like obsession with collecting and enumerating his subjects instead of the selected and singled masterworks of the Pictorialists he imitated, we skid from a simple, racial reading of Smith's images and are required to differentiate his amateur practice from the erotics of Primitivism.

I suggest that the Bessie Smith group represents photographic minstrelsy in Douglas's sense of "blacks playing whites-playing-blacks." More importantly, an individuation of the Black body takes place "through" the visual logic of

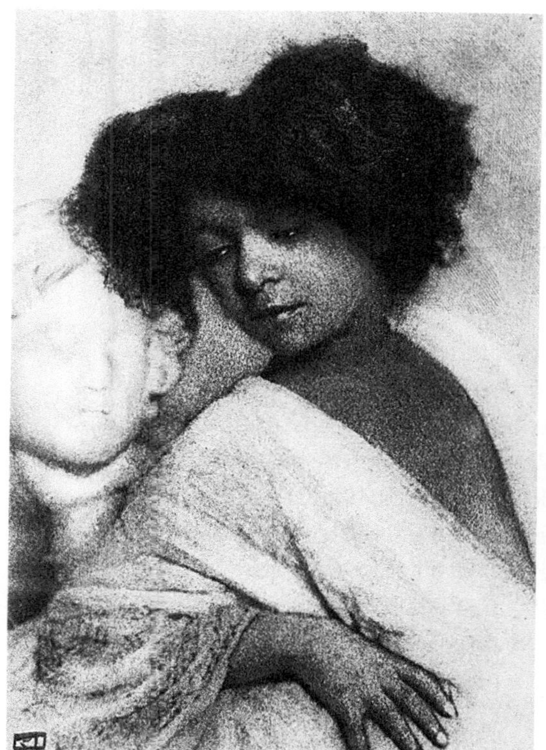

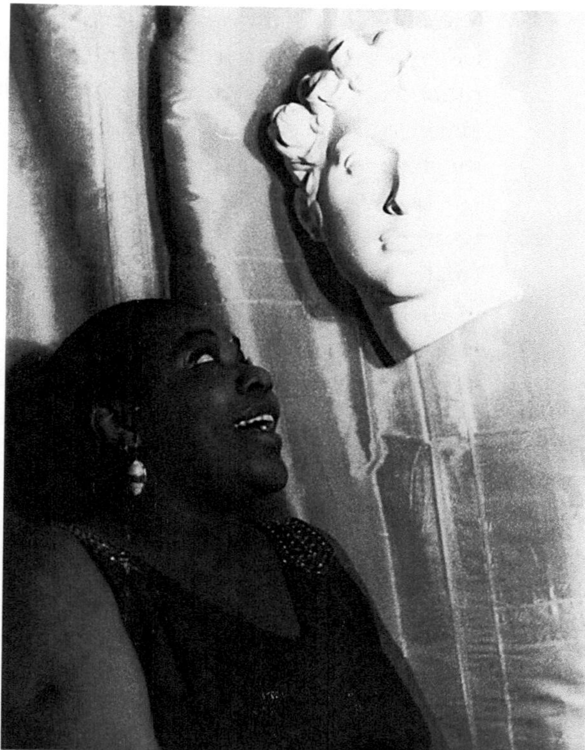

Figures 3.15 and 3.16. *Left*, Robert Demachy, *Contrasts (A Study in Black and White)*, 1904, photogravure from a gum bichromate print, *Camera Works*, no. 5 (1904). (Courtesy of The William Hood Dunwoody Fund, Minneapolis Institute of Art, acc. no. 64.34.5.5; public domain) *Right*, Carl Van Vechten, *Bessie Smith*, February 3, 1936, VJ:18. (Beinecke Rare Book and Manuscript Library, Yale University; © The Van Vechten Trust)

minstrelsy. The juxtaposition against the Antinous head introduces at least one additional dimension to Smith's performative identity. As the homosexual lover of the Roman emperor Hadrian, the white, classical sculpture points not only to Smith's blackness but also to her homoerotic interests.[85] If Jim Crow segregates Blacks and pins them to racial and cultural stereotypes, Van Vechten's Primitivist images release in these racialized bodies an unstable and conflicted process of individuation. Their performative affinities produce in them a fluidity of representations.

The poignancy of Van Vechten's photographs can be realized when we place them within the history of a racially divided country in the 1930s. Van Vechten's collaboration with Bessie Smith occurred just a year prior to her fatal car accident on US Route 61 between Memphis, Tennessee, and Clarksdale, Mississippi, on September, 26, 1937.[86] A Memphis surgeon who happened to drive by treated her on the scene, and when no ambulance appeared, he also decided to take her to the Clarksdale hospital; on the way, a second car crashed into the doctor's vehicle. The doctor later confessed to Smith's biographer, "Down in the Deep South cotton country, no ambulance driver, or white driver, would even have thought of putting a colored person off in a hospital for white folks."[87] Smith never woke up. Bernard nails the issue at stake by examining the photographic collaboration that occurred in Van Vechten's studio in the context of the racial violence of the era: "Against the backdrop of Jim Crow segregation, interracial socializing was an act of rebellion."[88]

Van Vechten's queering of the heterosexual discourse of Primitivism must be understood as a rebellion in one more way. It does not readily give the (male) photographer and his camera the control of the racialized body. Instead of the reductive representations of racial and sexual stereotypes in that photographic tradition, Van Vechten's subjects take photography in the direction of minstrelsy's endless doubling of stereotypes. Thus, I want to rethink Van Vechten's collaboration with his subjects using the psychologist E. Mark Stern, who describes the relationship between Van Vechten and Bessie Smith as that between "the awesome and the awestruck."[89] We might take the psychologist's clinical angle with a grain of salt, but the phrase helps us reevaluate the relationship between the white male photographer and his racialized subjects that obtains in Van Vechten's case. I suggest we call Van Vechten's photography "awestruck." Instead of the coercive power of the photographer's gaze, it represents the photographer's vulnerability to his glamorous subjects. In this way, his apartment-studio becomes a fundamentally intersectional space where participants come to collaborate in mutual fantasy-making, aided by the photographer and his props.

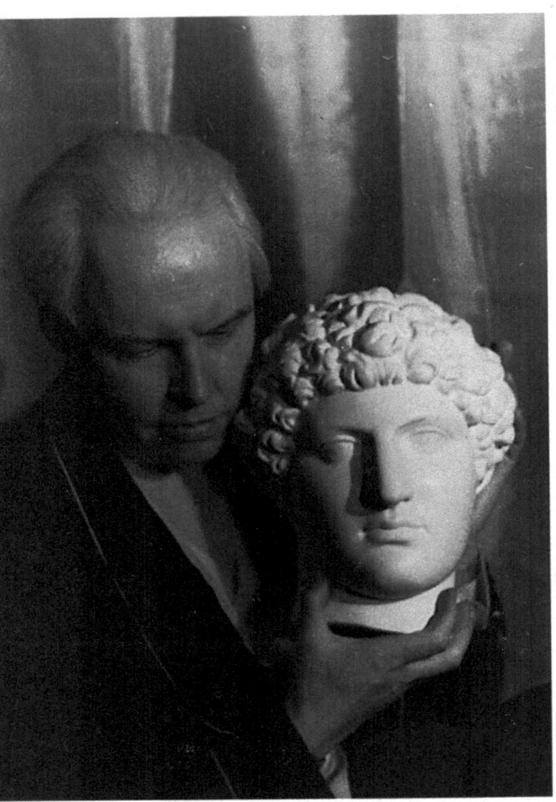

Figure 3.17. Carl Van Vechten, *Carl Van Vechten*, February 16, 1936, VII J:0. (Beinecke Rare Book and Manuscript Library, Yale University; © The Van Vechten Trust)

In this story of interracial interactions in a repressive racial regime, there is one more "rebellion" to note in Van Vechten's queer studio practice. The photographer, who normally remains invisible behind the lens, becomes a visible part of the primitivist minstrelsy (fig. 3.17). Two weeks after the Bessie Smith photograph, Van Vechten poses for a self-portrait holding the same Antinous sculpture next to his own head. It is as if the photographer is possessed by the racializing and sexualizing juxtapositions. He emulates them like a chameleon absorbing the racial and sexual regimes of the Unites States and embodies them in photographic representations as if he were a Peter Whiffle himself.

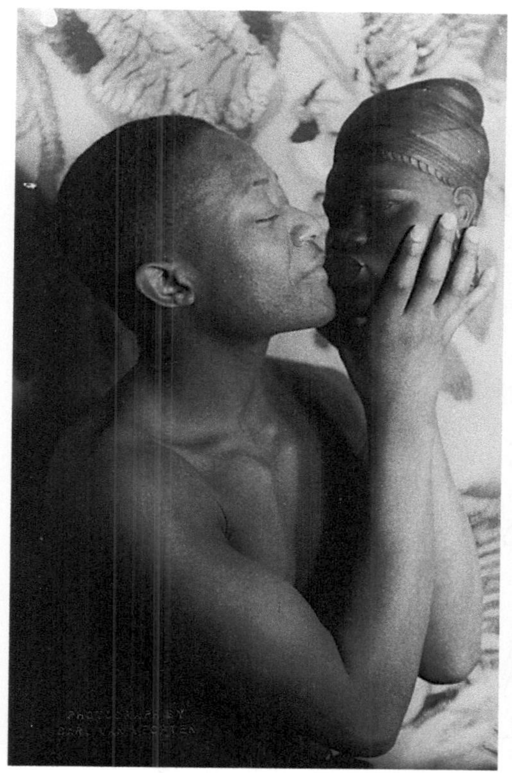

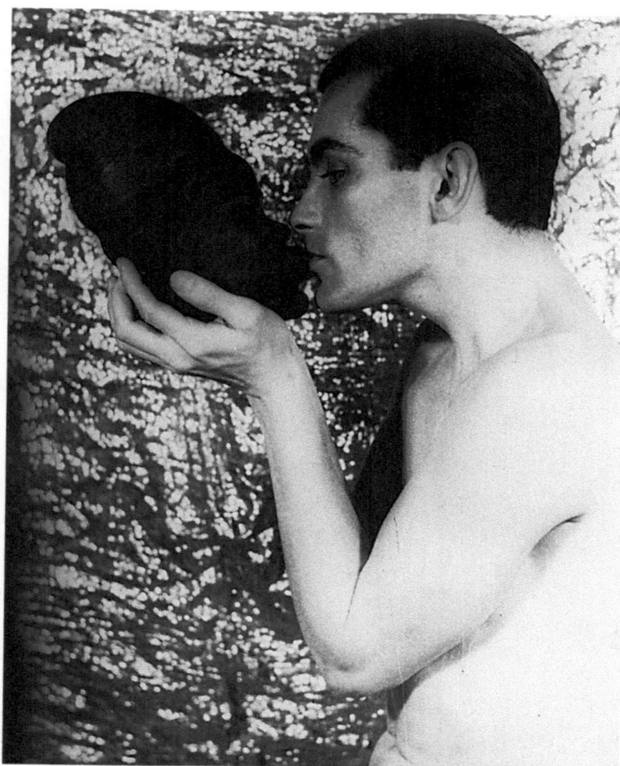

Figures 3.18 and 3.19. *Left*, Carl Van Vechten, *Feral Banga*, January 10, 1937, XIII, K:5; *right*, Carl Van Vechten, *Hugh Laing*, March 3, 1940, XXII Q:34.

When the sculptured heads turn toward his Black and white models, minstrelsy's doubling shifts into a surprising but unmistakable reference to Salomé (figs. 3.18 and 3.19). Van Vechten was haunted by the final scene in Richard Strauss's opera, which he saw in New York in 1907, in which Olive Fremstad breached "a carnal taboo," waiting to kiss the severed head of Saint John the Baptist: "I cannot yet recall her as she crept from side to side of the well in which Jochanaan was confined, waiting for the slave to ascend with the severed head, without that shudder of fascination caused by the glimmering eyes of a monster serpent, or the sleek terribleness of a Bengal tiger. And at the end, she suggested, as perhaps it has never been suggested before on stage, the dregs of love, the refuse of gorged passion."[90]

Van Vechten reconstructs the motif of the anticipated kiss in his studio but does not elaborate on the performance seen long ago. Instead, the visual motif draws directly from Aubrey Beardsley's illustration of the play's climax, titled *J'ai baisé ta bouche, Iokanaan* (I kiss your mouth, Jokannan; fig. 3.20), which had instantly become a sensation in England and Paris before the play was staged. In 1893, when Beardsley made the illustration, the English artist could have only conjured up the climax from reading the play, which Wilde originally

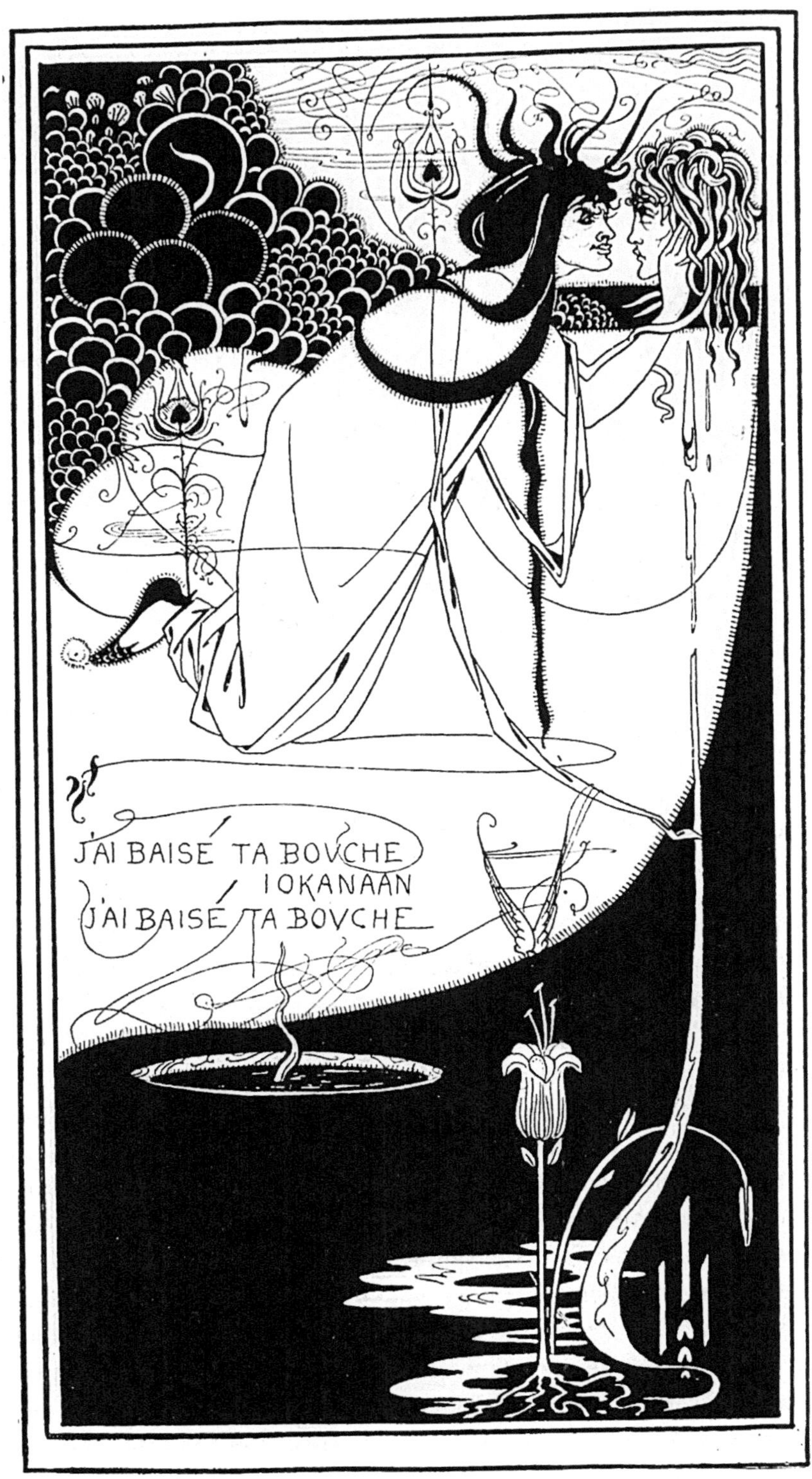

Figure 3.20. Aubrey Beardsley, *J'ai baisé ta bouche, Iokanaan*, line block print, 1893 (Museum no. E.456.1899; courtesy of Victoria and Albert Museum, London)

published in French translation and released in Paris in 1891. The play was produced only in 1896, that too in Paris, and remained banned in England until 1931. The Beardsley image was published as *The Climax* in the play's English edition in 1894, and it permanently locked the play's scandal in a powerful visual representation etched on the memory of readers and viewers.

Beardsley shows a spidery figure in a flowing gown using wiry lines that swirl around the severed head and stylized blood drops, borrowing from Japanese woodcut prints. For Wollen, the scandal of Beardsley's image is that it "modernized . . . the visual impact of Salomé," taken out of its biblical context and "encrusted with echoes of antiquity, and laced it in a topical and contemporary context." Wollen traces the journey of Beardsley's image through Wilde's Parisian publisher (also Beardsley's publisher) to Sergei Diaghilev of the Ballets Russes. Starting in the first decade of the twentieth century, the Salomé image circulated across the Atlantic, influencing cultural practitioners such as Ballets Russes' costume designer Leon Bakst as well as the performance of the Canadian dancer Maud Allan across Europe and England. In 1906, the American Orientalist dancer Ruth St. Denis, whom we saw in chapter 2, transposed the veiled image of Salomé to an Indian theme of Radha, the consort and lover of the Hindu god Krishna. "Soon New York was full of aspiring Salomés. Madame Dazi, who danced Salomé for the Ziegfeld Follies, even opened a Salomé school."[91]

Van Vechten does not show Gopal kissing a sculpture head, but he explores in Gopal's androgynous body the resonant image of the veiled Oriental figure (fig. 3.1). Gopal wears his metallic jewelry and the short skirt with starched pleats that we have seen in other images. Now he wears a crown from his dance of the Garuda (fig. 2.16). The sharp panels, lined with sequins arranged in a fan shape, show the sharp crest (or abbreviated wings) of the mythical bird from Hindu mythology. The transparent fabric held across the dancer's body brings about a Beardsley-like transformation of the human figure into a stylized work of art.

Edward White writes, "The publication of Wilde's play had been a crucial feature of Europe's art nouveau movement of the 1890s, especially the editions augmented by Aubrey Beardsley's vivid illustrations, his 'whiplash line' in sensuous concert with the violent carnality of Wilde's text."[92] The modern appeal of Salomé, picked up by Art Nouveau, rests in the fantasy image of an exquisite murderess. "It was the hallucinating combination of animal, goddess, artist, dandy, priestess, killer, seductress and hysteric which gave the image of Salomé its uncanny power."[93] The Beardsley image is key to understanding the promiscuous life and afterlife of the Wildean figure into a full-blown Art Nouveau aesthetic. By the 1930s, its "whiplash" aesthetic gave shape to ornate creatures—combining humans, insects, flowers, flesh, and metal—in jewelry, fashion, and architecture, as well as the Orientalized costumes and set designs in dance, theater, and Hollywood film by the 1930s.[94] The composite animal lingers in Van

Vechten's imagination in a powerful way.[95] Recalling Olive Fremstad's stage performance of Salomé at the Metropolitan Opera, Van Vechten describes a stealthy and violent feline. "Her entrance was that of a splendid leopard standing poised on velvet paws on the terrace, then creeping slowly down the staircase."[96] As White remarks, Van Vechten equated feline stealth with erotic activity, "both beautiful and savage." Van Vechten was disappointed that the nine-minute dance of the seven veils was not performed on the first night of the show by Fremstad but rather by the less adventuresome prima ballerina Bianca Froelich. While Froelich's "writhing" proved too scandalous for the New York patrons and led ultimately to the closing of the opera, Van Vechten found it altogether "tame compared with the wild manner in which she had torn off her layers in the dress rehearsal."[97] He would have ideally liked the whole performance taken in the direction of the exquisite, animal-like Fremstad.

As Van Vechten looked at the Indian dancer through the lens of his Leica in 1938, he would have recalled that palpable early memory of the "beautiful and savage" creature. Wrapping this composite, partly human, partly Garuda bird in a transparent fabric, he played out his fascination with the exquisite feline. Its soft, velvet paws and sharp nails might just tear through the layers of the gauze around it. How did Van Vechten recruit the camera in bringing the "violent carnality" of that glamorous fantasy image to life, and how did the camera refract the awestruck photographer's fantasy? The camera's distinct role as an active participant in the photo shoot requires explanation, to which we must now turn.

CHAPTER 4.
THE CAMERA

Let us begin with a detail we did not mention in our discussion of Van Vechten's portrait from 1936 by Romaine Brooks in chapter 3, namely, the object in his hand (fig. 3.2). Gleaming against the dark wicker chair, the right arm of Van Vechten's cream-color jacket opens like a calla lily, showing his fingers and thumb lovingly cradling a Leica camera. In this chapter, I want to isolate this detail and explore the intimacy between the photographer and the camera that shaped Van Vechten's pictorializing imagination. While the Brooks portrait captures for us the place of photography in Van Vechten's modernist lifestyle and interests, I want to show here how the camera transformed him. The Leica was virtually attached to Van Vechten's right hand.[1] He carried it everywhere. I argue here that it is primarily the Leica that turned him into an "awestruck" photographer, inflecting his pictorial fantasies and materially producing the glamour of his subjects.

The chapter is not about technological determinism. It explores the Leica's entanglements with the human participants in the New York studio. The German camera is activated as a distinct participant that guides the flow of desires and fantasies in the studio. Placed between the awestruck photographer and his glamorous subject, it creates a space of estrangement and exoticism—the space of Primitivism and Orientalism—between them, refracting their transcultural fantasies and turning their interracial, homoerotic interests into what I call *photo-eroticism*. We focus here on the photographer's relationship with the Leica, and chapter 5 elaborates on the dancer's intimacy with it. In both chapters, we witness the photo shoot transforming into a photo-erotic threesome within the privacy of the New York studio.

The Leica Moment

Although other handheld cameras existed prior to the Leica, what made the German camera alluring when it was first introduced at an industrial fair in Leipzig in 1925 was its precision, agility, and modern look. The Leica was the camera of the modern moment, as enthusiastic commentators were quick to point out: "To many of the old photographers it looked like a toy designed for a lady's handbag. But on closer examination it bore all the evidence of a keen precision instrument designed and manufactured by the ablest technicians of a world-famous microscope company. . . . This camera [was] an instrument of modern expression that dealt the final blow to the old 'imitation of art' school of photography. This camera was the Leica!"[2] The small, slick, metal machine must have seemed as exciting in 1925 as an iPhone in 2007. For the self-appointed aficionados of the new camera, the world of photography was suddenly divided into two. All other photography became old-fashioned, belonging to "the horse and buggy days," and riddled with "romantic pictorial conceptions" as odd as "painting a Rembrandt picture today, or building a Gothic cathedral in the shadow of a New York skyscraper with all its modern steel construction."[3]

Designed in 1914 by Oskar Barnack, an engineer at the Ernst Leitz Optical Company in Wetzlar, Germany, the Leica was promoted as a technological adventure of the Weimar Republic. The company's reputation was built on its design of precision lenses for microscopes, telescopes, and movie cameras since the nineteenth century. The Leica aimed at professionals as well as serious amateurs, by which I mean those who invested in the expensive German machinery over many handheld cameras available in the market since 1888, when the Eastman Kodak Company democratized photography through its advertisements. The ads claimed that, in order to take a photograph with a Kodak, one only needed to press a button. The camera box could then be sent away to a Kodak center for developing, printing, and refilling for future use.

Picking up the Leica was a transformative moment for Van Vechten. He had used the Kodak in his youth in the 1890s, when it was "much larger than a man's shoebox." He photographed his paternal grandmother in Cedar Rapids, "much as Whistler's mother had sat for that painter's most celebrated painting."[4] He also used the Kodak in Paris in 1908, when he was appointed by the *New York Times* to cover the arts. He mentions following theater personalities around the city and taking pictures of Olive Fremstad and Charles Dalmorès in the Luxembourg Gardens and of the coloratura soprano Louisa Tetrazzini entering her coupé after he had treated her to a view of the city from the top of the New York Times Tower. The anecdotes suggest that he would have probably used Kodak's No. 2 Model A Folding Pocket Brownie. A huge advancement over the "shoebox," it came closest to the Leica in its small size and transportability. It had a viewfinder to compose each image quickly and could load a spool of film that gave six or seven shots per roll. With the Kodak Brownie, then, Van Vechten would have been able to take snapshots of his subjects on the move and between their other activities.

Yet the Leica differed from the Kodak Brownie in significant ways. The Brownie had a fake-leather-covered cardboard body. Glued to it was a hard fabric having accordion folds to move the metal lens mount attached at the other end, pulled back and forth along a support base provided by the camera's front cover. The viewfinder helped in framing the image, but the focus could be calculated only imprecisely, with the help of a metal gauge placed to one side of the support base. The exposed rolls could be taken to any number of photographic stores that had mushroomed overnight in large and small towns in the United States and Europe by 1900. But limitations remained. While one could also request enlargements from the Kodak stores, one generally preferred the contact print of two and a quarter by three and a quarter inches, not only because of expense but also because of the possibility of losing details from a slightly out-of-focus negative.

While the Brownie's transportability helped in taking photographs on the fly, the design slowed you down. The camera required the photographer to look down into the viewfinder on one side and manipulate the accordion folds to estimate the distance of the subject in relation to the focal length of the lens, pulling the eye away from the view itself in the process. By contrast, the Leica was held up directly against the eye and became literally what the Weimar photographers and writers such as Laszlo Moholy-Nagy and Walter Benjamin understood as a prosthesis for the human eye.[5]

The prosthetic eye was designed to be precise. It used interchangeable, screw-mounted lenses whose precision was legendary. It had a range finder "used on guns" and a spool of thirty-five-millimeter film, designed originally for movie cameras, with sprockets for quick movement and to project the small camera image on a large screen.[6] The Leica could take forty or more pictures at a time, in quick succession if needed. The removable spool could be sent to be developed at the George Eastman House in Rochester, New York. Eastman was the first company to adapt its motion picture films to a Leica spool, but *The*

Leica Manual, produced in 1935 in New York for amateurs, encouraged users to develop their own films and make enlargements in a makeshift darkroom that could be easily created in a home kitchen or bathroom.[7]

In 1932, when Miguel Covarrubias introduced Van Vechten to the German camera, the writer switched overnight to photography. "I had begun to believe I was indeed a photographer." Van Vechten's excitement was palpable. "Within a month or two, I had provided myself with a makeshift darkroom, actually a disused kitchen, bought an enlarger, a printing frame, photographic paper, and other mystical paraphernalia, and began to process my own pictures." Van Vechten was enamored not only by the camera but by the whole "mystical paraphernalia" that came with it, including the interrelated series of mechanical and chemical processes.[8] The Leica meant for him the camera, the darkroom, the solvent baths, and the celluloid film strip from which small, individual negative images could be picked and enlarged into positive prints of any size. The Romaine Brooks portrait suggests that the Leica was attached not only to the photographer's hand but also to his creative process. Beyond the ease of taking a photograph, the Leica cultivated the pride in "making" an image. An amateur could now control the entire process of image production within the privacy of their apartment studio.

At first, Van Vechten sent his rolls to develop at the George Eastman House. The E. Leitz Company in New York distributed the spools and mediated between the "Motion Picture Film Department at the Eastman Kodak Company" and its clients in case of problems. In a letter dated September 22, 1932, Willard D. Morgan, at that time the manager of the "Photo-Optical Department" of the New York branch of Leica, responded to Van Vechten's complaint about defective rolls "with leaders tearing" in his camera and promised "to run down the trouble to its source."[9]

For an amateur like Van Vechten, the technical problems were only part of the growing pains. Van Vechten's assistant in the 1930s, his young lover and friend Mark Lutz, could hear his "outraged cries of indignation" when his first films returned from Rochester.[10] The issues may not always have been the horror of seeing, weeks later, the myriad mistakes Van Vechten might have made, from wrongly loading the film or incorrect exposure setting to forgetting to forward the film to the next frame. A long correspondence between Van Vechten and the George Eastman House in 1939–1940 suggests that the problem was also Van Vechten's subjects. The correspondence pertains to a roll of Kodachrome slides containing nude figures that could not be sent back to Van Vechten under the federal postal regulations and that the company was obliged to destroy, against Van Vechten's protests.[11] For good reasons, then, Van Vechten "always did his own developing, all his printing, all his own enlarging."[12]

The Study of Enlargements

Willard Morgan did not stop at helping Van Vechten with problems with the film processing. He engaged Van Vechten's interest in Leica photography. He had heard of Van Vechten's intentions to display his images "at a special exhibition at the Imperial Theatre" and asked if he could publish a few in the company's "monthly bulletin 'Leica Photography.'"[13] In this exchange, we get a glimpse of Van Vechten becoming part of a growing network of Leica fans and users who may not have been professional artists. Beyond Morgan's role in the company, he made it his mission to encourage Leica users to imagine themselves as serious amateurs. He promoted the German camera in New York beginning in 1928 and launched the First Annual Leica Photographic Salon in 1933. He formed a publishing house in 1934 with Henry M. Lester, and in collaboration with his wife, the dance photographer Barbara Morgan, published the first *Leica Manual* in 1935. The detailed guide brought the heft of professional knowledge to an amateur practice. In 1935, Morgan invited Van Vechten to participate in the *Second International Leica Exhibit* to be opened at the Radio City and stated a particular focus: "This year, we wish to have most of the photographs enlarged to about 11 × 14 in. and mounted on 16 × 20 in. mounts. A contact print should also be included."[14]

We do not know if Van Vechten participated in that exhibition. He served as a judge in other exhibitions. The correspondence between him and Morgan, however, brings attention to the importance of enlarging images in Leica photography. Following Morgan, Van Vechten regularly enlarged his images, and many prints at the New York Public Library are indeed eleven by fourteen inches. He mounted large prints regularly on the sixteen-by-twenty-inch cardboard mount that Morgan specified. He documented his practice scrupulously. He maintained a regular diary to annotate photo shoots. Contact prints helped in recordkeeping. He developed a number system for identifying the roll and the negative number of each image, which he included on the back of each cardboard mount, along with a personal stamp. Enlargements served multiple purposes. Exhibition was one. The Beinecke set comprises eight-by-ten enlargements, to be archived as opposed to displayed, I imagine. Van Vechten also made picture postcards to circulate among friends.

In *The Leica Manual*, a chapter by Willard Morgan highlights the many advantages of enlarging images. Beyond what the camera captured, one could adjust the quality of the image by selecting an appropriate printing paper, as well as shading and dodging at the time of printing, "in order to emphasize or hold back any portion of the picture." Also, "unattractive or disturbing parts of a negative may easily be omitted to improve the composition of the finished picture." There were other enhancements. For example, one could tilt the enlarging easel "for correcting the perspective in a picture" of architecture taken with the camera pointing upward. Above all, "the Leica enlargement of post card size or larger produces a picture which can easily be studied by anyone."[15] A Leica enlargement gave users an abundance of information to study about the subject than did images from any other camera of the day, whose magnification only showed the limitations of the camera. Chapters in *The Leica Manual* are devoted to describing the "study" of practitioners in such wide-ranging fields as aerial photography, astronomy, criminology, dentistry, entomology, historical research, movies, ophthalmology, and theater.[16]

Reflecting the mode of "study," a self-portrait shows Van Vechten looking through the magnifying glass at an object that is placed exactly where we are (fig. 4.1). The image is odd, but it belongs to a genre that depicts Leica users absorbed in an examination of their photographic subject. One of the earliest images of this kind is a self-portrait by a medical professional turned photographer named Paul Wolff (1887–1951), who became a poster child for the Leica after he received a camera as a prize in the Frankfurt Photography Exhibition in 1926. The exhibition was one among many organized by the Ernst Leitz Company. Wolff was the star of *Die Camera* (The Camera), organized by Leitz in 1935 at the newly built Rockefeller Center in New York, and it is possible that Van Vechten took the idea directly from this photographer, who was known by this time for experimenting with chemistry and producing fine enlargements from the grainy film negatives in the darkroom.

Wolff's self-portrait, published on the cover of his 1934 book, titled *Meine Erfahrungen mit der Leica* (My Experiences with the Leica), expresses the intimacy between the photographer and the craft of image-making (fig. 4.2). In using a magnifying glass to scrutinize a strip of negative, Wolff demonstrates that the celluloid negative might have registered something that was invisible to the photographer's naked eye. Like a lab scientist, he selects an example and investigates. He will subject the negatives to a chemical process within the controlled conditions of his darkroom and use the enlarged results as a permanent record of his study.[17]

The interrelated set of technical processes that made the Leica an instrument of scientific study, social critique, military strategy, and so on opened unimaginable possibilities for professionals and amateurs alike in the late 1920s and 1930s. Laszlo Moholy-Nagy, the chief exponent of the *Foto-Cultur* of Bauhaus in Weimar Germany, called his practice "New Vision" photography. As Rosalind Krauss points out, the New Vision was founded on the belief "that the camera was a special instrument which could reveal what the naked eye could not see."[18] Walter Benjamin emphasized the disjuncture between the world seen through the human eye and through the camera and identified in Moholy-Nagy and others the visual breakthroughs of "New Photography." Benjamin soon developed from New Photography his general insights on photography as such. Using an analogy of the psychic unconscious, which was revealed only in dream images, according to Freud, Benjamin famously wrote that it is only "through the camera that we first discover the optical unconscious" of the visible world.[19]

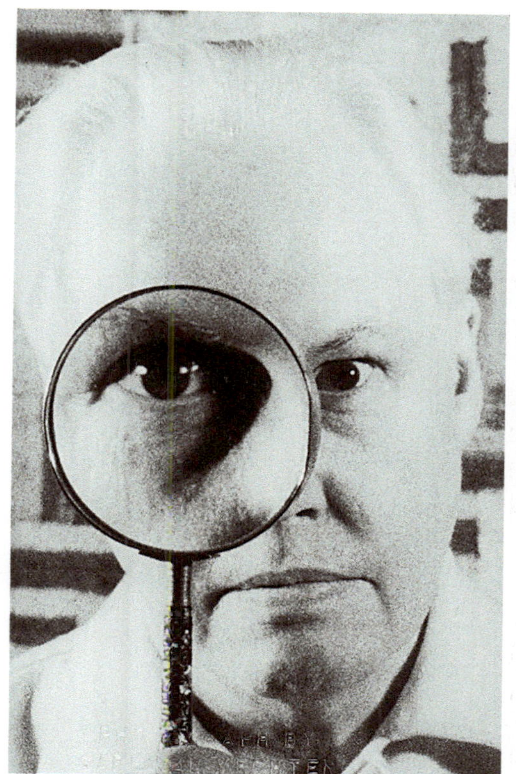

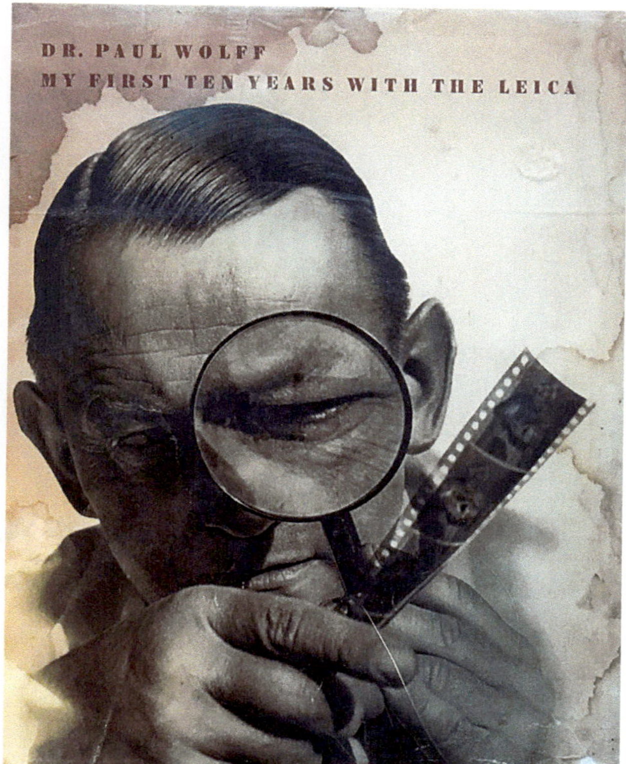

Figures 4.1 and 4.2. *Left*, Carl Van Vechten, undated postcard, probably 1944. (Beinecke Rare Book and Manuscript Library, Yale University; © The Van Vechten Trust) *Right*, Paul Wolff, *Meine Erfahrungen mit der Leica*, 1934. (Downloaded from https://www.catawiki.com/en/l/5558889-dr-paul-wolff-meine-erfahrungen-mit-der-leica-1934, accessed April 17, 2017; also https://www.amazon.com/First-Ten-Years-Leica-Photography/dp/B004RD27QG)

The technological prosthetic, as distinct from the human eye but nevertheless attached to it, fascinated Van Vechten also. What did he discover in his subjects when he blew up a Leica image into a "post card size or larger" print? Let us look at a picture postcard he sent to Gopal from the first day of the photo shoot, postmarked May 6, 1938, while the dancer was still in New York. On the back, he wrote in green ink, "As a photograph, I think *this* is my favorite!" (figs. 4.3 and 4.4).

Why did Van Vechten choose this photograph as his "favorite"? The image does not flatter the dancer exactly. In the negative, the body was already cropped oddly at the hands, making his hand gesture illegible. Van Vechten further crops the image at the navel to frame the body more tightly, removing the beautiful tiara on Gopal's head and most of the golden skirt. The key lighting from the left aims at the background curtain and shrouds the figure in darkness. The silhouette is slightly out of focus against the sharply chiseled folds of the luminous fabric in the back. If the photographer wished to compliment the dancer, there

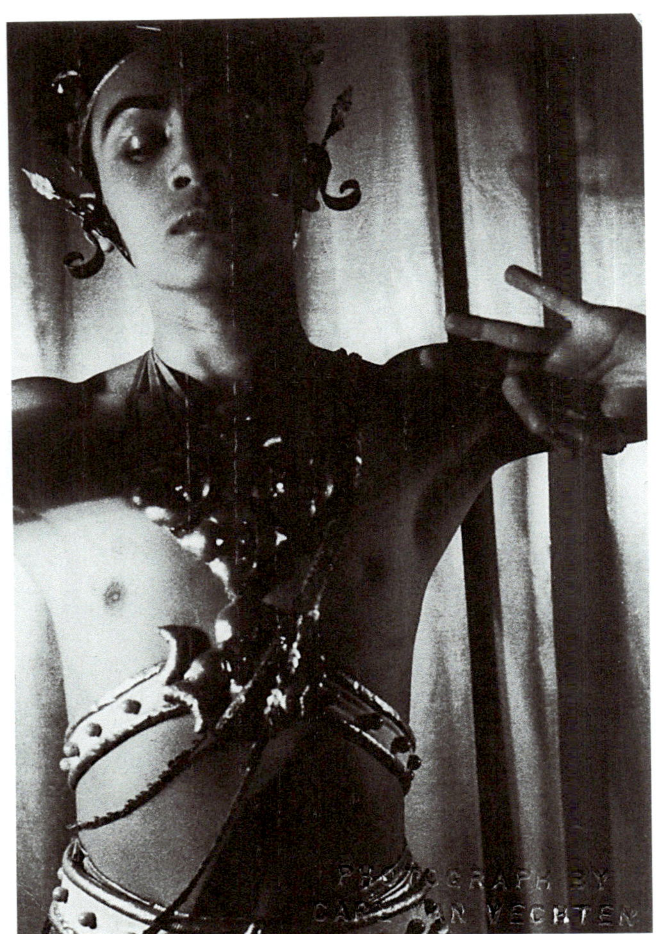

Figures 4.3 and 4.4. Carl Van Vechten, *Ram Gopal*, postcard, front and back. (The Rosenbach Library, Philadelphia)

CORRESPONDENCE

ADDRESS

Dear Ram. As a
photographer I think
this is my favorite!
Will call for you
Sunday at
one!
until then, Carlo,

Ram Gopal
Hotel Gladstone
114 East 52 Street
Manhattan

2006.186

were other, better images showing him in the same gorgeous costume but in sharp focus and in full view, commanding the luminous space around him (fig. 2.9). What was Van Vechten thinking or studying in this enlarged image, if not Gopal's dance?

Van Vechten's postcard makes one thing clear: it is an invitation for the dancer to see the image "as a photograph." In other words, the conversation is not about the dancer or his dance but about photography. The low-angle shot celebrates the mobility of the handheld camera. For the close-up, Van Vechten must have either lowered the tripod or more likely unmounted his Leica from the tripod and held it kneeling down, while the dancer looked at the lens inches away from his pelvis. In moving closer to the dancer's body, the camera pushes the boundary of physical intimacy between them. The recognition of an erotic suggestion may have appealed to the dancer. But there is more.

Comparing the postcard with the original negative, we notice that Van Vechten cropped the image at the navel, leaving out a portion of the dancer's lower garment. The cropping accentuates the foreshortening and makes the dancer's body appear monumental, as if it were a fragment from a marble relief carved against the flutes of a massive column or an ancient Greco-Roman torso placed on a high pedestal in a museum. This suggestion too would have appealed to the dancer, given his interest in ancient sculpture.

The extreme, exaggerated close-up does one more trick. It foregrounds the bold, shiny ornaments wrapping around the towering silhouette. Instead of a human dancer wearing a costume and jewelry, the tendrils projecting on either side of Gopal's head make the dancer's stylized body appear like a piece of Art Nouveau jewelry, where floral vines circle around insects and humans and fuse with their metallic bodies. The black-and-white image also makes the monumental figure appear as if it were a stone support for vegetation shaped in wrought iron, visible on Art Deco buildings built newly in New York in the 1930s. The disorienting transformation of the dancer's body in the photograph bring to mind Walter Benjamin's response to Karl Blossfeldt's photographic close-ups of plants in his 1928 publication "Urformen der Kunst." For Benjamin, Blossfeldt's enlargements were not disorienting but revelatory, as if the camera's magnification revealed in plants their "original stylistic forms [*Stilformen*]." He wrote, "In the crosier depicted by the fern, in the larkspur and in the blooms of saxifrage, we see forms reminiscent of the tracery in the rose windows of cathedrals. In the greatly enlarged pictures of chestnut and maple shoots we see pillars taking on the form of horsetails and totems. The bud of the *Eisenhuf* unfold like the body of an inspired dancer."[20] Van Vechten's picture postcard sets up a similarly transformative, "architectural" relationship between the dancer's body and his ornaments.

Van Vechten may not have heard of Benjamin, although he was absorbed in the general euphoria about the German camera and visited Munich in 1935–1936 to update his Leica to the one we see in Romaine Brooks's portrait. Andrés

Mario Zervigón argues that Benjamin's insights on the revelatory possibilities of photography were a "commonplace" in Weimar-era Germany.[21] When Miguel Covarrubias introduced Van Vechten to the Leica and excitedly "explained some of the advantages of this acquisition, a recent German invention," he communicated the new buzz and the promise Leica held not only for photographers but also for people of many other professions including writers.[22] As opposed to the camera of "the horse and buggy days," the Leica was born with the pulse of the time: "In 1925, automobiles were on the verge of a metamorphosis into streamlining, the familiar granite ware of our kitchens turned into an array of colors, women smoked on the streets, modern architecture was being championed by Frank Lloyd Wright, Le Corbusier, Richard J. Neutra, and others, and a few startling photographs taken at unusual angles appeared in advertisements, the movies were beginning to talk, Eisenstein's *Potemkin* and other Russian pictures startled movie fans. . . . Into this teeming world of change there was introduced a small insignificant camera."[23] The change in lifestyle, attitudes, and taste from Victorian America and fin de siècle Paris to a "streamlined" and technologically produced modernist sensibility marked by architecture, film, theater, advertisement photography, and other designed commodities can be traced to *The International Exhibition of Modern Decorative and Industrial Arts* in Paris in 1925, where experiments of Russian Constructivists such as Alexander Rodchenko and the Bauhaus photographer Moholy Nagy were first showcased. And even as their pathbreaking experiments were persecuted in Germany and in Soviet Russia by the 1930s, they gave a recognizably modern look to industrial design and advertising elsewhere in Europe and the United States, one that colloquially came to be known as Art Deco after the Paris exhibition. Art Deco was the visual aesthetic of the Jazz Age, becoming "a cosmopolitan style, travelling the world while marking aspects of the everyday built environment closer to home," from urban skyscrapers to interior design of apartments and ocean liners that Van Vechten and others took to Europe and to Hollywood film.[24]

Van Vechten's photography, then, relates broadly to the visual culture of Art Deco and not directly to avant-garde experiments of the Bauhaus and their Constructivist antecedents in the newly formed Soviet Russia. Their utopian political dreams never made it to him. Van Vechten was simply enchanted by the Leica and its possibilities. He was an amateur at the margins of the avant-garde taking up photography when Bauhaus was already "diluted" into art and commercial photography. According to Abigail Solomon-Godeau, Bauhaus and Constructivist ideas were put to "different discursive functions: seriality, unusual close-ups, and graphic presentation of the object were . . . promptly assimilated to advertising photography; defamiliarizing tactics such as unconventional viewpoints and the flattening and abstracting of pictorial space all became part of a stylistic lexicon available to commercial photographers, art photographers, designers, and photojournalists—a lexicon, it should be added, that had assimilated surrealist elements as well." For Solomon-Godeau, "formalism had become a stylistic notion rather than an instrumental one, an archive of picture-making strategies that intersected with a widely dispersed, heroized concept of camera vision."[25]

Van Vechten knew many photographers from this dispersed world of "formalism" and photographed them in his studio. Many worked for lifestyle, sport, and fashion magazines, including *Vanity Fair*, to which he contributed essays in the 1920s. He liberally absorbed and reproduced the modernist look of their photography. Like them, he built witty surprises and internal jokes into his highly dramatized self-portraits, street scenes, and images of celebrities and friends. But he fits uneasily within the canons of "art" or fashion photography. His prolific, but atypical practice provides a vivid example of amateur photography belonging to what I call the "Leica Moment."

Neither Benjamin nor Krauss mentioned the particular role of the Leica in revealing the "optical unconscious" of photography.[26] It is possible that, by the 1930s, the Leica simply became the technological unconscious (to paraphrase Benjamin a little) in the thinking and theorizing about photography. For Benjamin, Blossfeldt's enlargements of plants are a quintessential example of what he calls "New Photography," which in 1928 can only mean the photography of the Leica Moment, when the German camera brought into focus the visual preoccupations of the time among practitioners involved in a transatlantic world of photography.

When Van Vechten picked up the Leica, he picked up a visual aesthetic broadly associated with the German camera. His immediate sources were lifestyle magazines such as *Vogue*, *Vanity Fair*, and *House and Garden*, all published by Condé Nast, which had offices in Berlin, Paris, and New York. Most of the artists Van Vechten knew and photographed in his studio were represented in Condé Nast magazines.[27] He absorbed their styles and participated with many at the *Second International Leica Exhibit* held in the mezzanine gallery of Radio City in November–December 1935.[28] Many photographers worked with the Leica, and many did not; but their modernist visual ideas came into Van Vechten's camera. Like the American Richard Avedon, he produced a luminescent silhouette of his models. Like George Hoyningen-Heune, the Russian-born photographer who worked for the French *Vogue*, he carefully aimed his lighting to sharpen a particular detail, be it a model's bejeweled wrist or the flutings of a long chiffon dress. Like the British dandy Cecil Beaton, he attended to a decorative outline in his models, borrowing partly from Henri Matisse.[29]

As in New Vision and other modernist experiments, Van Vechten placed human figures within an overall geometry of the visual composition based on a cubist breakdown of the visual plane. In one such early experiment, he photographed himself in an extreme top-angle view that made his silken hair and cranium float against a geometric grid composed of light, diagonal lines, and darkened, flag-shaped triangles (fig. 4.5). The flattened image disorients us. We are unable to tell whether the pictorial grid represents a hanging curtain behind the head or the studio floor. We see Gopal standing on the same stiff fabric for

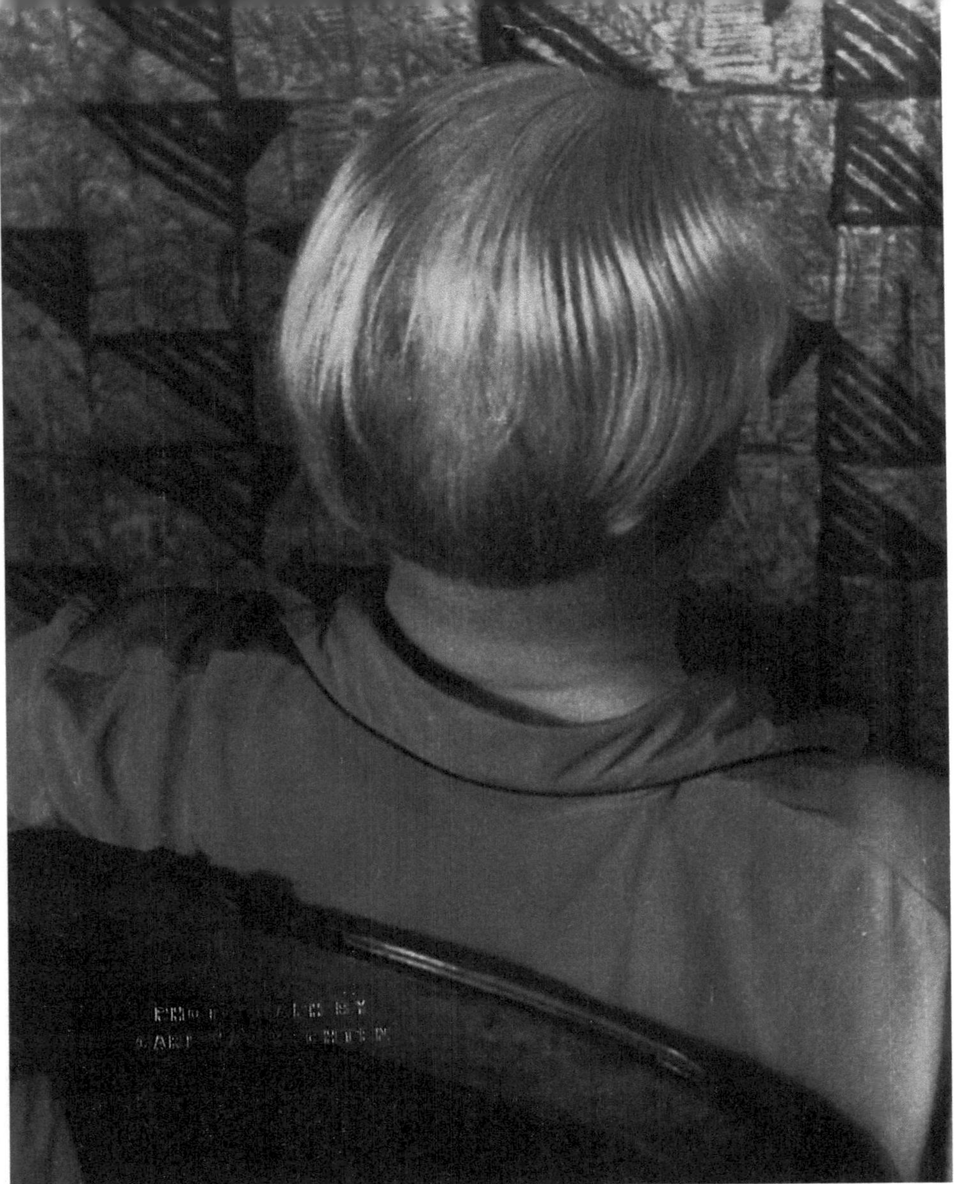

Figure 4.5. Carl Van Vechten, *Carl Van Vechten, Back of Head*, October 4, 1933. Ve:1. (Beinecke Rare Book and Manuscript Library, Yale University; © The Van Vechten Trust)

his Kathakali and Kathak poses (figs. 1.24 and 2.8). The departures from a legible figure-ground relationship, which was a norm in the "horse and buggy days" when photography imitated painting, reflects Constructivist experiments. The extreme downward tilt of the camera not only frees the sitter from the laws of gravity but also declares "the camera's own freedom from gravity," which Rosalind Krauss broadly associates with New Vision photography.[30]

The photographer's presence in an image also responds to a key formal trope of New Vision, namely, self-reflexivity. In one image, Van Vechten includes his shadow in the act of taking a photograph of a furrow made by a bulldozer (fig.

4.6). For Krauss, this is a trope in which the photographer inserts "an image of the photographic instrument into the space of the picture." The deliberate reference to the camera in the act of taking a picture brings to the photographic image an awareness of its own technological construction. Van Vechten's image literalizes Krauss's claim. It makes the photographer's spectral presence a "visual testimony to a technological apparatus that has usurped nature."[31] But far from New Vision's critical reflection on this technological manipulation of the world, the shadow of the photographer also becomes a visual pun for the heavy industrial machinery that has equally left its trace in the image in the form of a deep groove on wet earth.

In his studio, Van Vechten skewed the New Vision toward what seem to be "regressive" uses, closer to Victorian Gothic literature and spirit photography.[32] In a self-portrait, he animates his shadow as a separate creature in the background (fig. 4.7). Although the image was taken by Mark Lutz, Van Vechten burned and deepened the shadow in the darkroom to make it into a distinctly enlarged double of his head on the background curtain. The shadowy profile

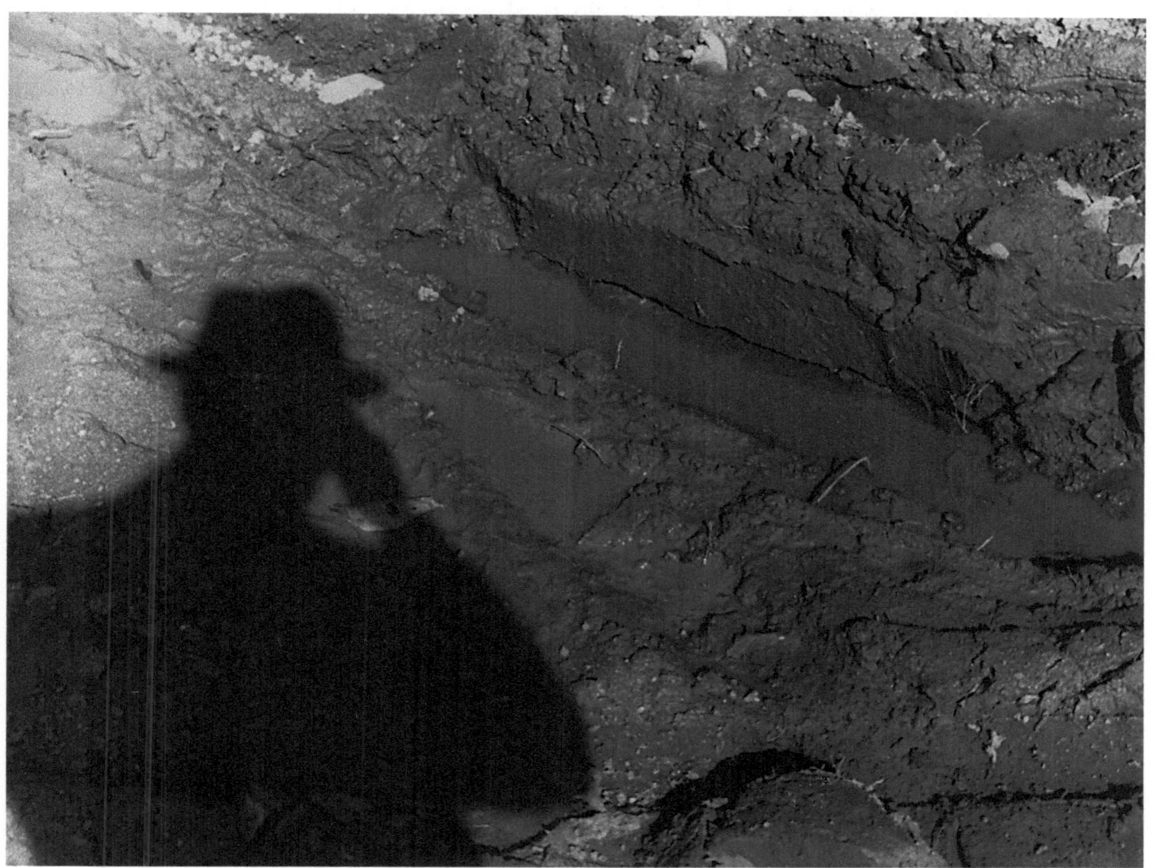

Figure 4.6. Carl Van Vechten, *Carl Van Vechten's Shadow at National Zoological Park, Washington, D.C.*, March 29, 1936, XI: 28. (Beinecke Rare Book and Manuscript Library, Yale University; © The Van Vechten Trust)

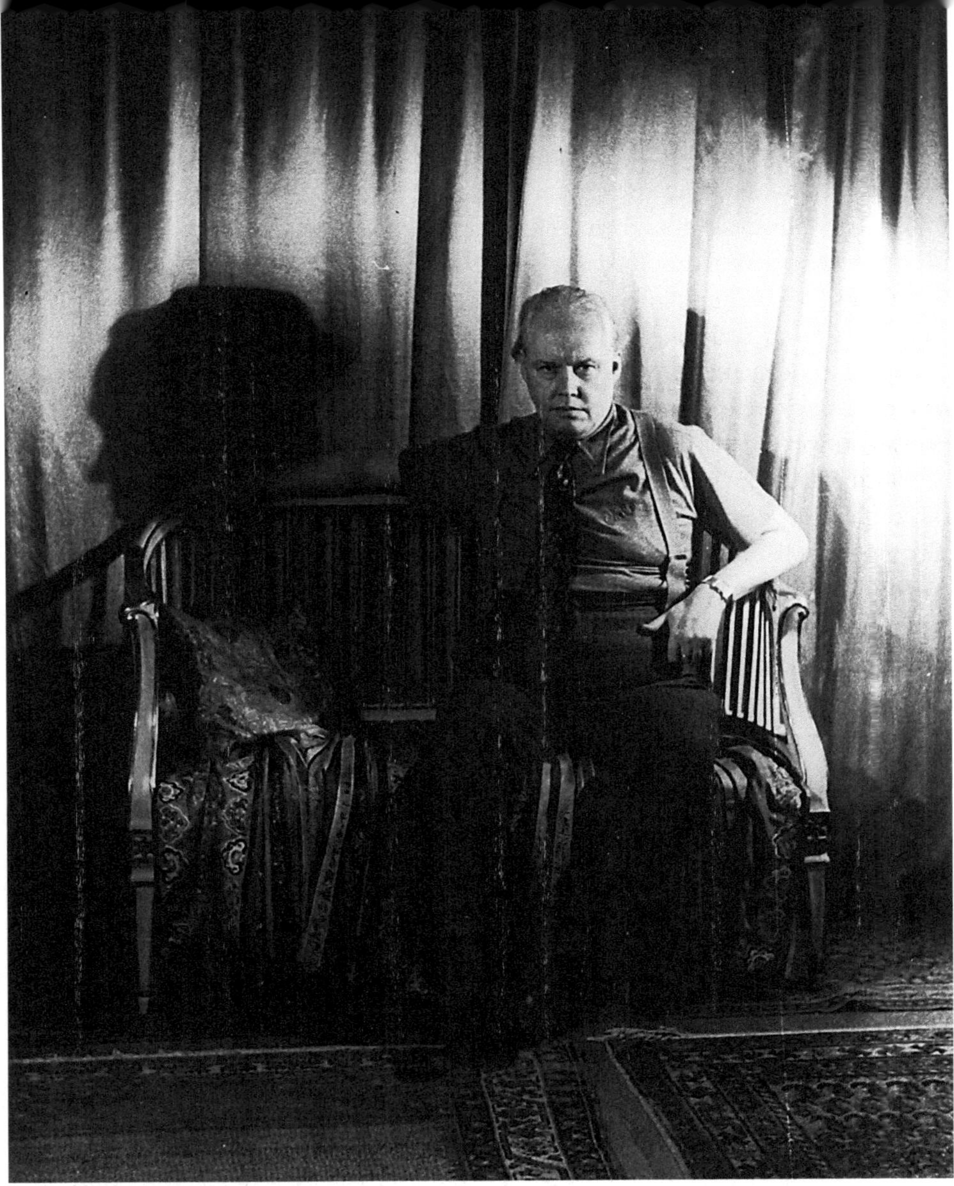

Figure 4.7. Mark Lutz, *Carl Van Vechten*, November 27, 1938, XVII N:O. (Beinecke Rare Book and Manuscript Library, Yale University; © The Van Vechten Trust)

hovers in midair over the sofa. The trick of two light sources hitting the folds of the curtain sideways stretches the profile, flattening the crown to make it appear like a hat worn by an anamorphic ghost snaking out of the sitter's body and floating away into space.

Van Vechten articulates his own view of shadows in his novel *The Blind Bow-Boy* (1923). The fictional character Campaspe Lorillard looks at her face in a mirror on her dressing table and remembers "how some one had said of her that he [the person] was like a pleasant pool . . . exposing a dormant silvery surface . . . or rippling placidly . . . with shadows, which portend hidden depths."[7] Van

Vechten writes, "No one, she reflected, save herself, knew how deep the pool was, or what might lie concealed at the bottom. . . . Shadows! There must be a philosophy of shadows! Shadows were the only realities. And there were always shadows, but most people overlooked the shadow in their search for the object which cast it."[33]

To my ears, Campaspe's reflections are literally photographic, as if the deep shadows are embedded in the "dormant silvery surface" of a black-and-white chemical image. Kirsten MacLeod explains that Campaspe's idea of shadows as "the only realities" sits against Plato's "The Allegory of the Cave" in *The Republic* and is closer to Celtic mysticism. Van Vechten mentions an author with the pseudonym A.E., whom MacLeod identifies as the Irish writer George William Russel (1867–1935), for whom "shadows function as a metaphor for the spirit."[34] Once cast by the body, the shadows become independent, uncanny, living presences, just as in Van Vechten's self-portrait.

Vechten thus engages with modernist photography, but as if he is flirting with it from the margins. His Leica skews the mastery of visionary photographers toward an enchanted gaze of an amateur. The tone of his images comes closer to the style and spirit of the commercial magazines to which many photographers contributed. Let us look at *Vanity Fair*, for instance, in which Van Vechten published articles in the 1920s. Between the two world wars, the magazine gained a reputation for establishing the standards for elegance and style in cosmopolitan living. Cleveland Amory and Frederic Bradlee explain that the secret of its popularity and success was that it was slightly behind its time "in the sense that she carried forward, into a faster and crasser age, the stately white-tie-and-tailed elegance of a fast by-going Edwardian era."[35] The magazine was transformed in 1928, when the Russian-born Turkish designer and art director Mehemed Fehmy Agha revolutionized all Condé Nast magazines, starting his career at the *Vogue* office in Berlin and soon arriving in New York to replace *Vanity Fair*'s "Edwardian" elegance with a modernist look.[36] The magazine recruited professional photographers from the field of advertising and fashion photography and especially lionized Edward Steichen, whose celebrity images contributed hugely to the slick, glamorous look of the magazine.

Steichen became one of Van Vechten's heroes. In a long poem for Van Vechten's sixty-eighth birthday on June 17, 1948, his wife, Fania Marinoff, wrote,

> *From the depths of your darkroom where you toil hours and hours,*
> *Your hands in strange liquids, with mysterious powers,*
> *With the lens of your Leica you create and give birth*
> *To beauty a Stieglitz or Steichen would deem of great worth.*[37]

The poem imagines Van Vechten as a sorcerer absorbed in the "mysterious powers" of Leica photography. We will elaborate on Leica's capacity to "give birth" later on. In comparing Van Vechten's work to Alfred Stieglitz and Edward

Steichen, Marinoff strokes the amateur's creative ambitions. The "art" photography of these Pictorialists clearly set the standard for Van Vechten. Let us consider Steichen's image of the Chinese American Hollywood star Anna May Wong, one of the first celebrity models whom Van Vechten also photographed, to explore Van Vechten's response to his hero (fig. 4.8). Appearing in the January 1931 issue of *Vanity Fair*, Steichen's photograph, titled *Orientale*, juxtaposes the softly lit, round face of the star and a bulbous chrysanthemum. The geometrical clarity of the image arrests us, not the dislocation of these disembodied shapes. The glossy surface of the photograph merges with the glassy depth of the indistinct table in which the reflection of these round forms is carefully distinguished by the background light. According to John Raeburn, Steichen lends stardom to his celebrities by making them glow within forms of "cultural conventionality." In many images of Anna May Wong, Steichen "highlighted her exoticism," sometimes placing her in a chiffon dress next to chrysanthemums and in this case comparing the star's head to the dazzle of the "Oriental" flower. "The flower's luminousness emphasizes her tawniness and straight black hair, thus serving as a double reminder of her race." The image also acquires "a plangent mysteriousness—even inscrutability"—appropriate for the "yellow woman" of Hollywood.[38] In the abstract qualities of the juxtaposition, Keith Davis is reminded of a Brancusi sculpture.[39]

Van Vechten is keenly aware of Steichen's celebrity images. In his novel *Spider Boy*

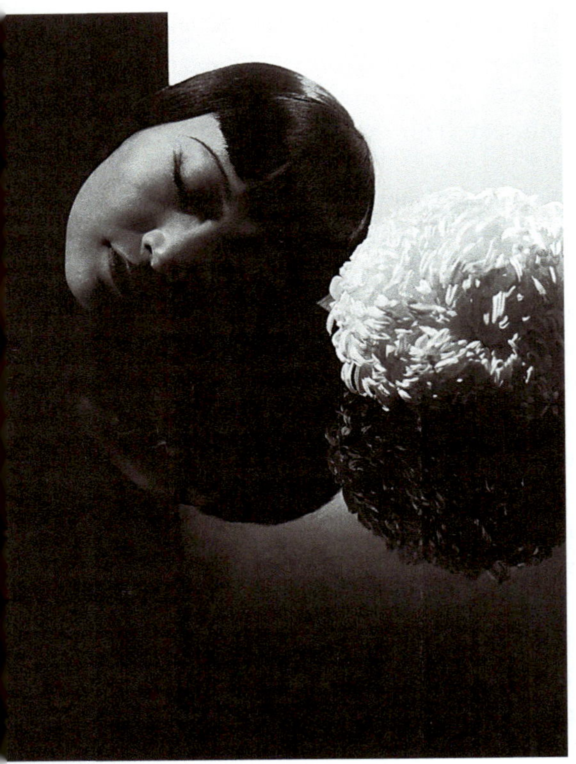

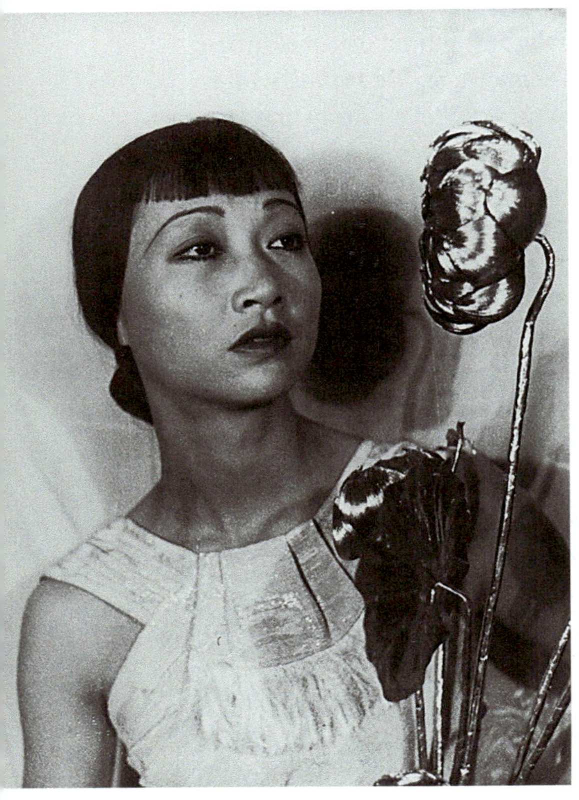

Figures 4.8 and 4.9. *Top*, Edward Steichen, *Orientale* (actress Anna May Wong), *Vanity Fair*, January 1931, 26. (© Condé Nast) *Bottom*, Carl Van Vechten, *Anna May Wong*, September 22, 1935, XIII i:28. (Beinecke Rare Book and Manuscript Library, Yale University; © The Van Vechten Trust)

(1928), he even defines a celebrity as one who sits for a portrait by Steichen.[40] As a Steichen knock-off, Van Vechten photographs Anna May Wong with chrysanthemums in 1935 (fig. 4.9). The image could never be published in *Vanity Fair*. According to Davis, Van Vechten's portrait falls short of the "transcendence" of Steichen.[41] According to John Raeburn, Van Vechten's photos are only envious imitations of Steichen. Raeburn compares the two in terms of "the technical superiority" of the professional versus the crudity of the amateur: "Unlike Steichen [Van Vechten] did not use a view camera, nor did he have the impressive battery of lights and other technical supports that a professional's studio would. He preferred the Leica for its ease of use, and the small camera also allowed greater spontaneity although its negatives permitted less clarity and detail than a view camera's."[42]

Van Vechten is clearly engaged with Steichen's imagery, but I want to ask a different question: What did he see in the master photographer? Or, more specifically, what did he "study" in Steichen when he "enlarged" it within his own image practice. Raeburn gives us an indirect and partial hint: "Steichen's commercial work appalled Stieglitz as a betrayal of the artistic standards they had collaborated in erecting." Critics of the time similarly found Steichen's image of Anna May Wong "artificial, posed, unnaturally lighted, and unwilling to let the main subject stand alone without tricky backgrounds, shadows, etc."[43] The criticism of artificiality might as well be applied to Van Vechten's photograph, and even more so. Aura is replaced by artifice: the glamour of stardom is reduced to the glitter of plastic flowers. Van Vechten seems to make a statement out of this artificiality by magnifying it. The image is a visual equivalent to his article "Pastiches et Pistaches," discussed in chapter 3, in which he favored the flamboyance of artifice over the pretensions that hide it. By parodying Steichen, Van Vechten not only strips away the gloss but also humanizes the star, showing her not as a head floating in midair but as a figure posing in a fashionable evening dress in the staged environment of his studio.

"Parody," however, is a strong word. Van Vechten's is an edgy citation but not a critique. Here is an amateur's affectionate visual reference to the master's work, and he tries it on as if it were a new suit. In an image, Van Vechten portrays himself with real, Steichen-like chrysanthemums (fig. 4.10). When he first arrived in New York, Van Vechten was drawn to Stieglitz' and Steichen's collaborative Gallery 291 in Greenwich Village. There he was exposed to Pictorialist photography, along with the transatlantic traffic of European artists and American writers, artists, and intellectuals whom he mentions in his novel *Peter Whiffle*. Just as Whiffle blends and hides in the modernist art scene of New York and Paris using a chameleon's tactics of camouflage, Van Vechten's self-portrait with chrysanthemums suggests one late-blooming photographer hiding in the allure of another.

In 1935, Van Vechten participated in the second Leica exhibition at Radio City along with Edward Steichen, Cecil Beaton, Man Ray, and George Platt

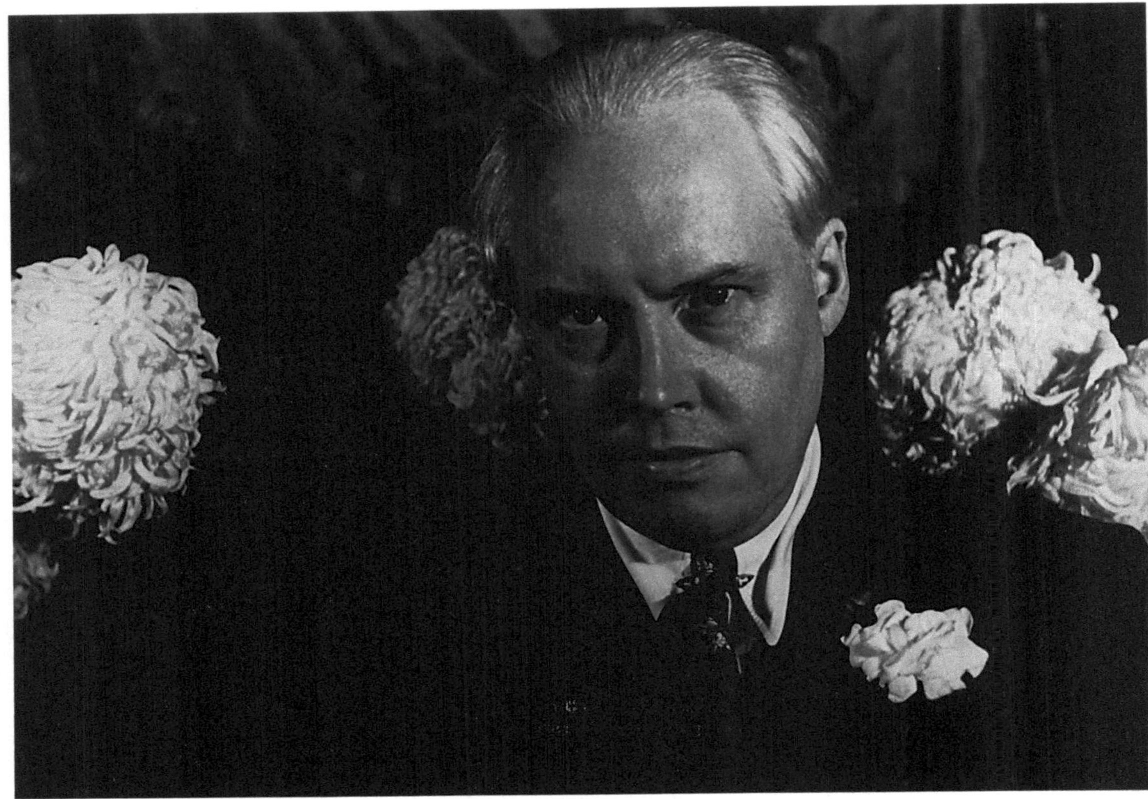

Figure 4.10. Carl Van Vechten, *Carl Van Vechten*, October 21, 1934, XI g:8. (Beinecke Rare Book and Manuscript Library, Yale University; © The Van Vechten Trust)

Lynes. Bruce Kellner writes, "Carl Van Vechten was in excellent company, and moreover, his experiments were widely heralded." In a review for the *New York Sun*, Henry McBride called Van Vechten "the Bronzino of this camera period. He works in the large and with a boldness of design . . . that makes his work carry emphatically."[44] The reference to the Italian sixteenth-century Mannerist artist is appropriate. It suggests that, in the 1930s, Van Vechten was a latecomer to this game of professionals. McBride's comment also catches the exuberant stylization of his posed models as well as a dandy's effeminacy in some of his male figures, for which Bronzino was also known. But while other photographers from the fashion industry were equally known for their posed subjects, McBride makes one more, subtle distinction. While their stylized subjects disappear into an overall glamour of the celebrity, as in Steichen's Anna May Wong, Van Vechten's "boldness of design" emphasizes the artificiality of pose.

A late bloomer and a witness to the art and celebrity scene in New York and Paris, Van Vechten would have understood not to take modernist art photography's claim to masterpieces at face value but as a consensus among professional artists whose avant-garde experiments were used to glamorize theater, film, high fashion, sports, and lifestyle magazines. In other words, masterworks printed in magazines may not be regarded literally as the original expression of artistic geniuses appearing from nowhere but rather as images selected by editors and distributors of a commercial magazine and protected by copyright laws. Seeing beyond originality, thus, Van Vechten would have recognized a mirroring between Steichen's *Orientale* in 1931 and Man Ray's photograph *Noire et Blanche* (1926), published a few years earlier to become a sensation among the consumers of a Parisian fashion magazine (fig. 4.11). How does Van Vechten absorb these internal conversations of modernism in his work?

Whitney Chadwick identifies in Man Ray's 1926 image the sexual economy of European modernist imagination, arguing that the disembodied head of a woman juxtaposed against an African mask simultaneously exoticizes female sexuality and eroticizes race.[45] Man Ray's visual framing informs Steichen's image of Wong's disembodied head against the giant chrysanthemum. In both images, the identity of the female models is fixed within the cultural stereotype

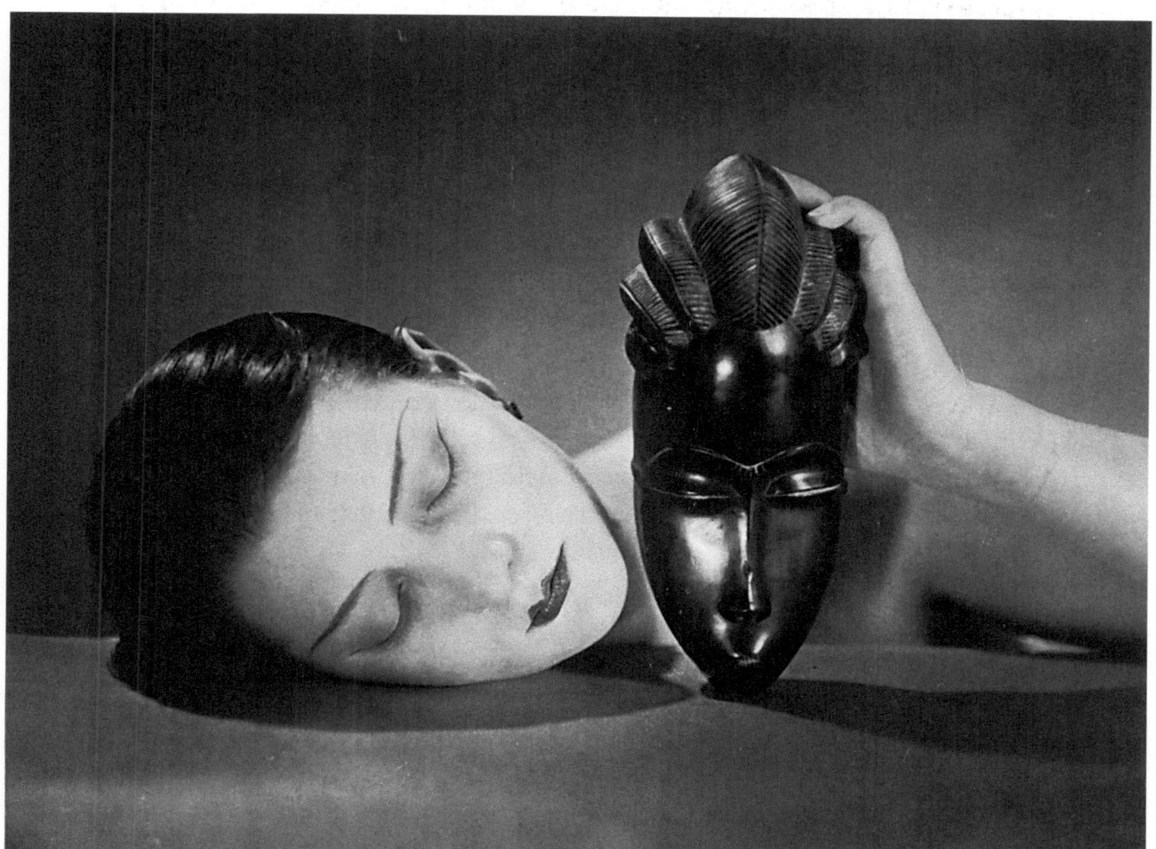

Figure 4.11. Man Ray (1890–1976), *Noire et Blanche* (Black and White), 1926, gelatin silver print, 6 3/4 × 8 7/8. (Gift of James Thrall Soby; digital image © The Museum of Modern Art/Licensed by SCALA/Art Resource, NY; © Man Ray 2015 Trust/Artists Rights Society (ARS) / ADAGP, Paris 2021)

informed, respectively, by Primitivism (a white man's fascination with Black people) and Orientalism (a Euro-American fascination with the exotic cultures of the East). Van Vechten's photographs clearly derive from the visual economies of modernism, but with a significant difference. They pull at the heterosexual fantasy of racialized bodies on which Primitivism and Orientalism are based. Instead, Van Vechten created a space for picture-making within the intimacy of his studio, complete with props and backdrops, where men and women, Black and white, stepped in front of his camera to perform a fantasy of mirrored identities with scandalously overt racial and sexual overtones. Thus, Bessie Smith's photographs with sculptural busts destabilize Man Ray's Primitivism through what we called the mode of "minstrelsy" in chapter 3 (fig. 3.14). Also, in his self-portrait, while Van Vechten surrounds himself with Wong-like chrysanthemums, he wears white pansies as a boutonniere, suggesting his affiliation with the "Pansy Craze" of 1930s New York and thus his queerness within the heterosexual economies of professional male artists.[46]

Unlike the professional photographers Van Vechten knew, he wore his modernism lightly. He may have admired the celebrity photographs of Steichen in *Vanity Fair*, but the tone of his images is closer to the edgy writing and caricatures in that magazine. In the mission statement of the magazine when it was launched in March 1914, the editor in chief, Frank Crowninshield, explained, "Vanity Fair has but two major articles in its editorial creed: first, to believe in the progress and promise of American life, and, second, to chronicle that progress cheerfully, truthfully, and entertainingly. . . . It will print humor, it will look at the stage, at the arts, at the world of letters, at sport, and at the highly vitalized, electric, and diversified life of our day from the frankly cheerful angle of the optimist, or, which is much the same thing, from the mock-cheerful angle of the satirist."[47]

Van Vechten's visual aesthetic developed from the "mock-cheerful" and "electrifying" tone of *Vanity Fair*. He particularly absorbed the look of the magazine's zingy covers, for which it was famous. Liberally using the flair and flourishes of Art Nouveau, late-cubist, and Art Deco styles, the illustrators of the *Vanity Fair* covers captured the tone of the magazine in visual terms and created an appetite for cosmopolitan lifestyles for its consumers right at the newsstands. The compositions mostly portray dance and music halls, bars, and theaters, caught in beams of spotlight. Cavernous interiors draw attention to a stage viewed from a dizzyingly high-angle perspective. Synchronized limbs of dancers onstage, as in a Busby Berkeley number, compete with pages from a musical score, as in a late-cubist collage. In one cover from 1928, by Eduardo Garcia Benito, a stylishly dressed couple is not simply seen on a rooftop terrace against skyscrapers but also caught by the shafts of city lights hitting them from the bottom of the page (fig. 4.12). In a similarly high-angle view, Van Vechten photographs himself against the chiaroscuro panels of shadows that fragment his face and disorient our sense of the figure (fig. 4.13).

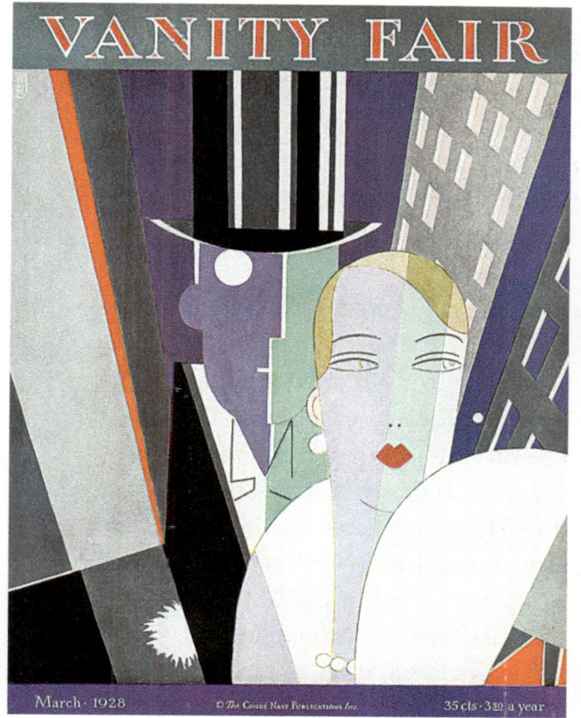

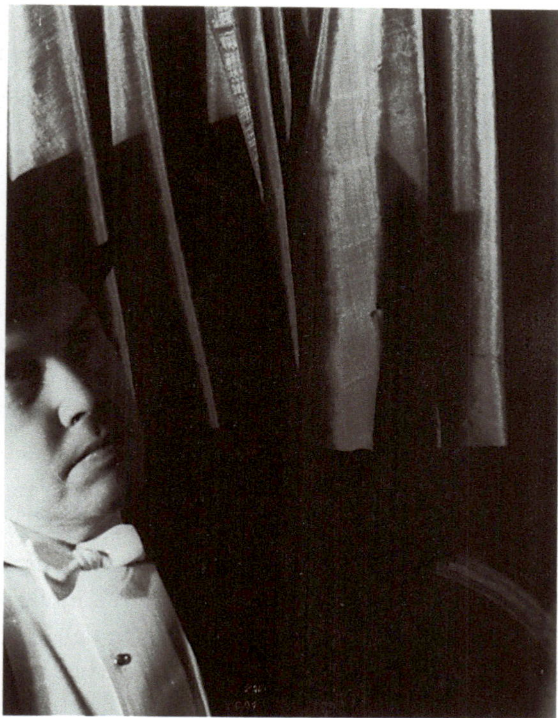

Figures 4.12 and 4.13. *Left*, Magazine cover featuring illustration by Eduardo Garcia Benito, *Vanity Fair*, March 1, 1928. (© Condé Nast). *Right*, Carl Van Vechten, *Carl Van Vechten*, November 13, 1933, XVIII e16. (Beinecke Rare Book and Manuscript Library, Yale University; © The Van Vechten Trust)

Queering the Eye

The Leica's precision lens allowed extreme close-ups that could be both disorienting and revelatory to practitioners. A dentist could focus on teeth patterns, and an entomologist could study insects. Enlargements also showed "more" details than the contact prints, and the temptation to make enlargements increased exponentially among Leica users, making contact prints a means to an end, instead of the final image. Van Vechten claimed that his photographs were "intended primarily as documents," and we should take this seriously to mean that his images are studies of his subjects.[48] Close-ups of Gopal's feet and hand gestures indicate Van Vechten's study of the technicalities of dance.

In making such study images, however, it is not true that Van Vechten did not "approve of cropping, even by [himself]." Comparing his enlarged prints of Gopal with the negative strip suggests that he regularly cropped the images to tighten the frame around the dancer, leaving out, but barely, the light stand and the cables snaking on the wood floor of his apartment and often visible in the negatives. The tight frame intensified attention. Even if Van Vechten created a straight "document," at the very least he looked for moments when the figure and the background came together for him in a surprising way. He also burned parts of his image to develop ideas in the darkroom that may have started in the studio. In a photograph from 1940, he made the ballet dancer Hugh Laing make a Buddha-like hand gesture, sitting cross-legged on a stool. He then burned the area of the stool in such a way that it disappeared in the dark and made Laing appear to be levitating against a batik background.[49] We will explore Van Vechten's more radical darkroom experiments with the Indian dancer shortly, but we will also insist on regarding his work with the Leica as "study" rather than simply as a flight of fancy.

Van Vechten's self-portrait with the magnifying glass captures the spirit of study, only departing from Wolff's self-image as an investigator in one significant way (figs. 4.1 and 4.2). While Van Vechten may have lifted the magnifying glass to examine a negative also, we do not see the sharp-edged strip that Wolff holds up to study. Instead, an extreme close-up shifts the view from the object of the photographer's attention to the photographer himself. It is as if the object of the photographer's study looks back at him. Thus, instead of making his scrutinizing eye and creativity the subject of Leica photography, Van Vechten captures the photographer being seized by the Leica's gaze. Van Vechten's stare communicates rapture. Like a deer caught in headlights, the enthralled photographer is arrested by the object of his attention. For Van Vechten, then, to possess a Leica meant being possessed by it. Recalling his overall experience as a photographer in 1962, Van Vechten writes of his photography with the German camera as a love affair, "an addiction (even an affliction) or an enchantment."[50] Here, then, is the awestruck photographer we met in chapter 3, captivated by the prosthetic and transformed by it.

If Wolff's close observation of the negative promises to show details hidden in the tonal depths of an image, the nearly flat image of Van Vechten constructs the view of the mechanical apparatus as if it were independent of the photographer. The apparatus does not pick and prioritize visual details for the benefit of the human, stereoscopic eyes. Instead, it captures everything in its purview, indiscriminately, resulting in a flat image with details hovering on the luminous surface of the photograph. Lit from both the left and the right, Van Vechten's large forehead and white hair dissolve into the white paper. The human face becomes dismembered and redistributed along a geometric grid, formed by the vertical handle of the magnifying glass in the foreground and an arrangement of short vertical and horizontal bands that briefly invoke strips of negative behind the head. The camera also distorts the human face, making it anamorphic. As if in a wobbly mirror, one eye is caught in the circular frame and magnified, turning the photographer into a bug-eyed creature, as it were, when placed under the scrutiny of an equally one-eyed camera.

How do we describe this "queering" of the scrutinizing gaze of the human investigator in Van Vechten's photography? What kind of prosthetic apparatus is the Leica? Laura Wexler suggests a relationship of the human eye to the prosthetic eye using Walter Benjamin and inflecting it in an important way:

"Look at the world through naked eyes; it appears one way. But interpose a small mechanical one-eyed box that hoards memories of the sight within its belly and something gives way. Things look different through a camera. The camera sets in motion a great parallax that can be attributed to the disjunction between the eye and the lens."[51] Wexler's delicious mixture of metaphors for the camera—a "one-eyed box" that also contains images in its "belly"—is a "parallax" I want to explore further.

In the mid-1980s, Wexler's essay was written to feminize the language of photography. Against the camera as a manly, gun-like mechanical instrument used for pointing, shooting, and capturing its subjects, Wexler's image revolves around the metaphors of an organism whose fecundity gives new meanings to Benjamin's insights and worries about "the camera's steely capacity for ingestion and reproduction."[52] The feminine metaphor of a birth-giving organism also appears in Marinoff's poem at Van Vechten's birthday, quoted earlier, except that, in the poem, that fecund organism is the photographer, whereas in Wexler, it is the camera.

There is one important twist in Wexler's feminist project that I find particularly significant. Wexler includes a cartoon by the Dutch cartoonist Tomi Ungerer, titled *Studio Robinson* (1981) to represent the feminized organism.[53] It shows a crocodile whose long snout is shaped like the accordion folds of a Kodak Brownie. In other words, Wexler's fecund, cyclopean "box" is not human. It is a wild creature that consumes the visible world and pulverizes it into small bits that we call photographs. The eye of this camera-animal, in which the distinction between the human photographer and the mechanical prosthesis no longer remains, is what I want to pursue in Van Vechten's image-making.

The Leica's "Feral" Gaze

Van Vechten's image with the magnifying glass represents a relationship between the photographer and his Leica gone "feral." The word is from Pooja Rangan, who uses it to argue against the humanized, "ocular" idea of gaze that usually informs the relationship between visual media and the human eye. According to Rangan, the ocular idea conflates Jacques Lacan's description of gaze with Michel Foucault's study of surveillance in modern prisons and schools. The intent of modern ocular regimes is to discipline and "humanize" the human. By contrast, for Rangan, Lacan's idea also contains a "nonocular" and a more bodily avenue of emergence that is useful to understand the erotics of Van Vechten's photography.[54]

Lacan first came upon his idea of gaze with reference to an experience in his youth, while on a fishing boat in southern France, when he was seized by a feeling that a sardine can, bouncing on the ocean waves, was looking back at him.[55] Gaze, then, is a bodily affect. For Lacan, the sensation of being possessed by a distant, nonhuman object could simply be the result of an unexpected synchrony between his unsteady feet on the floor of the fishing boat and the metal bobbing and glittering on the surface of the water. Like a magpie, then, the psychoanalyst pursues the glitter as if it were a living thing.

The camera's nonhuman gaze holds Van Vechten in its thrall, and he pursues its bodily fantasies in his studio and darkroom experiments with Gopal. The difference between the human and the nonhuman aspects of his fantasy can be best exemplified in Van Vechten's double-exposure prints, in which the negative is exposed twice, one exposure being the inverse of the other, and a single print is made. One such double exposure is of a crouching, nude African American model, which I use as a contrast to Gopal. The double exposure makes the nude model look as if locked in fellatio with his double, which Van Vechten calls "69" elsewhere.[56]

In this and other images of African American men, scholars have identified Van Vechten's explicitly interracial, homoerotic desires.[57] In Rangan's words, such images only represent the photographer's "humanizing" gaze. The double exposure of the African American model skews the technological image toward his human and personal fantasies. Van Vechten does not take this humanizing turn with Gopal. By way of contrast, then, let us consider Van Vechten's double-exposed print of the Indian dancer (fig. 4.14). As in the case of "69," Van Vechten exposes the negative of the dancer once and then rotates the printing paper to expose the same figure once again before developing the final print. But here, the homoerotic suggestion recedes or, more precisely, reorients the double exposure toward an autoerotic creature that interacts with the material surface of the photograph.

The original image on which Gopal's double exposure is based is now in the New York Public Library for the Performing Arts at the Lincoln Center (fig. 4.15). Van Vechten's choice of this image instead of a few other poses from the same moment on the first day of the photo shoot is useful for our discussion. The dancer skips on his toes, bending his legs at the knees and pulling the heels together (a movement called *kuditamitta adava*), and assumes the *ardhamandala* stance from Bharatanatyam. But the hands are broadly outstretched as in Kathakali. Arms fold out to the sides. His right palm takes on a *mayurakhyam* (peacock) gesture, the left *mudrakhyam* (doe-eye). The two combine to convey in his outstretched body the dance of a peacock.

In the image, the body swells up into light. The dancer's head aligns vertically with the towering crown and the sash hanging from his lower garment. The dancer's eyes are locked with the camera's lens. The figure is back-lit and the lighting sources are tilted slightly upward to set off Gopal's face and limbs in a clear, contrasting pattern of light and shade against the cascading folds of a plain fabric curtain, while the bottom half is submerged in a pool of darkness. The thighs slant forward, briefly catching light (like the glint of the metal can in Lacan's anecdote). The heels disappear into the dark pool, making the figure strangely hover like a five-point star pinned to the curtain. Van Vechten

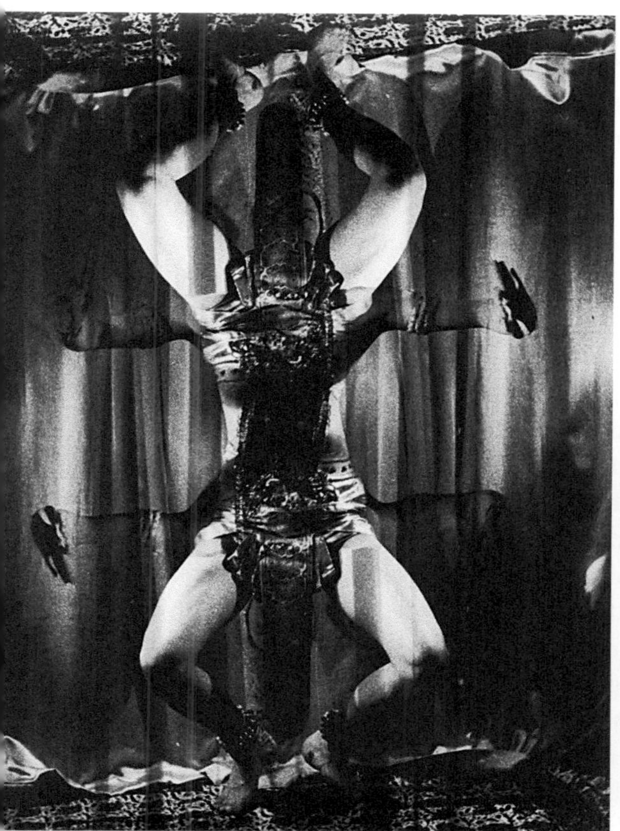
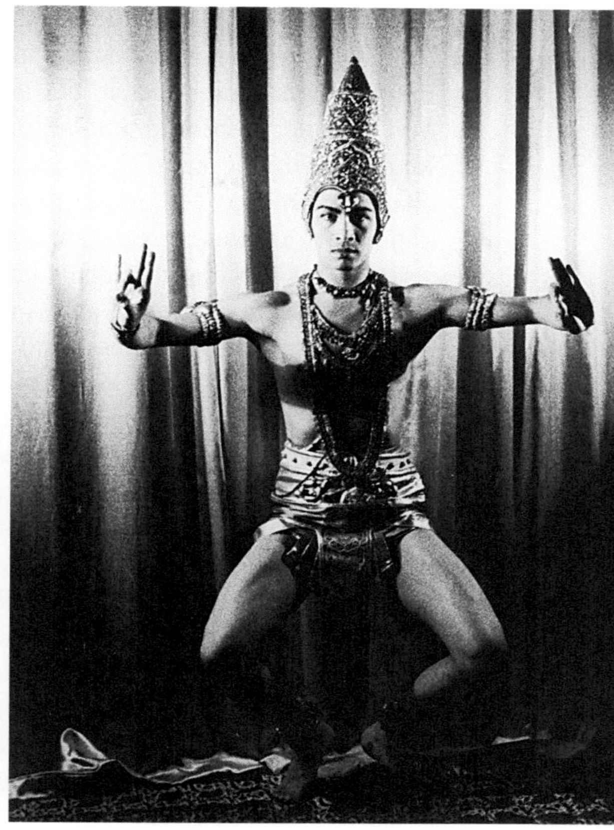

Figures 4.14 and 4.15. *Left*, Carl Van Vechten, double-exposure print from April 21, 1938, XI M25. (Beinecke Rare Book and Manuscript Library, Yale University; © The Van Vechten Trust). *Right*, Carl Van Vechten, *Ram Gopal*, April 21, 1938. (Jerome Robbins Dance Division, New York Public Library for the Performing Arts)

pursues this overall geometrical reconfiguration of the dancer in the double-exposed print.

The print does not pursue a homoerotic imagery, at least not explicitly. Instead of men performing fellatio, the double exposure redistributes the dancer's body along the visual geometry of the composition and the tonal saturation of the chemical print. At most, the tall Javanese crown becomes a dark, phallic form between the dancer's bent thighs in the double exposure, but only abstractly. Van Vechten produces in essence a dizzying arabesque of Gopal's peacock dance. The outstretched arms divide the visual composition into three horizontal registers in which partly legible graphic shapes are arranged. The dancer's brightly lit palms become black ciphers in space, as if a positive print has been turned back to its negative state in a tonal reversal. The heavy background curtain turns into a thin veil pulled over the image. Limbs become watery, appearing and disappearing into the residual bands of shadows drawn by the curtain folds over them.

While the translucent image appeals to touch, it only makes the chemical process of image-making visible, instead of Van Vechten's homoerotic pursuits. The "mystical paraphernalia," or the material and chemical processes with which Van Vechten wrestles in the darkroom, bring to the surface of the print a new kind of creaturely form. The spidery figure appears viscous and tangible, as the shapes in an x-ray. We may not have a name for this creature. But as shadows gather into a columnar shape in the center and limbs multiply bizarrely, we see its body, as if it were what Benjamin might call "the optical unconscious" of the dancer's body appearing in a dream-image. The dream creature results from a "parallax" between the camera and the human eye, as Wexler explains. It comes to the surface only when Van Vechten skids from his homoerotic fantasies. It captures the moment when the human photographer becomes a camera-animal and when the prosthetic fused with Van Vechten's eye makes his homoerotic fantasies "feral." If human desires lead to homoeroticism, the desires of the camera-animal lead to what I call photo-eroticism. Let me explain.

If Leica enlargements magnify details in a study image, Van Vechten's double-exposure prints of Gopal show details that go beyond his personal and interpersonal desires. Instead of two interpenetrating men out of a single body, Gopal's double exposure produces a single organism of a different order. We could call that "order" glamour. Writing about the glamour photographer George Hurrell's image of the Hollywood star Jean Harlow, Judith Brown explains that, while Harlow may be human, "her appeal is produced not through the depiction of warm humanity so much as through the cold chemical wash of the photographic bath." Brown describes glamour as an "aesthetic" pleasure akin to high modernism's attachment to cold, polished, "impenetrable," surfaces, except that the glamorous image also contains "something that is seductive, powerful, and often simply gorgeous."[58] If Van Vechten's homoerotic desire reaches out to the "warm humanity" of his racialized subjects, his photo-erotic desire looks for a gorgeous, nonhuman object of desire contained in the lure of the visual media itself. In chapter 5, we will pursue in detail one more double exposure and the production of glamour in a collaborative, photo-erotic threesome between the Indian dancer, the American photographer, and the German camera (fig. 5.12).

We do not know how long after Van Vechten's meeting with Gopal he made his double exposures. The ornate, virtually nude figure that appeared before his camera on the first day of the photo shoot seems to have dazzled him in such a way that he pursued it both in the double exposures and in the picture postcard of his "favorite" image. By the third and last day of the photo shoot, following Gopal's performance at the 46th Street Theatre, Van Vechten participated differently in the visual spectacle, enriching and complementing the dancer's body with a choice of different backdrops. He asked the dancer to wrap himself in a Salomé-like veil and took close-up shots of his foot placement to understand the technicalities of Indian dance. In short, by the third day, Van Vechten met the dancer on the familiar grounds of Orientalism.

But if Orientalism is a mode of making distant and unknown objects of desire knowable, as is classically demonstrated by Edward Said, Van Vechten returns to the first day again and again to recapture in the darkroom what may have been an experience of dazzling confusion in the studio. The strange vision, combining unknown postures, costumes, and hand gestures, may have only become increasingly incomprehensible as the dancer became immersed in the more technical details of Bharatanatyam and Kathakali from his dance repertory. In the darkroom, then, Van Vechten takes the knowable, Orientalist body beyond the fantasy of the distant Orient. Instead, he stretches it toward that other limit of incomprehensibility, where the physical form of the human dancer begins to appear not quite human. The incomprehensibility of the living body comes close to what Jacques Derrida calls a "chimera," a creature for which no name exists and that can only be comprehended as a composite.[59]

Looking through the Leica, Van Vechten recognizes this creature as a photographic referent coming into being as what Brown calls the "radiance of form." Brown distinguishes this idea of "glamour," produced through the material organization of an image, from the conventions of professional glamour photography in lifestyle and fashion magazines. It is a photo-erotic yearning of the camera-animal that transports the dancer into what Brown calls "the conditional tense—and particularly the past conditional tense—to which photography most particularly, gives access." Brown draws from literary writers of the early twentieth century, such as Virginia Woolf, whose reflections are not on photography per se but a "grammar . . . of still time . . . shared with photography." In Woolf's novel *Mrs. Dalloway*, the protagonist, Clarissa Dalloway, muses over her past not as what was there, as Roland Barthes has it, but as "what-might-have-been." Van Vechten pursues in Gopal the "luminous effect" of a photographic referent dwelling in "an ecstatic stasis as the image of desire" in the conditional temporality of photography.[60]

The half-portrait of the dancer captures Derrida's chimera (fig. 4.16). Gopal wears a fanciful headgear from his dance of the mythical bird Garuda. The petal-shaped panels, lined with sequins fanning back from a diadem on the forehead, represents the crest of that bird, which is described in Hindu mythology as a vehicle for the god Vishnu. The Garuda dance becomes a favorite part of Gopal's repertory. Later in his career, he designed for it a beak mask and an enormous set of wings attached to his arms. A biographical film made in 1970 by the French filmmaker Claude Lemorisse shows Gopal outdoors, swinging his arms in that costume, which the filmmaker dissolves into a bird flying in the distant sky, literalizing the avian reference.[61] By contrast, in Van Vechten's photograph, the bird is abbreviated to merely the sprightly wing-like leaves of the headgear spreading behind the bejeweled forehead of the dancer.

Van Vechten is clearly not interested in depicting Indian mythology. He frames the humanoid bird as a studio portrait. Gopal looks off to the right, in the direction of the light source that illuminates his youthful body. The soft, even

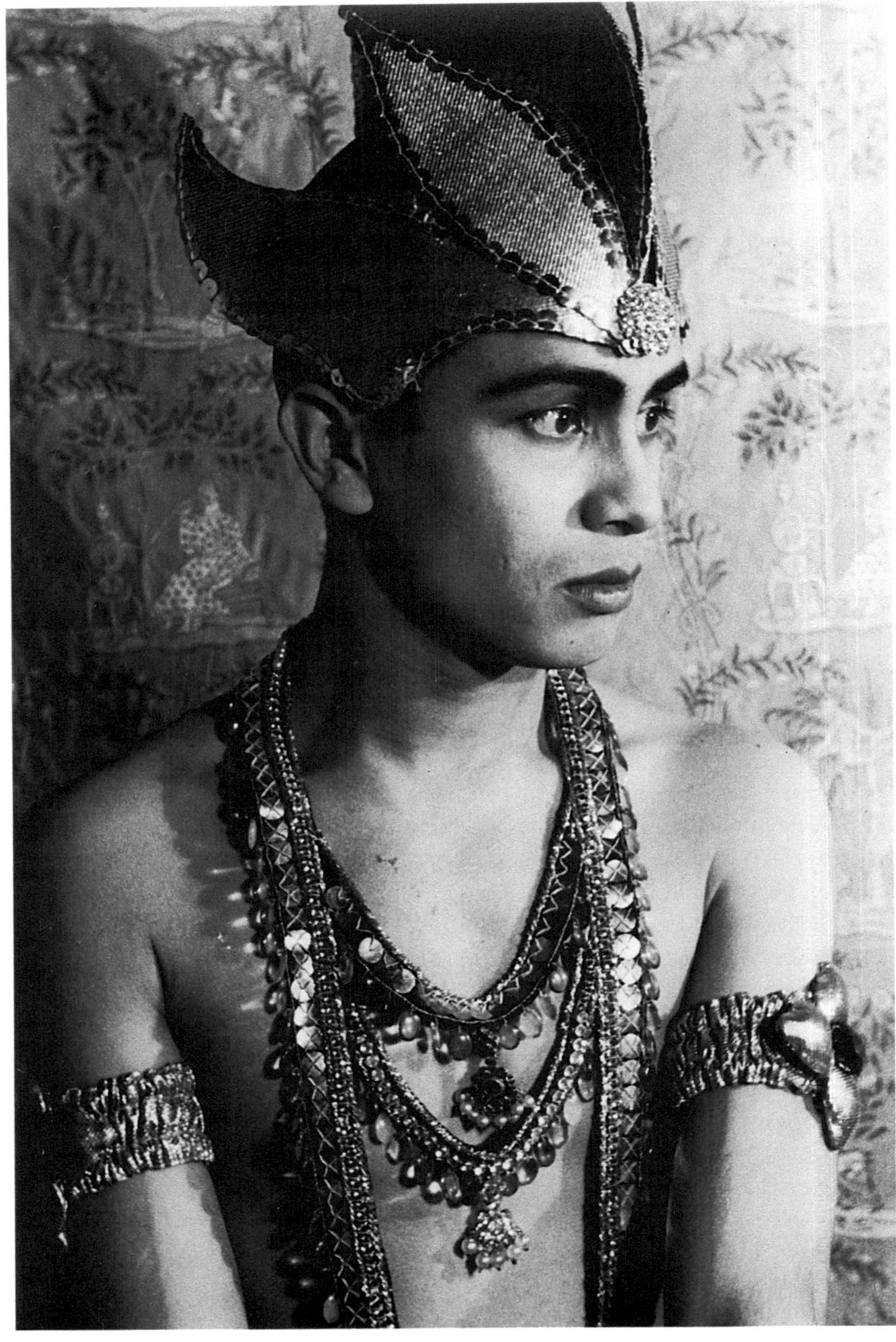

Figure 4.16. Carl Van Vechten, *Ram Gopal*, May 11, 1938, XX M21. (Beinecke Rare Book and Manuscript Library, Yale University; © The Van Vechten Trust)

light brings to focus a set of natural contrasts between the sharp, pointed ends of the crown and the smooth, melting curves of the shoulders and between the crude, grainy weave of the brocade fabric of the crown panels and the soft delicacy of the skin set against the sparkling chain of necklaces. The left shoulder catches not only the watery shadows of the ornament but also the specks of light reflected from the metal. Van Vechten chooses a complementary fabric backdrop. It is the Indian Kantha, or what Pika Ghosh calls *colcha*, whose embroidered design creates gently puckering ripples on the delicate muslin. The dermal quality of the fabric complements the translucent skin of this flesh-metal combination shimmering on the surface of the photograph.

Like Derrida's chimera, the flesh-metal combination gathers in its body a multiplicity of partly recognizable references from Van Vechten's bohemian circuit of modernist writers, painters, and performing artists since his early years in New York. Edward White suggests that, in those years, Van Vechten aspired to bring European modernism in all its forms to the staid culture of New York. During a brief stint as the editor of the magazine *Trend*, in 1914–1916, he made the magazine a place for free expression of transatlantic "fiction writers, politicians and poets who may find themselves face to face with wild beasts."[62] Over the years, as the United States lived through an economic boom after World War I, then the bust and Prohibition of the 1920s, the "beasts" multiplied, including the Fauvists he saw at Stieglitz's Gallery 291 in 1908; the "Marxists, feminists, psychoanalysts" in Mabel Dodge's salons; Gertrude Stein, the American poet in exile in Paris; the New York gay subculture; and the African American music and theater and other encounters in the speakeasies of Harlem. White points out that a major touchstone in Van Vechten's image of modernist rebelliousness was the Ballets Russes' performance of *Le sacre du printemps*, which he saw at the Théâtre des Champs-Élysées in Paris just before the war, whose story of pagan ritual sacrifices was drawn out by Stravinsky's score, "hammering out in complex, brutal rhythms," and "Nijinsky's impudent choreography, its every thrust and twist replete with a violent, primeval carnality." Van Vechten found the performance "wildly beautiful."[63]

Van Vechten would have found the Indian dancer's figure similarly beautiful in its dazzling multiplicity. The human exoskeleton may also have seemed as brilliant and fantastical as a praying mantis of the Surrealists, with whom Van Vechten was familiar (he photographed Man Ray and Salvador Dalí). The Surrealists were drawn to this creature as a kind of dream-image reflected in the natural world of plants and insects. The praying mantis was a wondrous figure of erotic appeal, since the creature was known for devouring her partner during mating, thus combining eros and death, with which the Surrealists were obsessed.[64] In particular, Van Vechten's response to the gorgeous, androgynous, humanoid exoskeleton would have been shaped by the visual language of Orientalism embedded in the Surrealist movement. Dudley Andrews reproduces the surrealist Max Ernst's program design for Louis Buñuel's film *L'Age d'or*, which shows a gorgeous, humanoid praying mantis in a dance-like stride, front claws and tentacles flamboyantly in air and webbed wings outstretched.[65] The spiraling, tendril-like forms draw from Art Nouveau, which also inspired the dance and dance costumes of the Ballets Russes. In Gopal's ornate figure, Van Vechten would have similarly recognized Art Nouveau's fantastical exoskeletons as they percolated into dance costumes, jewelry design, theater sets, and Hollywood films of Orientalist themes made in the 1930s.[66] The appeal of the feline Salomé, which we discussed in chapter 3, cannot be lost here.

The humanoid exoskeleton may have also appeared to Van Vechten as the fanciful Gazurmah, the African Icarus, described in the futuristic novel *Mafarka* (1909), by Filippo Tommaso Marinetti. Gazurmah "is constructed from wires, flesh, metal and muscle, born not from woman but from the constructing will of his father, an airplane as human being, a human being as airplane which/who surges through the universe to Mars."[67] The Futurist connection is indirect. We can infer it from Van Vechten's acquaintance with Marinetti and a long friendship with Marinetti's mistress, the English painter and writer Mina Loy, whom he met in Florence in 1914 just as she was becoming "a zealous convert to futurism."[68] A letter from Loy in 1914 mentions Marinetti sending Van Vechten some "littérature futuriste."[69] During Van Vechten's brief stint at *Trend* in 1914–1916, he was also swayed by the Futurist belief that war was designed "to recapture the word 'spontaneous,' to make people realize the meaning of life."[70] Loy and Van Vechten exchanged long letters for over two decades, starting when her career as a poet was "much too full of Marinettian vitality" (the word replaces "vulgarity," which was crossed out) and after Loy escaped the war and moved to the United States.[71]

Van Vechten's photographs of the Indian dancer offer a unique possibility of exploring the gaze of the camera that takes possession of the "awestruck" photographer during what I have called the Leica Moment of the 1930s. It is as if the technological eye of the camera, glued to the photographer, transforms him into a cyclopean camera-animal. The "feral" aspects of the Leica are underscored in Van Vechten's collaboration with the Indian dancer, but they could equally be demonstrated in images of African American and other subjects also. The Leica placed between the photographer and the dancer transforms both and refracts their interpersonal interactions in the studio. In Van Vechten's double-exposed prints of the dancer, we see the photographer facing the incomprehensibility of the subject and his interracial, homoerotic desire, which scholars explore in his relationship with other Black men, turns into a photo-erotic yearning of the camera-animal. In this chapter, we have seen Van Vechten's photography evolve in the thrall of the Leica. In chapter 5, I pick up the story of the camera's gaze from the dancer's point of view and identify a photo-erotic logic in his body that generates a shape-shifting, malleable creature that the dancer calls "god."

Let the subject generate its own photograph. Become a camera.

—Minor White

CHAPTER 5. PHOTO-DANCE

I want to turn Minor White's dictum in the epigraph into a question: How does Ram Gopal "generate [his] own photograph"? How does the dancer "become a camera" in New York? This chapter identifies the dancer's attraction to the Leica and his desire to exceed live performance and reach for the photographic image. We have witnessed in chapter 4 the way the camera attaches itself to the awestruck photographer and makes his gaze "feral." Here, we will similarly witness the Leica turning the dancer into a camera-animal and pursue its trail in the photographs. But first, how does the dancer develop this strangely uncanny "dermal" quality through photography? We can start this investigation by first exploring what Gopal does not do in the New York studio.

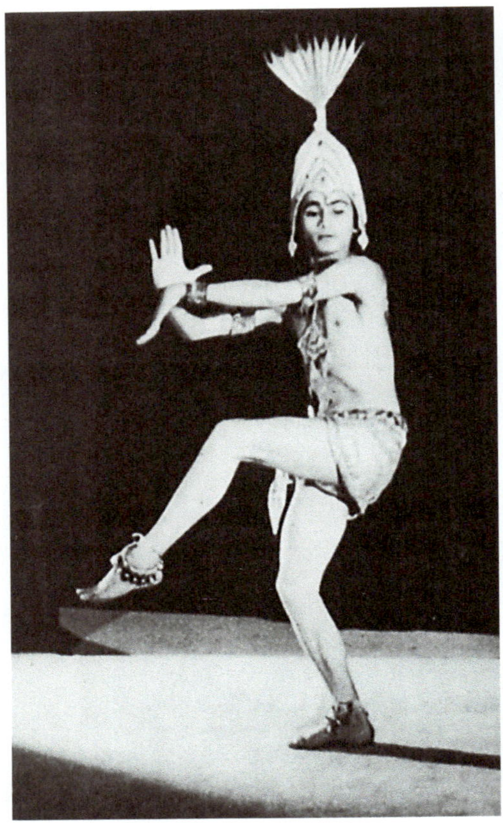
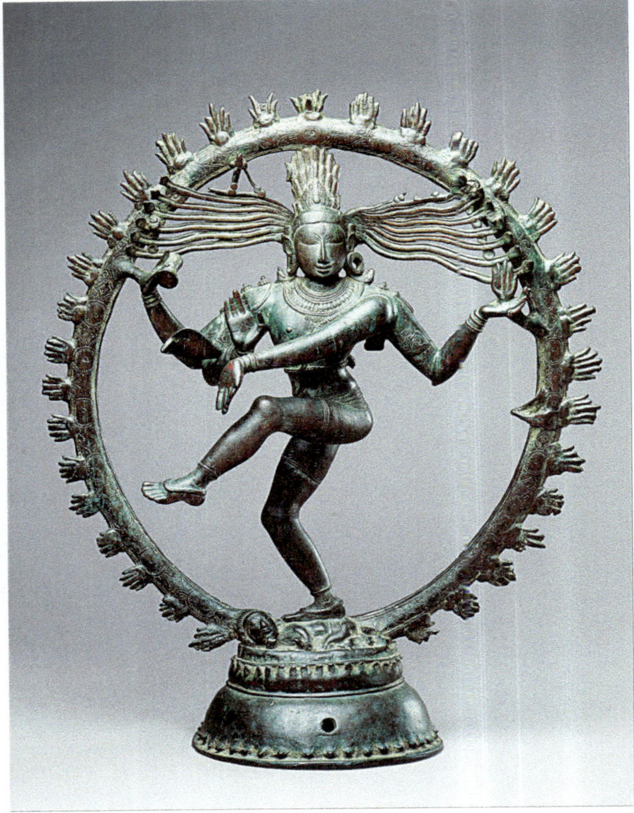

Figures 5.1 and 5.2. *Left*, Reproduction for "Shiva" from a page in the booklet *La Meri, World Tour, 1936–37, Assisted by Ram Gopal*. (Jerome Robbins Dance Division, The New York Public Library for the Performing Arts). *Right, Shiva as Lord of Dance (Nataraja)*, ca. eleventh century, Tamil Nadu. (The Metropolitan Museum of Art, New York, Gift of R. H. Ellsworth Ltd., in honor of Susan Dillon, 1987, acc. no. 1987.80.1; public domain)

Still Motion

As in Van Vechten's studio, Gopal is not really dancing in the image in figure 5.1; he is holding a pose for a camera. The image appears in a publicity brochure designed for the American dancer La Meri in 1936–1937, after Gopal joined her troupe and traveled across Asia. The image is useful as a point of departure for our investigation, for it shows the dancer briefly freezing a bodily movement for a still camera probably for the first time, as far as we know from his archives. The image helps us put "dance" in quotation marks to distinguish Gopal's presentation for a photograph from his live performance onstage, except that he engages the camera differently in New York, as we will see.

La Meri's booklet was designed to invite promotors in different countries to sponsor performances in advance of the troupe's visit. To suit their local venues, the promoters could select from a list of ninety-one possible dance numbers. The dances were organized in seven sections, titled "Dances of Spain," "Interpretative Dances," "Racial Dances," "North America," "South America," "Pacific

Islands," and "Europe." In a subsection of "Racial Dances" called "India (Classical Dances)," the brochure prints the Gopal image and describes the pose. "Sri Nataraj dances his cosmic dance, creating, destroying and re-making the world."[1] Remaining true to the brochure's purpose of making unfamiliar forms of world dance known to an international audience, Gopal represents the tenth- to twelfth-century South Indian bronze sculptures of Nataraja, recognizable from their display in art and ethnographic museums around the world since the late nineteenth and early twentieth centuries (fig. 5.2).

Gopal was not the first dancer to perform a solo number borrowing from a sculptural representation.[2] That credit goes to the American dancer Ted Shawn, as we pointed out in chapter 2 (fig. 2.13). As in Shawn's photograph from 1926, Gopal also reaches for the iconic form, imitating Nataraja's hand and leg positions as accurately as it is humanly possible. He stands firmly on his right foot as if to weigh down the mythical demon of ignorance depicted in the sculpture. He swings his left foot across the body, where it becomes part of a configuration of mimetic gestures addressing the audience. Arms come together on that side. The right palm opens into an upright *pataka* (flag), expressing *abhaya* (removal of fear). The left arm reaches across the body and ends in a drooping palm of a *gajahasta* (elephant's trunk), pointing to the toes and suggesting divine grace.

When the dancer completes the Nataraja pose, La Meri's photographer centers the body and clicks. Photographed from the front, the body is perfectly parallel to the picture plane. The dancer is as luminous as a spotlit sculpture in a museum gallery. The brochure makes a proud claim at the outset. All images are "LEICA action pictures taken during the performance." The mention of the Leica is significant. The brochure captures the Leica Moment and signals the international buzz about the German machinery. Leica's precision lens and fast shutter speeds added value, allowing La Meri's promoters to imagine real performances from these "action pictures." If we look carefully, however, we see that the booklet mostly reproduces publicity stills. The images may have been taken onstage, probably prior to a performance, but the dancers clearly hold a still pose. In the Gopal image, the reality effect of a live performance is produced by the angled shadows on the stage floor. A raking key light from the left casts a sharp, dark shadow of the dancer on the right. But while another key light also fully illuminates his body from the right, it curiously does not cast any shadow on the opposite side.

Gopal must have realized the limitations of the Leica, in spite of the hype. By the time he came to New York, he knew to remain still in front of the camera. As a counterpoint to La Meri's image, consider what happens in an exceptional moment, when Van Vechten's Leica catches the dancer in motion (fig. 5.3). The shoot may have started perfectly. Gopal wears a long tunic typical of the North Indian form of Kathak. The camera is placed on a tripod. The body is centered at a point where the frame is divided exactly by two different fabric curtains. The photographer had only to signal "action" and click away. But when the

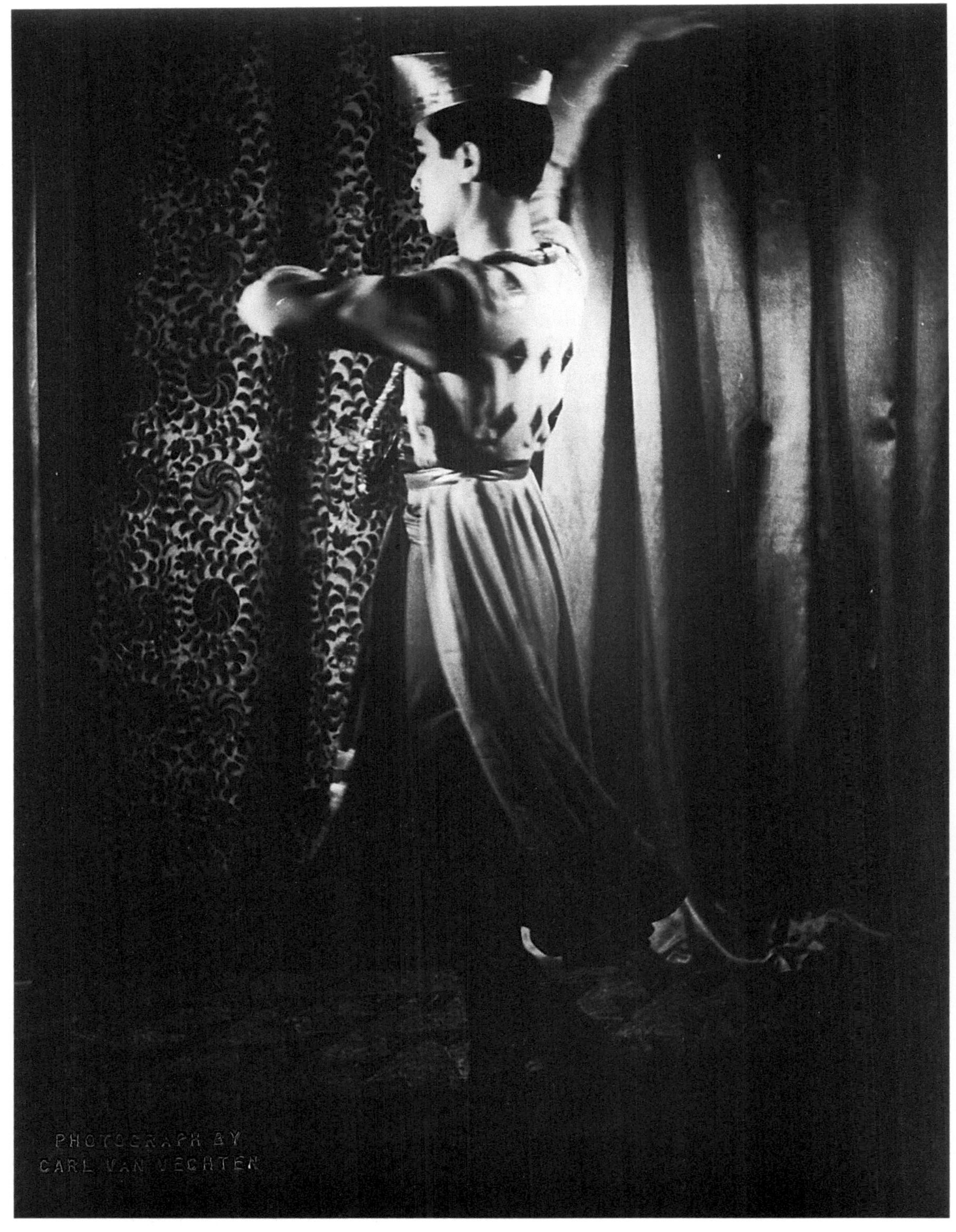

Figure 5.3. Carl Van Vechten, *Ram Gopal*, May 11, 1938, XVIII M18. (Beinecke Rare Book and Manuscript Library, Yale University; © The Van Vechten Trust)

body makes a pirouette common to Kathak, the photographer struggles. A flourish that would have received an applause in live performance leaves a ghostly smudge in the photograph. Hands become a blur, and the skirt pulls behind the figure. The image betrays the limitation of the Leica against the claims of La Meri's publicity brochure. In the brochure, La Meri shows a slight blur in her saree in one image also. In all others, her costume remains oddly motionless even when the body seems to be in motion.

For all performers, then, here was a conundrum to face between photography and live performance, between stasis and movement, if you will. Shiva's iconic pose may pass as a flash in a live choreography of the cosmic dance. In that fraction of a second, it would be hard to frame and focus on the pose as perfectly as we see in La Meri's brochure, unless the dancer lingered on it for the benefit of the camera. Over time, a consistent agreement seems to have evolved in India between a dancer onstage and a still camera. Dancers, at least in the Bharatanatyam and Kathak, halt their movements periodically to highlight a salient flourish or a crescendo in their choreographies, not only for the pleasure of a discerning audience but arguably also for a photographer. Professional dance photographers boast of their mastery in capturing performers in perfect focus in the middle of their movements.[3]

The Kathak image is unusual in the whole Van Vechten set. Gopal knew better by now to produce a legible dance image by remaining motionless in front of the camera. But even when representing Nataraja, it is remarkable that in New York, Gopal does not reach even once for the iconic clarity of sculpture. Examine, for instance, a photograph where the only way we recognize Nataraja is through the hands that come together in the *gajahasta* gesture for grace and the *pataka* for removing fear, this time moving the combination to his left (fig. 5.4). The rest of the pose departs from the icon. We imagine the dancer preparing to swing his left foot across and rotate his hands to the right side. Even so, the photographer managed to shoot the figure in perfect focus. The image suggests a different intention. In contrast to the Kathak image, where Van Vechten clicked in the middle of a movement, we get a sense here that Gopal is breaking down a full movement into its individual "still" parts for the benefit of the photographer.

In Van Vechten's Nataraja, nevertheless, the oddness of catching a figure in midmotion persists. The dancer swings far to the left of the frame. The key light misses him and hits the curtain with such blinding intensity that a dazzling spot appears on the right and distracts us from the off-centered figure. If the intention was to illuminate the dancer as in La Meri's brochure, it has failed. The background glare obscures our reading of the dancer, and a ripple of chiaroscuro pattern scatters our attention across the image.

And here is the oddest part of this botched image. We see Gopal interacting with the flash deliberately, as if it were a dance partner. He arches to the left far enough to give the glare its own space.[4] The hand holding the *pataka* gesture

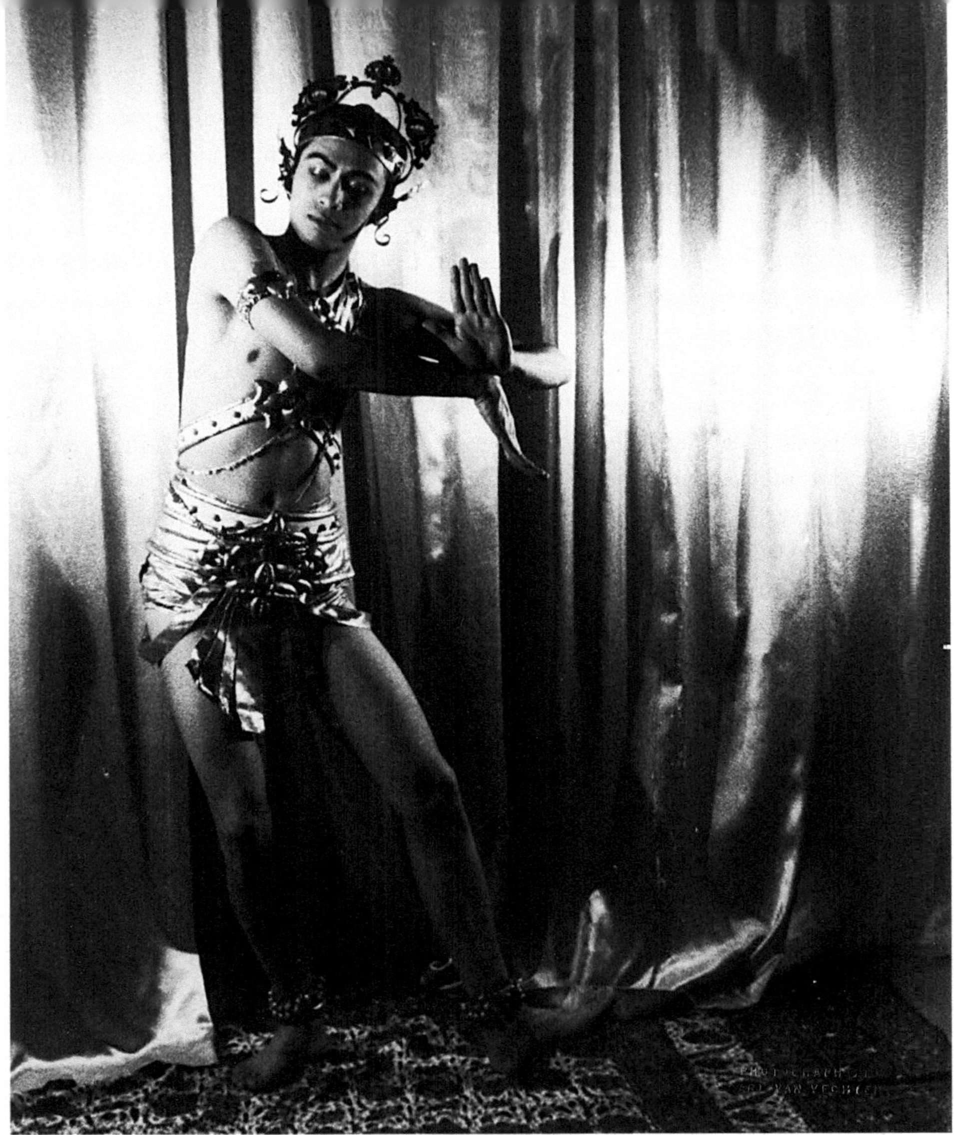

Figure 5.4. Carl Van Vechten, *Ram Gopal*, April 21, 1938, XIII M41, gelatin silver print, 10 7/8 in. × 13 7/8 in., mount dimensions 16 in. × 20 in. (Museum of the City of New York; © The Van Vechten Trust)

practically emerges from the luminous orb. It is hard to know whether the dramatic interaction with the studio glare was intended during the photo shoot or whether it was an accident. In any case, the image could never be used in a publicity brochure. Van Vechten, however, found it sufficiently intriguing to make a double-exposure print, which we will discuss later in the chapter.

Taken together as a set, the New York photographs suggest a different conversation between the dancer and the photographer than simply making publicity stills. Gopal indulged in a creative play between his body and the camera in Van Vechten's studio. It was by far the most extensive photo shoot for him, resulting in nearly two hundred photographs he could see in succession in contact sheets and enlargements. Exchanges with Van Vechten fueled his imagination, offering him an uncharted realm for rethinking dance in relation to the camera as well as the material conditions of the photo studio and the chemical process of making an image. Van Vechten's picture postcard of his "favorite" photograph came from the same moment in the photo shoot as Nataraja and suggested a photographic transformation of Gopal's dance, as we discussed in chapter 4. Here was a different articulation of his dance or even a different way of visualizing bodily movements through a still image.

The still image could be compared to the system for writing notations, created by dancers such as Rudolph Laban in the 1920s to chart out choreographies for future students.[5] Let us turn once more to the botched image of Gopal's Kathak pirouette, this time to read it in this "notational" way (fig. 5.3). At first, the blurs would have puzzled the dancer. But it too is a visual representation after all, except that it is of a kind he may not have seen before. The shallow focus fails to hold the dancer steadily in view in his most glorious moment of performance. Instead, it registers a vector of motion starting in his raised hand and moving across the body to finish in the ruffle of the skirt at the bottom of the image. The wave can be imagined in a three-dimensional way also, starting in a blurry shadow behind the head, then cresting in the perfect focus of the dancer's cap and the glint of diamond-shaped embroidery on his back, and ending in the blurry edge of his skirt. As in a sculptural relief or braille, the prickly details make the vector palpable to touch against a veil of darkness.

The main difference between a notation system and this photograph is that, instead of making choreography legible, this is a representation gone feral. The uneven photograph records an imperfect relationship between a body in motion and the camera's lens and shutter speed. The photographic smudge is a graphic representation similar to an x-ray. It is the resistance offered by the photographic apparatus to a moving body that makes the vector of a dance movement visible (paradoxically) in the image. The partly legible, partly illegible inscription requires deciphering, like ancient hieroglyphs. The new kind of (haptic) representation of dance would not do as a publicity photograph, but Gopal indulged it within the privacy of Van Vechten's studio. He might even have been stimulated by a new way of imagining choreography with the assistance (or resistance) of the camera and studio lighting.

Celluloid Desires

How do we understand the dancer's unusual engagement with photography? In the 1930s, posing for any camera, moving or still, was a new experience for Indian dancers. Hari Krishnan documents the experience of dancers from the *devadasi* community in Madras who confronted the camera when they sought employment in the commercial film industry during their political and legal struggles against the dance reform movement. The era of the talkies ushered in a demand for song-and-dance numbers, and the *devadasis* already had traditional training in solo performance and a sophisticated vocabulary of *abhinaya* (mimetic gestures) that could be adapted to narrative film. The demand for these women was short-lived, and the *devadasis* were soon replaced by actresses from the urban middle class, many already belonging to families of film producers and benefiting from the new legitimization of Bharatanatyam in this period. Krishnan explores the role of commercial cinema in making Bharatanatyam a "classical" dance in Madras. Films narrated the distress of the *devadasi* women and appealed to the moral and ethical values of an urban class by portraying their plight as the loss of "tradition."[6] The longing for a lost tradition was made sharper with spectacularly produced dance sequences, shot under elaborate lighting and gloriously designed studio sets.

Krishnan documents the symbiotic relationship between film and dance in Madras. Cinema popularized Bharatanatyam in urban and rural areas, while classical dance reset the moral reputation of a somewhat disreputable industry of commercial films. Krishnan collected songbooks and illustrated magazines to show a growing fandom not only for films but also for dance. His interviews with dancers and choreographers describe their upward mobility and stardom within the social dynamics of the industry. Krishnan's insights into the "intermediality" of dance and film is underplayed by historians of Indian dance and performers alike but must be taken seriously. In Van Vechten's studio, Gopal represents the intermedial circuit that Krishnan calls "celluloid classicism," except that, instead of using the celluloid image for cleansing and glamorizing performance, the Bangalorean dancer reworks intermediality itself as a new kind of choreography in front of the Leica, as I hope to show.

Among Krishnan's interlocutors in Madras, Kucalakumari gives us a rare glimpse of the experience of "dancing for the camera." Adept as a hereditary temple dancer as well as a star of the Madras film industry, Kucalakumari argues, "There *is* a difference between Bharatanatayam on stage and in cinema. On stage, one has to be very careful because it's live. If you make any mistakes, the audience will know it. . . . In films, it's as if we are dancing for the camera. That is, the dance is specifically tailormade for close-ups and long shots, so the visual focus is not on the whole body but rather on isolated parts of face, feet, and torso."[7]

Kucalakumari is unique in her reflection. She gives us a distinction between film and stage, instead of outright dismissing the former as most dancers do. The experience in front of the camera is disembodied and mediated, while a stage performance is immediate and embodied. The camera's gaze is indifferent to her performance, unlike a live audience. The dance is constrained and interrupted by the limits of a shot. The performance is also "tailormade," allowing no spontaneity. During the takes, the camera fragments the dancer into body parts, and ultimately only a short fraction of her performance might be used in the film's larger narrative. While Kucalakumari enjoyed the fame of commercial cinema, she acknowledged in the end, "No matter how many films I have done, I've always enjoyed stage performance more."[8] Displaying her training within the social and interpersonal environment of the stage held more reward for the dancer than becoming a distant, spectral image for a cinema audience.

The engagement with the celluloid media was a novel experience for classical dancers in the 1930s. While Kucalakumari preferred the stage, Gopal brought photography and dance together into an intermedial exchange that went beyond a live performance. His interaction with the glare of the spotlight in the Nataraja image suggests a reinterpretation of Shiva's cosmic dance to include the material conditions of Van Vechten's studio. In the next section, I relate Gopal's intermedial interest to a global circuit of dance and photography that is underplayed in the history of Indian dance and erased particularly when the celluloid image is considered simply as a means to document a stage performance, as La Meri's brochure claims in her "Leica action pictures." I hope to show that, instead of a desire for intimacy with a live audience, Gopal reaches for representations that are *not* available to a connoisseur in a live concert and are only produced in a bodily intimacy with the camera.

Intermediality

We started this chapter with a discussion of Nataraja and his cosmic dance. Now we must elaborate on the intermedial circuits of that sacred icon itself to reveal the crucial role of photography in constructing its cultural value for both art history and performance studies. The connection between Nataraja and Indian dance developed first within the global flows of art history, art museums, and photography in the early twentieth century and not within dance per se.

Since the publication of the Boston-based art historian Ananda Coomaraswamy's influential volume of essays *The Dance of Shiva* (1918), sacred sculpture of India became integral to classical dance, as we discussed in chapter 2. The Madras reformers refined their practice using the art historian's command of Sanskrit texts and expertise in visual evidence from ancient India. Gopal (and Ted Shawn before him) took the "sculptural turn" literally to archaeological sites and used artworks from museums. During his visit to Paris after his New York stint in 1938, Gopal was exhilarated by the city's art museums. He visited the Musée Guimet, which "was crammed full of some of the most rare Tibetan '*thankas*,' hanging tapestries, Palava and Chola Bronzes from South India, and the most fantastic sculptures from Cambodia, Siam, and wonderful life-size and larger than life-size Hindu heads of Buddha, the Enlightened One!"[9] Recalling the Dutch Orientalist dancer Mata Hari, who had danced in front of a bronze statue of Nataraja in that museum in 1905, he sought it out as a performance venue.[10] When he got his chance, he glowingly wrote that his performance was a huge success among Parisian critics and explained why: "The powers of those gods must have helped me and given rhythm and fire to every movement of my body, my hands and expressions."[11]

The central role of photography in these early global interactions between museum sculpture, art history, and dance is underplayed in Gopal's account and in the history of Indian classical dance. But let us examine how the Paris Nataraja that Gopal mentions as well as Coomaraswamy's influential essay participated in those global circuits. The Nataraja sculpture was given to the Musée Guimet by the Russian-French Indologist and archaeologist Victor Goloubew, a friend and colleague of Coomaraswamy's.[12] In 1911, Goloubew also gave twenty-seven photographs of a bronze Nataraja to the French sculptor Auguste Rodin and asked for his response to them. The photographs, now in the Musée Rodin in Paris, show fragments of face, feet, and hands, along with full views from the front, back, and the side, taken from two different sculptures, including one from the Government Museum in Madras that Goloubew had recently shot. Rodin wrote a poem that imagined the different parts of the two sculptures as the body of a single dancer. Thus, even before Coomaraswamy, or a live performance of a dancer onstage, the modernist sculptor's poem should be regarded as the earliest known attempt to bring the cosmic dance of Shiva to life from a composite mixture of photographic details. Katia Légeret-Manochhaya writes that Rodin could not have seen a live choreography of Shiva's cosmic dance, "given that the first traditional-style performance by an Indian troupe in Paris did not take place until 1938—a work of *bharatanatyam* under the direction of the famous dancer Ram Gopal."[13] In 2012, Légeret-Manochhaya conducted research in the Rodin archives and used her training as a Bharatanatyam dancer in Paris to design a performance based on Rodin's fascination with the photographs.

Coomaraswamy's interest in Indian dance developed first in this global milieu. He had seen Ruth St. Denis's sensational performance of *Radha* in 1906 in London, but as with other Euro-American scholars and practitioners, he could not have used his knowledge of actual performing traditions of India in his interpretation of the Nataraja sculpture.[14] By the 1920s, he was nevertheless positioned as an authority in a discourse forming around Indian dance and sculpture. In 1921, the scholarly journal *Ars Asiatica* published a series of essays on Indian sculpture by Coomaraswamy, Goloubew, Rodin, and E. B. Havell and illustrated them with twelve "Rodin" photographs along with images of Shiva from Elephanta and Mamallapuram. The journal established a visual connection between artworks in a faraway museum and real archaeological sites in India.[15] Coomaraswamy's essay, titled "Instructions on the Entity and the Names of Shiva," offered a reading of the Rodin photographs using "citations on the attributes and functions of the god Shiva, taken from ancient and major texts such as the *Linga Purana*, and *Periya Puranam*, as well as *Tiruvacagam* of Manikka Vacagar and the *Mahabharata*."[16] In the first decades of the twentieth century, such journals produced a museological discourse of Indian sculpture and made the nexus of sculpture and dance (and archaeology) imaginable for both dancers and art historians in Europe, the United States, and India. What is striking here, however, is that the "intermedial" role of photography disappears from this discursive nexus, and ancient sculpture becomes naturalized as the cultural foundation for classical Indian dance along with Sanskrit texts.

Nachiket Chanchani explains exactly how Goloubew's photographs generated motion in sculpture. Of images published in *Ars Asiatica*, he writes, "These photographs, which were taken under Goloubew's direction during his visit to India in 1911, radically depart from earlier presentations of Indian art. They serialised a single object to reveal its many formal and iconographical elements and suggest Siva's multifaceted nature as an unswerving, incessantly moving erotic ascetic." The images were published together "as a set" in that journal "in the same year that [Alfred] Stieglitz first exhibited *The White Hand* and other photographs of [Georgia] O'Keeffe's body that scholars have read as fragmented portraits of the embodied O'Keeffe."[17] Just as Stieglitz brought O'Keefe to life, body part by body part, motion was produced in the Nataraja sculpture through an accumulation of separate, fragmentary details. To Chanchani's insight, we might only add that it required Rodin's poetic sensibility, and more accurately the modernist sculptor's protocinematic imagination akin to Eadweard Muybridge, to generate from the photographic fragments of two different sculptures the movement of a single dancing figure.

For Ram Gopal, as for Ted Shawn, the importance of photography in making an embodied connection between the dancer and ancient sculpture was not lost. As we discussed in chapter 2, Shawn did not perform at the temple site of Mamallapuram in 1926; he took a pose for the camera and brought images back to the United States. We also have no evidence of Gopal's performance at the Chennakesava temple in Belur in 1946 except for the photographs. Nevertheless, the photographs circulated widely in publications and posters as concrete evidence of both his performance in the sacred precinct and his embodied relationship to the deep history of the sacred site (fig. 2.12).

There are significant differences between Shawn's and Gopal's engagement with photography. Shawn's images represent stone temples as a pictorial background similar to Ruth St. Denis's fabric backdrops for *Radha*, *bayadere*, and other performances since 1906. Shawn's "Cosmic Dance of Siva" in New York was also performed frontally, as a photographic representation shot against the wooden ring with a stationary camera (fig. 2.14). By contrast, Gopal's Belur photographs make the dancer's body part of the reconstructed architectural site. We no longer imagine the dancer performing against a flat background but see him instead as a lithic detail within the archaeological environment. The overall black-and-white tonality of the photographic image shows the three-dimensional site as a cinematic mise-en-scène incorporating the dancer. While Gopal knew these sites from his research trip in 1937, Van Vechten's studio might have given him an uncanny body feel of a stone temple as a cinematic space probably for the first time.

The "Prismatic Aura" of Film

We get clear evidence of Gopal's fascination with the photographic and cinematic media in an account of his experience with film in Bangalore just a few months after his New York photo shoot.[18] The story is told by Tom D'Aguir, an engineer in the Post and Telegraph Department in Bangalore and an amateur photographer and filmmaker living in the 1930s next door to Gopal's Torquay Castle in the British cantonment. D'Aguir tells of the young dancer who came one day to ask if the filmmaker would come to his bungalow to film him dancing. The dancer had just seen an exhibition of D'Aguir's color photographs in a gallery at the Mayo Hall on M. G. Road and made the request because "he has never seen himself in colour before." The excerpt is from the filmmaker's interview with Ayisha Abraham, a contemporary video artist in Bangalore, when D'Aguir was in his nineties.[19]

What did Gopal mean by his desire to see himself "in colour"? Clearly a distinction was being made between the colorful costumes, the golden ornaments, the pink blush, and the black eyeliner in which Gopal would have seen himself in his green-room mirror and with which he dazzled his audience when he appeared under the glow of stage lighting.[20] For a stage performer, the reference suggests a different and an unusual desire. Given that Gopal approached D'Aguir after seeing an exhibition of his color photography, I suggest that his emphasis on "colour" indicates a desire to embody the aura of photography and film.

Abraham notes that "there is little filmmaking that candidly captures the new experiment of a traditional dancer" even by midcentury. What might "the new experiment" look like to a dancer in the 1930s, when most performers remained conflicted between the stage and the screen?[21] Abraham interviewed two dancers, the Kathak maestro Kumudini Lakhia and the doyen of Bharata Natyam Mrinalini Sarabhai, both students and associates who performed with Gopal in the 1940s and 1950s, only to discover that their memory neither extended back to the 1930s nor revealed anything about Gopal's sustained interest in film. The lack of memory may also be in part because the two dancers were personally invested in stage presentation. By Lakhia's and Sarabhai's time, the proscenium had evolved virtually into a sacred space for classical dance, as we discussed in chapter 2.[22]

We get a hint of Gopal's distinction from his contemporaries only when Lakhia calls him a "showman."[23] She learned less about Kathak from him and more about techniques for staging a visual spectacle. Lakhia's reference to his showmanship is affectionate (Sarabhai is more dismissive) and contains a grain of truth in that it suggests that the dancer imagined his body as a coherent part of a visual display beyond his dance training. Gopal composed the proscenium as a mise-en-scène similar to his Belur photographs, and D'Aguir's "colour" held the promise of one more performance space located beyond the proscenium and within the media of photography and film.

Color photography was unusual in the 1930s, enough for D'Aguir to claim being the first to introduce it in Bangalore. The most dazzling expression of color photography at this time was of course the motion pictures. Black-and-white films of the silent era were regularly tinted, and the Technicolor Motion Picture Corporation made commercial films truly spectacular through chemical processing in the 1920s and 1930s. As Sarah Street and Joshua Yumibe point out, the Hollywood industry of the interwar period "added a prismatic aura to the moving image of the Jazz age."[24] In the nineteenth century, "the aniline revolution reconfigured the colorant industry" when dyes extracted from coal tar replaced the more expensive natural colorants drawn from "organic materials imported through colonial trade."[25] Throughout late nineteenth and early twentieth centuries, cheap aniline colorants altered the chromatic spectrum of printed posters, wallpaper, fashion designs, lantern slides, stage sets, and filters for theater lights, and modernist artists began to experiment with saturated palettes. Colors brought both a new sense of realism and a thrilling intensification of reality in silent-era films. On the one hand, they conveyed the difference between day (yellow or orange) and night (blue) and various emotional moods (red for passion, blue for sadness, for example). On the other hand, as Tom Gunning has shown, filmmakers also used hand tinting, stenciling, and more industrialized coloring techniques for shock value, intercutting colored segments against the ground of black and white to emphasize fantasy.[26] For Lucy Fischer, the unnatural, industrial colorants "marked not the film's proximity to normal, experiential reality outside it but its temporal and psychological distance from that reality."[27] According to Natalie M. Kalmus of the Technicolor Motion Picture Corporation, the wide-ranging experiments brought about a new kind of "color consciousness" into the motion picture industry.[28] When Technicolor modulated the colorants to adapt to notions of realism in the commercial industry, subdued colors conveyed realistic narratives, whereas bright, contrasting colors served as attributes of exotic geographical locations seen in Orientalist films.

Documenting the global reach of this industrially constructed "color consciousness" through the circulation of Hollywood films, Street and Yumibe write that "cinema's spectacular ambition" is often displayed around the world when its color "incorporates other cultural and technical forms" and generates "moments of medial expansiveness" for its global audience.[29] For Gopal, ever hungry for "Metro films" in his youthful days in Bangalore, "colour" awakened a desire to incorporate a "medial expansiveness" in his body and performance. It painted the "synthetic dreams" that transported him to an expanded space of modernity beyond the floors of the royal palace in Mysore or the performance stage. That dream space was becoming palpable everywhere in the princely state—in the new and glossy industrial colors of automobiles, the commercial streets and foyers of movie theaters pulsating with neon, and the sparkling lights of the distant Chamundi Hills that dazzled him on his way to the Mysore palace for his first concert.[30] D'Aguir's color photography brought the "prismatic aura" of those dispersed dreams within his reach, and he wished to bathe in it when he asked to be filmed.

What followed Gopal's conversation with D'Aguir? After D'Aguir passed away, Abraham received a rusty spool of eight-millimeter film from his family members, from which she retrieved and digitized a few segments. Her excitement is barely contained in her description: "The strip of footage stumbles awkwardly through the projector, and projects an image that goes in and out of focus, as the fungus and the broken sprocket holes influence the quality of the projection. . . . As I threaded the recalcitrant film, through the gates of a projector, it was like from a genie's lamp that came alive this exquisite dancer" (fig. 5.5).[31] She identified the dancer with the help of a choreographer friend, Bharat Sharma. The blistered image shows Gopal dancing with two other dancers on the terrace of his Torquay Castle. Gopal wears an embroidered, Mughal-style turban and the long *angarkha* of Kathak, whereas the other dancers wear a gold crown, as in popular Parsi theater and mythological films. Abraham notes that the terrace was chosen in order to maximize the available natural light. Beyond the terrace walls, we see a banyan tree that hints at a Bangalore that no longer exists, and Torquay Castle itself is replaced by the YMCA building surrounded

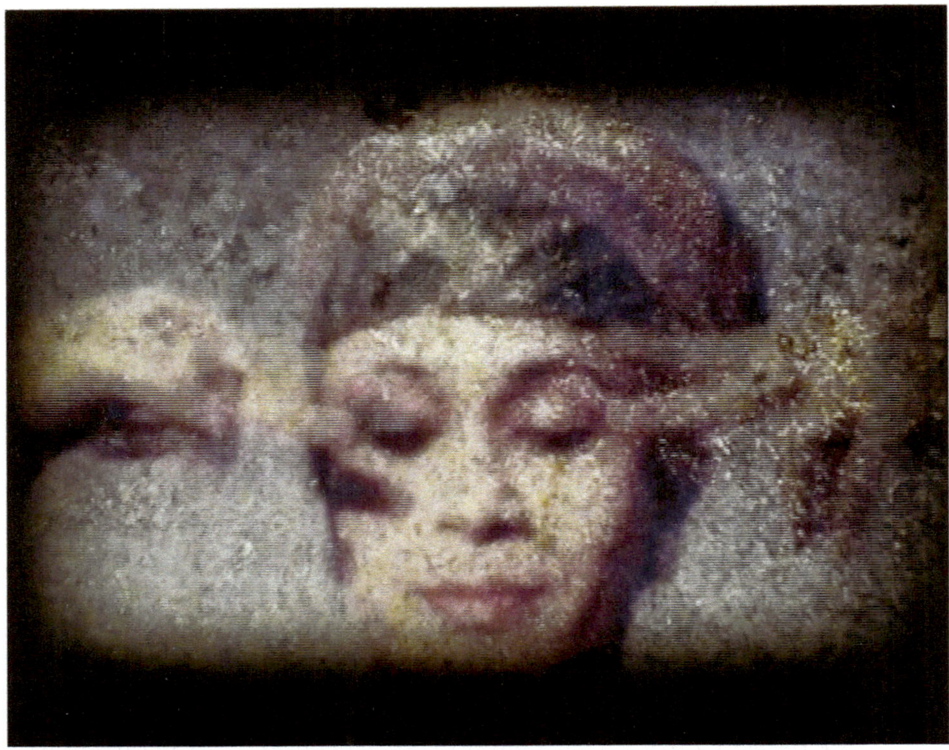

Figure 5.5. Screen shot from Ayisha Abraham's film *I Saw a God Dance* (2012).

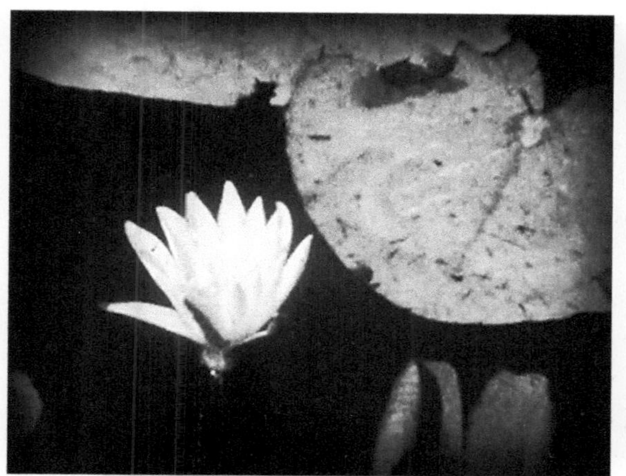
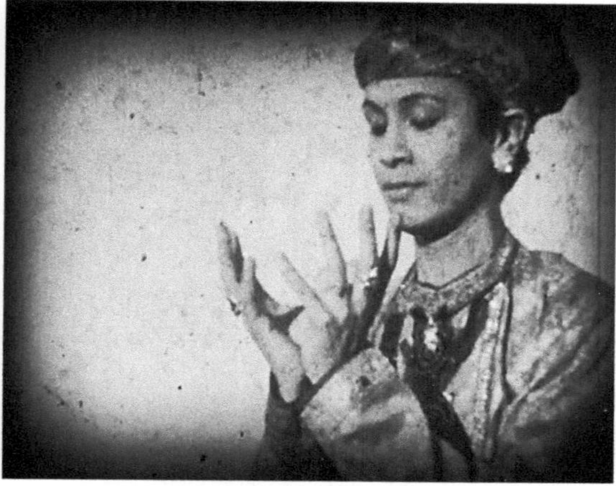

Figures 5.6 and 5.7. Screen shots from Ayisha Abraham's film *I Saw a God Dance* (2012).

by high-rises. When the film cuts to a close-up of the dancer's face and hands, all external details vanish, and the screen fills up with the aniline glory of the celluloid image with the dancer pulsating in it.

Abraham sees D'Aguir's film as a joint project. "The collaboration between Tom D'Aguir and Ram Gopal brings the languages of cinema and dance together and the experimentation of filmmaking into the improvisations of dance, as it is being born into something new."[32] The collaboration is fully visible in the film. The dancer's mimetic movements (*abhinaya*) are coordinated with parallel cinematic representations. A shot of Gopal's fluttering hands is juxtaposed with a butterfly. The arm movement showing the sway of an elephant's trunk (*gaja-hasta*) is intercut by a stop-motion close-up of a toy elephant. We could tentatively call these juxtapositions a montage.[33] The use of a stuffed toy instead of a live elephant, however, is significant in that it highlights the ability of film to make inanimate things animate. In another close-up, when the dancer cups his hands to show the unfolding petals of a flower, D'Aguir matches the gesture with a stop-motion close-up of a blossoming lotus lily (figs. 5.6 and 5.7). This parallel play takes their collaboration beyond a montage reading. D'Aguir not only sets up an analogy between the dancer's hand and a flower but also compares stop-motion photography to the mimetic technique of *abhinaya*. While the dancer calls into being an imaginary blossom, the filmmaker captures the imperceptible unfolding of the lotus petals. Both mime and montage produce in their own way a reference that cannot be seen. Thus, beyond simply calling this cinematic representation a montage, we must name the interaction "screen-dance," a neologism used for a visual and formal collaboration where cinema inseparably participates in choreography.[34] As opposed to a stage performance, this collaboration represents for Gopal a "prismatic" way of choreographing movements and inhabiting dance.

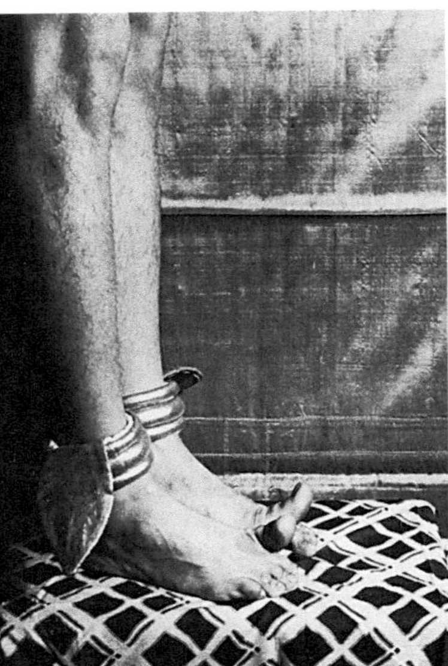
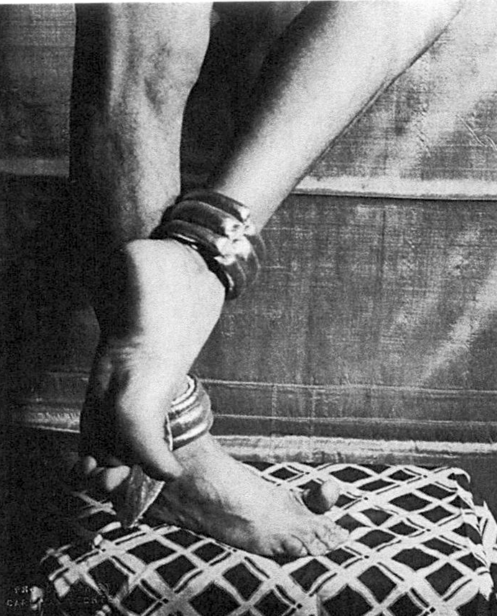
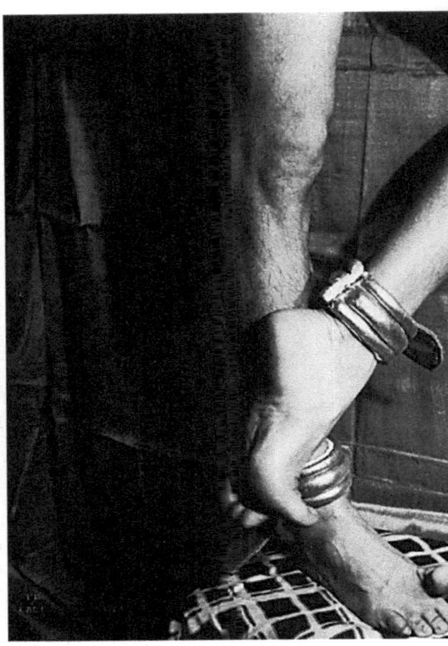

Figures 5.8–5.10. *Left to right*, Carl Van Vechten, *Ram Gopal*, May 11, 1938, XX M12; Carl Van Vechten *Ram Gopal*, May 11, 1938, XX M13; Carl Van Vechten, *Ram Gopal*, May 11, 1938, XX M14. (Beinecke Rare Book and Manuscript Library, Yale University; © The Van Vechten Trust)

Photo-Dance and the Photogenic God

The eight-millimeter film could have been shot within months after Gopal's photo shoot in New York. While he may have posed for publicity images prior, the New York photo shoot would have been the first to make Gopal aware of the "prismatic" articulation of his body. When Van Vechten's camera pulled close to the dancer's feet on a stool, Gopal saw a fragmented detail of his body for the first time, just as Kucalakumari the movie star would have in Krishnan's account (figs. 5.8–5.10). In sequence, the images opened up a channel for thinking dance differently, in movements produced as if by a flip book or the flicker of a motion picture projector.

When Van Vechten matched the circular halo of Gopal's Kathakali headgear with a solar disk printed on an Art Deco fabric backdrop, the dancer would have become aware of his head as an expressive form within a geometrical composition (figs. 1.29 and 5.11). Van Vechten offers at least two different expressions. From the front, the headgear projected forward like a visual echo of the disk behind the dancer. From the side, the foreshortened crown and the half-visible fabric disk intersected at a right angle to form a cube seen in perspective within the rectangular frame of the image. In these interactions between the figure and the ground, the dancer is disconnected from a live performance and introduced to a different order of visual display.

Adapting the neologism of "screendance" mentioned earlier, I call this visual order *photo-dance*. It is the result of both the photographer's desire to place the

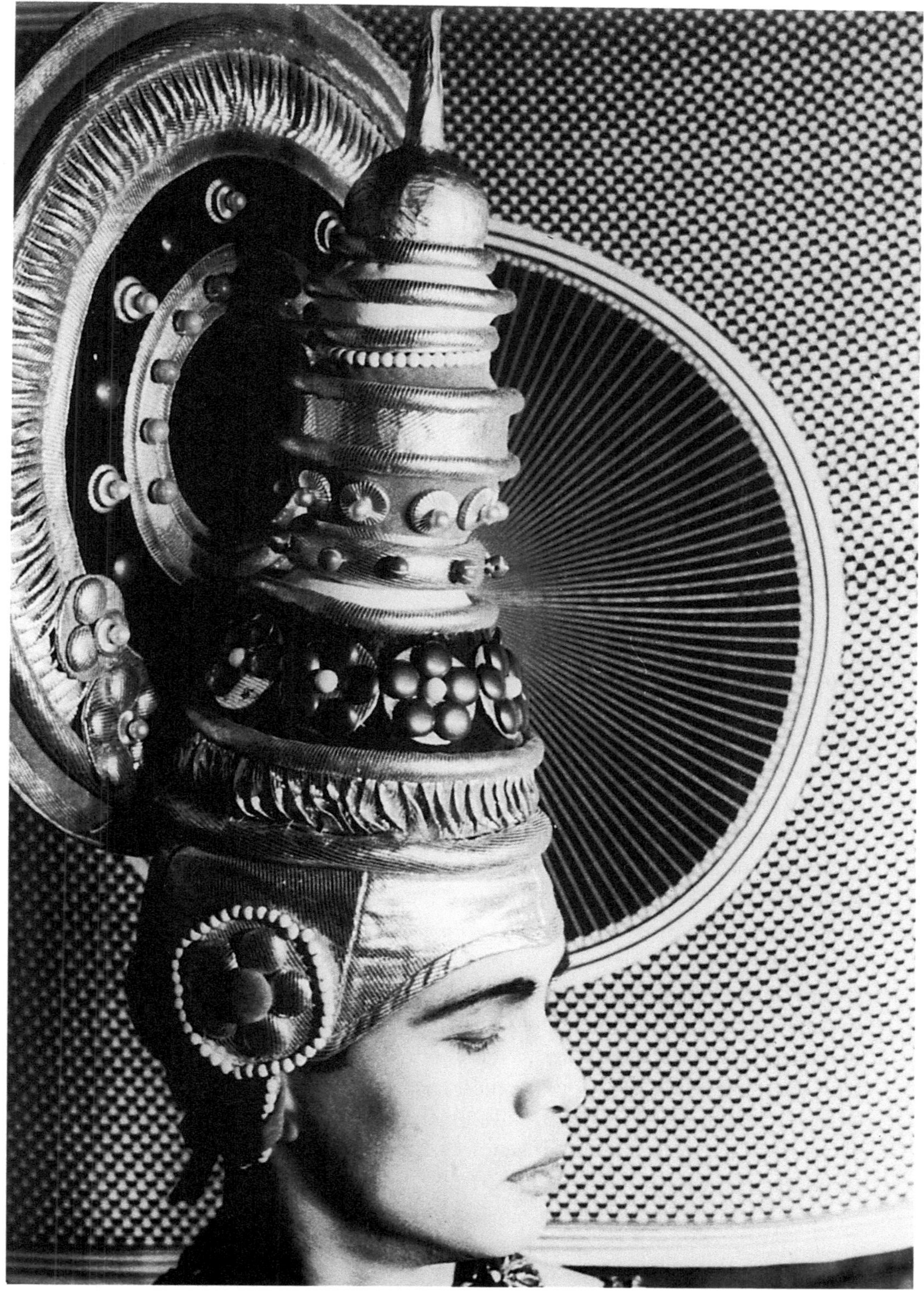

Figure 5.11. Carl Van Vechten, *Ram Gopal*, May 11, 1938, XIX M. (Beinecke Rare Book and Manuscript Library, Yale University; © The Van Vechten Trust)

dancer's body parts within the architecture of his shot and the dancer's awareness of his bodily transformations due to the camera's angle and distance from him. The rearrangeable sequence of photographs might make the dancer recognize the multiplicity of possible movements and stirrings that otherwise might remain hidden in any single moment of his presentation. Some stirrings, such as a butterfly's flutter or the blossoming of a flower, might be dormant in Van Vechten's close-up of his hand and might be released as a coherent motion only in D'Aguir's film. Photo-dance, then, differs from screendance in a significant way. While D'Aguir's camerawork and montages reconstitute the dancer's body within a new temporal configuration, the diverse multiplicity of temporal depictions never come together as a single choreographic movement in Van Vechten's photographs. Instead, their potential vectors remain congealed within the frozen image fragment.[35]

Van Vechten develops some of the imaginary vectors of Gopal's photo-dance in the darkroom, magnifying with his Leica what the human eye does not see. Let us return to Gopal's depiction of Nataraja against the flash of the studio light to explore exactly what is magnified in Van Vechten's enlargement beyond the human body in exotic costumes seen in the studio (5.4). Van Vechten makes a double exposure of the negative and develops the glare into an inverted double of the dancer's curved body (fig. 5.12). The disorienting, upside-down figure partners in a sort of yin and yang duo with the dancer. Through the watery layers of fabric folds, the two figures appear like aquatic creatures swimming around each other in a choreography completed by photography. We do not know if Gopal saw this double exposure, but in the original Nataraja image on which it is based, we sense the dancer's awareness of this potential interplay when he engages with the flash.

Writing in 1928, the French filmmaker and theorist Jean Epstein calls such uncanny figurations "photogénie."[36] For Epstein, photogenic figurations are the "cinematic properties of things" made visible by the technology of the camera and the chemical film. The camera captures an inner life of things unknown to human perception prior to film. Epstein writes about the wonder of seeing such a formation, "A short documentary describing in a few minutes twelve months of the life of a plant, from its germination to maturity and decay, up to the formation of the seed of a new generation, is enough to take us on the most extraordinary trip, the most difficult escape, that man has ever attempted."[37] The techniques available to filmmakers, such as close-up and stop motion, bring forth a life that exists in an altogether different temporality, that of "the vegetative life" of our "somatic unconscious."

For Epstein, cinema in this sense is "animistic; in other words, it attributes a semblance of life to the objects it defines." Inanimate objects acquire a life similar to "the life in charms and amulets, the ominous, tabooed objects of certain primitive religions."[38] Epstein's film *Tempestiere* (1947) brings us close to this nonhuman temporality of objects. A fisherman's anxious wife awaits her

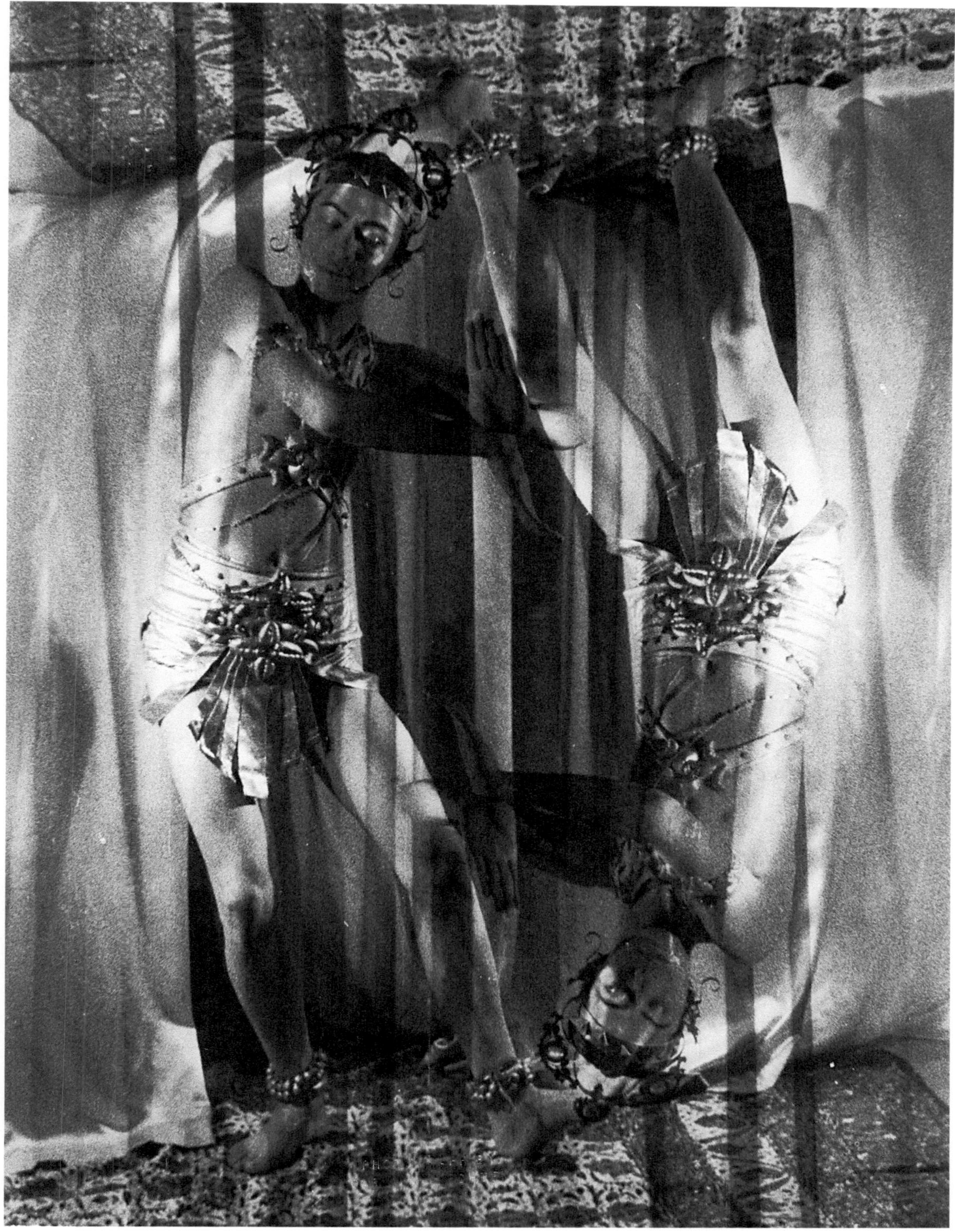

Figure 5.12. Carl Van Vechten, double exposure of figure 5.4. (Jerome Robbins Dance Division, The New York Public Library for the Performing Arts; © The Van Vechten Trust)

husband's return. Her fear is made materially palpable in a mesmerizing representation of ocean waves crashing on rocky beaches and building into a raging storm. Using long takes and techniques including the reverse playing of shots, Epstein saturates the screen with a primordial waterscape seen as if in our "somatic unconscious." Amid the cresting and thrashing waters, we suddenly see a close-up of a conch shell from a maritime museum that was briefly introduced to us earlier in the film. The spiky, spiral cone carries the trace of its prior creaturely existence, but the shocking montage connects it with the roaring sea. As if under our eyes, the swelling, folding ocean waves seize and solidify into the layered involutions of the mineral form. The sudden seizure produces in the oceanic forms what Roland Barthes calls the referent of "death," both in its "temporal" dimension as well as what Epstein calls its "moral character."[39] For the anxious fisher wife as well as viewers like Barthes, the shell would have signified their own mortality. But the film has a happy ending. The fisherman returns. The conch shell may be ominous for mortal humans, but the film activates it differently. Enlarged on the screen, the croissant-like form becomes a "talisman" containing the power and exuberance of the waterscape. In its stillness, it contains both a lingering sense of death and the awe and wonder of nature that remains independent of, and indifferent to, the anxious, existential point of view of the humans.

A close-up takes on a particularly graphic quality for Epstein. Emily Apter explains that the French word for "close-up" is *gros plan*, literally a "big plan or map," and for Epstein, "the gros plan turned the screen into a relief map squirming with everyday objects coming alive." The shift of scale may turn a conch shell or a human face into a landscape, while a landscape acquires a human skin. Apter reads in the "dermal" transformations of wartime aerial photographs of Morocco in Hollywood films a white man's colonizing gaze on its racial subjects. And yet, when D'Aguir's film reads Gopal's face for a similarly microscopic "histophysiology of passions . . . like a fortune teller," it reveals a stage performer's desire for the cinematic exuberance of "colour" (fig. 5.5).[40] The pleasure of D'Aguir's intercuts of Gopal's hands with lily flowers is not only in the dancer's *abhinaya* but also in the stop-motion pulse of the film that brings together the curling fingers and opening buds into a new "kinetic fleshland" that we could call a "hand-flower," adapting from Apter. The composite dream-image cannot be imagined outside the film. It is a photogenic creation, produced only when the dancer inhabits the prismatic aura of cinema.

Epstein insists that the *photogénie* exists only in motion pictures, not in a still image and never in a painting. "The photogenic is like a spark that appears in fits and starts." And yet I suggest that Epstein is less concerned with motion picture per se and more with the pulse of that "spark" entering the camera the moment the shutter opens. In short, he thinks of photography and cinema together. When light enters the camera and strikes the emulsion of a celluloid film, it traces a distinct vector of "time." For Epstein, film is a "space-time system," in which every frame is "an instant without duration" captured in a graphic form.[41] Both a still photograph and a moving image share the chemical process of catching and releasing the temporal spark on the celluloid.

Epstein's writings on film became influential among writers of photography in the 1930s. Christophe Wall-Romana sleuths out the influence of Epstein's "somatic unconscious" of film on Benjamin's idea of the "optical unconscious" of a photographic image, which, however, Benjamin attributes to Sigmund Freud, disavowing Epstein's animism.[42] Nevertheless, the awareness of a "temporal" dimension of a photographic image comes into Benjamin and other thinkers of "New Photography" from Epstein and other French Impressionist filmmakers of the 1920s who thought of photography and film together in their reflections on the celluloid image.[43] The distinction between cinema and photography began to blur with the invention of the Leica, which was the first camera to use the thirty-five-millimeter roll designed originally for the movie camera. As in chapter 4, I propose that Gopal's experiment with photo-dance in Van Vechten's studio derives from this historical conjunction of the Leica Moment.

Around 1938, both the New York photo shoot and the collaboration with Tom D'Aguir in Bangalore helped Gopal realize the photogenic possibilities of his body in Epstein's nonhuman, talismanic sense. In front of Van Vechten's Leica, Gopal makes a gesture similar to the one in a close-up of his face in D'Aguir's film (figs. 5.5 and 5.13). He raises his hands and uses his two fingers to mimetically outline his eyes, while Van Vechten's camera focuses on the shine of his eyelids. Gopal translates the gesture for Van Vechten. In the back of one print, now at the New York Public Library, Van Vechten writes, "Ram Gopal: The gesture means: I have beautiful eyes" (fig. 5.14). The statement cannot be taken literally. I would like to read it as a "histophysiology of passions" in Epstein's sense by asking, What is the "I" to which the gesture points? The comment refers to Gopal's *mudra* (the meaning contained in the stylized gesture), not the dancer's bodily features as a half-Burmese and half-Rajput Bangalorean youth. In other words, the "I" referred to here is a photogenic representation, which Gopal deciphers as a "fortune teller" for the sake of the American photographer.

The distinction between Gopal's person and his deictic gesture in the photograph is important. Gopal writes in his autobiography about those eyes, "I used to be fascinated by them that when I caught a glimpse of them in a mirror they seemed truly to belong to those Gods my great teacher talked about always. It was with a start that I realised they belonged in my own face!" This is an extraordinary self-reflection in which Gopal is describing the training of his eyes at the Kathakali school in the Malabar. He tells us that, after his teacher Kunju Kurup poured sufficient ghee and exercised his eyes, they reddened and gleamed "like two lights burning from within and filled with fire."[44] And, for a moment, he had a sudden experience of some other presence, that of "gods," underneath his skin.

The extraordinary part is that Gopal describes his eyes as if from outside, as if he were seeing them in a mirror that alienates him from himself. For Epstein,

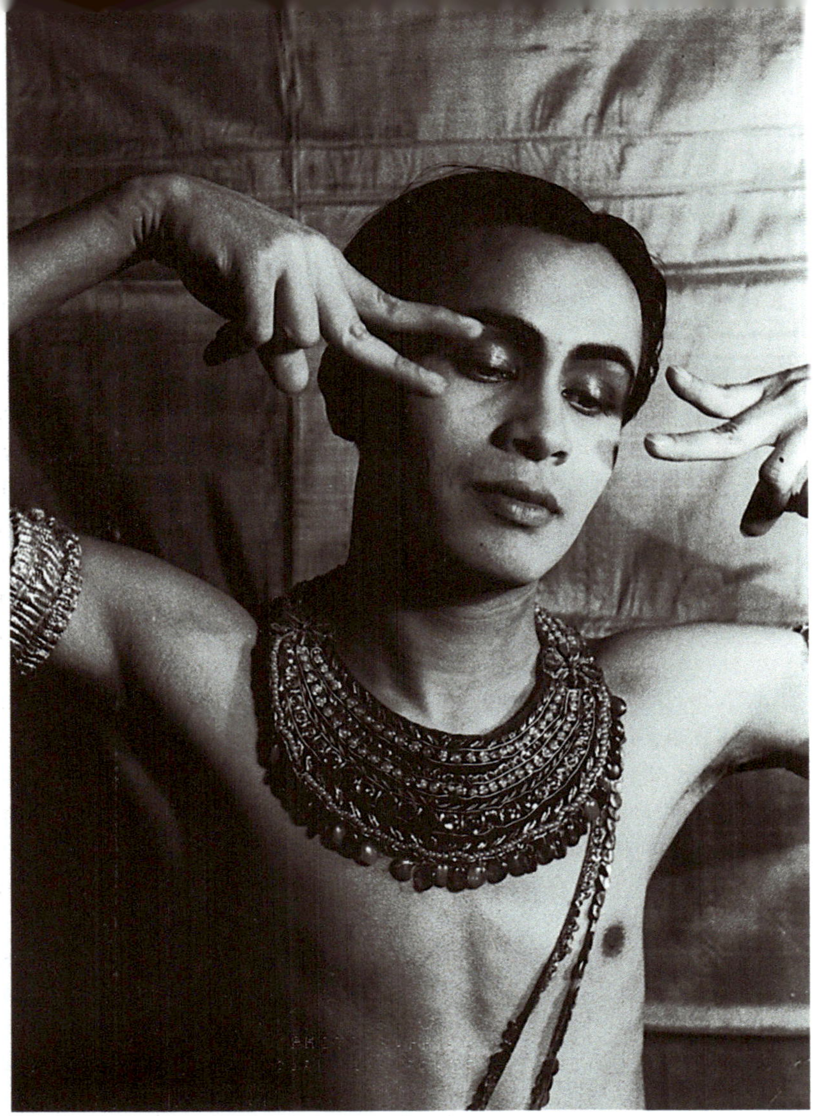

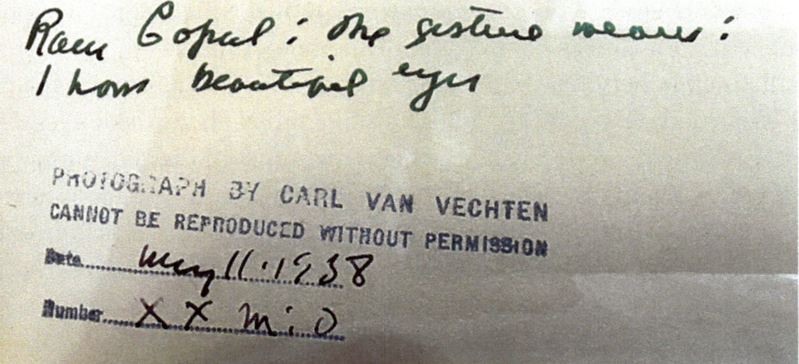

Figures 5.13 and 5.14. *Top*, Carl Van Vechten, *Ram Gopal*, May 11, 1938, XX M0, front. *Bottom*, May 11, 1938, XX M0, back, inscription: "Ram Gopal: The gesture means: I have beautiful eyes." (Jerome Robbins Dance Division, The New York Public Library for the Performing Arts; © The Van Vechten Trust)

photogénie is activated exactly when the viewer's eyes are externalized and fused with the camera, "like virtual reality," as Apter explains. Describing a viewer's absolute attachment to the filmic spectacle while seated in the dark theater, Epstein writes, "When a character is going to meet another, I want to go along with him not behind him or in front of him or by his side, but in him. I would like to look through his eyes and see his hand reach out from under me as if it were my own; interruptions of opaque film would imitate the blinking of our eyelids."[45] In the sensation of "gods" under Gopal's skin, he activates an externalized gaze akin to Epstein's camera. Absorbing that gaze, the dancer is suddenly estranged from himself, as if he were encountering another body in his own. Gopal reproduces that uncanny body as a photographic referent in his collaboration with the American photographer and then the Bangalorean filmmaker.

In Gopal's autobiography as well as in interviews and letters, he describes dance as if it were an out-of-body experience for him. It is not merely a performance or a way of training the body but an ecstatic mode of being. Through dance, he reaches for the material representation that we should call *photogénie* but that Gopal repeatedly calls "God." In his autobiography, he recalls experiencing the thrill of this figurative presence in his body for the first time during the monsoon season in his childhood home. Jumping and rolling in the muddy rain water of a thunderstorm in the backyard of his Bangalore home, the boy found himself caught up "in this wild primordial dance of Nature, of Siva, of God himself": "and in the wake of this rain and thunder and wind I am transfigured."[46] It is not simply the boy who dances, but the whole world rotated around him in a shift and blend of perspectives similar to Epstein's camera work: "I would like to see a dance shot successively from the four cardinal directions. Then, with a stroke of a pan shot or of a turning foot, the room as it is seen by the dancing couple."[47]

The chapter on childhood in Gopal's autobiography, titled "I Saw a God Dance," whips up lively, lengthy description of the natural and social worlds surrounding his "transfigured" self. "Everything in nature is God, look and you will see," a Sanskrit professor tells him. "When you see the lightening flash and hear the thunder drums up in the clouds and it rains, it is the God Siva dancing his Tandava, his dance of creation." His childhood is mainly organized around memories of his mother, a Karen woman; Karen women were known among Burmese as the "Irish of the East" for their beauty. Gopal's mother is the primary figure of enchantment for him, a figure that sends the Bangalorean boy into reverie. Her walk is "the most graceful, dignified and beautiful of any women anywhere in this world today, except those of Bali." Visiting the Shwe Da Goan pagoda in Rangoon with her, Gopal is taken by the fragrance of marigold and jasmine flowers and incense. "How alluring is the perfume and smell of our Eastern Temples, be they Buddhist or Hindu. And what colourful places wherein to worship God. Surely God was a wonderful being full of colour and a love of ritual and beauty."[48] A year after his mother passed away, he wrote to Mercedes de

Acosta, "In October '45 my mother who was a Goddess to me, and the most wonderful Spiritual influence in my Life, died. With her died the Boy and emerged the more sorrowful Ram."[49] I suggest that the "colour" he pursued in D'Aguir's film as well as in Van Vechten's studio was an attempt to regain the "alluring" fragrance of that distant, now lost, memory.

For Gopal, "God" was an interrelated series of "wonderful" affects that had exhilarated his body since childhood. Not long after his mother passed Gopal had a "psychic experience" as he watched a streak of light coming into his bedroom from a room next door that had a "bronze image of Gauri, the Mother aspect of Divinity." Then suddenly, he sensed "a great shape, sitting cross-legged, dressed in white," levitating next to him and disappearing through the doorway. The deceased mother, the goddess statue, possibly the angelic Buddhist Guanyin, all become interrelated motherly figures haunting the Torquay Castle. The bronze statue of "Gauri" is a wondrous amulet in female form. "She has the most glorious Female body I have yet seen, . . . wonderful undulating curves, full breasts, and the most extraordinary beauty of her face an ever present smile on an ever changing face, . . . quite extraordinary." It was miraculously acquired in "an ancient temple in Conjeevaram," where "an old priest" told him that the statue was destined for him and that one day he "must build a wonderful marble temple of art and God with her enshrined in it." Gopal prayed to the venerated image daily after his mother died, calling her "the Indian Virgin Mary Incarnate, the Immaculate Virgin, who listens to all our prayers, grants us all our desires."[50]

To summarize, the subject Gopal referred to as "I" with "beautiful eyes" in Van Vechten's photograph is a protean constellation of embodied figurations that he calls "gods." They include Hindu gods and goddesses, Bodhisattvas, and not least the deceased mother remembered from his childhood days. They are all distant figurations but whose awe and wonder he reproduces as a bodily sensation. Quoting the Indologist Heinrich Zimmer, he claims dance as fundamentally "a form of magic. The dancer becomes amplified into a being endowed with supranormal powers. His personality is transformed. Like *Yoga*, the dance induces trance, ecstasy, the experience of the Divine, the realization of one's own secret nature, and finally, mergence into the Divine essence." The magical ideology informs his dance training. Describing his early training in Kathakali, he writes that his guru, Kunju Kurup, used to insist, "You must *become*, you must concentrate and feel so intensely all I tell you . . . that you are not conscious of the self. The self is forgotten, unimportant, small, of this world. But that 'other self,' the God you are portraying, must come to life by sheer will-power and concentration, and this is possible only if you are completely lost in the rhythm of the moment."[51] Gopal's consistent training around self-possession and transfiguration, in short, made his body a talisman for "fortune telling" in Epstein's sense.

The Skin of God

In La Meri's brochure, Gopal represents the iconography of Shiva's cosmic dance literally. But in Van Vechten's studio as well as in D'Aguir's film, Gopal does not represent sacred sculpture in a readymade tableau. Instead, he uses the photographic medium to reconstitute in his body the ineffable presence of gods from ancient sculpture. To explain this final bodily transmutation, I want to elaborate on the allure of one particular distant figuration that Gopal mentions more frequently than others in the constellation of divine references. This is the Hollywood star Greta Garbo.

Gopal returns obsessively to Garbo, whom he first saw on the big screen in Bangalore. In La Meri's brochure image of Nataraja, only Gopal's crown is different from the South Indian sculpture. As we saw in chapter 2, the crown is modeled after Garbo's costume in *Mata Hari* (1931; figs. 2.19 and 2.20). The reference would not be missed by this avid fan of Garbo and the "Metro films," but it is also an odd choice for a Kathakali dancer to include it in his performance. Gopal gives no evidence of exactly when he first choreographed his Nataraja or made costumes for it, but the crown is certainly not his design. It was made for him during his trip to Java with La Meri and is probably La Meri's design based on Hollywood production of Orientalist films. On reaching Los Angeles, Gopal and Aleksander Janta attended a party at the house of Greta Garbo's costume designer, Adrian, but the crown was already in his suitcase by then. It disappeared after his 1938 trip, but his obsession with Garbo is amply documented in his letters to Garbo's lover Mercedes de Acosta.[52]

In Gopal's autobiography and in his letters to Mercedes de Acosta, Garbo emerges as an ineffable dream-image. "[She was] the divine star of my childhood days and first glimpse into the movie-houses of my home town where bills on the cinemas carried her name." The image is etched in his memory: "Those lotus-shaped eyes, those unbelievable lashes, that fabulous mouth so filled with sensual promise and yet pregnant with spiritual secrets, and that profile, matchless in its perfection, with the flowing liquid grace of her movements on the screen."[53]

Gopal's description is similar to the wonderful statue of Gauri in the Torquay Castle, but in attending to Garbo's eyelashes and lips, he is also obviously describing a cinematic close-up. Garbo's description comes close to the star's screen presence that Roland Barthes details: "Garbo still belongs to that moment in cinema when capturing the human face still plunged audiences into the deepest ecstasy, when one literally lost oneself in a human image as one would in a philtre, when the face represented a kind of absolute state of the flesh, which could be neither reached nor renounced." Garbo's face is not human. On the cusp of becoming human, "Garbo offers to one's gaze a sort of Platonic idea of the human creature." She is "almost sexually undefined" and often called "*Divine*, probably to convey less a superlative state of beauty than the essence of her corporeal person . . . formed and perfected in the clearest light." In contrast to Katherine Hepburn's face, which is for Barthes "constituted by an infinite complexity of morphological functions" to represent an "existential" woman (defined further when she plays "woman as child, woman as kitten"), Garbo's face is masklike. It is cinema that gives it the "thematic harmony" of a face. The prismatic, dermal configuration on the screen "represents this fragile moment when cinema is about to draw an existential from an essential beauty, when the archetype leans towards the fascination of mortal faces, when the clarity of flesh as essence yields its place to a lyricism of Woman."[54]

In Gopal's and Barthes's vivid descriptions, both are referring to the Hollywood star as Epstein's "kinetic fleshland" appearing glamorously on the screen during the silent era. For Gopal, "[Garbo is] as silent as the wonderful images of the Goddesses in the temples where I haunted and meditated and drowsed, and as communicative through that very potent silence itself, for my first vision of this magic called Garbo occurred in the days of the silent films."[55] For both Barthes and Gopal, the mute "face object" (Barthes's phrase) retains in its human appearance a divine aura, except that Gopal couches the aura in the idiom of Hindu gods: "This was Vedic magic, every hymn that the sages wrote to Lakshmi, Goddess of Beauty, Saraswati Goddess of Learning, and Parvati, that sensual wife of Siva, all these and every other distilled dream of my boyhood were incarnated in this swan called Garbo." In 1948, during a performance stint in Stockholm, Gopal visited the apartment where Garbo was born as a sort of pilgrimage. "It would be a breathless experience for me, like visiting the abode or *ashrama*, sacred place of some saint."[56] He might as well have mentioned the Buddhist temple he visited with his mother in Burma as a child.

Unlike Nataraja, who is a mythic ideal for Indian dance, Garbo appears for Gopal as what Barthes calls an "archetype," simultaneously human and nonhuman, incarnating both his deceased mother and sacred sculpture. In his long letters to console Mercedes de Acosta as Garbo's distraught lover, Gopal continued to address Garbo less as a human figure and more as a nonhuman archetype:

> Does she look as divine as ever? . . . There is something so beautiful, spiritually speaking, about her, . . . something so divine . . . that I don't believe this world will ever see her like again ever. So do help her. . . . Give her my greetings when you see her . . . and tell her that from distant remote south India, in a beautiful provincial bourgeois town of Bangalore, where there are temples of Siva and great occult men of truth and powerful sages, tell her that Ram sends her his greetings "through" the medium of you, . . . his greatest friend in America.

By the late 1940s, when Garbo's fame was on the decline, Gopal offered his dance as an Epstein-like charm for healing the bruised actor, helping her regain both her magical aura and her love for Mercedes: "I wonder what she would think of Indian dancing, . . . I mean the real thing, . . . the classic and highly spiritual temple dancing which I do. . . . One day I will dance for both you and Greta. . . . I will explain what the symbols mean, . . . give you the hymn I am going to dance out and then see what it 'says' to you. . . . What I do in my dancing must make 'her' come closer to you."[57]

Gopal never met Garbo in person. He organized his thoughts about her "humanity" primarily as a cinephile. She is a photogenic creature produced by the materiality of the luminous screen. As if it were a permeable tissue, the cinematic screen lends Garbo's skin a haptic reality. Gopal reads that skin endlessly as a "histophysiology of passions" in his long letters to Mercedes de Acosta. While fully retaining that pulsating, epidermal materiality of the screen, the photogenic creature steps into a social world as a real and human person through Gopal's sorcery.

"Second Skin"

In chapter 2, we heard the dance critic John Martin describing Gopal as a "pictorial man" after his New York concert on May 1, 1938. The reference conjured for Martin all the negative connotations of a motion picture industry—popular kitsch as opposed to the haloed artistic traditions—with which Hari Krishnan's Madras dance culture also struggled. I want to propose here, however, that Martin's derogatory reference would have delighted Gopal, except that he would have liked to refer the "pictorial man" as "god," brought to life through the vitalist logic of Epstein's *photogénie*. I want to turn to the New York photographs to describe the logic unfolding in a still image.

Laura Wexler brings Epstein's animism to a still image perfectly: "As the photographer composes the scene, and juxtaposes within his own unity things that were not connected before, a still and stubborn world rises up and begins to dance, spinning this time around a human axis."[58] As Van Vechten assembles the disconnected "things" into a "unity" in his studio, the dancer inhabits the *tableau vivant* as one such "thing" akin to Walter Benjamin's view of a "screen actor." Unlike a stage performer, a screen actor performs "not in front of an audience but in front of an apparatus" and is thus reduced to a cinematic prop and alienated from his body during production, only to be brought to life in the editing room as a distant reflection of himself.[59] I suggest that Gopal revived himself similarly in his collaboration with the Leica. In New York, his midshots and close-ups would have alerted him to the fragmentation and reconstitution of his body within the architecture of the photographic image (fig. 5.15).

In a *tableau vivant*, the figure cannot be isolated from the ground. A printed backdrop flattens the tableau. A batik print creates a ripple across the surface, pulsating with symmetrical loops of snakes, pouncing tigers, grazing cows, and thorny vegetation, all suspended in a fibrous net of tendrils. Against this filigree work, the necklace becomes imprinted like a tattoo across the dancer's chest. The musculature and ornaments as well as the fabric background become part of a single interplay of texture and luminosity (fig. 5.16). The camera catches

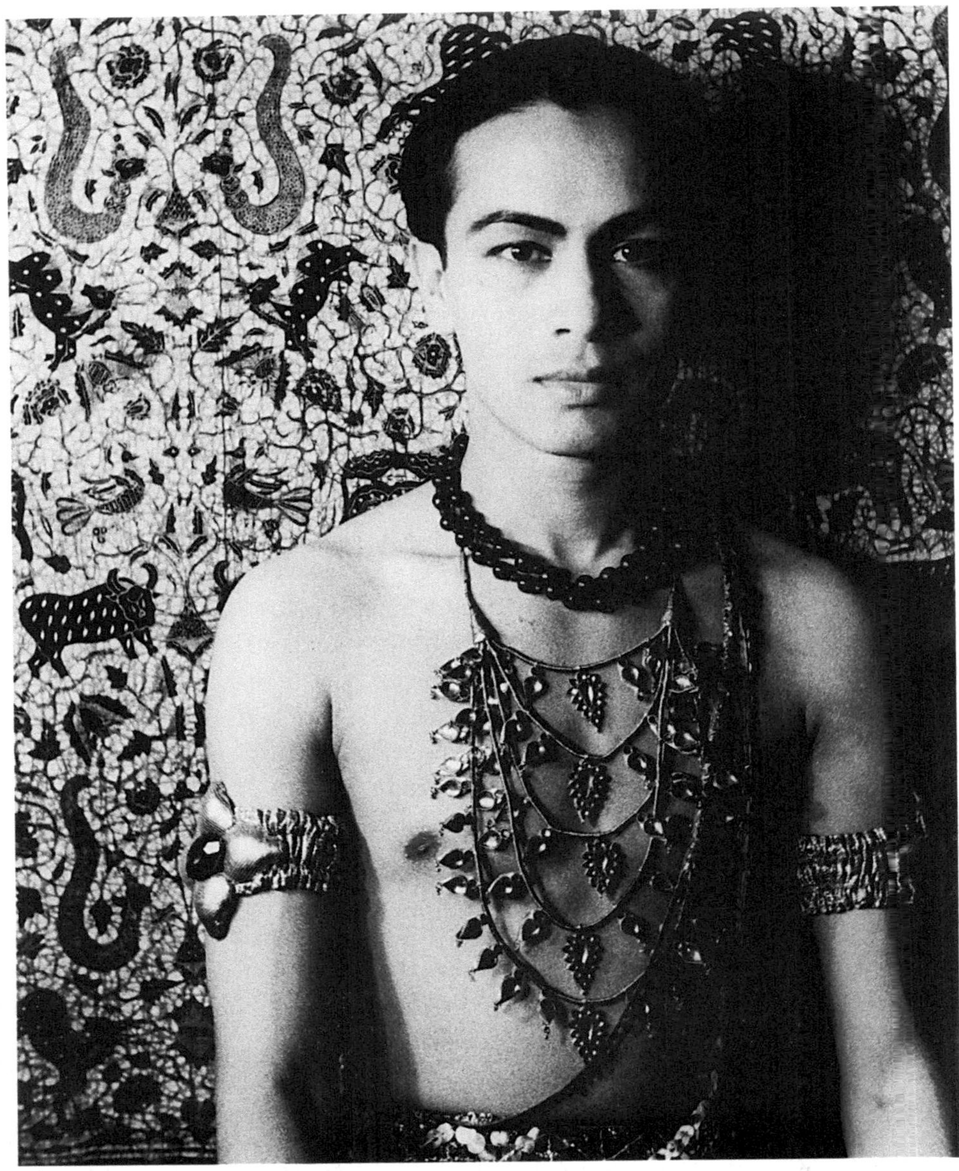

Figure 5.15. Carl Van Vechten, *Ram Gopal*, April 21, 1938, XII M23. (Beinecke Rare Book and Manuscript Library, Yale University; © The Van Vechten Trust)

the silhouette of a single body-costume combination. The wiry extensions around the dancer's head stiffen into antenna-like hair curls of this new and hybrid configuration. The studded breast plate and skirt pleats become scales of a fantastic, exoskeletal creature. As the outlines of the dancer's body distribute themselves into the overall surface of the photograph, mysterious humanoid shadows appear in the deep folds of the curtain. Carved as if against the luminous flutes of a marble column, the dancer inhabits what Epstein calls an image of our "somatic unconscious."

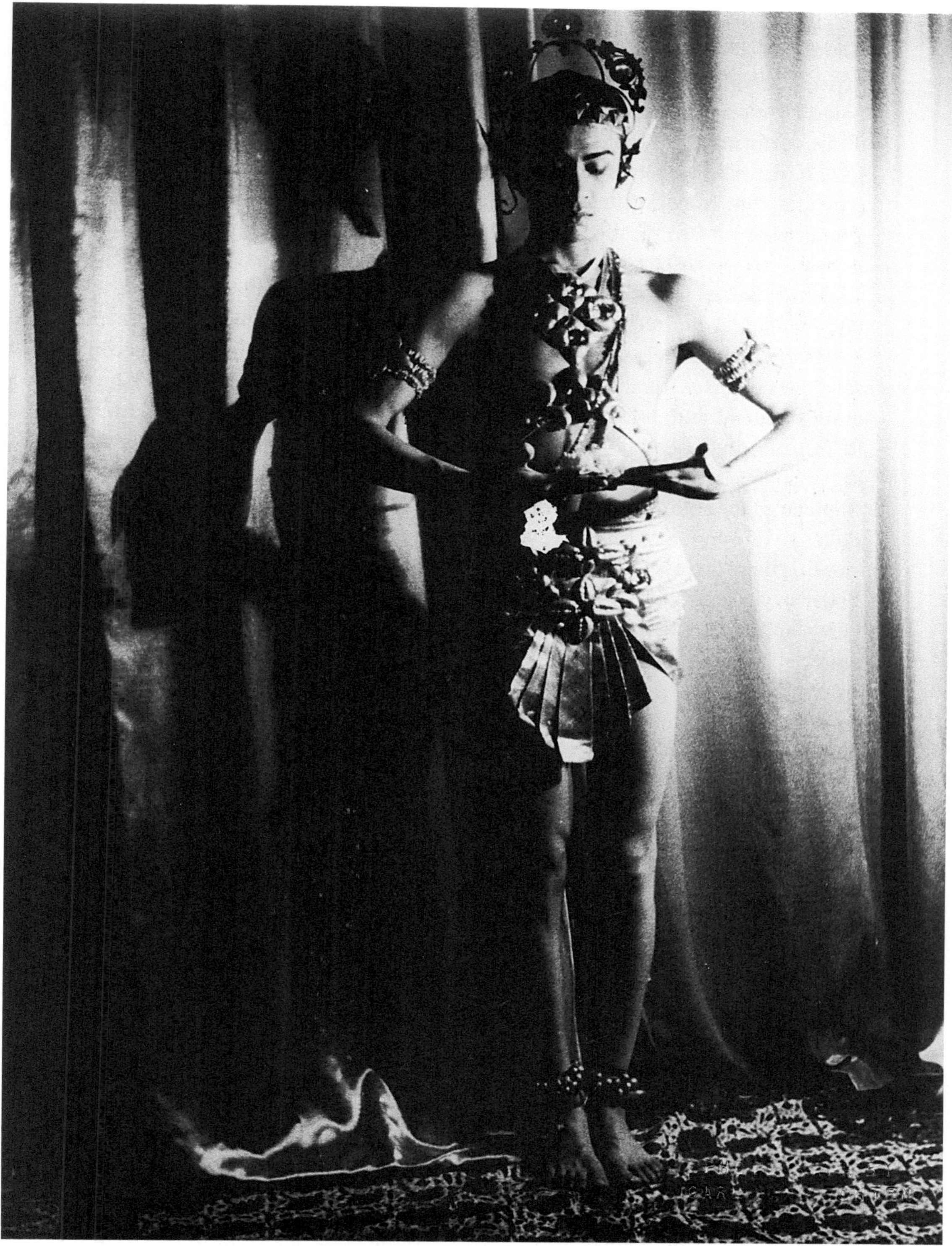

Figure 5.16. Carl Van Vechten, *Ram Gopal*, April 21, 1938, XII M32. (Beinecke Rare Book and Manuscript Library, Yale University; © The Van Vechten Trust)

For Anne Anlin Cheng, a similarly "taut intimacy" between the silvery celluloid surfaces and the human body produces a hybrid "second skin" of the African American actor Josephine Baker. Cheng finds this dermal quality in Baker's Victorian-style studio portraits and then, by the 1920s, in her stage and filmic performance.[60] Baker's sensational dances at La Revue Nègre in Paris in 1925 borrowed liberally from the sexualized racial stereotypes of ethnographic accounts. But molding her skin according to that ethnographic "study" and glamorizing it with "plasticity and metallurgy," her Primitivist burlesque on the Parisian stage creates a "rupture" in the ethnography's "illusions of objectivity or science."[61] Baker "wears her naked skin as a sheath."[62] Her striptease shows nothing. Instead, as her naked body shines with the inclusion of metal, plastic, oil, and feathers, it participates in what Cheng calls "Modernism's dream of a second skin."[63] The dermal qualities of the Black, female body produce a camouflage of other denuded and polished surfaces in fashion design and the modern architecture of Adolf Loos and Le Corbusier. For Cheng, the interpenetration of modernist bodies is highlighted in a house that Loos designed for Baker. At its center was a large swimming pool with viewing gallery that would have not only shown Baker swimming in her bathing suit, or naked, but also offered glimpses of her viewer-guests across the shimmering water. The house was never built, and Baker never mentions it; but Cheng finds in it a concrete example of intimacy between Baker's glamorous, impenetrable nakedness and modernist visual and material desires.

I take Cheng's insights to Gopal's objectification in front of Van Vechten's camera. In the interpenetration that Loos designed of a nearly naked swimmer and modernist viewing practices, one cannot help but think of Van Vechten's double-exposure print of Gopal as an aquatic creature, except that Cheng's Baker wears her second skin as a resistant mode of being a subject in a racialized world. Cheng's insights are framed by critical race studies and Black feminism. Baker's objectification is informed by scholars such as Hortense J. Spillers who write about the "violent writing" that transforms a Black slave and captive into "a 'thing,' . . . then 'flesh' with all its material fissures, tears, scars, and ruptures" that remind of "injuries inflected on that body." In attempts to heal the racialized body from that violent "body writing," Cheng avoids returning to an "essentialized notion of prediscursive flesh or recuperated embodiment" in which race studies seems invested, according to her. Instead, Baker's synthetic, "plastic . . . figuration . . . turns her from a body suffering from or disguising the 'hieroglyphics of flesh' [Spiller's phrase] into a figure that stands resistant to them."[64]

My study differs from Cheng's, as well as from that of race scholars, in two ways. One, Gopal's body may be racialized by colonial processes in India and by his American viewers including Van Vechten and the critic John Martin. But it is not subject to the bodily violence on which the fantasies of "tattoo" and other forms of body writing are posited within critical race studies and Black feminism. Second, importantly, the mediated "second skin" is not a protective shell

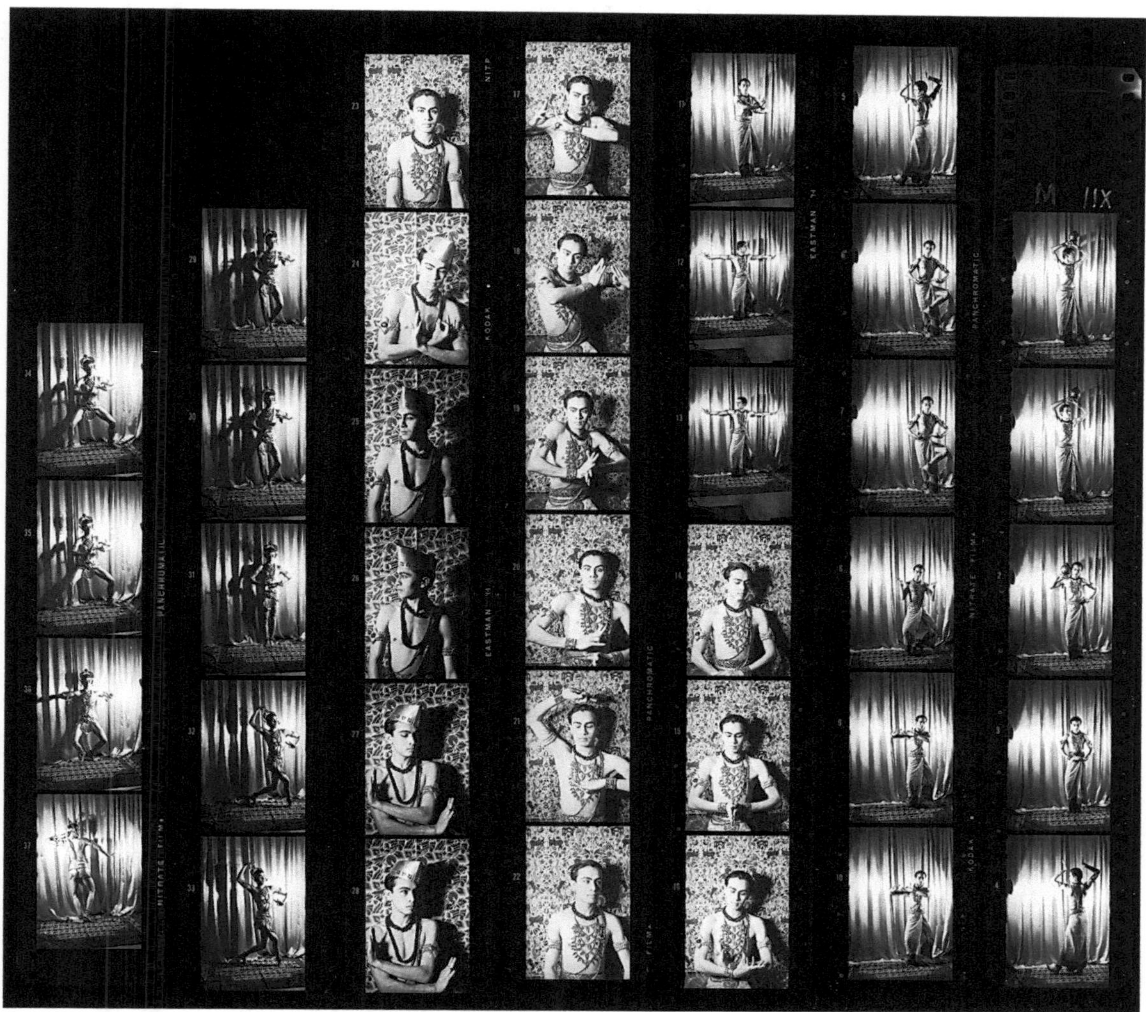

Figure 5.17. Carl Van Vechten, roll XII, April 21, 1938. (Beinecke Rare Book and Manuscript Library, Yale University; © The Van Vechten Trust)

in which to recuperate an abject and vulnerable creature from body-writing.[65] Instead, Gopal finds an ecstatic mode of inhabiting the photograph.

Looking across Van Vechten's negatives and enlargements, the dancer would have sensed the stirrings of a photogenic life in his bodily figurations (fig. 5.17). In sequence, the dancer's body "spins into dance" with a new, technological vitality, as Wexler has it. Instead of a skin recuperating from an onslaught of media, Van Vechten's Leica produces in the dancer's body what Walter Benjamin describes as the "innervation" of the human sensorium.[66] This too is a form of body-writing. According to Miriam Hansen, Benjamin exemplifies bodily innervation in the Buddhist prayer wheel on which Tibetan monks meditate. That external object disrupts the natural being and transfigures (or disfigures) the body into what Hortense Spillers calls the "hieroglyphics of the flesh," except that Benjamin does not explore victimhood in this disruption but rather a new desire. For Benjamin, and partly also for Cheng, a mimetic attachment to external "wounds" stirs a sense of wonder in the human body. Innervation is a promiscuous formation. The result is grotesquery, that is, a human body reimagined as something else. Benjamin's other examples of the intimacy across "dissimilar" species of organisms and objects include a child playing "at being . . . a windmill and a train."[67] Wall-Romana connects Benjamin's innervation to what Epstein calls the "sympathetic life" of a "non-visual coenaesthesis." It is a "corporeal vision" defined as the "inner sense of one's own senses [or] the physiological face of the subconscious."[68] In the innervation of the body through a dialectic, intercorporeal relation with the shock and pulse of the moving image, Benjamin imagined a possibility of regaining the unique aura of the human body, otherwise lost with the onset of mechanically reproduced images. By the mid-1930s, Benjamin lost that fragile optimism, seeing screen bodies absorbing the phantasmagoric imaginings of a charismatic fascist state.

In the privacy of Van Vechten's studio, Gopal brought the mimetic energies of that corporeal vision to his interactions with Van Vechten's Leica. Let us end our exploration of this newly constituted self-image with a photograph from the first day of the photo shoot. It belongs to the group of fourteen shots Van Vechten took at the start of the second roll, numbered XII. Gopal wears a sarong, as if he were in an informal rehearsal (fig. 5.17). All the images in the group show the figure pushed to the right side of an asymmetric composition.[69] In the fifth shot, marked XII M4, the dancer is pushed so far to the right that the luminous curtain enters the picture much more than in any of the previous images (fig. 5.18). The lighting can on the left, barely kept outside the frame, makes a distinct cone of light grazing across the curtain. The dancer puts his left foot forward as if to walk into the cone and freezes into that pose. Or he may be poised to make a turn on his left heal. The big toe is lifted and strains forward. The hips are pushed back. The body is firmly rooted in the right foot, stable and bracing for a forward swing (as if someone said, "Get set"). We could expect the figure to turn around any moment, but, of course, Gopal remains motionless. The body straightens. The figure is held still and aligned perfectly with the rectangular picture plane of the viewfinder of the Leica.

For the first few images in this group, Gopal started by facing the camera, holding a metal pot (fig. 1.3). In this image, however, he turns his back to the camera, as if to give Van Vechten a reverse shot of the previous images. The pot disappears. Instead, Gopal raises his two hands in a mimetic gesture of placing the imagined pot or perhaps a royal crown over his head, as in traditional Kathakali. The head turns to the cone of light. Transfixed in this way, the body produces a clean profile framed by the chevron pattern of his raised arms. Parallel to the picture plane, the majestic figure appears as a decorative frieze within the visual architecture of the photograph, recalling Egyptian hieroglyphs or Greek

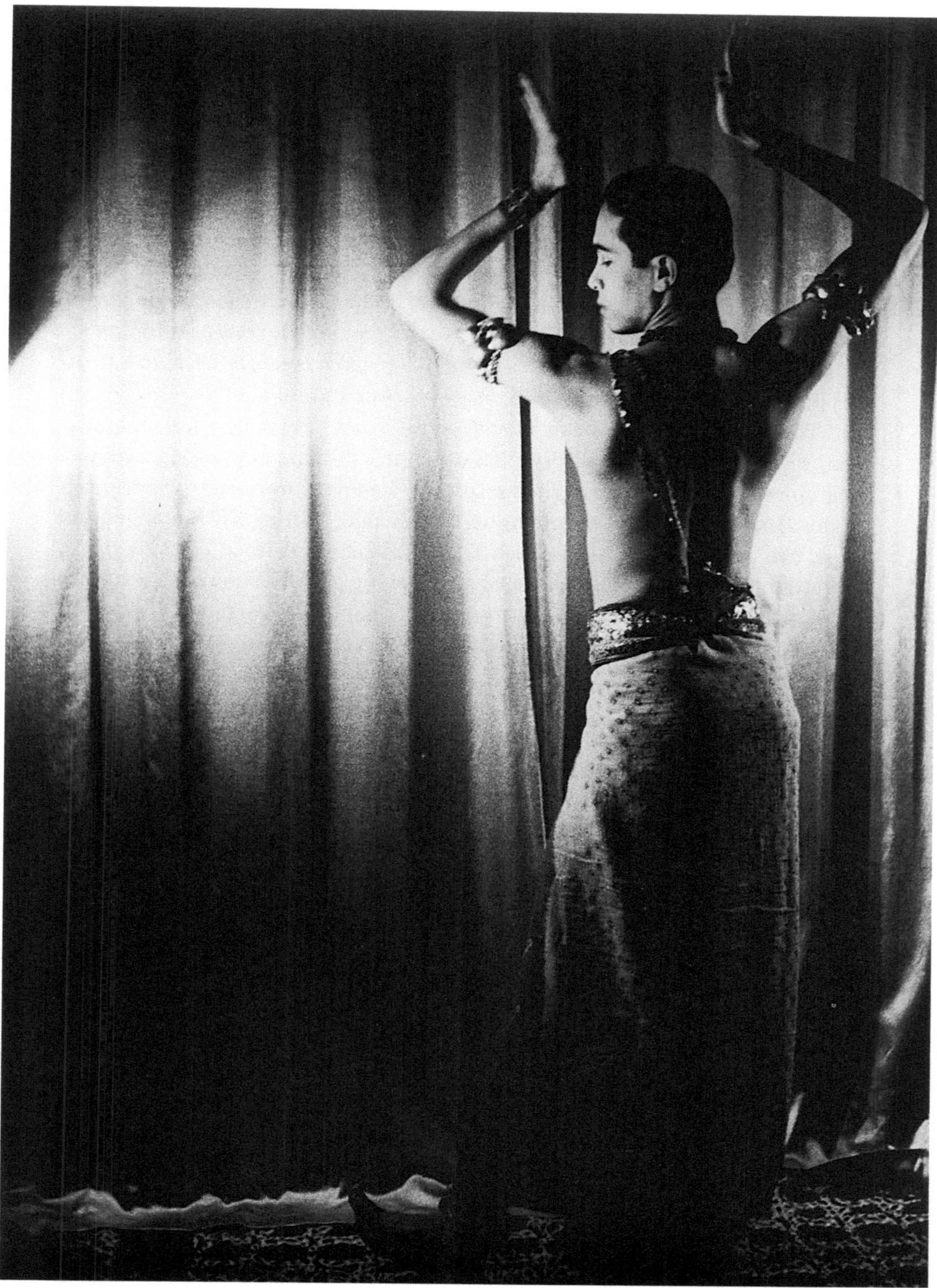

Figure 5.18. Carl Van Vechten, *Ram Gopal*, April 21, 1938, XII M4. (Beinecke Rare Book and Manuscript Library, Yale University; © The Van Vechten Trust)

caryatids that were beginning to "Orientalize" the Art Deco architecture of New York in the 1930s. Gopal's forward foot is briefly outlined against the crumpled edges of the fabric curtain that glimmer softly on the studio floor like crests from an ocean wave in the darkness of the night.

Photography sparked in Gopal an altogether different order of bodily awareness from both his live performances and publicity stills that imitated sacred sculpture. While the desire to reproduce ancient sculpture is deeply ingrained in an Indian dancer's imagination, as we have seen, only in Van Vechten's studio does Gopal discover a means to carve sculpture in "space-time," as a living photogenic creature, produced by an intercorporeal exchange with the camera. As the gaze of Van Vechten's Leica hits the spectacular creature, it returns the gaze.

To cultivate a bodily awareness of the photogenic creature became a regular part of dance training in India. Gopal's student and collaborator the veteran Kathak dancer Kumudini Lakhia conveys this awareness in her classroom diaries: "The tricky and the most beautiful element is the gaze of the body." Lakhia's biographer Reena Shah gives us the context. Lakhia is developing a composition in Jhap Taal, a ten-beat cycle containing an odd, shifting rhythm of two and three, two and three beats, to which Lakhia matches her choreography. Thus, "the eyes barely look straight ahead, always looking off at oblique angles that are constantly, subtly shifting." She arranges a sequence of distinct movements: "In the first movement, you look with your ears by pointing your ears towards your hand, as if you are hearing something. Then when the body shifts you are looking with your nose pointing at your elbow. You should feel that you are seeing with your ears and nose, not with your eyes."[70] Lakhia's instruction for her students is useful here. The panoptic, proprioceptive awareness of the surrounding space is defined as the gaze of the dancer's body. In the words of Minor White, this is where the dancer "becomes a camera." The gaze that Lakhia describes is in fact the feral gaze of *photogénie*. It is an intercorporeal gaze, produced historically by the global flows of dance, photography, and film in the early twentieth century and realized by Gopal in New York in an intermedial exchange with Van Vechten's Leica. In Lakhia's account, the dancer absorbs that gaze in her body through training, and her limbs move in space like feelers of an insect balancing on the furtive wave of the ten-beat rhythmic cycle.

CHAPTER 6. AFTERIMAGES

The New York photo shoot of 1938 was a brief encounter between Ram Gopal and Carl Van Vechten that was soon forgotten by both. Not much is found about their collaboration in the archives and in the histories of visual and performing arts in India or the United States. Gopal remembered almost nothing from his New York visit in 1938. He was only exhilarated by the city, "awed by its rhythm and its babble and movement and smell of power and money."[1] The elaborate photo shoot that took place around his concert is never mentioned in his autobiography, and the vast literature on Van Vechten remains silent on this matter. So quickly did the memory of the encounter of 1938 lose its intensity and fade away for both practitioners.

We can glean some of the conversations that took place beyond the studio in a few fragments found in the archives. Soon after New York, when Gopal visited Aleksander Janta's family estate in Poland, Van Vechten sent Janta a package. "Speechless as I am over the last pack of pictures," Janta wrote to Van Vechten on August 8, 1938. "Ram's being divine, and even I like myself in Kathakali poses, which I do very seldom, believe me." Janta sees in those "beauties" the possibility of a book, titled "Ram Gopal . . . by Carl van Vechten," for which he recommends individual images using Van Vechten's negative numbers.[2] We also know that Van Vechten sent a picture postcard to Gertrude Stein by way of introducing the dancer to the American expatriate poet in Paris when Gopal was on his way to Europe after the photo shoot. Van Vechten sent a set of photographs also to Gopal's family in Bangalore. His sister, signing "Jessie-Jeswanti Ram Gopal," wrote back thanking him: "[for] the beautiful photos you sent me of my brother." She also mentions her brother writing from Poland about "how wonderful and kind" Van Vechten and his "good wife" were "to him at New York." She might have been hinting at Van Vechten's amateurism in a remark regarding the reactions of people to whom she showed the images: "[They] comment on the great artistic skill and finish of your photography. What a wonderful hobby yours is."[3]

The memory of each other began to fray in the minds of both Van Vechten and Gopal as soon as the dancer left the photographer's apartment. When Janta returned to New York in 1945, he wrote a letter to Van Vechten, dated November 18, 1945, reporting receiving "a cable from Ram who is now backed by a trust promoting Indian ballet for tour abroad and he may be here next year."[4] In turn, Gopal inquired about "Van Vechtens" in a letter from this time to Mercedes de Acosta. But no direct communication survives between the Indian dancer and the American photographer. The two receded into their own respective worlds. Picture postcards that Van Vechten made of the Indian dancer remained in circulation among Van Vechten's circle of friends and lovers until his death in 1964. One such box of 429 photographs that he gave to the ballet dancer William "Bill" Earl in December 1960 is now at the Frances Young Tang Teaching Museum and Art Gallery, Skidmore College.[5] The set contains index cards identifying various individuals by name, except for a few images of unnamed dancers grouped together at the back of the box. Gopal's photographs are included in that miscellaneous and anonymous group. When I spoke with Van Vechten's biographer Bruce Kellner just before he died in 2019 at the age of eighty-eight, he had no memory of even hearing about the Indian dancer. This was especially surprising because Kellner, a navy veteran from World War II and the Korean War, had developed a close friendship with Van Vechten in the 1940s and 1950s around a mutual interest in Gertrude Stein and was immersed in Van Vechten's circle of friends not long after Gopal's visit to New York and during the time when his photographs were still shared among friends and displayed around Van Vechten's apartment.

How do we account for the silence in historical archives? One reason could simply be human memory. It may also be that the conditions that fostered

Euro-American travels and global interactions in New York changed soon after Gopal left the city. There is no evidence that Janta's proposal to Van Vechten for publishing the dancer's photographs ever materialized. Van Vechten was not in the business of publishing his images. While Janta might have done so himself, their conversation might have died down because of the dramatic changes already taking place in Europe when Gopal was in Poland with Janta and Mercedes de Acosta. Gopal could sense the change. After spending a few leisurely days at Janta's estate, when the whole party left for Paris, Gopal saw the premonitions of the imminent war in the European landscape. As the train approached Warsaw, several curious "large beams and shafts of light searching the sky" made him think of "the Grauman's Chinese Theatre Film premier [he] had seen recently in Hollywood where such lights lit the theatre, the stars, and milling hysterical crowd." But Janta explained that it was what had become by now the "usual manoeuvres . . . trying to spot an aeroplane high up."[6]

After the party's last stop in Paris that winter of 1938, they dispersed. Mercedes left for the United States, and Gopal returned to India along with his "Polish manager" and the Javanese dancer Retna Mohini, whom he met in Paris along with her husband, the photographer Henri Cartier-Bresson. Janta and Mohini visited Bangalore as well as Gopal's Kathakali school in the Malabar. When Gopal returned to Paris in the fall of 1939, Europe was unrecognizable. Reporting to Mercedes de Acosta from Bangalore after his short trip, he not only expressed sadness at the fall of Paris but also feared that the war might spread to India. Probably thinking of Warsaw, which was razed to the ground by the Nazis, he writes, "Just think, Alba, Our Paris, wonderful, gay, loving and artistic, in dark somber gloom? Unthinkable. But—thank God it was NOT invaded by Bombing and destruction and also that the French had the sense to retreat slowly first and save their city."[7] He mentions that Janta had become a war reporter and was captured as a prisoner of war. His property in Poland was confiscated, his mother and pregnant sister were apprehended, and the whereabouts of his brother were unknown.

Back in New York, did Van Vechten really forget Gopal after the 1938 photo shoot? Not really. If you squint at Emelie Danielson's photograph from 1942 of his living room, which we discussed in chapter 1 (fig. 1.11), you will see Gopal appearing among a set of three enlarged photographs on the window sill behind the tiger-skin sofa. The curtain against which Van Vechten took so many of his photographs is drawn to one side to show a Rococo mirror on the sill along with plants that catch the sunlight from the window. Gopal is to the left of the mirror. To his left is a photograph of a pet lion cub of the Hollywood actress Tallulah Bankhead, named Sir Winston Churchill Jr., a photograph that Van Vechten had taken along with many images of the star on July 15, 1941. On the right of the mirror is the ballerina Alicia Markova as Giselle in a photograph from April 15, 1941. Clearly, the Indian dancer was in Van Vechten's environments until at least 1942, four years after the photo shoot. By the time of Bill Earl's gift box of

1960, however, Gopal's name withered from the photographer's memory even while his images remained in circulation among friends and lovers.

The spectacular photographs we have seen in this book remain the only record of the exchanges between the two men in New York in the spring of 1938. I have identified in these images an unusual desire that is only partly explained by the homoerotic interests of the two cultural practitioners. The book has been an attempt to name the desire that attracted the two men to each other. Their mutual intimacy is routed through photography and is available in its interpersonal as well as historical and cultural granularity only in the images.

The two cultural practitioners obviously had robust lives outside the photographic image. This book, however, has insisted on exploring how that "outside" leaves its trace in the image. Roland Barthes has eloquently engaged with the complexities and dangers of naming such a photographic referent, and he hovers in my book as a guide. In his classic meditation on photography, he shows us that the transparency and readability of the referent is an alluring affect of the photograph. As a mechanical and chemical trace of what was once there in front of the camera, the referent attaches itself irreducibly to the photographic image. Nevertheless, that contingent trace is elusive. Now you see it, now you don't. The allure drew Barthes into an endless process of deciphering the photographic image. This book's chapters have similarly been organized around that puzzle of the referent. Recursion and iteration became an interpretive method. I returned to the photographs to find in them, each time and once again, the presence of the participants of the New York photo shoot in 1938.

The Barthesian approach helped me trust my viewing practices in the investigation, or at least not mistrust them like an iconoclastic art historian and humanist. Barthes encourages a "phenomenology" in which the body of the interpreter becomes an instrument of knowledge about the photographic image. This visceral dimension of his methodology comes across in his vivid analogy of the "wound" and "stigmata" inflicted by a photograph.[8] Barthes has helped me get beyond the literal subject to explore photographs for the presence of desires and "embodied processes" involved in the photo shoot.[9] I too have indulged in what the editors of a volume based on Barthes's meditations call "feeling photography."[10] However, I wanted not simply to long for but to mark the "irreducible thereness" (and thatness) of the past moment to which the photographs bear witness, even if it were impossible to separate that moment from my ways of feeling into the images.

In other words, I wrestled with what Barthes recognizes as a "paradox" built within his phenomenology of a photographic image. Barthes wonders, "affect was what I didn't want to reduce; being irreducible, it was thereby what I wanted, what I ought to reduce the Photograph *to*; but could I retain an affective intentionality . . . ?"[11] Barthes's bodily attachment to the irrecoverable past of the photographic referent is so intense that he calls it the photograph's "essence" and ultimately names it "Death," encoded in all photographic images including his own. But if that irreducible content inflicts a mortal wound in the viewer, how do we distinguish its felt intensity, namely, the "affect" of a photographic referent, from the "affective intentionality" of that referent?

Here, to my mind, Barthes seems unclear, and strategically so, in order to position the meaning of the photographic image in the existential body of the viewer. In my book, by contrast, I pursue the "affective intentionality" of the photograph as the "history" of the photographic referent. The distinction is strategic on my part also. With "history," I want to recognize the difference that Barthes implies between "affect" and the "affective intentionality" of the photographic image. History could only be sensed by separating the "intentionality" of the image from the many personal involutions in which a Barthes-style meditation of photography develops.[12] The desires of the historical actors during the 1938 photo shoot are not quite available to me, and to call what I see in those stunning images "their essence" seems presumptuous.

The two terms may be equivalents but not quite the same. Like "essence," the "history" of the photographs emerges in the practices of viewing and reading. Readers may even regard my narrative as a longing for the presence of the participants in the New York photo shoot similar to Barthes's longing for his mother in the well-known, unseen, Winter Garden photograph. Just as the essence of the photographic referent offers a resistance to Barthes's longings, history too offers a resistance to my modes of knowing.

And yet the two terms cannot be considered interchangeable. I feel uncomfortable giving my existential body and my historical place in the twenty-first century too much agency of phenomenological meaning-making, unavoidable as it may be. I worry that I might foreclose a line of inquiry that the photographs might invite, now or in the future, for me or for someone else. Of course, like the essence of a photographic image, history is also only an afterimage, contingent on what I see, as well as linked, chemically and neurologically, to my perception. Now I see it, now I don't. Unlike Barthes, however, I have conceptualized this anamorphic presence of the photographic referent as what Michal-Rolph Trouillot has called a "bundle of silences" surrounding a historical moment in the past.[13]

So, as I summarize the larger findings and takeaways of the book, I want to describe them as afterimages. One afterimage is Barthes himself. I include my reflections on Barthes at the end of the book, not in the beginning, because my investigation was not about demonstrating a Barthesian methodology, at least not explicitly, nor was it my purpose to make interventions in Barthesian studies of photography. In *Camera Lucida*, Barthes insists on limiting his reading of photographs "only" as a viewer and spectator, disclaiming the point of view of a photographer or the technological history of the photographic apparatus. By contrast, this book is not about me, my time, or my cultural position in relation to the photographic referent. Instead, I have tried to be a historian of the 1930s moment in which the images were produced, avoiding giving too much credit to my own encounters in the photographic archives. It is possible that Van Vechten's photographs of Gopal are so deliberately stylized that I cannot include them in my photo album. And yet their studied artfulness got me hooked enough to pursue the referent in them.

Barthes lingers in this book as my interlocutor and guide at "feeling photography." While he leads me to the historical actors discussed in the book, he does not appear as one of them. By contrast, other major thinkers (and "feelers" and "healers") of photography such as Walter Benjamin emerge as participants in the historical conjunctions of the 1930s in which the New York photo shoot is placed. I have not used Benjamin as my ally or guide, as scholars have done in their efforts to decolonize photography and media across the humanities. Rather, he appears as a historical actor in the book. The more I investigated the presence and interventions of the Leica during the New York photo shoot, the more he became an exponent of the German camera he never names in his writings. A historical afterimage I develop in the book is the embeddedness of the French Impressionist filmmakers such as Jean Epstein within Benjamin's thinking and feeling of photography, at least in his earlier writing in the late 1920s and early 1930s, before his optimism was dampened. I trace the bind between their thinking in the 1930s as part of the photographic referent of Van Vechten's images in the chapters 4 and 5. While the connection between those thinkers and the New York photo shoot is arguably less direct, it is integral to the international fascination with the German camera during what I have defined as the Leica Moment.

The most unexpected discovery for me was indeed the active role of the Leica in producing the allure of the photographic image for the historical actors in my book. And thus, unlike for Barthes, the photographic apparatus became part of the history I pursue. Barthes disavows camerawork as belonging outside the limits of the viewer and relating to a photographer's expertise and technical knowledge. By contrast, in my account, the Leica becomes a historical actor in the New York photo shoot precisely when it slips from the photographer's control and declares Van Vechten as an amateur.[14] The Leica enchants the studio and structures the space of estrangement in which the "awestruck" photographer and his glamorous actors indulge in fantasy-making.

I also discover the photographer not as the human author of the image Barthes imagines but as a composite grotesque that I call the camera-animal, which leaves its trail in the image. Similarly, the dancer also does not appear as a human performer whom I know to be physically present in the studio, and whose dance I could study outside the image, but as an exquisite grotesque whose gaze captivates me in the photographs. The skin of that nonhuman creature fuses with the material surface of the photograph. Van Vechten's double-exposed print of Nataraja literalizes the Barthesian bind whereby "the Photograph always carries its referent with itself, both affected by the same amorous or funereal immobility, at the very heart of the moving world: they are glued together, limb by limb, like the condemned man and the corpse in certain tortures; or even like those pairs of fish (sharks, I think, according to Michelet) which navigate in convoy, as though united by an eternal coitus" (fig. 5.12).[15]

The "eternal coitus" of the chemical image and the photographic referent transforms the intercultural and homoerotic attractions of the human actors into what I call photo-eroticism. The privacy and intimacy of Van Vechten's apartment-studio remains a constant, material ground for photo-erotic desires and border-crossing. In examples such as the double-exposure print, among others, we see a promiscuous transaction between media and bodies that exposes the photo shoot to a dose of technological sublime. The promiscuous relations that unfold in the privacy of the studio stand in contrast to the way Van Vechten and Gopal curate their public lives and cultural presence in their separate countries after the brief encounter in New York. In short, those relations are only available to us as fleeting, anamorphic afterimages.

I wonder if the lapse of memory of the photo shoot in Gopal and Van Vechten is a deliberate silencing of a deeply personal and transformative event by the historical subjects, as Michal-Rolph Trouillot alerts us.[16] The global flows of interracial and intercorporeal exchanges in the studio might have become politically risky in the heat of the moment. Soon after the photo shoot, both Gopal and Van Vechten returned to the dynamic political and cultural life of their respective countries and claimed their privilege in it from their somewhat-marginal positions. The cultural repositioning is especially seen in Gopal's relation to the history of Indian classical dance by the mid-twentieth century. In his *Indian Dancing* (1951), he invests in the idea of classical dance as a cultural inheritance, and in his 1957 autobiography, he fully inhabits the aura of that inheritance.

In Gopal's unpublished letters to Mercedes de Acosta, his connection to that cultural inheritance is nuanced with his awareness of his conflicted times. Writing from the winter cold and gray of Paris during his second European tour in 1939–1940, Gopal remembers "the glorious blue of [his] native India, its warm breath, and cooling rivers and streams in the South, in Malabar." The landscape glows in his imagination. He had recently visited Shiva shrines, attended festivals, and reconnected with his old Kathakali guru, "far away from the rest of a very modern India": "Malabar retains so much of the pure and clean in tradition, living, and most important of all, Religion; that no other single city of India has, or emanates, in contact."[17] Just as he mourns the devastation of Europe, he reflects on India on the verge of gaining Independence. "To begin with India, Eternal India, Goddess of all the world, spiritual reservoir of Eternity, how sad a position she is in. . . . Here in India the true beauty of her spiritual beauty, the greatness of her ARTS is lost, flung on the rack as it were, in the mad scramble for money making by madder capitalists, Indian capitalists, who under the guise of so called Nationalism, are wreaking havoc with India's masses and their hungry souls and bodies!!!"[18] Gopal is especially critical of the left-leaning nationalists who had affiliated their cultural practices with the Soviet socialist ideas of cultural progress and societal transformations.[19] Instead, he attaches himself to that remembered land of "India" and fashions it into a monumental vision.

The ideals of that glorious land continue in only a few exceptional men of his times. One is Mahatma Gandhi, who introduced Gopal to the teachings of the *Bhagavata Gita*. Gandhi was a modern Krishna, mediating in the political conflicts as "the Divine one, whose eternal melody today, in the twentieth century, was one of peace and love, whose doctrine of non-violence the barbaric and machine-dominated West was incapable of understanding." Between 1940 and 1947, Gopal gave concert tours all over India. At a concert at the Regal Theatre in Delhi, he met Jawaharlal Nehru, "one of the great architects of New India" whom he compares with "Emperor Ashoka" and "Lord Buddha." And if Gandhi was Krishna, Nehru was his disciple "Arjuna, who fought bravely and vanquished the evil he saw about him through his great powers of mind and spirit."[20] These national heroes traversed different temporalities, real and mythic, and Gopal found in them a model for being in this world. Key to his mode of worldliness was a distance from the present-day country and its politics. In that "other" India, he wrote to Mercedes de Acosta, "I shall continue to exist in Divinity—that is literally, among gods. For those temples in the South, in Malabar, with their power, beauty, austerity, and ritual, hold for me the greatest attraction."[21]

For Gopal, dance represented a way of inhabiting that other world. It transcends politics, and he defined it as a spiritual journey, "a pilgrim's progress," that benefits humankind across regional and linguistic divisions. He performed for "the convalescent British and Indian troops in hospitals scattered throughout the length and breadth of India."[22] On Gandhi's suggestion, he began to preface his dance with advocacy for the beauty of the South Indian idiom. And, finally, he established a school of dance at the Torquay Castle in Bangalore, inviting a number of teachers to teach for him: Ellappa Mudaliar and Gowrie Ammal from Mylapur, Madras, to teach "Dasi Attam," as well as Muthukumaran Pillai from Mayvaram in the Tanjore district, who taught in the same style as his teacher, Meenakshisundaram Pillai. Among the first students at his school were the legendary Bharatanatyam dancer Mrinalini Sarabhai, who studied both Dasi Attam and Kathak and danced with him in Madras and Calcutta during the war. Gopal continued his research visits to Tanjore and to Kumbhakonam and resumed his lessons in Kathakali with his teacher, Kunju Kurup. His network in India grew strong. He organized the All India Dance Festival in Delhi and performed in the All India Festival in Bombay. He coauthored a book on Indian dance with the Bombay art and film critic Serozh Dadachanji. In Bombay, he also tried choreography for film. By India's Independence, Gopal was at the height of his career as a dancer and teacher, gaining national recognition and also representing Indian dance abroad, in tours to England and the United States in 1947–1948. In 1947, he danced at the reopening of the Indian section of the Victoria and Albert Museum. In 1948, he was sent to New York by the government of India for a concert tour, and in 1954, he was invited to be a resident dancer at Jacob's Pillow, the center for dance in the Berkshires, Massachusetts, on the invitation of its founder, Ted Shawn.

Less well-known in this mode of worldliness is that in the 1950s, Gopal also acted in Hollywood films. He wrote to Mercedes de Acosta, "In 1951, I did a very neat job of acting with Claudette Colbert, 3rd biggest role in 'Outpost Malaya.'" In 1952, he was invited to choreograph dances for *Elephant Walk.* Then there was *Purple Rain* with Gregory Peck, in which he played a Burmese philosopher, Phang San. The list goes on.[23] He embraced Orientalism fully: "I think there is a place waiting to be filled in Motion pictures in Europe and America somebody who can play these Mongol, Eastern, and Egyptian roles, characters the PUBLIC would pay millions to see, and I am going to try and become THAT character on the screen. As Ramses or Tutankhamen, as a Mongol Khan, as an Indian prince or Raja, or as an ascetic Buddhist monk, a Tibetan, I KNOW I could do these things better than any other."[24]

These are extraordinary claims that need explanation. How does racializing and ethnologizing his body along Primitivist and Orientalist stereotypes not seem contradictory to Gopal's equally deep connection to India's cultural heritage? Here is a thought. Both are modes of wearing what Anne Anlin Cheng calls "modernism's dream of a second skin" in relation to Josephine Baker.[25] This second skin is produced by a modernist desire for its other and a mimetic exchange between a performer's racialized body and the gaze of its white viewers. Cheng reads Baker's glamorous body synchronously, in its contiguity with other material and aesthetic forms including the deliberate sensuousness of stylish clothing as well as the clean, white surfaces in architectural designs, enriched by the glamor of ebony, metal, plastic, and cellophane in the 1920s and 1930s.

Unlike Gopal, Cheng does not include the aura of an imagined homeland among Baker's modernist desires. Instead she places Baker's "dermal" exchanges against questions of race and identity raised by cultural critics such as Frantz Fanon, whose idea of race as a "wound" inflicted by a white man's gaze on a Black body energized critical race studies. "What I am calling the dream of the second skin—or remaking one's self in the skin of the other—is a *mutual* fantasy, one shared by both Modernists seeking to be outside of their own skins and by racialized subjects looking to escape the burdens of epidermal inscription." By separating this "skin" from the "flesh," in essence distinguishing the racialized body's promiscuous, intercorporeal relations from the corporeal violence of that body, Cheng refines the basic assumption of race studies. "The racist interpellation 'See the Negro!' [quoting Fanon] is thrown into crisis when we attend to the contours of what is seen, and when we challenge the most readily available terms of describing the body fixed by that injunction."[26]

Gopal's investment in the "*mutual* fantasy" of modernism is fleetingly visible in Van Vechten's photographs. By the mid-twentieth century, he denied this promiscuous flow of modernism in his curated self-presentation. His autobiography does not mention the epidermal exchanges with photography and film that we have explored in this book. Instead, those exchanges disappear into a "transcendent" body of a classical Indian dancer. Gopal's worldliness (or *other*worldliness) percolated into the dance training of students and bodily practices of dancers in post-Independence India, now guided and transmitted through a *guru-shishya* (master-disciple) tradition. As the dancer and scholar Avanthi Meduri reflected on her personal life and training in the Bharatanatyam in Madras not long thereafter, she wrote in the 1980s, "My Indian teachers . . . extolled the virtues of transcendental knowledge (*alaukika gnana*), which is characterized by intellectual detachment. This view of reality terrified me then as it is today, for it undercuts plurality and forces one to consciously efface or transcend Self."[27] And indeed, Gopal's 1957 autobiography spells out exactly this "detached" and otherworldly dimension of Indian dance. However, Van Vechten's photographs show that the transcendence was routed differently in the 1930s. Instead of a singular nonnegotiable ideology derived from a larger-than-life cultural heritage to which a "terrified" child student was exposed in Madras, the "transcendental" mode of being was literally shaped in an earlier era in the very "plurality" of global flows that shaped the dancer's self-fashioning as an ecstatic form of bodily alienation in front of the camera. During the New York photo shoot of 1938, Gopal's "intellectual detachment" crossed the line of national cultural heritage and flirted with what Van Vechten recognized as the "jazz quality" in his performance, as shown in chapter 3. By midcentury, Gopal disavowed that modernist fantasy and pursued his place in the history of Indian classical dance. Surprisingly, at the same time, he also moved permanently to the United Kingdom and lived a life of a cultural celebrity, while dance historians such as Sunil Kothari worried that the future generation of Indian dancers would not remember him in India.[28]

Van Vechten's forgetfulness may also relate to his involvement with institution-building relating to a cultural cosmopolitanism attained within the racialized dynamics of New York. In the 1940s, Van Vechten began to build public archives based on his relations with the artistic community in New York City, especially African American intellectuals and performers. He donated thousands of images of artists, writers, and performers to the Beinecke, the New York Public Library, and other chosen public collections. His photographs of New York City were concentrated in the Museum of the City of New York. The George Gershwin Memorial Collection of Music and Music Literature at Fisk University in Nashville, Tennessee, was built around Van Vechten's interests in African American music, and the Carl Van Vechten Galleries at that university held regular exhibitions on modernism and photography.

Curating a self, not only for Van Vechten but also for his subjects, is best represented in the James Weldon Johnson Memorial Collection of Negro Arts and Letters at the Beinecke.[29] Photographs of prominent figures of the African American community from that collection appear everywhere: on book jackets of novels and autobiographies of the writers of the Harlem Renaissance and in catalogs of exhibitions on men and women intellectuals. In the fall of 2020, the Beinecke displayed Van Vechten's colored images of some of those writers and intellectuals in the windows of the library and organized a spectacular series of "Beinecke Mondays," in which scholars presented biographies to celebrate the many contributions of those individuals to the intellectual, political, and cultural life of the country.[30]

At all these curated venues, Van Vechten's photographs can be recognized by their distinctive look, with figures seen against myriad fabric backgrounds. But they also achieve a "transcendent" quality as visual testaments to the singular achievements of the individual sitters, detached from what I have explored in Gopal as a cross-racial collaboration and mutual fantasy-making within the privacy of Van Vechten's studio. The photographic collaboration that regularly took place in his studio has become politically incorrect in the current moment of my writing, characterized by the resurgence of white supremacy and the radical activism of Black Lives Matter within the divisive politics of the twenty-first-century United States. I hope scholars who study Van Vechten's other racialized subjects may see the collaborations that occurred within the intimacy of the New York studio as what I have called the politics of privacy, which took place in plain sight in perhaps a more brutal period of racial segregation and violence in the United States.

In India's dance history, Gopal's immersion in the global circuits became anachronistic by the mid-twentieth century. Just as the American dance critic John Martin saw Gopal's performance in New York in 1938 as cheap "pictorial" kitsch, the Bangalorean art critic G. Venkatachalam wrote of the dancer, "Like Ravi Varma's paintings, his dances are pretty but not convincing. Their superficiality is obvious."[31] The reference to Ravi Varma is telling. The painter and entrepreneur Raja Ravi Varma (1848–1906) belonged to the royal household of a princely state of Travancore comparable to Mysore. In the nineteenth century, Ravi Varma's oil paintings and mass-produced prints were celebrated for their portrayal of fleshy Indian gods and mythological figures through a use of Western realism, but they were dismissed as low kitsch precisely for their promiscuity by the mid-twentieth century.[32]

Venkatachalam's view of Gopal may be seen as duplicitous, since he was not averse to global, cross-cultural interactions. When the American dancer Esther Sherman, known as Ragini Devi, came to India in the 1930s, Venkatachalam hosted her at the Theosophical Society's compound at 6 St. John's Road in the Bangalore cantonment, where he lived, and encouraged her to learn Kathakali at the Kerala Kalamandalam.[33] He also took credit for inspiring Ragini Devi and his dance partner from the Kalamandalam days, Guru Gopinath, to depart from the complicated costume and long ritualized performances of traditional Kathakali and to choreograph short numbers for an audience beyond the remote South Indian region of Kerala.[34] But here is the difference. In asking the Ragini Devi and Gopinath duo to modulate traditional performance,

Venkatachalam imagined for Kathakali a pan-Indian, "national" audience, for whom the regional form might be new and unknown in the 1930s. By contrast, Gopal's eclectic practice and his reach for a global audience was a flat-out compromise of India's cultural tradition.

This book has described in Gopal an intimacy between the global flows of Orientalism and Indian classical dance. This in itself is not a revelation. However, Orientalist exchanges are misrecognized in post-Independence India, and cultural forms shaped by those exchanges are marginalized when they do not achieve the national paradigms of cultural heritage. Gopal inhabits this blind spot, of which I had a brief but sharp acknowledgment during a conference of Indian dance in 2017 in Delhi, where I asked the legendary modernist dancer Astad Deboo (d. 2020) what he thought about Gopal. "Everyone knows Ram Gopal's name," Deboo said, but "what has he done for India?" By way of contrast, Deboo pointed to Uday Shankar. In the 1930s, Shankar returned from his world tours to India and opened a school for experimental dance in Almora in the North Indian hills. Deboo was absolutely right. Gopal migrated to the United Kingdom in the 1950s, while dancers from Shankar's school gained fame for innovative choreographies on the Indian and international stage and in the commercial film industry of India. But here is what I find most striking in Deboo's comment. The legitimacy of a performer is based on a "national" paradigm. As a senior dancer and pioneer of contemporary dance in India, and much loved for incorporating dance as well as philosophical and cultural traditions from world cultures into his choreographies, Deboo did not see Gopal's innovations. Both Deboo in his dismissal of Gopal and Venkatachalam in his promotion of Ragini Devi arrived at the national paradigm from two opposite sides, local and global if you will, and the Indian dancer who moved to the United Kingdom disappeared in the blind spot of that paradigm. Cultural promiscuity was fraught, unless it was employed for a national purpose. By midcentury, Gopal too found his earlier global affinities, and his Ravi Varma–like "princely" vision of modernity, anachronistic and regressive.[35] The transnational references all but disappeared from both his representations and dance writing, and the various androgynous metamorphoses we see in the New York photographs became impossible to imagine.

Archives of those early global flows are only now appearing in scholarly literature.[36] Cultural crossovers need new terms of description. The title of the historian Vivek Bald's book *Bengali Harlem* puts a name to the cultural promiscuity that skids from national paradigms in India as well as the United States. Bald documents Muslim merchants from Bengal who traded in embroidered fabric (*chikan*) and other luxury items in the United States beginning in the 1890s.[37] Using immigration and naturalization records, marriage certificates, newspapers, records at law courts, ship logs, and other documents, Bald identifies journeys of eleven such merchants (*chikandars*) who arrive from Calcutta and ply their goods in New York City as well as in beach resorts such as Atlantic City and Asbury Park in New Jersey, making their way to cities in the US South, such as Charleston, Atlanta, and New Orleans. Their mobile lifestyle recalls early-modern trade across the Indian Ocean, with individuals living full lives on two or more continents, instead of the patterns of immigration or refugee settlements in recent times.[38] By the 1920s and 1930s, the individual histories of those Bengali *chikandar* merge into the larger history of the United States. The men intermarry, have children, and form communities in Black neighborhoods, such as Tremé and Storyville in New Orleans and Harlem in New York, where they host other migrant merchants from India. Bald maps their individual journeys through the racial politics of segregation in the United States and also shows their participation in the struggles against British rule in India waged from New York and other locations.[39]

Bald's historical period, 1890–1930, intersects with the cast of characters who appear in my book also, including the promoters of "Oriental," "Eastern," and "Ethnic" dances, such as Ruth St. Denis, Ted Shawn, La Meri, the performers of "Hindoo ballet" such as Uday Shankar and Ram Gopal, and African American performers of Harlem and their white patrons, such as Van Vechten. Bald describes his Muslim traders also as "peddlers of notions." They not only ply exotic goods but also play up their appearance and romanticize the "East" by wearing beards, long gowns, and fez caps. In a dizzying example of cross-cultural mimesis, Bald documents African American men passing as Indians and wearing that "Eastern" garb in order to escape the segregationist regime of the South. Thus, while it is true that the African American cultural life of New York's Tenderloin District and Harlem was formed by the Great Migration from a racially segregated South, in Bald's account, that "South" was blended. It included the Bengali traders along with "thousands of immigrants from the English- and Spanish-speaking Caribbean" as well as "Argentinians, Colombians, Mexicans, Panamanians, and Chinese."[40]

In my pursuit of the history of the 1938 photo shoot, I have tried to imagine Gopal, Van Vechten, and other cultural practitioners within the interracial networks of New York as precisely as was possible in the archives. In light of Bald, I wonder to what restaurant Mercedes de Acosta might have taken the dancer after his concert at the 46th Street Theatre on May 1, 1938? Could it have been the Bengal Garden, located at 144 West Forty-Sixth Street and owned by a Bengali immigrant, Habib Ullah, and his Puerto Rican wife?[41] To find a trace of such historical actors in Van Vechten's Upper West Side studio, we might have to look at the photographs from a raking angle. Some of Van Vechten's exotic fabric curtains could have easily come from the South Asian merchants who sold their goods in Greenwich Village and elsewhere in the city. In his photographs, we could also look for the hidden networks that brought the photographer and his various subjects to collaborate with each other in his studio. Looking at his photographs of the jazz singer Ella Fitzgerald on January 19, 1940, for example, makes me wonder whether he knew that Fitzgerald's career was launched in the 1930s, when a certain "Bardu" Ali introduced her to Chick Webb, known as "one of Harlem's leading swing jazz bandleaders."[42] Bardu (or Bahadour) Ali was a son of another Bengali immigrant, Moksad Ali, who moved in 1903 from New Orleans across the Mississippi and raised his three children in Hancock County, Mississippi, with his wife, Ella. In the Harlem's records, Bardu Ali was classified as a "negro actor" living on St. Nicholas Avenue between 151st and 152nd Streets. By the 1930s, he had "made a name for himself in black theatrical and music circles as a suave and crowd-pleasing emcee."[43] In Van Vechten's studio, Fitzgerald is seated on the sofa with the tiger skin we see in Emelie Danielson photograph discussed in chapter 1, but Bardu Ali appears nowhere.

The global network of communities forming in New York City by the time of Gopal's visit becomes hard to imagine when dance becomes a bounded cultural practice and an art form seen exclusively from the point of view of the dancer and his expert critics. When John Martin called Gopal a crowd-pleasing showman, we could ask, What did that crowd that Martin disdained look like? We could also investigate whether Gopal's transcultural representations in New York mirrored not only the fantasies of his elite, white admirers but also the desires and longings of that "other" crowd of possibly Indian and African American fantasy peddlers in the audience. Would that mixed, diasporic crowd have recognized in his glamorous body the same "jazz quality" that Van Vechten saw in the Indian dancer? While the affinities visible in Van Vechten's photographs cannot be named and organized, the images leave us with these fleeting thoughts in the archives in which we study our historical documents.

ACKNOWLEDGMENTS

Like a gift that keeps giving, Carl Van Vechten's photographs of Ram Gopal at Yale's Beinecke Library set me on a path of serendipitous encounters beginning in the spring of 2015. Adrienne Sharp, a Mount Holyoke College alumna who happened to work at the Beinecke at that time, set me up with a library account, and the Access Services staff circled around the project right away. I thank Moira Fitzgerald, Rebecca Hirsh, Matthew Daniel Mason, Annamarie Menta, Natalia Sciarini, and many others for their generous assistance at the Beinecke from start to finish. During the COVID-19 pandemic, when non-Yale visitors were not allowed in the library, Nancy Kuhl, the curator of Yale Collection of American Literature, reached out remotely and sent me digital files of Van Vechten's negatives of Gopal. June Can patiently accepted requests for the bulk of the images in the book.

The book would not have been possible without the generosity of the caring staff at many other collections. In Bangalore, India, I am grateful to Ashish Khokar for sharing documents from the Mohan Khokar Archives of Dance. At the Rosenbach Library, Philadelphia, I thank Elizabeth Fuller, Jobi Zink, and Kristina Robold for documents from the Mercedes de Acosta Papers. At the New York Public Library, a special thanks to Andrea Felder and Tom Lisanti and to Erik Skolarski for helping me access the Jerome Robbins Dance Division Archives remotely when it was not possible to visit New York due to COVID-19. At the Philadelphia Museum of Art, which holds the single largest set of Van Vechten's photographs of Gopal, I am grateful to Peter Barberie, curator of photography, and Darielle Mason, the Stella Kramrisch curator of South Asian and Himalayan art. I thank Lauren Robinson for assistance at the Museum of the City of New York and Ian Barry and Jessica Lubniewski at the Francis Young Tang Teaching Museum and Gallery at Skidmore College for showing me Van Vechten's picture postcards from their Jack Shear Photography Collection. A special shout of thanks to Norton Owen at the Jacobs Pillow Archives for a wonderful welcome to study their holdings of Gopal, La Meri, Ted Shawn, and other dancers. The robust programming at Jacobs Pillow, including many seasons of dazzling performances and lectures, exposed me to various traditions of world dance as well as contemporary choreography, and an exhibition of photographs stimulated my interest in dance photography. A huge gratitude to Todd Gustavson, the curator of the Technology Collection at the George Eastman House Museum in Rochester, New York, for sharing his knowledge of the technological and industrial history of photography, cameras, lenses, films, lights, tripods, chemicals, and companies for an entire morning and for letting me handle the Leica models in their collection, including the prototype of 1909 and the ones Van Vechten was likely to have used in the 1930s. I feel beholden to Ayisha Abraham for hosting me at her home in Bangalore and sharing her research and documentation around the salvaged eight-millimeter film by Tom D'Aguir of Gopal performing at his Torquay Castle, shot within months of his New York photo shoot in 1938.

I am grateful to the numerous public and private collections that liberally gave me digital files and permission to publish the artworks in this image-driven book. Above all, I owe a huge gratitude to Edward Burns, the trustee of the Van Vechten Trust, for his steady support from the start. Dan Munn freely allowed me to publish Florine Stettheimer's *Asbury Park, South*, from the halley k harrisburg and Michael Rosenfeld Collection, New York. Katie Womack and Caroline Gallagher at the Reynolda House Museum, North Carolina, helped me with Charles Demuth's *Cabaret Interior with Carl Van Vechten* (1917) in the Barbara B. Millhouse Collection. I thank Miranda Muscente and Cole Hill at Condé Nast for facilitating the permission to reproduce images from *Vanity Fair* and *Vogue* and Robbi Siegel at the Art Resource and Alan Baglia at the Artists Rights Society for collaborating on the rights for Man Ray's photograph *Noire et Blanche* (1926). Maria Elena Roca Covarrubias of the Miguel Covarrubias family estate in Mexico City generously allowed me to reproduce that brilliant and understudied artist's caricatures.

The book began taking shape during a residential fellowship at the Research and Academic Program, Clark Art Institute, in the spring of 2017. I thank Christopher Heuer, Karen Bucky and her library staff, and Deborah Fehr for their hospitality. My wonderful research assistant Michael Pratt, an MA art history student at Williams College, geeked out with me over the Leica and enriched my understanding of 1930s Euro-American photography. I would not have been able to accept the Clark Fellowship without a salary top-off at Mount Holyoke College, and I am grateful to the dean of faculty, Jon Western (d. 2022), for it. Two faculty grants from Mount Holyoke took me to conferences and research trips, and two more supported the publication. I thank the Linda Kelso Wright Fund in the Art History and Architectural Studies Department for funding a research assistant, which brought the book to fruition in the summer of 2021. And speaking of serendipity, my wonderful assistant, the architecture studies major Sarannya Sharrma, turned out to be a Bharatanatyam dancer whose insights into the technical vocabulary of Indian dance proved invaluable. I feel indebted to the two exceptional, anonymous reviewers at Rutgers University Press who recognized the strengths of the project and challenged me to push the book's conceptual boundaries in new directions. My visionary editor at RUP, Nicole Solano, deserves a very special thanks for embracing a project that did not fit a disciplinary category, and Sonia Tam coordinated our efforts at the press. I feel grateful to RUP's editing, design, production, and marketing team, especially Alissa Zarro, Courtney Brach, and Savannah Porcelli, as well as the copy editor, Andrew Katz, and indexer David Prout for bringing the project to fruition.

From the start, the project pulled me out of my comfort zone of South Asian art history. The book would be unimaginable without the support of the many colleagues and friends in various scholarly disciplines and the performing arts. I thank the organizers of the 2015 conference at Yale, Inderpal Grewal, Kishwar Rizwi, and Tamara Sears, for the invitation that led me to the Van Vechten photographs at the Beinecke. I am grateful for my exchanges with the numerous participants that spring, including graduate students of art history and South Asian studies as well as Carol Armstrong, Crispin Branfoot, Rebecca Brown, Iftikhar Dadi, Deepali Deewan, Kasturi Gupta, Sunil Gupta, Christopher Pinney, Holly Schaffer, and Laura Wexler. Sandra Matthews from Hampshire College, a photographer herself and the founding editor of the online journal *Trans Asian Photography Review*, got her ears warmed during our car drives between the Pioneer Valley in Massachusetts and New Haven, Connecticut.

Testing my findings at conferences and inviting colleagues for lunches became a habit thereafter. At the American Council for Southern Asian Art (ACSAA) symposium in Toronto in 2015, my copanelists Kathryn Hansen and Ameera Nimjee alerted me to a learning curve relating to Indian dance and theater histories. At the ACSAA symposium in Cambridge, Massachusetts, in 2017, Antonia Behan illuminated me on the exotic textiles circulating in New York City in the early twentieth century. At a Five-Colleges Art History Seminar, Brigitte Buettner, Barbara Kellum, Anna Lee, Dana Leibsohn, Erica Morawski, Yael Rice, and Alex Seggerman challenged me to think about the materiality of photographs. At the Annual South Asia Conference in Madison, Wisconsin, Annu Palakunnathu Matthew, Sophia Powers, and Rashmi Vishwanathan gave me a nudge toward performative photography. The revolving door of scholars at the Clark Institute and the nearby Williams College created a stimulating intellectual environment during my Clark Fellowship. I thank my resident buddies in Williamstown, Delinda Collier, Ivan Garat, Jinhee Hong, Marden Nichols, and Tamara Sears, for a great support system. I value the exchanges during my Clark talk and seminar with Deborah Brothers, Mark Gottlieb, Guy Hedreen, Michael Ann Holly, Liz McGowen, Olivier Meslay, Keith Moxey, Christopher Nugent, Munjulika Rahman, and a fantastic cohort of students in the art history MA program at Williams College. Rakhi Balaram and Susan Bean joined me as great allies. Holly Edwards, Mary Roberts, and Avinoam Shalem offered new ways of examining Orientalism. Ralph Lieberman shared insights about the relationship between architectural photography and dance photography. Eva Heekin translated Aleksander Janta's *Pamietnik Indyjski* (Indian Diary, 1970) from Polish into English for me.

I owe a huge gratitude to the organizers of numerous symposia and scholarly gatherings that provided opportunities to try out my ideas on a diverse group of colleagues. Stephen Whiteman invited me to give a talk in the Asia Lecture Series at the University of Sydney, and Mark Ledbury of the Powers Institute hosted me in Australia. Martin Hribek asked me to collaborate with him on a panel, "Imaging India in Central and Eastern Europe," at the twenty-fourth European Conference of South Asian Studies in Warsaw, Poland, and Jinah Kim hosted my presentation for the Lakshmi Mittal and Family South Asia Institute and the History of Art Department, Harvard University. I was pleased to present my research at the Beinecke's online series of "Beinecke Mondays" organized by Michael Morand. Sumathi Ramaswamy invited me to an interdisciplinary arts and media international workshop, "China Rising? India Shining? The Art of Comparison," at Duke University, where Rey Chow's prompt to explore Orientalism as a two-way street of mutual fantasy-making set me on an uncharted path.

I thank Pushpamala N. for inviting me to a conference titled "Mysore Modernity, Artistic Nationalism & the Art of K. Venkatappa" at the National Gallery of Art in Bangalore, India, in 2016, where artists and historians of arts and science, including Ayisha Abraham, Parul Dave-Mukherjee, Chandan Gowda, Abhishek Hazra, Srajana Kaikini, Raghevendra Kulkarni, Raman Shiv Kumar, Partha Mitter, R. Nandakumar, Mamta Sagar, Shukla Sawant, Cop Shiva, and many others drew attention to a "Princely Modern" style of Enlightenment in Mysore. I thank Ashish Khokar for inviting me to "The Natya Ballet Dance Festival," which he organized in collaboration with the Sangeet Natak Akademi in New Delhi in 2016. I feel enriched by the participants of that seminar, including Lubna Marium, Sadanand Menon, Mandeep Raikhi, Gowri Ramnarayan, and Anita Ratnam, as well as the many performers who gave lecture-demonstrations from various Indian dance traditions. I want to single out Astad Deboo (d. 2020) not only for a mesmerizing evening performance during the conference but also for a conversation about Ram Gopal that proved important for me. In Delhi, I also thank the dance critic Sunil Kothari (d. 2020) for his encouragement. An afternoon with the Bharatanatyam dancer Geeta Chandran was precious. Gulam Sheikh may recognize in these pages our dinner conversation about global interactions among premodern and early-modern cultures. A most delightful dinner with Geeta Kapur and Vivan Sundaram at their home allowed me to compare Vivan's insights on Umrao Singh Sher-Gil's self-presentation for the camera to Ram Gopal's in New York.

I thank Smt. Rita Swamy Choudhary, secretary at the Sangeet Natak Akademi, for inviting me back to New Delhi in 2019 to present my research and to engage the eminent dance photographer Avinash Pasricha in a conversation on the relationship between performing arts and photography. My wonderful tabla guru, Pandit Ashis Sengupta, organized the series of events with boundless enthusiasm. I thank him as well as Arun Gupta, Indu Lala, Yuriko Lochan, Yaaminey Mubayi, Avinash Pasricha, and Sunny Singh for joining me in a stimulating discussion with the students of Kathak Kendra regarding performing bodies and still images. Rajeev Lochan's understanding of photography and Vinay

Mishra's insights as not only a practicing musician but also a scholar of Shastric texts on music and dance created a nice bridge across the arts in that forum.

I want to recognize the innumerable conversations that make up the archives with which we work even when they do not make it into the stories we tell. Like fireflies swarming in the night, the chance encounters that illuminated the project over the years include a conversation about gay activism in India at Lata Mani's home in Bangalore, an insight from Katherine Hauser on queer imagery in the United States, a brilliant reading by Hari Krishnan of narcissism in Ram Gopal's photographs, and Haresh Lalwani remembering Leon Bakst's Art Nouveau designs for Ballets Russes in Paris in relation to Gopal's costume. Darielle Mason identified the sculptures in the South Asian Art section of the Victoria and Albert Museum as being on loan from Stella Kramrisch when Gopal danced there in 1948, and Michael Meister was as excited about finding a Pathé news clip of that V&A performance as discovering medieval Hindu temples in Rajasthan. The poet and dance critic Jay Rogoff shared his dance reviews and recommended books on ballet and modern dance. Penny Jolly's scholarship on the body in Renaissance art made me think anew of the Indian dancer. Driving back from my talk in Cambridge, Massachusetts, to Providence, Rhode Island, Tapati Guha-Thakurta shed a surprising light on the cross-cultural interactions in Van Vechten's photographs. At an impromptu meeting at Newark, New Jersey, train station, Ann David and I bonded over our mutual fascination with Gopal's idiosyncratic persona. Julia Bailey, Renata Holod, and Yael Rice were instrumental in hunting down the original, sixteenth-century Persian miniature painting printed on a fabric backdrop behind a photograph of Gopal. Matthew Isaac Cohen caught Gopal's use of gauze in relation to many early-twentieth-century striptease artists who followed Mata Hari. Alexander Janta's biographer Michal Folega told me about Gopal's interactions with Janta and his family and mailed me his publications from Poland. Stephen Haynes showed me his Leica photography and spotted the uneven focus and burning in Van Vechten's photographs. Katya Légeret-Manochhaya shared a delightful photograph from the 1970s of Gopal at the Lamorisse castle outside Paris, leaning on a chaise lounge and correcting Katya's hand position using a stick. Katya was a disciple of Amala Devi, who had performed with Gopal at the Victoria and Albert Museum in 1948. In a similarly unexpected encounter with Gopal's persistent presence, in Sydney, Australia, Anandavalli, a senior dancer and teacher, gifted me a poster of her inaugural performance (*arangretram*), which was introduced by Gopal, her guru in London in the 1970s. In Bangalore, Ashish Mohan Khokar shared endearing stories about his family's close relationship with Gopal ("a grandfather to me") from the days when his mother, the Bharatanatyam dancer M. K. Saroja, studied with him. When Ram Rahman mentioned that the Delhi-based architect Raj Rewal had worked as an assistant to Gopal in his youth, I wondered about the myriad networks in which the book's characters were involved, about which I will never know. I was amazed when Ayisha Abraham introduced me to Bhanumati in Bangalore in 2016. The Kathakali dancer, then in her nineties, had danced with Gopal in the 1950s. Bhanumati's eyes glowed upon seeing "that beautiful man" in Van Vechten's photographs, and my most precious memory still remains of the moment when she proceeded to show me how to take the standing *mandala sthanam* pose from Kathakali. Uttara Asha Coorlawala has been a steady beacon in my own hesitant forays into dance history, and I thank her for sharing her research on La Meri.

The book was an effort to find order and design in what often appeared to be a surprising coincidence. At Mount Holyoke College and the Five Colleges Consortium, colleagues have inspired the project in many known and unknown ways. The photography historian Anthony Lee's office next door to mine has a shelf cluttered with cameras, stereoscopes, and stereographs that make his passion for photography infectious. As Tony and my Americanist colleague Paul Staiti worked on their own book projects alongside me, our watercooler conversations often felt like support sessions of friends who are pregnant at the same time. I thank Tony for reading my book proposal and a sample chapter. Bettina Bergmann offered an affectionate nudge with her shout-out of "How is the project going?" Michael Davis's excitement at spotting an essay of mine on the internet and thereafter leaving clippings about Van Vechten from the *New York Times* in my mailbox made everything suddenly meaningful. Jessica Maier permitted the use of the department's restricted funds to support a research assistant in the fall of 2021. Robin Blaetz, Katherine Binder, Ken Colodner, Paula Debnar, Ombretta Frau, Leah Glasser, Hannah Goodwin, Gail Hornstein, Kavita Khory, Catherine Leguis, Bernadine Mellis, and Yaaminey Mubayi queried me at a Faculty Friday presentation organized by the associate dean of faculty, Gary Gillis. Ram Gopal reminded the dancer Charles Flachs of a 1912 image of Vaslav Nijinsky as "le dieu bleu," and he made an unforgettable connection for me between dance photography and wildlife photography. Pooja Rangan gave pointers on Jean Epstein. Yael Rice shared a podcast of Ann David's talk on Gopal at the British Museum in 2018. Mary Renda invited me to join a writing group. Indira Peterson read chapter 2. Elizabeth Young shared her interests in animal studies and modeled for me the excitement of doing interdisciplinary scholarship in the humanities, while Karen Remmler made me aware that letting oneself loose on an interdisciplinary project without the anxiety of tenure in a department is indeed a privilege of a senior professor.

I have followed the project where its baby legs took it. Family members in India and in North America extending from Florida to Nova Scotia nourished it by simply being fully who they are. Stephen Haynes's online links of Leica aficionados worked their way into the project. Malini Sinha's feel for fabric threads and dyes made me study Van Vechten's backdrops seriously. Kanha's favorite word, "whatever," changed in my mind from a teenager's way of disregarding a parent's advice into a permission to follow my instinct in whatever direction it took me. The book would be swarming with footnotes saying, "personal conversation with Mimi Hellman." Mimi was the first to encourage me to follow the project "where it goes," and I think of her as a secret collaborator. Her presence permeates these pages in many forms: questions I failed to respond to, concerns I dismissed, thought bubbles with which I struggled, and insights from her expertise in Euro-American design history as well as eighteenth-century French art and material culture that may have slipped into an idea in South Asian visual and performing arts and American photography. I thank her for reading the whole manuscript but realize that the burden of not getting her point accurately and misreading her intent, as well as the many errors of judgment that make up the book, are entirely mine to bear in the end.

I dedicate this book to the many elders in my life for their strange ways of keeping me on my toes. I am grateful to Sheila Kelly for her sharp look that told me to stay intellectually curious and to Anil Desai for teasing me for the "yarn" I spin in my writing. Virbala Desai asked how the book was coming along so that she could bless it one more time. Lois Miraglia communicated the pleasure of literature, and Barry Hellman modeled for me a poet's style of achieving concreteness of thought and imagery in words.

I wonder what Mati would have thought if she had a chance to hold the book in her hands! Her death a year prior to the beginning of a photography-related project makes me unavoidably think of Roland Barthes's *Camera Lucida*. My book, however, is not about my "Winter Garden photograph," which Barthes famously found at his mother's death and in which he yearned for her youthful presence prior to his birth. Instead, other visceral memories seem to have creeped into my book from witnessing my mother's aging and dementia during her last fifteen years on the planet. The loss of bodily coordination and the disintegration of language and memory slowly transformed Mati from being a strong-willed adult into a nonhuman animal. Her most valuable parting gift came toward the end of her life, when she communicated her affection by biting my wrist, the way cats do. In the book, I may have pursued this quick lesson in "affect theory" and tried to describe the sudden glimpse of prelinguistic (or should we say postlinguistic) creatureliness that Barthes traced as "punctum" in his meditation on photography.

NOTES

Prelude

1. Ashish Khokhar, "Pioneers of Indian Dance: Ram Gopal (1912–2003)," *Sahapada*, June 28, 2018, https://www.sahapedia.org/ram-gopal-1912%E2%80%932003. For the phrase "Nijinsky of India," see "The Mohan Khokar Dance Archives of India," *Attendance: Dance Annual of India*, accessed December 26, 2020, http://attendance-india.com/dance-archives-of-india/. Ram Gopal may have been the first classically trained dancer to travel outside India, but the credit for bringing Indian dance to an international audience should go to Uday Shankar, who was older than Gopal by almost a decade but an untrained dancer, with whom I compare Gopal in detail in chapter 2.
2. The archival memory and biographical narrative is primarily shaped by Ram Gopal, *Rhythm in the Heavens: An Autobiography* (London: Secker and Warburg, 1957). Since the 1990s, see also Ashish Khokar, "Ram Gopal: The King of Classical Dance," *Attendance* (Mohan Khokar Dance Foundation), 1998, 64–71; Sunil Kothari, "Ram Gopal: At Home Abroad," *Sruti*, April 2000, 21–23; Ann R. David, "Spectacle or Spectacular? The Orientalist Imagery in Indian Dance Performance in Britain from 1900–1959," *Dance and Spectacle* (Society of Dance History Scholars), 2010, 79–87; Ann R. David, *Ram Gopal: Interweaving Histories of Indian Dance* (London: Bloomsbury, forthcoming).
3. Among publications since Van Vechten's death in 1964, see Bruce Kellner, *Carl Van Vechten and the Irreverent Decades* (Norman: University of Oklahoma Press, 1968); Bruce Kellner, ed., *The Harlem Renaissance: A Historical Dictionary for the Era* (Westport, CT: Greenwood, 1984); Jonathan Weinberg, "Boy Crazy: Carl Van Vechten's Queer Collection," *Yale Journal of Criticism* 7, no. 2 (1994): 25–49; Carl Van Vechten, *The Dance Writings of Carl Van Vechten*, ed. Paul Padgette (New York: Dance Horizons, 1981); Rudolph P. Byrd, ed., *Generations in Black and White: Photographs by Carl Van Vechten from the James Weldon Johnson Memorial Collection* (Athens: University of Georgia Press, 1993); Emily Bernard, *Carl Van Vechten and the Harlem Renaissance: A Portrait in Black and White* (New Haven, CT: Yale University Press, 2012); Keith F. Davis, *The Passionate Observer: Photographs of Carl Van Vechten* (Kansas City, MO: Hallmark Cards, 1993); Tatiana Petrovich Njegosh, "'Africa and Broadway': Carl Van Vechten's Harlem as an American Spectacle of Color," *European Contributions to American Studies* 53 (2004): 223–242; James Smalls, *The Homoerotic Photography of Carl Van Vechten: Public Face, Private Thoughts* (Philadelphia: Temple University Press, 2006); Edward White, *The Tastemaker: Carl Van Vechten and the Birth of Modern America* (New York: Farrar, Straus and Giroux, 2014).
4. Michel-Rolph Trouillot, *Silencing the Past: Power and the Production of History* (1995; repr., Boston: Beacon, 2015). I thank my anonymous reviewer at the press for nudging me to think in this direction of the "provenance" of the photographs.
5. Trouillot, 52.

6. Ram Gopal and Serozh Dadachanji, *Indian Dancing* (London: Phoenix House, 1951).
7. Allan Sekula, "Photography and the Limits of National Identity," *Gray Room* 55 (Spring 2014): 28–33.
8. Anthony W. Lee, *The Global Flows of Early Scottish Photography: Encounters in Scotland, Canada, and China* (Montreal: McGill-Queen's University Press, 2019), traces its lineage to Arjun Appadurai, *Modernity at Large: Cultural Dimensions of Globalization* (Minneapolis: University of Minnesota Press, 1996).
9. Nachiket Chanchani, "The Camerawork of Ananda Kentish Coomaraswamy and Alfred Stieglitz," *History of Photography* 37, no. 2 (May 2013): 204–220; Saskia Kersenboom, "Ananda's Tandava: 'The Dance of Shiva' Reconsidered," *Marg* 62, no. 3 (March 2011): 28–43; Brinda Kumar, "Of Networks and Narratives: Collecting Indian Art in America, 1907–1972" (PhD diss., Cornell University, 2015); Katia Légeret-Manochchaya, *Rodin and the Dance of Shiva* (New Delhi: Niyogi Books, 2016).
10. I proposed this "thickness" of media and performance in global flows in "Pushpamala N. and the 'Art' of Cinephilia in India," in *Transcultural Turbulences: Towards a Multi-sited Reading of Image Flows*, ed. Ronald Wenzlhumer and Christiane Brosius (Berlin: Springer, 2011), 221–248.
11. Christopher Pinney and Nicholas Peterson, eds., *Photography's Other Histories* (Durham, NC: Duke University Press, 2003).
12. Elizabeth Edwards, ed., *Anthropology and Photography, 1860–1920* (New Haven, CT: Yale University Press, 1992); Christopher Pinney, *Camera Indica: The Social Life of Indian Photographs* (Chicago: University of Chicago Press, 1998); James Ryan, *Picturing Empire: Photography and Visualization of the British Empire* (London: Reaktion Books, 1997); Deborah Poole, *Vision, Race, and Modernity: A Visual Economy of the Andean Image World* (Princeton, NJ: Princeton University Press, 1997); Krista A. Thompson, *An Eye for the Tropics: Tourism, Photography, and Framing the Caribbean Picturesque* (Durham, NC: Duke University Press, 2006).
13. Geoffrey Batchen, *Apparitions. Photography and Dissemination* (Sydney: Power, 2018); Zahid R. Chaudhary, *Afterimage of Empire: Photography in Nineteenth-Century India* (Minneapolis: University of Minnesota Press, 2012); Krista A. Thompson, "The Evidence of Things Not Photographed: Slavery and Historical Memory in British West Indies," *Representations* 113, no. 1 (2011): 39–71; Christopher Pinney, *The Coming of Photography in India* (London: British Library, 2008).
14. "Objects of Orientalism: A Symposium," organized by Mary Roberts and Mark Gottlieb, Clark Art Institute, 2016; Zeynep Inankur, Reina Lewis, and Mary Roberts, eds., *The Poetics and Politics of Place: Ottoman Istanbul and British Orientalism* (Seattle: University of Washington Press, 2011); Matthew Isaac Cohen, *Performing Otherness: Java and Bali on International Stages, 1905–1952* (New York: Palgrave Macmillan, 2010); Mary Roberts, *Intimate Outsiders: The Harem in Ottoman and Orientalist Art and Travel Literature* (Durham, NC: Duke University Press, 2007); Mary Roberts and Jill Beaulieu, eds., *Orientalism's Interlocutors: Painting, Architecture, Photography* (Durham, NC: Duke University Press, 2002).
15. David, "Spectacle or Spectacular?"; Janet O'Shea, *At Home in the World: Bharata Natyam on the Global Stage* (Middletown, CT: Wesleyan University Press, 2007).
16. I am inspired here by Rey Chow, who explores Orientalism as a "lure" that binds the participants in mutual fantasy-making in cross-cultural interactions. See Rey Chow, "The Dream of a Butterfly," in *The Chow Reader*, ed. Paul Bowman (New York:

Columbia University Press, 2010), 124–146.

17. Douglas Rosenberg, *Screendance: Inscribing the Ephemeral Image* (New York: Oxford University Press, 2012); Douglas Rosenberg, ed., *The Oxford Handbook of Screendance Studies* (New York: Oxford University Press, 2016); and articles in the *International Journal of Screendance*, partly available online: http://arts.brighton.ac.uk/projects/screendance/the-international-journal-of-screendance (accessed December 29, 2020).
18. Tina M. Campt, *Image Matters: Archive, Photography, and the African Diaspora in Europe* (Durham, NC: Duke University Press, 2012), 33; Miriam Thaggert, *Images of Black Modernism: Verbal and Visual Strategies of the Harlem Renaissance* (Amherst: University of Massachusetts Press, 2010), 146. Photography "played a crucial role in producing the truth of 'race,'" Deborah Poole writes in *Vision, Race, and Modernity* (214).
19. See Critical Ethnic Studies Editorial Collective, ed., *Critical Ethnic Studies: A Reader* (Durham, NC: Duke University Press, 2016); Belinda Kazeem-Kaminski, "Unearthing. In Conversation: On Listening and Caring," *Critical Ethnic Studies* 4, no. 2 (Fall 2018): 75–99; Thompson, "Evidence of Things Not Photographed"; Saidiya Hartman, *Wayward Lives, Beautiful Experiments: Intimate Histories of Social Upheaval* (New York: Norton, 2019).
20. Anne Anlin Cheng, "Wounded Beauty: An Exploratory Essay on Race, Feminism, and the Aesthetic Question," *Tulsa Studies in Women's Literature* 19, no. 2 (Autumn 2000): 191–217; Saidiya Hartman, "Venus in Two Acts," *Small Axe* 12, no. 2 (June 2008): 1–14; Kimberly Juanita Brown, *The Repeating Body: Slavery's Visual Resonance in the Contemporary* (Durham, NC: Duke University Press, 2015).
21. Miriam Hansen, "Benjamin and Cinema: Not a One-Way Street," in "'Angelus Novus': Perspectives on Walter Benjamin," special issue, *Critical Inquiry* 25, no. 2 (Winter 1999): 306–343.
22. Adam Geczy, *Transorientalism in Art, Fashion, and Film: Inventions of Identity* (London: Bloomsbury, 2019); Anne Anlin Cheng, *Second Skin: Josephine Baker and the Modern Surface* (Oxford: Oxford University Press, 2011); Anne Anlin Cheng, *Ornamentalism* (New York: Oxford University Press, 2019). Lyneise E. Williams, *Latin Blackness in Parisian Visual Culture, 1852–1932* (New York: Bloomsbury, 2019); Lucy Fischer, *Cinema by Design: Art Nouveau, Modernism, and Film History* (New York: Columbia University Press, 2017); Anne Anlin Cheng, "Shine: On Race, Glamour and the Modern," *PMLA* 126, no. 4 (2011): 1022–1041; Matthew Bernstein and Gaylyn Studlar, eds., *Visions of the East: Orientalism in Film* (New Brunswick, NJ: Rutgers University Press, 1997); Emily Apter, "Acting Out Orientalism: Sapphic Theatricality in Turn-of-the-Century Paris," *Esprit Créateur* 34, no. 2 (1994): 102–116.
23. Judith Brown, *Glamour in Six Dimensions: Modernism and the Radiance of Form* (Ithaca, NY: Cornell University Press, 2009).
24. One pathbreaking publication I use here is Hari Krishnan, *Celluloid Classicism: Early Tamil Cinema and the Making of Modern Bharatanatyam* (Middletown, CT: Wesleyan University Press, 2019).

Chapter 1. The Photo Studio

1. Portrait in the Henry W. and Albert A. Berg Collection of English and American Literature, New York Public Library. "Carl Van Vechten, painting in oil by Martha Baker," New York Public Library Digital Collections, accessed August 13, 2021, https://digitalcollections.nypl.org/items/510d47db-c736-a3d9-e040-e00a18064a99.
2. "Sitters and Subjects of Carl Van

Vechten Photographs, 1938," folder 2678, box 231, Notebooks, Series III: Personal Papers, 1879–1971, YCAL MSS 1050, Carl Van Vechten Papers, Beinecke Rare Book and Manuscript Library, Yale University, New Haven, CT.

3. Hand gestures (*hastas*) are named and learned as the basic vocabulary of Indian classical dance. The basic reference for them was provided by *The Mirror of Gesture: Being the Abhinaya Darpana of Nandikesvara*, translated, illustrated, and introduced by the art historian Ananda Coomaraswamy in 1917. Performed by a single hand or by combining both hands, *hastas* imply an open-ended multiplicity of mimetic associations that come together in a specific configuration (*mudra*) and convey a specific narrative meaning only in a live performance unfolding in real time. By definition, then, the *hastamudras* are hard to identify accurately in a single photograph. See my conversation about this difficulty with the dancer Geeta Chandran in chapter 2.
4. The Museum of the City of New York does not mention Van Vechten's negative numbers, but this image could be Van Vechten's negative number XII M 36. See Museum of the City of New York, "Ram Gopal," accessed July 20, 2019, https://collections.mcny.org/Collection/Ram%20Gopal.-2F3XC5TJ7QC.html.
5. An especially striking image is a Kodachrome slide of the jazz and blues singer and actress Ethel Waters, 1940, object id: 2018487, JWJ Van Vechten, no: LXXI, Negro Collection 1, Beinecke. The color slide shows the chain-link pattern olive green set against a white background.
6. Christopher Pinney, *Camera Indica: The Social Life of Indian Photographs* (Chicago: University of Chicago Press, 1997), chap. 1.
7. Edward White, *The Tastemaker: Carl Van Vechten and the Birth of Modern America* (New York: Farrar, Straus and Giroux, 2014), 36.
8. Carl Van Vechten, *Moving to 101 Central Park West, the Van in Front of 150 West 55th Street*, photograph, September 11, 1936, accession no. x2010.8.744, unique identifier: MNY214024, Museum of the City of New York.
9. Bruce Kellner, *Carl Van Vechten and the Irreverent Decades* (Norman: University of Oklahoma Press, 1968), 271.
10. Carl Van Vechten, "Portraits of Artists," *Esquire* 57 (December 1962): 257.
11. "Lists and notes regarding CVV photographs," folder 2689, box 232, Series III, Van Vechten Papers. Van Vechten notes that he is recalling here an earlier remark that "appeared in the catalogue of the Syracuse University showing of the Jerome Bowers Paterson Memorial Collection."
12. Van Vechten announces his work with "color pictures" in a letter to the American poet in Paris Gertrude Stein, dated August 12, 1939, in *The Letters of Gertrude Stein and Carl Van Vechten, 1913–1946*, ed. Edward Burns (New York: Columbia University Press, 1986), 646. A brief reference to Benny Garland Jr. here is also useful.
13. Alan Trachtenberg, "Mirror in the Marketplace: American Responses to the Daguerreotype, 1839–51," in *Lincoln's Smile and Other Enigmas* (New York: Hill and Wang, 2007), 3–25; Elizabeth Anne McCaulay, *A. A. E. Disdéri and the Carte de Visite Portrait Photograph* (New Haven, CT: Yale University Press, 1985), 3.
14. Neal Avon, "Folk art fantasies: Photographers' backdrops, *Afterimage* 24 (1997): 12–18; Pinney, *Camera Indic.*
15. Ajay J. Sinha, "Notes on a Painting of a Painted Photograph," *Trans Asia Photography Review* 3, no. 2 (Spring 2013), http://tapreview.org.
16. Anthony W. Lee, *The Global Flow of Early Scottish Photography: Encounters in Scotland, Canada, and China* (Montreal: McGill-Queen's University Press, 2019), 104.
17. Sophie Feyder, "Photography and the Making of Black Urban Femininities

in the 1950s East," *Safundi* 15, nos. 2–3 (2014): 227–254.

18. Anthony W. Lee, *A Shoemaker's Story: Being Chiefly about French Canadian Immigrants, Enterprising Photographers, Rascal Yankees, and Chinese Cobblers in a Nineteenth-Century Factory Town* (Princeton, NJ: Princeton University Press, 2008); David MacDougall and Judith MacDougall, dirs., *Photo Wallahs: An Encounter with Photography in Mussourie, a North Indian Hill Station*, film (Berkeley Media, 2000). See also David MacDougall, "Photo-Hierarchicus: Signs and Mirrors in Indian Photography," *Visual Anthropology* 5, no. 2 (1992): 103–129; and David MacDougall, "Photo-Wallah: An Encounter with Photography," *Visual Anthropology Review* 8, no. 2 (1992): 96–100.
19. Arjun Appadurai, "The Colonial Backdrop," *Afterimage* 24, no. 5 (1997): 4–7.
20. Regina Perry, introduction to *Van Der Zee*, ed. Lilaine De Cock and Reginald McGhee (New York: Morgan and Morgan, 1973), 10–11. See a fuller discussion also in Miriam Thaggert, "A Photographic Language: Camera Lucida and the Photography of James Van Der Zee and Aaron Siskind," chap. 5 in *Images of Black Modernism: Verbal and Visual Strategies of the Harlem Renaissance* (Amherst: University of Massachusetts Press, 2010).
21. Jeff Rosen, *Julia Margaret Cameron's "Fancy Subject": Photographic Allegories of Victorian Identity and Empire* (Manchester, UK: Manchester University Press, 2016).
22. Vittoria A.-T. Sancho, "Respect and Representation," *Third Text*, no. 44 (Autumn 1998): 55–68; Richard J. Powell and Virginia M. Mecklenburg, *African American Art: Harlem Renaissance, Civil Rights Era, and Beyond* (Washington, DC: Smithsonian American Art Museum, 2012).
23. "Lists and notes regarding CVV photographs."
24. Kellner, *Carl Van Vechten*, 271–272.
25. Henri Cartier-Bresson, *The Decisive Moment: Photography by Henri Cartier-Bresson* (New York: Simon and Schuster, 1952).
26. Kellner *Carl Van Vechten*, 271.
27. Pieter Mijer, *Batiks and How to Make Them* (New York: Dodd, Mead, 1925).
28. Abby G. Lillethun, "Batik in America: Javanese to Javanesque, 1893–1937" (PhD diss., Ohio State University, 2002). See also Abbe G. Lillethun, "Javanese Effects: Appropriation of Batik and its Transformations in Modern Textiles," *Textile Society of America, 9th Biennial Symposium Proceedings* 431 (2004), http://digitalcommons.unl.edu/tsaconf/431. I thank Antonia Behan for pointing me in this direction of fabric design. See also Matthew Isaac Cohen, *Performing Otherness: Java and Bali on International Stages, 1905–1951* (New York: Palgrave Macmillan, 2010), 74, for the New York batik exhibition of 1919.
29. Nicola J. Shilliam, "From Bohemian to Bourgeois: American Batik in Early Twentieth Century," *Contact, Crossover, Continuity: Proceedings of the Fourth Biennial Symposium of the Textile Society of America*, September 22–24, 1994, 253–263, http://digitalcommons.unl.edu/tsaconf/1052.
30. Carl Van Vechten, interview with William T. Ingersoll for the Columbia Oral History Project, 1960, quoted in Kellner, *Carl Van Vechten*, 261.
31. "Sitters and Subjects of Carl Van Vechten Photographs, 1938."
32. The popular nationalist magazine *Intiya* of the South Indian activist poet and journalist Subramania Bharati (1882–1921) reproduces an illustration in its April 20, 1907, issue showing men representing different regional and religious communities of India through their distinct dresses, being blessed by Mother India. See Sumathi Ramaswamy, *The Goddess and the Nation: Mapping Mother India* (Durham, NC: Duke University Press, 2010), 19 (fig. 7). In popular illustrations, Subramania Bharati is

distinguished by a turban that is not very different from Gopal's here.

33. Vivek Bald, *Bengali Harlem and the Lost Histories of South Asian America* (Cambridge, MA: Harvard University Press, 2013), 18.
34. Quotations from Bald, chap. 2, "Between Hindoo and Negro," 49–51.
35. The vibrant colors of this fabric are visible in Van Vechten's Kodachrome slides of W. E. B. Du Bois, dated July 18, 1946. Image set no. CCXXX-VIa, box 223, Series IV: Photographs, Color Slides, Portraits, Van Vechten Papers.
36. The golden yellow and red fabric pattern is seen in Van Vechten's Kodachrome slide of Alan Juante Meadows, 1940, Image set no. CLXXV, slides 59 and 60, box 223, Series IV, Van Vechten Papers.
37. Aleksander Janta to Carl Van Vechten, August 8, 1938, folder 847, box 60, Series I: Correspondence, Van Vechten Papers.
38. The negative strip suggests that, after the short session, the two may have gone for a walk, when Van Vechten took a series of shots of the bronze sculpture of Tritons and Nereids at his favorite Promenade fountain at Radio City, now Rockefeller Center.
39. Van Vechten, Columbia Oral History Project, 1960, quoted in Paul Padgette, *The Dance Photography of Carl Van Vechten* (New York: Schirmer Books, 1981), 5–6.
40. Van Vechten, Columbia Oral History Project, 1960, quoted in Padgette, 5.

Chapter 2. The Dancer

1. Michel-Rolph Trouillot, *Silencing the Past: Power and the Production of History* (1995; repr., Boston: Beacon, 2015).
2. See the photograph of Gopal with Aleksander Janta on a Japanese ocean liner, *Chichibu Mari*, from Tokyo to Honolulu in Janta's "India" diary, *Pamietnik Indyjski* (London: Officyna Poetow i Malarzy, 1970).
3. Ram Gopal, folder 155, box 15 (Oversize), Series I: Photographs of Blacks Collected Chiefly by James Weldon Johnson and Carl Van Vechten, 1893–1954, Photographs of Prominent African Americans, JWJ MSS 76, Beinecke Rare Book and Manuscript Library, Yale University, New Haven, CT.
4. For Eslanda Robeson's amazing career as an anthropologist, photographer, and activist of international reputation whose Indian friends include Jawaharlal Nehru and Indira Gandhi, see Malaika Kambon, "The Mind That Sees: The Third Eye of Eslanda Goode Robeson," *San Francisco Bay View*, May 27, 2015, https://sfbayview.com/2015/05/the-mind-that-sees-the-third-eye-of-eslanda-goode-robeson/.
5. David MacDougall and Judith MacDougall, dirs., *Photo Wallahs: An Encounter with Photography in Mussourie, a North Indian Hill Station*, film (Berkeley Media, 2000), captures this performance at a commercial studio.
6. See a set of twelve Kodachrome slides for a particularly wonderful example from 1940 showing a gorgeously dressed Ethel Waters against the olive-green links printed on a cream-colored fabric. Image set no. LXXI, box 223, Series IV: Photographs, Color Slides, Portraits, YCAL MSS 1050, Carl Van Vechten Papers, Beinecke.
7. See chapter 1, note 32. Originating in Ottoman Turkey and named after the Moroccan city, the fez could be considered an object of global modernity. In early twentieth-century New York, the fez was known as a smoking cap that brought an exotic fantasy of leisure to men's luxury outfits at smoking clubs. In the South Asian context, it is called a *Rumi topi* (Roman cap), introduced by the Nizam of Hyderabad after a visit to Rome, and it soon became part of the attire of Muslim nationalist leaders in early twentieth century.
8. Maria Morris Hambourg et al., *Nadar* (New York: Metropolitan Museum of Art, 1995); Christopher Pinney,

Camera Indica: The Social Life of Indian Photographs (Chicago: University of Chicago Press, 1997), particularly chap. 2.

9. Janaki Nair, *The Promise of the Metropolis: Bangalore's Twentieth Century* (New Delhi: Oxford University Press, 2005); Nair, *Mysore Modern: Rethinking the Region under Princely Rule* (Minneapolis: University of Minnesota Press, 2011).
10. Ram Gopal to Mercedes de Acosta, April 3, 1946, Acosta 11:01, "Gopal, Ram, Correspondence with Mercedes de Acosta, Ephemeral, 1938–1960," Mercedes de Acosta Papers, Rosenbach Museum and Library, Philadelphia, PA.
11. Mrinalini Sarabhai, interview recorded by Ayisha Abraham, Abraham's personal collection, Bangalore.
12. Nicola Rayner, "Strike a Pose," *Dancing Times* 109, no. 1307 (July 2019): 23–25. I borrow the term and idea of *autoethnology* from Pooja Rangan, "Transitions, Transactions: Bollywood as Signifying Practice," in *Sarai Reader: Frontiers (The Edge of Frame)* (New Delhi: Centre for the Study of Developing Societies, 2007), 272–285.
13. The image is cropped from a midshot of the dancer, in XVIII, M30, May 11, 1938.
14. Geeta Chandran, personal conversation, New Delhi, spring 2017.
15. This is amply demonstrated in the tradition of portraiture in Western art. For portraits as representations that individuate an individual in India's religious imagery, see Padma Kaimal, "Passionate Bodies: Constructions of the Self in South Indian Portraits," *Archives of Asian Art* 48 (1995): 6–16; and Kaimal, "The Problem of Portraiture in South India, circa 870–970 A.D.," *Artibus Asiae* 59, nos. 1–2 (1999): 59–133.
16. For the term in relation to dance and film, see Hari Krishnan, *Celluloid Classicism: Early Tamil Cinema and the Making of Modern Bharatanatyam* (Middletown, CT: Wesleyan University Press, 2019), 3. In chapter 6, we will see the dancer extending this idea into a reimagining of what I call "photo-dance."
17. Ram Gopal, *Rhythm in the Heavens: An Autobiography* (London: Secker and Warburg, 1957), 15–16.
18. Gopal, 16.
19. Manu Bhagavan, *Sovereign Spheres: Princes, Education and Empire in Colonial India* (Oxford: Oxford University Press, 2003). See also Nair, *Mysore Modern*; and Priya Maholay-Jaradi, ed., *Baroda: A Cosmopolitan Provenance in Transition* (Mumbai: Marg Foundation, 2015).
20. Janaki Nair, "Mysore's Wembley? The Dasara Exhibition's Imagined Economies," *Modern Asian Studies* 47, no. 5 (September 2013): 1549–1587.
21. Sunila S. Kale, "Structures of Power: Electrification in Colonial India," *Comparative Studies of South Asia, Africa and Middle East* 34, no. 3 (2014): 454–475. See also Roobina Kharode and Shukla Sawant, "City Lights, City Limits: Multiple Metaphors in Everyday Urbanism," in *Art and Visual Culture in India, 1857–2007*, ed. Gayatri Sinha (Mumbai: Marg, 2009), 190–205.
22. Gopal, *Rhythm in the Heavens*, 19.
23. Sunil Kothari, "Mysore School of Bharata Natyam," in *Bharata Natyam* (Mumbai: Marg, 1997), 136–143; Hari Krishnan, "From Gynemimesis to Hypermasculinity: The Shifting Orientations of Male Performers of South Indian Court Dance," in *When Men Dance: Choreographing Masculinities across Borders*, ed. Jennifer Fisher and Anthony Shay (New York: Oxford University Press, 2009), 378–391.
24. Gopal, *Rhythm in the Heavens*, 26–27.
25. See also Amrit Srinivasan, "The Hindu Temple Dancer: Prostitute or "Nun?," *Cambridge Anthropology* 8, no. 1 (1983): 73–99.
26. Gopal, *Rhythm in the Heavens*, 27. On O. C. Gangoly (1881–1974), the founding member of the Indian Society of Oriental Art in Calcutta, see Brinda Kumar, "Of Networks and Narratives: Collecting Indian Art

in America, 1907–1972" (PhD diss., Cornell University, 2015), 158.

27. Gopal, *Rhythm in the Heavens*, 37–38.
28. Gopal, 28.
29. Gopal, 139–140.
30. According to Uttara Asha Coorlawala, arguably, the exaggerated sway of the hip inflects Gopal's pose toward Odissi, another classical form drawn out of a shared heritage in ancient sculpture. Coorlawala, personal communication, 2018.
31. Amrit Srinivasan, "Reform and Revival: The Devadasi and Her Dance," *Economic and Political Weekly* 20, no. 44 (1985): 1869–1876; Matthew Harp Allen, "Rewriting the Script for South Indian Dance," *Drama Review* 41, no. 3 (Fall 1997): 63–100; Uttar Asha Coorlawala, "The Sanskritized Body," *Dance Research Journal* 36, no. 2 (Winter 2004): 50–63; Janet O'Shea, *At Home in the World: Bharata Natyam on the Global Stage* (Middletown, CT: Wesleyan University Press, 2007); Devesh Soneji, ed., *Bharatanatyam: A Reader* (New Delhi: Oxford University Press, 2010); Devesh Soneji, *Unfinished Gestures: Devadasis, Memory, and Modernity in South India* (Chicago: University of Chicago Press, 2012).
32. Matthew Harp Allen, "Standardize, Classicize, and Nationalize: The Scientific Work of the Music Academy of Madras, 1930–52," in *Performing Pasts: Reinventing the Arts in Modern South India*, ed. Indira Vishwanathan Peterson and Devesh Soneji (New Delhi: Oxford University Press, 2008), 90–132.
33. Isaac Lubelsky, *Celestial India: Madame Blavatsky and the Birth of Indian Nationalism* (Sheffield, UK: Equinox, 2012).
34. See Sukanya Rahman, *Dancing in the Family: The Extraordinary Story of the First Family of Indian Dance* (New Delhi: Speaking Tiger, 2019), for the American dancer Esther Sherman, also known as Ragini Devi, in relation to the Theosophical Society in Bangalore in the 1930s, before her Kathakali training at the Kerala Kala Mandalam—a path Ram Gopal was soon to follow. See also Hari Krishnan, *Celluloid Classicism*, chap. 2, for the Madras dance movement and the Theosophical Society. Amrit Srinivasan is critical of the "puritanism" of the Theosophical Society, which, "by propagating Aryan, Sanskritic elements within Indian culture as a nationalistic self-understanding, did disservice to the understanding of 'classical' art traditions and the role they played in building up local networks and political engagements." Srinivasan, "Why Sadir?," *Seminar* 676 (December 2015): 34.
35. Coorlawala, "Sanskritized Body." For the history of Bharatanatyam also see Allen, "Rewriting the Script for South Indian Dance"; Ann-Marie Gaston, *Bharatanatyam: From Temple to Theatre* (New Delhi: Manohar, 1996); Saskia Kersenboom, "Ananda's Tandava: 'The Dance of Shiva' Reconsidered," *Marg* 62, no. 3 (March 2011): 28–43; Soneji, *Unfinished Gestures*.
36. Avanthi Meduri, "Temple Stage as Historical Allegory in Bharatanatyam: Rukmini Devi as Dancer-Historian," in Peterson and Soneji, *Performing Pasts*, 133–164.
37. Ram Gopal and Serozh Dadachanji, *Indian Dancing* (London: Phoenix House, 1951), 33.
38. This is famously attested in the 1950s by a dancer and guru in the eastern Indian region of Orissa, Kalicharan Patniak, who argued for a classical status for Odissi dance by providing extensive "proof" of the connection between the contemporary practice and sculpture on the ancient monuments of Orissa. See Nandini Sikand, "Bodies and Borders: The Odissi Costume Controversy," 58–59, in *Dance Matters Too: Markets Memories, Identities*, ed. Pallabi Chakravorty and Nilanjana Gupta (New York: Routledge, 2018).
39. Among others, for a brief reference to Ernest Hemingway and

Eugene O'Neill as visitors to the shop, see Corinna Wessels-Mevissen, "Introducing a God and His Ideal Form: A. K. Coomaraswamy's 'Dance of Siva,' 1912/1918," *Indo-Asiatische Zeitschrift: Mitteilungen der Gesellschaft für indo-asiatische Kunst, Berlin* 16 (2012): 37.

40. Ananda K. Coomaraswamy, "The Dance of Shiva," in *The Dance of Shiva: On Indian Art and Culture*, rev. ed. (New York: Noonday, 1957), 180n3.
41. Kumar, "Of Networks and Narratives," 148.
42. Ananda K. Coomaraswamy, "Śiva as Nataraja," *Central Hindu College Magazine* 9, no. 7 (1909): 174. I thank Laura Weinstein for sharing this earliest reference. Kersenboom, "Ananda's Tandava"; Elisa Ganser, "Ananda K. Coomaraswamy's *Mirror of Gesture* and the Debate about Indian Art in the Early Twentieth Century," in *Asia and Europe—Interconnected: Agents, Concepts, and Things*, ed. Angelika Malinar and Simone Müller (Wiesbaden: Harrassowitz Verlag, 2018), 96; Wessels-Mevissen, "Introducing a God and His Ideal Form." For interactions between British Orientalists and American nationalists, see Tapati Guha-Thakurta, *The Making of a New "Indian" Art: Artists, Aesthetics, and Nationalism in Bengal, c. 1850–1920* (Cambridge: Cambridge University Press, 1992).
43. Gopal, *Rhythm in the Heavens*, 5.
44. Gopal, 125–126.
45. For the Pathé clip, see British Pathé, "Indian Dancer (1947)," YouTube, April 13, 2014, https://youtu.be/5IrabwIKwK8. Darielle Mason, Philadelphia Museum of Art, personal conversation, July 2020, for the identification of the Stella Kramrisch collection. See also Kumar, "Of Networks and Narratives," chap. 3.
46. Srinivasan, "Why Sadir?," 34. See also Srinivasan, "Reform and Revival."
47. See Sunil Kothari, *Bharata Natyam: Indian Classical Dance Art* (Mumbai: Marg, 1979); Kothari, "Institutionalization of Classical Dances of India: Kalakshetra—The Principal Case Study," in *Traversing Tradition: Celebrating Dance in India*, ed. Urmimala Sarkar Munsi and Stephanie Burridge (London: Routledge, 2011), 22–36.
48. Gopal, *Rhythm in the Heavens*, 20, puts the phrase in the Maharaja's mouth and thus endows himself with a royal blessing.
49. Gopal, 49.
50. Gopal, 48–52.
51. Krishnan, "From Gynemimesis to Hypermasculinity."
52. Gopal, *Rhythm in the Heavens*, 140.
53. Mrinalini Sinha, *Colonial Masculinity: The "Manly Englishman" and the "Effeminate Bengali" in the Late Nineteenth Century* (Manchester, UK: Manchester University Press, 1995).
54. Sugata Ray, "The 'Effeminate' Buddha, the Yogic Male Body, and the Ecology of Art History in Colonial India," *Art History* 38, no. 5 (November 2015): 916–939.
55. "Ram Gopal: Hindu Temple Dancer," 46th Street Theatre, May 1, 1938, in "Programs of Ram Gopal," call no. MGZB, Carl Van Vechten Collection, New York Public Library of Performing Arts.
56. Stella Kramrisch, *Indian Sculpture: Ancient, Classical, and Medieval* (1933), revised and reprinted (New Delhi: Motilal Banarasidas, 2013), 184.
57. Kramrisch, 16.
58. Kramrisch, 64 and elsewhere.
59. Gopal, *Rhythm in the Heavens*, 30–37.
60. All quotes from Gopal, 28–36.
61. In Gopal's use of gauze, Matthew Isaac Cohen recalls early twentieth-century striptease artists who followed the Dutch Orientalist dancer Mata Hari. Email correspondence, April 28, 2021.
62. Kathryn Hansen, *Stages of Life: Indian Theatre Autobiographies* (Ranikhet, India: Permanent Black, 2011). Gopal, with connections in Burma, may have been familiar with the amazing story of Dosabhai Hathiram, the "lady actor" and father of the well-known photojournalist of the

1950s Homai Vyarawala, discussed in Katheryn Hansen, "Parsi Theatrical Networks in Southeast Asia: The Contrary Case of Burma," *Journal of Southeast Asian Studies* 49, no. 1 (February 2018): 4–33.

63. Kathryn Hansen, "Making Women Visible: Gender and Race Cross-Dressing in the Parsi Theatre," *Theatre Journal* 40, no. 2 (May 1999): 140. See also Hansen, *Stages of Life*.
64. Purnima Shah, "Transcending Gender in the Performance of Kathak," *Dance Research Journal* 30, no. 2 (Autumn 1998): 3.
65. Gopal, *Rhythm in the Heavens*, 40–41.
66. Quoted in Usha Venkateswaran, *The Life and Times of La Meri: The Queen of Ethnic Dance* (New Delhi: Indira Gandhi National Center for the Arts, 2005), 15.
67. La Meri, "Personal Recollections" and "Biographical Notes," La Meri Papers, Series I, New York Public Library. See also Baba Yaga Music, "La Meri, American Ethnic Dancer," accessed June 7, 2018, http://babayagamusic.com/Encyclopedic-Dictionary-Ethnic-Arts/Ethnic-Music-and-Dance-Performers/La-Meri-Twentieth-Century-Ethnic-Dancer.htm.
68. While Madras, Bombay, and Calcutta may be obvious examples, see a detailed description of the networks of theater in Rangoon, Burma, in the late nineteenth and early twentieth centuries in Hansen, "Parsi Theatrical Networks in Southeast Asia." Jazz arrived in India in the 1920s. See Warren R. Pinckney Jr., "Jazz in India: Perspectives on Historical Development and Musical Acculturation," *Asian Music* 21, no. 1 (Autumn 1989–Winter 1990): 35–77.
69. Nina C. George, "How Bengaluru's Opera House Came Back to Life," *Deccan Herald*, September 11, 2018, https://www.deccanherald.com/metrolife/how-it-came-back-life-692254.html.
70. Gopal, *Rhythm in the Heavens*, 40.
71. Krishnan, *Celluloid Classicism*, 5 and chap. 2.
72. The photograph, in the collection of Kiran Natarajan, is reproduced in Nina C. George, "How Bengaluru's Opera House Came Back to Life," *Deccan Herald*, September 11, 2018, https://www.deccanherald.com/metrolife/how-it-came-back-life-692254.html.
73. Venkateswaran, *Life and Times of La Meri*; Nancy Lee Chalfa Ruyter, *La Meri and Her Life in Dance: Performing the World* (Gainesville: University Press of Florida, 2019).
74. Krishnan, *Celluloid Classicism*, 106–109. See also Ruyter, *La Meri and Her Life in Dance*, 102–103.
75. Gopal, *Rhythm in the Heavens*, 41.
76. Venkateswaran, *Life and Times of La Meri*, 19.
77. Romita Ray, "Orientalizing the Bayadere/Fabricating Mata Hari," *Photographies* 5, no. 1 (March 2012): 87–111.
78. Madelon Djajadiningrat-Nieuwenhuis, "Mangkunegoro VII and Rabindranath Tagore: A Brief Meeting of Like Minds," *Indonesia and the Malay World* 34, no. 98 (March 2006): 99–107; Matthew Isaac Cohen, *Performing Otherness: Java and Bali on International Stage, 1905–1952* (New York: Palgrave Macmillan, 2010).
79. Cohen, *Performing Otherness*.
80. Ruyter, *La Meri and Her Life in Dance*, 109.
81. Venkateswaran, *Life and Times of La Meri*, 20. In the program note of Gopal's performance at the Dillingham Hall in Honolulu dated January 19, 1938, a number is described as follows: "Klana Surwibawa (Java)," where "King Klana having fallen in love with Chandra Kirana, Princess of Kandiri, prepares himself while awaiting the coming of one he always sees at the corner of his eye." In another concert in 1939, at the Aldwych Theatre, London, he performed a number titled "King Klana and Devi Srikandi" with the Javanese dancer Retna Mohini, the wife of the photographer Henri Cartier-Bresson. See "Programs of Ram Gopal."

82. Roy E. Jordaan, "The Tara Temple of Kalasan in Central Java," *Bulletin de l'École française d'Extrême-Orient* 85 (1998): 163–183. The photograph is numbered OD 9714, originally published in *Oudheidkundig Verslag*, 1929.
83. South Asian Diaspora Arts Archive, "Ram Gopal in Javanese Costume Playing King Klana—Photograph," accessed August 17, 2018, https://sadaa.co.uk/archive/dance/ram-gopal/ram-gopal-in-javanese-costume-playing-king-klana-photograph.
84. Ruyter, *La Meri and Her Life in Dance*, 112.
85. Ruyter, 113, for her side of the story.
86. Gopal, *Rhythm in the Heavens*, 43–44.
87. Gopal, 45.
88. Michal Folega, *Zycie Na Swait Otwarte: Aleksander Janta Polczynski* (Life for an Open World: Aleksander Janta Polczynski) (Tuchola, Poland: Meander, 2014), 29–35.
89. Michal Folega, email to the author, April 30, 2021. The invisible interconnections that brought the dancer into the social circle of the photographer are briefly revealed by the fact that Van Vechten had photographed Handforth in 1936.
90. "Programs of Ram Gopal."
91. "Indian Dancer Here: Wears Giant Pearl," *Herald Express* (Los Angeles), February 10, 1938; "Indian Dancer Pays Visit Here," *Los Angeles Times*, February 12, 1938. Both in "Ram Gopal, Clippings," call. no. MGZR, Jerome Robbins Dance Division, New York Public Library for the Performing Arts
92. Gopal, *Rhythms of the Heavens*, 58.
93. Robert A. Schanke, *"That Furious Lesbian": The Story of Mercedes de Acosta* (Carbondale: Southern Illinois University Press, 2003).
94. Gopal, *Rhythm in the Heavens*, 61. See the Van Vechten photograph of Bernadine Szold Fritz, October 15, 1934, LOT 12735, no. 397 (P&P), Library of Congress, http://www.loc.gov/pictures/item/2004662894/; and her papers at the Beinecke Rare Book and Manuscript Library, Yale University, New Haven, CT.
95. "Ram Gopal Hindu Temple Dancer," Wilshire-Ebell Theatre, March 11, 1938, in "Programs of Ram Gopal."
96. *New York Times*, May 1, 1938, in "Ram Gopal, Clippings."
97. John Martin, "Ram Gopal Is Seen Here in Hindu Dances: Cobra Number the High Point in His New York Debut," *New York Times*, May 2, 1938, in "Ram Gopal, Clippings."
98. Ruth K. Abrahams, "Uday Shankar: The Early Years, 1900–1938," *Dance Chronicle* 30, no. 3 (2007): 363–426; Diana Brenscheidt, *Shiva Onstage: Uday Shankar's Company of Hindu Dancers and Musicians in Europe and the United States, 1931–1938* (Berlin: LIT Verlag, 2011).
99. Joan L. Erdman, "Performance as Translation: Uday Shankar in the West," *Drama Review* 31, no. 1 (Spring 1987): 64–88.
100. Patricia Vertinsky and Aishwarya Ramachandran, "Uday Shankar and the Dartington Hall Trust: Patronage, Imperialism, and the Indian Dean of Dance," *Sport in History* 38, no. 3 (2018): 289–306.
101. Martin published Sheshagiri's comments along with his rebuttal in "The Dance: Art of India, Shan-Kar Criticized as Departing from Canons of the Indian Classic Dance," *New York Times*, April 2, 1934. See Prarthana Purkayastha, "Dancing Otherness: Nationalism, Internationalism, and the Work of Uday Shankar," *Dance Research Journal* 44, no. 1 (Summer 2012): 69–92.
102. Martin, "Ram Gopal Is Seen Here."
103. Purkayastha, "Dancing Otherness"; Sonal Khullar, "Almora Dreams: Art and Life at the Uday Shankar India Cultural Centre, 1939–1944," *Marg* 69, no. 4 (June–September 2018): 14–32.
104. Joan L. Erdman, "Who Remembers Uday Shankar?," *Freethinker*, accessed June 12, 2018, https://mm-gold.azureedge.net/new_site/mukto-mona/Articles/jaffor/uday_shanka2.html.

105. Joan L. Erdman, "Cross-Cultural Discourses: Writing of Uday Shankar," in *Proceedings of the Society of Dance History Scholars, Twentieth Annual Conference, Barnard College, New York City, June 19–22, 1997* (Riverside, CA: Society of Dance History Scholars, 1997), 269–275.
106. Shan-Kar and His Hindu Ballet, 1937, folder 3085, box 293, Series V: Printed Materials, 1871–1986, Van Vechten Papers.
107. See images from the Amala Shankar Archives in Purkayastha, "Dancing Otherness."
108. Gopal, *Rhythm in the Heavens*, 62–63.
109. "Hindu Temple Dancer at 48th [*sic*] St. Theatre," in "Ram Gopal, Clippings."
110. Aleksander Janta to Carl Van Vechten, August 8, 1938, folder 847, box 60, Series I: Correspondence, 1907–1971, Van Vechten Papers.
111. On "hyperfemininity," see Priyanka Basu, "Moving from the Temple to the Studio-Space: Transformation of the Women Dancer's Labour in Films," in *The Moving Space: Women in Dance*, ed. Urmimala Sarkar Munsi and Aishika Chakraborty (Delhi: Primus Books, 2018), 138–155.
112. Saloni Mathur, *India by Design: Colonial History and Cultural Display* (Berkeley: University of California Press, 2007).
113. "Ram Gopal Hindu Temple Dancer," May 1, 1938, 46th Street Theatre, in "Programs of Ram Gopal."
114. Julia Bailey, email to the author, August 5, 2017, including figure composition and inscription, for which I thank her. See British Library, "1539–1543, The Khamsah, or Five Poems, of Niẓāmī f. 2," accessed August 5, 2017, http://www.bl.uk/manuscripts/Viewer.aspx?ref=or_2265_f026v.
115. Anne Anlin Cheng, *Ornamentalism* (New York: Oxford University Press, 2019).
116. See Ajay J. Sinha, "Mysore Modern across the Arts," in *K. Venkatappa and His Times*, ed. Pushpamala N. and Deeptha Achar (New Delhi: Routledge, forthcoming), for a discussion of Gopal's malleable representations in relation to his contemporary Mysorean visual artist K. Venkatappa's affinity with early-modern visual culture of the princely state and departures from the national-modern paradigms of early twentieth-century art.

Chapter 3. The Photographer

Epigraph: Columbia Oral History Project, quoted in Bruce Kellner, *Carl Van Vechten and the Irreverent Decades* (Norman: University of Oklahoma Press, 1968), 261.

1. Pika Ghosh, *Making Kantha, Making Home: Women at Work in Colonial Bengal* (Seattle: University of Washington Press, 2021), 31–41, and 33 for an exquisite example from ca. 1600, made probably in India for a European market.
2. Edward White, *The Tastemaker: Carl Van Vechten and the Birth of Modern America* (New York: Farrar, Straus and Giroux, 2014), 70.
3. White, 59.
4. Peter Wollen, "Salome," in *Paris/Manhattan: Writings on Art* (London: Verso, 2004), 101–102.
5. Carl Van Vechten, *Peter Whiffle: His Life and Works* (New York: Knopf, 1922), 147–148.
6. Wollen, "Salome," 111.
7. Lincoln Kirstein, "Carl Van Vechten: 1880–1964," *Yale University Library Gazette* 39, no. 4 (April 1965), reprinted in *By With To & Whom: A Lincoln Kirstein Reader*, ed. Nicholas Jenkins (New York: Farrar, Straus and Giroux, 1991), 31–37.
8. Rhonda K. Garelick, *Rising Star: Dandyism, Gender, and Performance in Fin de Siècle* (Princeton, NJ: Princeton University Press, 1998).
9. Carl Van Vechten, "In Defence of Bad Taste," in *The Merry Go Round* (New York: Knopf, 1918), 16.
10. Peter Wollen, "Art and Fashion: Friends or Enemies?," in *Paris/Manhattan*, 162.
11. Sarah D. Coffin and Stephan Harri-

son, "Across the Ocean," in *The Jazz Age: American Style in the 1920s* (Cleveland, OH: Cleveland Museum of Art, 2017), 1.

12. Bruce Kellner, *Carl Van Vechten and the Irreverent Decades* (Norman: University of Oklahoma Press, 1968); Kevin Mumford, *Interzones: Black/White Sex Districts in Chicago and New York in the Early Twentieth Century* (New York: Columbia University Press, 1997); Vechten, *Peter Whiffle*. See also Patricia Stuelke, "The Queer Optimism of Jessie Tarbox Beals' Greenwich Village Postcards," *Photography and Culture* 7, no. 3 (November 2014): 285–302.
13. Jonathan D. Katz, "Hide/Seek: Difference and Desire in American Portraiture," in *Hide/Seek: Difference and Desire in American Portraiture*, by Jonathan D. Katz and David C. Ward (Washington, DC: National Portrait Gallery, 2010), 24.
14. According to Barbara Haskell, the watercolor portrays Van Vechten with Marcel Duchamp, Demuth, and others mingling with Black patrons at the Black-owned Marshall Hotel north of Times Square. See Haskell, *Charles Demuth, 1883–1935* (New York: Whitney Museum of Art and H. N. Abrams, 1987), 49–96.
15. Mumford, *Interzones*.
16. White, *Tastemaker*, 69. See Saidiya Hartman, *Wayward Lives, Beautiful Experiments: Intimate Histories of Social Upheaval* (New York: Norton, 2019), for a gorgeous representation of the bohemian lifestyle of African American women in the grit of the Tenderloin District and Harlem.
17. Ann Douglas, *Terrible Honesty: Mongrel Manhattan in the 1920s* (New York: Farrar, Straus and Giroux, 1995), 87.
18. Douglas, 83.
19. Mumford, *Interzones*, 73–92.
20. Bruce Kellner, introduction to *The Harlem Renaissance: A Historical Dictionary of the Era*, ed. Bruce Kellner (Westport, CT: Greenwood, 1984), xiii–xxvii.
21. Kirstein, "Carl Van Vechten," 31–37.
22. Kirstein, 34.
23. See Anne Anlin Cheng, *Second Skin: Josephine Baker and the Modern Surface* (Oxford: Oxford University Press, 2011), 85–86, for the "permutation" of Baker's own modern skin and leopard, concretized by photographs and magazine illustrations in the 1930s. See also the street photograph with Chiquita in Lyneise E. Williams, *Latin Blackness in Parisian Visual Culture, 1852–1932* (New York: Bloomsbury, 2019).
24. Kirstein, "Carl Van Vechten," 34.
25. Kirstein, 34.
26. Paul Padgette, *The Dance Photography of Carl Van Vechten* (New York: Schirmer Books, 1981), 7.
27. Emily Bernard, *Carl Van Vechten and the Harlem Renaissance: A Portrait in Black and White* (New Haven, CT: Yale University Press, 2012), 53. See his relation especially with Paul Robeson, Ethel Waters, and Zora Neale Hurston here.
28. The magazine does not mention the title, which is from Kellner, *Harlem Renaissance*, inside cover.
29. Bernard, *Carl Van Vechten and the Harlem Renaissance*, 59; and Zora Neale Hurston to Carl Van Vechten, February 28, 1934, in *Zora Neale Hurston: A Life in Letters*, ed. Carla Kaplan (New York: Doubleday, 2002), 290.
30. Robert Littell, "Every One Likes Chocolate," *Vogue*, November 1, 1936, 66.
31. Kirstein, "Carl Van Vechten," 34.
32. Van Vechten, *Peter Whiffle*, 124.
33. Van Vechten, 123.
34. Van Vechten, 42–49.
35. Gary Zabel, "Adorno on Music: A Reconsideration," *Musical Times* 130, no. 1754 (April 1989): 200.
36. Fumi Okiji, *Jazz as Critique: Adorno and Black Expression Revisited* (Stanford, CA: Stanford University Press, 2018).
37. Quoted in White, *Tastemaker*, 58.
38. Zabel, "Adorno on Music," 200.
39. Dina Gusejnova, "Jazz Anxiety and the European Fear of Cultural Change: Towards a Transnational

History of a Political Emotion," *Cultural History* 5, no. 1 (2016): 26–51.
40. Okiji, *Jazz as Critique*, 6–8.
41. Saidiya Hartman, *Scenes of Subjection: Terror, Slavery, and Self-Making in Nineteenth-Century America* (New York: Oxford University Press, 1997), 33, quoted in Okiji, *Jazz as Critique*, 79.
42. Quoted in Douglas, *Terrible Honesty*, 104–105.
43. Douglas, *Terrible Honesty*, 104–105.
44. Cheng, *Second Skin*, 87, quoting Le Corbusier, *When the Cathedrals Were White* (1947), 158–161.
45. Peter McNeil, "'That Doubtful Gender': Macaroni Dress and Male Sexuality," *Fashion Theory* 3, no. 4 (1999): 412, quoting *Town and Country* (1772): 243. See also McNeil, *Pretty Gentlemen: Macaroni Men and the Eighteenth Century Fashion World* (New Haven, CT: Yale University Press, 2018).
46. Carl Van Vechten, "Pastiches et Pistaches," *Reviewer*, no. 2 (February 1922): 270.
47. Stephen Brown and Georgiana Uhlyarik, *Florine Stettheimer: Painting Poetry* (New York: Jewish Museum; New Haven, CT: Yale University Press, 2017), 28, 118–119.
48. Van Vechten, "Pastiches et Pistaches," 270.
49. Van Vechten, 269–270.
50. Van Vechten, 270.
51. I borrow the idea of "modern surface" from Cheng, *Second Skin*.
52. Jonathan O. Wipplinger, *The Jazz Republic: Music, Race, and American Culture in Weimar Republic* (Ann Arbor: University of Michigan Press, 2017), 3. Wipplinger's distinction between "jazz effect" as an interpretative outlook and "jazz tradition" in music is useful (14).
53. Coffin and Harrison, *Jazz Age*.
54. Keith F. Davis, *Passionate Observer: Photographs by Carl Van Vechten* (Kansas City, MO: Hallmark Cards, 1993), 16.
55. Philip V. Bohlman and Goffredo Plastino, introduction to *Jazz Worlds/World Jazz* (Chicago: University of Chicago Press, 2016), 8.
56. George E. Lewis, "Foreword: Who Is Jazz?," in Bohlman and Plastino, *Jazz Worlds/World Jazz*, xix.
57. Travis A. Jackson, "Race, Culture, Commodity, Palimpsest: Locating Jazz in the World," in Bohlman and Plastino, *Jazz Worlds/World Jazz*, 393. I borrow the idea of "vernacular" from Miriam Bratu Hansen, who writes, "the term vernacular combines the dimension of the quotidian, of everyday usage, with connotations of discourse and dialect, with circulation, promiscuity, and translatability," reflecting on global cinema's production of "Americanism." Hansen, "The Mass Production of the Senses: Classical Cinema as Vernacular Modernism," *Modernism/Modernity* 6, no. 2 (1999): 60.
58. By contrast, Ken Burns's ten-part film series *Jazz* enshrines the music as American through a chronological account of American performers.
59. Lewis, "Foreword: Who Is Jazz?," xi–xii.
60. See Goffredo Plastino, "Jazz Napoletano: A Passion for Improvisation," in Bohlman and Plastino, *Jazz Worlds/World Jazz*, 316.
61. See Bernard, *Carl Van Vechten and the Harlem Renaissance*, 69, for a fuller discussion. Bernard contrasts Van Vechten to Mezz Mezzrow, "a white middle-class jazz musician, son of a Russian Jewish immigrant, who wrote in his 1946 autobiography of wanting to be a 'voluntary negro.'"
62. National Portrait Gallery, "Carl Van Vechten," object no. NPG.2000.36, accessed August 19, 2021, https://npg.si.edu/object/npg_NPG.2000.36?destination=edan-search/default_search%3Fpage%3D3%26return_all%3D1%26edan_local%3D1%26edan_q%3Dmiguel%252Bcovarrubias%252B.
63. See Williams, *Latin Blackness in Parisian Visual Culture*, introduction.
64. Bernard, *Carl Van Vechten and the Harlem Renaissance*, 69.
65. Bernard, 67; Ethel Waters, with

Charles Samuels, *His Eye Is on the Sparrow: An Autobiography* (New York: Da Capo, 1992), 195.

66. "Adelaide Hall," inscribed photograph, 1929, Series I: Photographs of Blacks Collected Chiefly by James Weldon Johnson and Carl Van Vechten, 1893–1954, Photographs of Prominent African Americans, JWJ MSS 76, Orbis record 4714434, Beinecke Rare Book and Manuscript Library, Yale University, New Haven, CT.
67. Bernard, *Carl Van Vechten and the Harlem Renaissance*, 61.
68. I thank Mimi Hellman for the term "corporeal imagination."
69. White, *Tastemaker*, 18.
70. Davis, *Passionate Observer*, 11. See also Kristin MacLeod, "The Library Dream-Prince: Carl Van Vechten and America's Modernist Cultural Archives Industry," *Libraries & Cultural Record* 46, no. 4 (2011): 360–387, for Van Vechten's practice of collecting as close to Peter Whiffle's interest "not to define or describe, but to enumerate" (366).
71. Vincent Warren, "Yearning for the Spiritual Ideal: The Influence of India on Western Dance, 1626–2003," *Dance Research Journal* 38, nos. 1–2 (Summer–Winter 2006): 108.
72. Notebooks, Series III: Personal Papers, 1879–1971, YCAL MSS 1050, Carl Van Vechten Papers, Beinecke Rare Book and Manuscript Library, New Haven, CT.
73. Carl Van Vechten, "Portraits of Artists," *Esquire* 57 (December 1962): 174.
74. Van Vechten donated most of these images to the Museum of the City of New York. See Carl Van Vechten, *Push Cart*, March 5, 1932, gelatin silver print, accession no. X2010.8.580, and *Harlem Market*, accession no. X2010.8.581, Museum of the City of New York. Kodachrome slides of Harlem are at the Beinecke.
75. Kirstein, "Carl Van Vechten," 36.
76. I borrow Sarah Blackwood's idea of "performed portrait," referring to a set of "symbolic and aesthetic practices" in nineteenth-century American art and literature that "helped produce new ideas about human interiority." Blackwood, *The Portrait's Subject: Inventing Inner Life in the Nineteenth-Century United States* (Chapel Hill: University of North Carolina Press, 2019), 2.
77. Michael Kreyling, "Fugitive Voices," in *The Oxford Critical and Cultural History of Modernist Magazines*, vol. 2, *North America, 1894–1960*, ed. Peter Brooker and Andrew Thacker (Oxford: Oxford University Press, 2012), 516.
78. Van Vechten, "Pastiches et Pistaches," 268–269. See also Carl Van Vechten, *The Tiger in the House* (New York: Knopf, 1920), for his affectionate revelry in this odd zone of incomprehensibility, and compare his historical reflection to an equally powerful confrontation with the incomprehensibility of a cat and the anxious tailspin into the history of philosophy, in Jacque Derrida, *The Animal That Therefore I Am*, ed. Marie-Louis Mallet, trans. David Wills (New York: Fordham University Press, 2008).
79. Carl Van Vechten, "The Reminiscences of Carl Van Vechten," 193, interview by William Ingersoll, Oral History Research Office, Columbia University, New York, March 3, 1960, quoted in Bernard, *Carl Van Vechten and the Harlem Renaissance*, 2–3.
80. White, *Tastemaker*, 180.
81. Bernard, *Carl Van Vechten and the Harlem Renaissance*, 3.
82. Bernard, 74–76.
83. Douglas, *Terrible Honesty*, 74–77.
84. Wendy A. Grossman, "Race and Beauty in Black and White: Robert Demachy and the Aestheticization of Blackness in Pictorialist Photography," in *Blacks and Blackness in European Art of the Long Nineteenth Century*, ed. Adrienne L. Childs and Susan H. Libby (Farnham, UK: Ashgate, 2014), 201–230. Grossman complicates the heterosexual meanings of Orientalism in scholarly literature by arguing that the figure is androgynous and that the classicized bust relates to a nineteenth-century

full sculpture by the Italian sculptor Lorenzo Bartolini (1777–1850) titled *The Grape Presser*.

85. Female jazz and blues singers were known for their liaisons with other women. Bessie Smith is said to have had an alleged lesbian relationship with her mentor, the mother of the blues, Ma Rainey, who wrote a blues song after her arrest in 1925 at a police raid of a lesbian party: "Went out last night with a crowd of my friends. They must've been women, 'cause I don't like no men. It's true I wear a collar and a tie. . . . Talk to the gals just like any old man. . . . Don't you say I do it. Ain't nobody caught me. You sure got to prove it on me." See Hartman, *Wayward Lives*, for the less famous but no less promiscuous lives of African American women in the Jazz Age.
86. Chris Albertson, *Bessie: Empress of the Blues* (London: Sphere Books, 1972), 277.
87. Albertson, 196.
88. Bernard, *Carl Van Vechten and the Harlem Renaissance*, 68.
89. E. Mark Stern, "The Awesome and the Awestruck: Bessie Smith and Carl Van Vechten," simultaneously published in the *Psychotherapy Patient* 11, nos. 3–4 (2001): 27–35; and Robert B. Marchesani and E. Mark Stern, *Frightful Stages: From the Primitive to the Therapeutic* (Hawthorne, NJ: Hawthorne, 2001). Page numbers refers to the *Psychotherapy Patient version.*
90. Van Vechten, quoted in White, *Tastemaker*, 60.
91. Wollen, "Salome," 108–109.
92. White, *Tastemaker*, 58.
93. Wollen, "Salome," 101–102.
94. Lucy Fischer, *Cinema by Design: Art Nouveau, Modernism, and Film History* (New York: Columbia University Press, 2017).
95. The cover of Van Vechten's novel *Blind Bow Boy* (1923) has a drawing by Alastair (Hans Henning Voight) (1887–1969) a German artist who illustrated in Beardsley's style. Van Vechten also wrote an introduction to a collection of Alastair's drawings. See Alastair (Hans Henning Voight), *Fifty Drawings by Alastair*, introduction by Carl Van Vechten (New York: Knopf, 1925).
96. Quoted in White, *Tastemaker*, 60.
97. White, 62.

Chapter 4. The Camera

1. The Leica here is most probably Model FF, with its slightly bulging film chamber to hold an extra-large thirty-three feet of film. Van Vechten mentions getting a "new model" in a visit to Munich just around 1936, in "Portraits of the Artists," *Esquire* 57 (December 1962): 174.
2. Manuel Komroff, "Before We Press the Button," in *The Leica Manual: A Manual for the Amateur and Professional Covering the Entire Field of Leica Photography*, by Willard D. Morgan and Henry M. Lester, rev. ed. (New York: Morgan and Lester, 1938), quoted in Alessandro Pasi, *Leica: Witness to a Century* (New York: Norton, 2003), 20.
3. Willard D. Morgan, "Introduction to Leica Photography," in *The Leica Manual: A Manual for the Amateur and Professional Covering the Entire Field of Leica Photography*, by Willard D. Morgan and Henry M. Lester (New York: Morgan and Lester, 1935), 17. Unless otherwise noted, all subsequent cites refer to the 1935 edition.
4. Van Vechten, "Portraits of the Artists," 170.
5. Walter Benjamin, "The Work of Art in the Age of Its Technical Reproducibility," second version (1935–1936), in *Walter Benjamin: The Work of Art in the Age of Its Technological Reproducibility and Other Writings on Media*, ed. Michael W. Jennings, Brigid Doherty, and Thomas Y. Levin (Cambridge, MA: Harvard University Press, 2008), 19–55. Jennings relates Benjamin's idea to the Bauhaus photographer Laszlo Moholy-Nagy's view of "the camera lens [as] a crucial prosthesis, an extension of the range

and power of the human visual apparatus." Jennings, Doherty, and Levin, "Editors' Introduction," in *Walter Benjamin*, 11. See also Mia Fineman, "Ecce Homo Prostheticus," *New German Critique* 76 (1999): 85–114, relating the camera lens in the Weimar era of the 1920s to the metal prostheses designed in medical practice for dismembered soldiers during World War I.

6. Komroff, "Before We Press the Button," 13.
7. Morgan and Lester, *Leica Manual*.
8. Van Vechten, "Portraits of the Artists," 174.
9. Folder 554, box 42, Series I: Correspondence, 1907–1971, YCAL MSS 1050, Carl Van Vechten Papers, Beinecke Rare Book and Manuscript Library, Yale University, New Haven, CT. See also folder 559 for the correspondence between Van Vechten and George Eastman House, regarding problems with loading spools and other issues.
10. Bruce Kellner, *Carl Van Vechten and the Irreverent Decades* (Norman: University of Oklahoma Press, 1968), 259.
11. For these images deemed "indecent, immoral [and] lewd," see folder 559, box 42, Series I, Van Vechten Papers.
12. Kellner, *Carl Van Vechten and the Irreverent Decades*, 272.
13. Willard Morgan to Carl Van Vechten, January 28, 1933, folder 554, box 42, Series I, Van Vechten Papers.
14. Willard Morgan to Carl Van Vechten, November 1, 1935, folder 554, box 42, Series I, Van Vechten Papers. While Van Vechten's photographs at the Beinecke are mostly eight by ten inches, many prints he gave to the New York Public Library are eleven by fourteen inches. In both cases, they are mounted on board mounts with documentation in the back, a practice that, along with maintaining contact prints, he may have developed from these interactions with Morgan and other fans.
15. Willard D. Morgan, "Enlarging and Contact Printing," chapter 7 in Morgan and Lester, *Leica Manual*, 145.
16. Sections titled "Leica in Science and Education" and "The Leica in Specialized Fields," in Morgan and Lester, *Leica Manual*.
17. See Laura Wexler, "I Am a Camera: The Photographic Process and the Reconfiguration of the Self," *Berkshire Review*, 1982, 120, for Richard Avedon's reference to the "illicit connection between photography and playing hospital, when people came into his studio to 'find out how they were.'"
18. Rosalind Krauss, "Jump over the Bauhaus," *October* 15 (Winter 1980): 104.
19. David Mellor, ed., *Germany, the New Photography 1927–1933: Documents and Essays* (London: Arts Council of Great Britain, 1978); Benjamin, "Work of Art in the Age of Its Technological Reproducibility," 37.
20. Walter Benjamin, "New Things about Plants: A Review of Karl Blossfeldt, *Art Forms in Nature*" (1928), in Mellor, *Germany, the New Photography*, 21.
21. Andrés Mario Zervigón, "Photography's Weimar-Era Proliferation and Walter Benjamin's Optical Unconscious," in *Photography and the Optical Unconscious*, ed. Shawn Michelle Smith and Sharon Sliwinski (Durham, NC: Duke University Press, 2017), 32. None of the authors in this volume mention the role of the Leica in the ideas of the late 1920s and the 1930s.
22. On the encounter of English literary figures with German photography, see David Mellor, "London-Berlin-London: A Cultural History. The Reception and Influence of the New German Photography in Britain 1927–33," in Mellor, *Germany, the New Photography*, 113–132.
23. Morgan, "Introduction to Leica Photography," 17.
24. Michael Windover, *Art Deco: A Mode of Mobility* (Québec City: Presses de l'Université du Québec, 2012), 3. See also Lucy Fischer, *Cinema by Design:*

Art Nouveau, Modernism, and Film History (New York: Columbia University Press, 2017), for the Art Deco look of early Hollywood cinema.

25. Abigail Solomon-Godeau, "The Armed Vision Disarmed: Radical Formalism from Weapon to Style," in *The Contest of Meaning: Critical Histories of Photography*, ed. Richard Bolton (Cambridge, MA: MIT Press, 1989), 97.
26. Nor does Solomon-Godeau point to its role in "diluting" those visionary experiments.
27. Van Vechten, "Portraits of Artists."
28. The organizer Willard Morgan's letter dated November 1, 1935, inviting Van Vechten to participate mentions the exhibition at Radio City. Bruce Kellner mentions Bergdorf Goodman, the large department store, which may possibly have been a sponsor for the exhibition, showcasing "Cecil Beaton, Edward Steichen, Man Ray, George Platt Lynes and Carl Van Vechten." Kellner, *Carl Van Vechten and the Irreverent Decades*, 261.
29. See Van Vechten, "Portraits of Artists," for artists he knew, photographed, and learned from. See Patrick Keating, "Artifice and Atmosphere: The Visual Culture of Hollywood Glamour Photography, 1930–1935," *Film History* 29, no. 3 (2017): 105–135, for one example: of Hoyningen-Heune and his "style" in *Vogue* and *Vanity Fair*.
30. Krauss, "Jump over the Bauhaus," 102.
31. Krauss, 109.
32. Clément Chéroux, Andreas Fischer, and Pierre Apraxine, *The Perfect Medium: Photography and the Occult* (New Haven, CT: Yale University Press, 2005).
33. Carl Van Vechten, *The Blind Bow-Boy* (1923), edited with introduction by Kirsten MacLeod (Cambridge, UK: Modern Humanities Research Association, 2018), 54, quoted in Keith F. Davis, *Passionate Observer: Photographs of Carl Van Vechten* (Kansas City, MO: Hallmark Cards, 1993), 27–28.
34. Van Vechten, *Blind Bow-Boy*, 54nn87–88.
35. Cleveland Amory and Frederic Bradlee, introduction to *Vanity Fair: Selections from America's Most Memorable Magazine: A Cavalcade of the 1920s and 1930s* (New York: Viking, 1960), 7.
36. Amory and Bradlee, 7.
37. Fania Marinoff, "To Carlo (1943)," folder 1290, box 99, Series I, Van Vechten Papers.
38. John Raeburn, "Steichen and Celebrity Photography," chapter 5 in *A Staggering Revolution: A Cultural History of Thirties Photography* (Urbana: University of Illinois Press, 2006), 77.
39. Davis, *Passionate Observer*, 24.
40. Quoted in Raeburn, "Steichen and Celebrity Photography," 75.
41. Davis, *Passionate Observer*, 24
42. Raeburn, "Steichen and Celebrity Photography," 76.
43. Raeburn, 63.
44. Kellner, *Carl Van Vechten and the Irreverent Decades*, 261. Willard Morgan's letter to Van Vechten mentions Radio City as the location. Kellner mentions Bergdorf Goodman, the department store that may have sponsored the exhibition.
45. Whitney Chadwick, "Fetishizing Fashion/Fetishizing Culture: Man Ray's 'Noire et blanche,'" *Oxford Art Journal* 18, no. 2 (1995): 3–17.
46. George Chauncey, "'Pansies on Parade': Prohibition and the Spectacle of the Pansy," in *Gay New York: Gender, Culture, and the Making of the Gay Male World, 1800–1940* (New York: Basic Books, 1994), 300–329.
47. In Amory and Bradlee, *Vanity Fair*, 13.
48. Van Vechten, "Portraits of the Artists," 174.
49. The full view can be seen in an image included in a gift box of close to five hundred postcards of dancers from Van Vechten to the ballet dancer Bill Earl, now at the Frances Young Tang Teaching Museum and Art Gallery, Skidmore College. The close-up showing the hand gesture is at the

Beinecke: folder 4903, box 358, Series VI: Photographs, circa 1845–1967, Van Vechten Papers.

50. Van Vechten, "Portraits of the Artists," 170.
51. Wexler, "I Am a Camera," 119.
52. Wexler, 123.
53. Wexler, 118.
54. Pooja Rangan, *Immediations: The Humanitarian Impulse in Documentary* (Durham, NC: Duke University Press, 2017), 162.
55. Jacques Lacan, *The Four Fundamental Concepts of Psychoanalysis*, trans. Alan Sheridan (New York: Norton, 1978), 72, 75. See also Hal Foster, "Obscene, Abject, Traumatic," *October* 78 (Autumn 1996): 106–124.
56. The image is published as fig. 12 in James Smalls, *The Homoerotic Photography of Carl Van Vechten: Public Face, Private Thoughts* (Philadelphia: Temple University Press, 2006). I am unable to locate the image in the archives but am guessing from other images that the model is the dancer Archie Savage, whom Van Vechten photographed on March 2, 1942. Van Vechten's scrapbooks, all at the Beinecke, have collages that capture homoerotic innuendoes in clippings of text and images from newspapers and magazines. Van Vechten quips about fellatio as "69" on a page in one of his scrapbooks.
57. See Smalls, 12–14, for "epidermal" fetishism and sexual fetishism.
58. Judith Brown, *Glamour in Six Dimensions: Modernism and the Radiance of Form* (Ithaca, NY: Cornell University Press, 2009), 5.
59. Jacques Derrida, "The Animal That Therefore I Am (More to Follow)," *Critical Inquiry* 28, no. 2 (Winter 2002): 369–418.
60. Brown, *Glamour in Six Dimensions*, 70–71.
61. Excerpt in Ayisha Abraham's film *I Saw a God Dance* (2012). See Ayisha Abraham, "From the Roof Top into the Mine," *New Cinemas: Journal of Contemporary Film* 11, nos. 2–3 (2013): 169–182.
62. Carl Van Vechten, "The Editor's Workbench," *Trend* 8, no. 1 (October 1914): 101, quoted in Edward White, *The Tastemaker: Carl Van Vechten and the Birth of Modern America* (New York: Farrar, Straus and Giroux, 2014), 115–116.
63. White, 104.
64. Roger Caillois, "The Praying Mantis: From Biology to Psychoanalysis," in *The Edge of Surrealism: A Roger Caillois Reader*, trans. Claudine Frank and Camille Naish (Durham, NC: Duke University Press, 2003), 69–81.
65. Dudley Andrews, "Praying Mantis: Enchantment and Violence in French Cinema of the Exotic," in *Visions of the East: Orientalism in Film*, ed. Matthew Bernstein and Gaylyn Studlar (New Brunswick, NJ: Rutgers University Press, 1997), 232–252.
66. Paul Greenhalgh, ed., *Art Nouveau, 1890–1914* (London: Victoria and Albert Museum, 2000); Fischer, *Cinema by Design*.
67. Quoted in Peter Wollen, "The Question of Technology," in *Paris/Manhattan: Writings on Art* (London: Verso, 2004), 56–57.
68. White, *Tastemaker*, 111.
69. Mina Loy to Carl Van Vechten, 1914, folder 1083, box 76, Series I, Van Vechten Papers.
70. Carl Van Vechten, "War Is Not Hell," *Trend* 8, no. 2 (November 1914): 150, quoted in White, *Tastemaker*, 116.
71. Mina Loy to Carl Van Vechten, 1915, folder 1082, box 76, Series I, Van Vechten Papers. In 1916 in New York, Loy became part of the Greenwich Village bohemian circle, to which Van Vechten belonged. Van Vechten also photographed her, along with her daughter Fabian Lloyd, in 1937.

Chapter 5. Photo-Dance

Epigraph: In James Baker Hall, *Rites and Passages* (New York: Aperture, 1978), 117, quoted in Laura Wexler, "I Am a Camera: The Photographic Process and the Reconfiguration of the Self," *Berkshire Review*, 1982, 118.

1. Booklet, *La Meri, World Tour, 1936–37, Assisted by Ram Gopal*, Series

I, La Meri Papers, MGZMD 207, Jerome Robbins Dance Division, The New York Public Library for the Performing Arts.

2. Hari Krishnan, in *Celluloid Classicism: Early Tamil Cinema and the Making of Modern Bharatanatyam* (Middletown, CT: Wesleyan University Press, 2019), claims that it is Ram Gopal's senior Uday Shankar who first introduced the Nataraja into Indian dance. Shankar's brochure in the Van Vechten collection, discussed in chapter 2, describes a group dance narrating the story of Shiva and his consort Parvati and not a solo performance focusing on the sculptural representation, as Gopal explores.
3. On a major exponent of dance photography in India, Avinash Pasricha, see Navina Jafa, "Freezing Performance—Art of Avinash Pasricha," *Narthaki*, July 4, 2019, https://narthaki.com/info/articles/art460.html. In this regard, Charles Flachs, a dancer, photographer, and my colleague in the dance department at Mount Holyoke College, takes pride in photographing wild birds in perfect focus but finds still images of dancers disturbing. Personal conversation, 2019. The connection between dance and wildlife photography deserves more attention.
4. The intensity of the light on the right is such that one almost wonders whether it was created intentionally by placing an additional light source behind the curtain.
5. On "Labanotations," see Suzanne Youngerman, "Movement Notation Systems as Conceptual Frameworks: The Laban System," *Journal for the Anthropological Study of Human Movement* 19, no. 2 (Fall 2012): 33–45. Notation books for group dances existed at least since the French courts of the eighteenth century. See Sarah R. Cohen, *Art, Dance, and the Body in French Culture of the Ancient Régime* (Cambridge: Cambridge University Press, 2000).
6. Krishnan, *Celluloid Classicism.*
7. Krishnan, 66–67.
8. Krishnan, 67.
9. Ram Gopal, *Rhythm in the Heavens: An Autobiography* (London: Secker and Warburg, 1957), 80.
10. Romita Ray, "Orientalizing the Bayadere/Fabricating Mata Hari," *Photographies* 5, no. 1 (March 2012): 87–111.
11. Gopal, *Rhythm in the Heavens*, 82–83.
12. Corinna Wessels-Mevissen, "Introducing a God and His Ideal Form: A. K. Coomaraswamy's 'Dance of Siva,' 1912/1918," *Indo-Asiatische Zeitschrift: Mitteilungen der Gesellschaft für indo-asiatische Kunst, Berlin* 16 (2012): 30–42.
13. Katie Légeret-Manochhaya, *Rodin and the Dance of Shiva* (New Delhi: Niyogi Books, 2016), 8, where she may be referring to the 1939 visit, when he returned to Paris with a troupe, not the 1938 visit after New York, in which he danced solo. Also see Alexander Gerstein, ed., *Rodin and Dance: The Essence of Movement* (London: Courtauld Gallery and the Musée Rodin, 2016); Hubert Goldschmidt, "Rodin and the Dance," *Ballet Review* 47, nos. 1–2 (Spring–Summer 2019): 177–206.
14. Saskia Kersenboom, "Ananda's Tandava: 'The Dance of Shiva' Reconsidered," *Marg* 62, no. 3 (March 2011): 28–43. For a debate among revisionist dance scholars of Coomaraswamy, also see Wessels-Mevissen, "Introducing a God and His Ideal Form."
15. R. Sewell, "Review of Ars Asiatica, No. III by A. Rodin, A. Coomaraswamy, E. Havell, V. Goloubew," *Journal of the Royal Asiatic Society of Great Britain and Ireland*, no. 1 (January 1923): 126–128.
16. Légeret-Manochhaya, *Rodin and the Dance of Shiva*, 27.
17. Nachiket Chanchani, "The Camerawork of Ananda Kentish Coomaraswamy and Alfred Stieglitz," *History of Photography* 37, no. 2 (2013): 213.
18. The chronology is imprecise here. My

reason for placing the film right after the New York photo shoot is that he danced solo to prerecorded music in New York, while the film shows the dancer accompanied by other dancers and musicians from his troupe, which he formed only in 1939 after his return from the New York trip.

19. Ayisha Abraham, "From the Rooftop into the Mine," *New Cinemas: Journal of Contemporary Film* 11, nos. 2–3 (2013): 169–182.
20. Abraham's documentary film *I Saw a God Dance* (2012) starts with extreme close-up shots of Gopal putting on his makeup, and excerpts of his stage performances display his flamboyant costumes.
21. In addition to the film star Kucalakumari, whom we discussed, Hari Krishnan finds a stigma about performing for a film in the example of Rukmini Devi Arundale, who made a film on her performance but, tellingly, bought back all existing copies to prevent circulation. Krishnan, *Celluloid Classicism*, chap. 2.
22. Sunil Kothari, *Photo Biography of Rukmini Devi* (Chennai: Kalakshetra Foundation, 2004); Ann-Marie Gaston, *Bharatanatyam: From Temple to Theatre* (New Delhi: Manohar, 1996). See also Krishnan, *Celluloid Classicism*, chap. 2.
23. Interview in Ayisha Abraham's documentary film *I Saw a God Dance* (2010).
24. Sarah Street and Joshua Yumibe, *Chromatic Modernity: Color, Cinema, and Media of the 1920s* (New York: Columbia University Press, 2019), 6.
25. Joshua Yumibe, "The Color Image," in *The Image in Early Cinema: Form and Material*, ed. Scott Curtis, Philippe Gauthier, Tom Gunning, and Joshua Yumibe (Bloomington: Indiana University Press, 2018), 142.
26. Tom Gunning, "Colorful Metaphors: The Attraction of Color in Early Silent Cinema," in *Il colore nel cinema muto: Atti del 2. Convegno internazionale di studi sul cinema*, ed. Monica Dall'Asta and Guglielmo Pescatore (Udine, Italy, 1995), 20–31.
27. Lucy Fischer, "Art Nouveau and the Age of Attractions," chap. 1 in *Cinema by Design: Art Nouveau, Modernism, and Film History* (New York: Columbia University Press, 2017), 46.
28. Natalie M. Kalmus, "Color Consciousness," *Journal of the Society of Motion Picture Engineers* 25, no. 2 (August 1935): 139–147.
29. Street and Yumibe, *Chromatic Modernity*, 2, on Abel Gance's epic film *Napoleon* (1927). See also Yumibe, "Color Image."
30. Street and Yumibe, *Chromatic Modernity*, 7, which also discusses the "chromatic density" of the modern street. See also Janet Ward, *Weimar Surfaces: Urban Visual Culture in the 1920s Germany* (Berkeley: University of California Press, 2001). See chapter 2 for Gopal's observation of the Chamundi Hills.
31. Abraham, "From Rooftop to Mine," 172.
32. Abraham, 174.
33. The filmmaker Sergei Eisenstein calls montage the "art of comparisons." See his "The Montage of Film Attractions" (1924), in *Selected Works*, vol. 1, *Writings 1922–34*, ed. Richard Taylor (London: BFI; Bloomington: Indiana University Press, 1988), 39–58.
34. Douglas Rosenberg, *Screendance: Inscribing the Ephemeral Image* (Oxford: Oxford University Press, 2012); Douglas Rosenberg, ed., *The Oxford Handbook of Screendance Studies* (New York: Oxford University Press, 2016).
35. The open-endedness of a photograph's meaning, until it is closed by a caption, draws on Roland Barthes, *Camera Lucida: Reflections on Photography*, trans. Richard Howard (New York: Hill and Wang, 1981). For the distribution of the "indexical" trace of a photograph into two potential vectors, that of a past moment and a discoverable future, see Walter Benjamin, "Little History of Photography," in *Walter Benjamin: The Work of Art in the Age of Its Technological Reproducibility and Other Writings on Media*, ed. Michael W. Jennings,

Brigid Doherty, and Thomas Y. Levin (Cambridge, MA: Harvard University Press, 2008), 276–278.

36. Jean Epstein, "On Certain Characteristics of Photogénie," trans. Tom Milne, in *Jean Epstein: Critical Essays and New Translations*, ed. Sarah Keller and Jason N. Paul (Amsterdam: Amsterdam University Press, 2012), 292–296.
37. Christoph Wall-Romana, "Epstein's *Photogénie* as Corporeal Vision: Inner Sensation, Queer Embodiment, and Ethics," in Keller and Paul, *Jean Epstein*, quotation from 57–58 and 63.
38. Epstein, "On Certain Characteristics of *Photogénie*," 295.
39. Barthes, *Camera Lucida*, 15.
40. Emily Apter, "Landscape of Photogeny: Morocco in Black and White," *ANY: Architecture New York*, no. 16 (1996): 24–25.
41. Jean Epstein and Stuart Liebman, "Magnification and Other Writings," *October* 3 (Spring 1977): 9.
42. Wall-Romana, "Epstein's *Photogénie* as Corporeal Vision," 57.
43. An echo of Epstein's organic, animating "space-time system" can be seen in Benjamin's well-known idea of "aura" as "a strange tissue of space and time: the unique apparition of a distance, however near it may be," discussed in chapter 4. See Walter Benjamin, "The Work of Art in the Age of Its Technical Reproducibility" (second version, 1935–1936), in *The Work of Art in the Age of its Technological Reproducibility and Other Writings on Media*, edited by Michael W. Jennings, Brigid Doherty, and Thomas Y. Levin (Cambridge, MA: Harvard University Press, 2008), 23.
44. Gopal, *Rhythm in the Heavens*, 33.
45. Epstein and Liebman, "Magnification," 10–11.
46. Gopal, *Rhythm in the Heavens*, 5.
47. Epstein and Liebman, "Magnification," 10.
48. Gopal, *Rhythm in the Heavens*, 11.
49. Ram Gopal to Mercedes de Acosta, [June or July?] 16, 1946, Acosta 11:01, "Gopal, Ram, Correspondence with Mercedes de Acosta, Ephemera, 1938–1960," Mercedes de Acosta Papers, Rosenbach Museum and Library, Philadelphia, PA.
50. Gopal to de Acosta.
51. Gopal, *Rhythm in the Heavens*, 207.
52. Robert A. Schanke, *"That Furious Lesbian": The Story of Mercedes de Acosta* (Carbondale: Southern Illinois University Press, 2003). Letters in the Rosenbach Museum and Library. I wondered about the crown when Alexander Janta's biographer Michal Folega mentioned seeing a wooden box full of Gopal's "moth-eaten" costumes in the basement of Janta's and his wife Valentine Pacewicz's New York house years later. Folega, email to the author, April 26, 2021.
53. Gopal, *Rhythm in the Heavens*, 174.
54. Roland Barthes, "The Face of Garbo," in *Mythologies*, trans. Annette Lavers (London: Paladin Books, 1973) 62–64.
55. Gopal, *Rhythm in the Heavens*, 174–175.
56. Gopal, 174.
57. Ram Gopal to Mercedes de Acosta, April 3, 1946, Acosta Papers.
58. Laura Wexler, "I Am a Camera: The Photographic Process and the Reconfiguration of the Self," *Berkshire Review*, 1982, 119.
59. Walter Benjamin, "The Work of Art in the Age of Its Technological Reproducibility" (second version, 1935–1936), in Jennings, Doherty, and Levin, *Work of Art in the Age of Its Technological Reproducibility*, 30–31.
60. Anne Anlin Cheng, *Second Skin: Josephine Baker and the Modern Surface* (Oxford: Oxford University Press, 2011), 118–119.
61. Cheng, 38.
62. Cheng, 2.
63. Cheng, 1.
64. Cheng, 119–120.
65. For a grounding of this recuperative direction more directly in a broader discussion of the human sensorium and modern media, see Susan Buck-Morss, "Aesthetics and Anaesthetics: Walter Benjamin's Artwork Essay

Reconsidered," *October* 32 (1992): 3–41.

66. Miriam Hansen, "Walter Benjamin and Cinema: Not a One-Way Street," in "'Angelus Novus': Perspectives on Walter Benjamin," special issue, *Critical Inquiry* 25, no. 2 (Winter 1999): 306–343.
67. Walter Benjamin, "On the Mimetic Faculty," in *Reflections*, ed. Peter Demetz, trans. Edmund Jephcott (New York: Harcourt Brace Jovanovich, 1978), 333–336. One can also imagine similarly the "cobra," "downward dog," and other animal positions in yoga.
68. Wall-Romana, "Epstein's *Photogénie* as Corporeal Vision," 58.
69. On the negative strip, two telling exceptions, where the body is centered, draw attention to the band of studio light across the middle of the photographs, as we discussed in chapter 2.
70. Reena Shah, *Movement in Stills: The Dance and Life of Kumudini Lakhia* (Ahmedabad, India: Mapin, 2005), 286.

Chapter 6. Afterimages

1. Ram Gopal, *Rhythm in the Heavens: An Autobiography* (London: Secker and Warburg, 1957), 62.
2. Folder 847, box 60, Series I: Correspondence, 1907–1971, YCAL MSS 1050, Carl Van Vechten Papers, Beinecke Rare Book and Manuscript Library, Yale University, New Haven, CT.
3. Jessie-Jeswanti Ram Gopal to Carl Van Vechten, October 12, 1938, folder 655, box 48, Series I, Van Vechten Papers.
4. Folder 847, box 60, Series I, Van Vechten Papers.
5. Ajay Sinha, "Carl Van Vechten," *Accelerate: Access & Inclusion at the Tang Teaching Museum* (Frances Young Tang Teaching Museum, Skidmore College), no. 2 (2018): 14–15.
6. Gopal, *Rhythm in the Heavens*, 77–78.
7. Ram Gopal to Mercedes de Acosta, June 20, 1940, Mercedes de Acosta Papers, Rosenbach Museum and Library, Philadelphia, PA. Also see his letter of January 30, 1940, from Paris.
8. Roland Barthes, *Camera Lucida: Reflections on Photography*, trans. Richard Howard (New York: Hill and Wang, 1981), 21. See also his claim, "So I make myself the measure of photographic 'knowledge'" (9).
9. Elspeth H. Brown and Thy Phu explain that Freud's idea of "affect" is based on "embodied processes" that translate as "feelings" or "physiologically charged emotions" in the body of the individuals who access its meaning. Introduction to *Feeling Photography* (Durham, NC: Duke University Press, 2014), 5.
10. Brown and Phu.
11. Barthes, *Camera Lucida*, 20–21.
12. Barthes acknowledges this tension. "History is hysterical: it is constituted only if we consider it, only if we look at it—and in order to look at it, we must be excluded from it" (65).
13. Michel-Rolph Trouillot, *Silencing the Past: Power and the Production of History* (1995; repr., Boston: Beacon, 2015), 27.
14. We do not know if Gopal owned a Leica, but he certainly knew about it before he came to New York in 1938. In a photograph of the dancer with Alexander Janta on the ocean liner *Chichibu Mari* from Tokyo to Honolulu on their way to Los Angeles, we see a Leica camera dangling from Janta's hands. See chapter 2.
15. Barthes, *Camera Lucida*, 5–6.
16. For a distinction between historical actors as "bundle of capacities that are specific in time and space" and "purposeful subjects aware of their own voices," see Trouillot, *Silencing the Past*, 23–24.
17. Ram Gopal to Mercedes de Acosta, October 12, 1939, Acosta Papers.
18. Ram Gopal to Mercedes de Acosta, [June or July?] 16, 1946, Acosta Papers.
19. The critique seemed aimed at the Indian Progressive Theatre Association (IPTA), the Progressive Writer's Group, the Progressive Artists Group,

active by mid-century and all identified by later critics as India's cultural "avant-garde." Geeta Kapur, *When Was Modernism: Essays on Contemporary Cultural Practice in India* (New Delhi: Tulika, 2000).

20. Gopal, *Rhythm in the Heavens*, 133–137.
21. Ram Gopal to Mercedes de Acosta, January 30, 1940, Acosta Papers.
22. Gopal, *Rhythm in the Heavens*, 125, 139.
23. Ram Gopal to Mercedes de Acosta, January 9. 1954, from London, Acosta Papers.
24. Ram Gopal to Mercedes de Acosta, July 6, 1954, from London, Acosta Papers.
25. Anne Anlin Cheng, *Second Skin: Josephine Baker and the Modern Surface* (Oxford: Oxford University Press, 2011), 1.
26. Cheng, 13.
27. Avanthi Meduri, "Bharatha Natyam—What Are You?," *Asian Theatre Journal* 5, no. 1 (Spring 1988): 2.
28. Sunil Kothari, reporting on his talk "Remembering Ram Gopal" in 2017 in Kuala Lumpur in *Narthaki*, the online journal and archive for classical Indian dance founded by the dancer activist Anita Ratham: Kothari, "Remembering Ram Gopal." *Narthaki*, December 8, 2017, https://narthaki.com/info/gtsk/gtsk164.html.
29. The Philadelphia Museum of Art probably holds the single largest collection of Van Vechten's photographs, but they were given to the museum by his assistant, Mark Lutz, in a spectacular feat of curation that I discuss at the beginning of the book.
30. See Beinecke Rare Book and Manuscript Library, "Mondays at Beinecke: Van Vechten Color Photographs in the James Weldon Johnson Memorial Collection (Part 2)," accessed December 2020, https://beinecke.library.yale.edu/event/mondays-beinecke-van-vechten-color-photographs-james-weldon-johnson-memorial-collection-part-2; and Beinecke Library at Yale, "Van Vechten Color Photographs (Part 1): Mondays at Beinecke, November 23, 2020," YouTube, November 25, 2020, https://www.youtube.com/watch?v=wvpRyK5rNlk&t=17s.
31. G. Venkatachalam, *Dance in India* (Bombay: Nalanda, n.d.), 67.
32. Raja Ravi Varma has been completely revived in the past two decades as one of the earliest Indian avant-garde artist precisely because of his promiscuity. See Geeta Kapur, "Representational Dilemmas of a Nineteenth-Century Painter: Raja Ravi Varma," in *When Was Modernism: Essays on Contemporary Cultural Practices in India* (New Delhi: Tulika, 2000), 145–178. His "photos of the gods" also blur the distinction between high and low forms of cultural practices. See Christopher Pinney, *"Photos of the Gods": The Printed Image and Political Struggle in India* (London: Reaktion, 2004).
33. Sukanya Rahman, *Dancing in the Family: The Extraordinary Story of the First Family of Indian Classical Dance* (New Delhi: Speaking Tiger, 2019), 33–34.
34. Venkatachalam, *Dance in India*, 45–46.
35. Ajay Sinha, "Mysore Modern across the Arts," in *G. Venkatappa and His Times*, ed. Pushpamala N. and Deeptha Achar (New Delhi: Routledge, forthcoming).
36. Katia Légeret-Manochhaya, *Rodin and the Dance of Shiva* (New Delhi: Niyogi Books, 2016); Vivan Sundaram and Deepak Ananth, *Umrao Singh Sher-Gil: His Misery and His Manuscript* (New Delhi: Photoink, 2008); Rahman, *Dancing in the Family*.
37. Vivek Bald, *Bengali Harlem and the Lost Histories of South Asian America* (Cambridge, MA: Harvard University Press, 2013).
38. Nancy Um, *Shipped but Not Sold: Material Culture and Social Protocols of Trade during Yemen's Age of Coffee*, Perspectives on Global Pasts (Honolulu: University of Hawaiʻi Press, 2017).
39. Sukanya Rahman's account of Ragini

Devi in *Dancing in the Family* includes anti-British protest groups in New York that overlap with Vivek Bald's account of a Muslim seaman, Dada Amir Haidar Khan, and other activists who jumped ship from British ships in New York and became involved in political protest in the 1920s and 1930s. See Bald, "The Travels and Transformations of Amir Haidar Ali," in *Bengali Harlem*, 137–159.

40. Bald, *Bengali Harlem*, 162.
41. Bald, 160–162.
42. Bald, 87.
43. Bald, 87.

BIBLIOGRAPHY

Abraham, Ayisha. "From the Rooftop into the Mine." *New Cinemas: Journal of Contemporary Film* 11, nos. 2–3 (2013): 169–182.

Abrahams, Ruth K. "Uday Shankar: The Early Years, 1900–1938." *Dance Chronicle* 30, no. 3 (2007): 363–426.

Alastair (Hans Henning Voight). *Fifty Drawings by Alastair*. Introduction by Carl Van Vechten. New York: Knopf, 1925.

Albertson, Chris. *Bessie: Empress of the Blues*. London: Sphere Books, 1972.

Allen, Matthew Harp. "Rewriting the Script for South Indian Dance." *Drama Review* 41, no. 3 (Fall 1997): 63–100.

——. "Standardize, Classicize, and Nationalize: The Scientific Work of the Music Academy of Madras, 1930–52." In *Performing Pasts: Reinventing the Arts in Modern South India*, edited by Indira P. Vishwanathan and Devesh Soneji, 90–132. New Delhi: Oxford University Press, 2008.

Amory, Cleveland, and Frederic Bradlee. Introduction to *Vanity Fair, America's Most Memorable Magazine: A Cavalcade of the 1920s and 1930s*. New York: Viking, 1960.

Andrews, Dudley. "Praying Mantis: Enchantment and Violence in French Cinema of the Exotic." In *Visions of the East: Orientalism in Film*, edited by Matthew Bernstein and Gaylyn Studlar, 232–252. New Brunswick, NJ: Rutgers University Press, 1997.

Appadurai, Arjun. "The Colonial Backdrop." *Afterimage* 24, no. 5 (1997): 4–7.

——. *Modernity at Large: Cultural Dimensions of Globalization*. Minneapolis: University of Minnesota Press, 1996.

Apter, Emily. "Acting Out Orientalism: Sapphic Theatricality in Turn-of-the-Century Paris." *Esprit Créateur* 34, no. 2 (1994): 102–116.

——. "Landscape of Photogeny: Morocco in Black and White." *ANY: Architecture New York*, no. 16 (1996): 20–27.

Avon, Neal. "Folk Art Fantasies: Photographers Backdrops." *Afterimage* 24 (1997): 12–18.

Baba Yaga Music. "La Meri, American Ethnic Dancer." Accessed June 7, 2018. http://babayagamusic.com/Encyclopedic-Dictionary-Ethnic-Arts/Ethnic-Music-and-Dance-Performers/La-Meri-Twentieth-Century-Ethnic-Dancer.htm.

Bald, Vivek. *Bengali Harlem and the Lost Histories of South Asian America*. Cambridge, MA: Harvard University Press, 2013.

Barthes, Roland. *Camera Lucida: Reflections on Photography*. Translated by Richard Howard. New York: Hill and Wang, 1981.

——. "The Face of Garbo." In *Mythologies*, selected and translated by Annette Lavers, 62–64. London: Paladin Books, 1973.

Basu, Priyanka. "Moving from the Temple to the Studio-Space: Transformation of the Women Dancer's Labour in Films." In *The Moving Space: Women in Dance*, edited by Urmimala Sarkar Munsi and Aishika Chakraborty, 138–155. Delhi: Primus Books, 2018.

Batchen, Geoffrey. *Apparitions: Photography and Dissemination*. Sydney: Power, 2018.

Benjamin, Walter. "Little History of Photography." In *Walter Benjamin: The Work of Art in the Age of Its Technological Reproducibility and Other Writings on Media*, edited by

Michael W. Jennings, Brigid Doherty, and Thomas Y. Levin, 274–298. Cambridge, MA: Harvard University Press, 2008.

Benjamin, Walter. "New Things about Plants: A Review of Karl Blossfeldt, *Art Forms in Nature*." 1928. In *Germany, the New Photography, 1927–33: Documents and Essays*, edited by David Mellor, 20–21. London: Arts Council of Great Britain, 1978.

———. "One Way Street." In *Selected Writings*, vol. 1, *1913–1926*, edited by Marcus Bullock and Michael W. Jennings, 444–488. Cambridge, MA: Harvard University Press.

———. "On the Mimetic Faculty." In *Reflections*, edited by Peter Demetz, translated by Edmund Jephcott, 333–336. New York: Harcourt Brace Jovanovich, 1978.

———. "The Work of Art in the Age of Its Technical Reproducibility" (second version, 1935–1936). In *Walter Benjamin: The Work of Art in the Age of Its Technological Reproducibility and Other Writings on Media*, edited by Michael W. Jennings, Brigid Doherty, and Thomas Y. Levin, 19–55. Cambridge, MA: Harvard University Press, 2008.

Bernard, Emily. *Carl Van Vechten and the Harlem Renaissance: A Portrait in Black and White*. New Haven, CT: Yale University Press, 2012.

Bernstein, Matthew, and Gaylyn Studlar, eds. *Visions of the East: Orientalism in Film*. New Brunswick, NJ: Rutgers University Press, 1997.

Bhagavan, Manu. *Sovereign Spheres: Princes, Education and Empire in Colonial India*. Oxford: Oxford University Press, 2003.

Blackwood, Sarah. *The Portrait's Subject: Inventing Inner Life in the Nineteenth-Century United States*. Chapel Hill: University of North Carolina Press, 2019.

Bohlman, Philip V., and Goffredo Plastino. Introduction to *Jazz Worlds/World Jazz*, edited by Philip V. Bohlman and Goffredo Plastino, 1–48 Chicago: University of Chicago Press, 2016.

Boone, Joseph Allen. *The Homoerotics of Orientalism*. New York: Columbia University Press, 2014.

Brenscheidt, Diana. *Shiva Onstage: Uday Shankar's Company of Hindu Dancers and Musicians in Europe and the United States, 1931–1938*. Berlin: LIT Verlag, 2011.

British Library. "1539–1543, The Khamsah, or Five Poems, of Niẓāmī f. 2." Accessed August 5, 2017. http://www.bl.uk/manuscripts/Viewer.aspx?ref=or_2265_f026v.

British Pathé. "Indian Dancer (1947)." YouTube, April 13, 2014. https://youtu.be/5IrabwIKwK8.

Brown, Elspeth H., and Thy Phu. Introduction to *Feeling Photography*, edited by Elspeth H. Brown and Thy Phu, 1–26. Durham, NC: Duke University Press, 2014.

Brown, Judith. *Glamour in Six Dimensions: Modernism and the Radiance of Form*. Ithaca, NY: Cornell University Press, 2009.

Brown, Kimberly Juanita. *The Repeating Body: Slavery's Visual Resonance in the Contemporary*. Durham, NC: Duke University Press, 2015.

Brown, Stephen, and Georgiana Uhlyarik. *Florine Stettheimer: Painting Poetry*. New York: Jewish Museum; New Haven, CT: Yale University Press, 2017.

Buck-Morss, Susan. "Aesthetics and Anaesthetics: Walter Benjamin's Artwork Essay Reconsidered." *October* 32 (1992): 3–41.

Byrd, Rudolph P., ed. *Generations in Black and White: Photographs by Carl Van Vechten from the James Weldon Johnson Memorial Collection*. Athens: University of Georgia Press, 1993.

Caillois, Roger. "The Praying Mantis: From Biology to Psychoanalysis." In *The Edge of Surrealism: A Roger Caillois Reader*, translated by Claudine Frank and Camille Naish, 69–81. Durham, NC: Duke University Press, 2003.

Campt, Tina M. *Image Matters: Archive, Photography, and the African Diaspora in Europe*. Durham, NC: Duke University Press, 2012.

Cartier-Bresson, Henri. *The Decisive Moment: Photography by Henri Cartier-Bresson.* New York: Simon and Schuster, 1952.

Chadwick, Whitney. "Fetishizing Fashion/Fetishizing Culture: Man Ray's 'Noire et blanche.'" *Oxford Art Journal* 18, no. 2 (1995): 3–17.

Chandnani, Nachiket. "The Camerawork of Ananda Kentish Coomaraswamy and Alfred Stieglitz." *History of Photography* 37, no. 2 (May 2013): 204–220.

Chaudhary, Zahid R. *Afterimage of Empire: Photography in Nineteenth-Century India.* Minneapolis: University of Minnesota Press, 2012.

Chauncey, George. *Gay New York: Gender, Culture, and the Making of the Gay Male World, 1800–1940.* New York: Basic Books, 1994.

Cheng, Anne Anlin, *Ornamentalism.* New York: Oxford University Press, 2019.

——. *Second Skin: Josephine Baker and the Modern Surface.* New York: Oxford University Press, 2011.

——. "Shine: On Race, Glamour and the Modern." *PMLA* 126, no. 4 (2011): 1022–1041.

——. "Wounded Beauty: An Exploratory Essay on Race, Feminism, and the Aesthetic Question." *Tulsa Studies in Women's Literature* 19, no. 2 (Autumn 2000): 191–217.

Chéroux, Clément, Andreas Fischer, and Pierre Apraxine. *The Perfect Medium: Photography and the Occult.* New Haven, CT: Yale University Press, 2005.

Childs, Adrienne L., and Susan H. Libby, eds. *Blacks and Blackness in European Art of the Long Nineteenth Century.* Farnham, UK: Ashgate, 2014.

Chow, Rey. "The Dream of a Butterfly." In *The Chow Reader*, edited by Paul Bowman, 124–146. New York: Columbia University Press, 2010.

Coffin, Sarah D., and Stephen Harrison. *The Jazz Age: American Style in the 1920s.* Cleveland, OH: Cleveland Museum of Art, 2017.

Cohen, Matthew Isaac. *Performing Otherness: Java and Bali on International Stages, 1905–1952.* New York: Palgrave Macmillan, 2010.

Cohen, Sarah R. *Art, Dance, and the Body in French Culture of the Ancient Régime.* Cambridge: Cambridge University Press, 2000.

Coomaraswamy, Ananda. *The Dance of Shiva: Fourteen Indian Essays.* New York: Sunwise Turn, 1918.

——. *The Dance of Shiva: On Indian Art and Culture.* Rev. ed. New York: Noonday, 1957.

Coomaraswamy, Ananda, and Gopala Kristnayya Duggirala, trans. *The Mirror of Gesture: Being the Abhinaya Darpana of Nandikesvara.* Cambridge, MA: Harvard University Press, 1917.

Coorlawala, Uttara Asha. "Dancing and Writing from Otherness." *India International Centre Quarterly* 32, no. 4 (Spring 2006): 42–50.

——. "Ruth St. Denis and India's Dance Renaissance." *Dance Chronicle* 15, no. 2 (1992): 123–152.

——. "The Sanskritized Body." *Dance Research Journal* 36, no. 2 (Winter 2004): 50–63.

Critical Ethnic Studies Editorial Collective, ed. *Critical Ethnic Studies: A Reader.* Durham, NC: Duke University Press, 2016.

David, Ann R. *Ram Gopal: Interweaving Histories of Indian Dance.* London: Bloomsbury, forthcoming.

——. "Spectacle or Spectacular? The Orientalist Imagery in Indian Dance Performance in Britain from 1900–1959." *Dance and Spectacle* (Society of Dance History Scholars), 2010, 79–87.

Davis, Keith F. *The Passionate Observer: Photographs of Carl Van Vechten.* Kansas City, MO: Hallmark Cards, 1993.

Derrida, Jacques. *The Animal That Therefore I Am.* Edited by Marie-Louis Mallet. Translated by David Wills. New York: Fordham University Press, 2008.

——. "The Animal That Therefore I Am (More to Follow)." *Critical Inquiry* 28, no. 2 (Winter 2002): 369–418.

Dinkar, Niharika. "Masculine Regeneration and the Attenuated Body in the Early Works of Nandalal Bose." *Oxford Art Journal* 33, no. 2 (2010): 169–188.

Djajadiningrat-Nieuwenhuis, Madelon. "Mangkunegoro VII and Rabindranath Tagore: A Brief Meeting of Like Minds." *Indonesia and the Malay World* 34, no. 98 (March 2006): 99–107.

Douglas, Ann. *Terrible Honesty: Mongrel Manhattan in the 1920s*. New York, Farrar, Straus and Giroux, 1995.

Edkins-Richardson, Diana, ed. *Vanity Fair: Photographs of an Age, 1914–1936*. New York, C. N. Potter, 1982.

Edwards, Elizabeth, ed. *Anthropology and Photography, 1860–1920*. New Haven, CT: Yale University Press, 1992.

Edwards, Holly. *Noble Dreams, Wicked Pleasures: Orientalism in America, 1870–1930*. Williamstown, MA: Sterling and Francine Clark Art Institute; Princeton, NJ: Princeton University Press, 2000.

Eisenstein, Sergei. "The Montage of Film Attractions." 1924. In *Selected Works*, vol. 1, *Writings 1922–34*, edited by Richard Taylor, 39–58. London: BFI; Bloomington: Indiana University Press, 1988.

Epstein, Jean. "On Certain Characteristics of Photogénie." Translated by Tom Milne. In *Jean Epstein: Critical Essays and New Translations*, edited by Sarah Keller and Jason N. Paul, 292–296. Amsterdam: Amsterdam University Press, 2012.

Epstein, Jean, and Stuart Liebman. "Magnification and Other Writings." *October* 3 (Spring 1977): 9–25.

Erdman, Joan L. "Blurred Boundaries: Androgyny and Gender in the Dance of Uday Shankar." In *Border Crossings: Dance and Boundaries in Society, Politics, Gender, Education and Technology, Joint Conference with The Association of Dance in Universities and Colleges*, compiled by Linda J. Tomko, 117–124. Riverside: University of California, Society of Dance History Scholars, 1995.

———. "Circling the Square: A Choreographed Approach to the Work of Dr. Kapila Vatsyayan and Western Dance Studies." *Dance Research Journal* 32, no. 1 (Summer 2000): 87–94.

———. "Cross-Cultural Discourses: Writing of Uday Shankar." In *Proceedings of the Society of Dance History Scholars, Twentieth Annual Conference, Barnard College, New York City, June 19–22, 1997*, 269–275. Riverside, CA: Society of Dance History Scholars, 1997.

———. "Dance Discourses: Rethinking the History of the 'Oriental Dance.'" In *Moving Words: Re-writing Dance*, edited by Gay Morris, 288–305. New York: Routledge, 1996.

———. "Performance as Translation: Uday Shankar in the West." *Drama Review* 31, no. 1 (Spring 1987): 64–88.

———. "Who Remembers Uday Shankar?" *Freethinker*. Accessed June 12, 2018. https://mm-gold.azureedge.net/new_site/mukto-mona/Articles/jaffor/uday_shanka2.html.

Feyder, Sophie. "Photography and the Making of Black Urban Femininities in the 1950s East." *Safundi* 15, nos. 2–3 (2014): 227–254.

Fineman, Mia. "Ecce Homo Prostheticus." *New German Critique* 76 (1999): 85–114.

Fischer, Lucy. *Cinema by Design: Art Nouveau, Modernism, and Film History*. New York: Columbia University Press, 2017.

Folega, Michal. *Zycie Na Swait Otwarte: Aleksander Janta Polczynski* (Life for an Open World: Aleksander Janta Polczynski). Tuchola, Poland: Meander, 2014.

Foster, Hal. "Obscene, Abject, Traumatic." *October* 78 (Autumn 1996): 106–124.

Ganser, Elisa. "Ananda K. Coomaraswamy's *Mirror of Gesture* and the Debate about Indian art in the Early Twentieth Century." In *Asia and Europe—Interconnected: Agents, Concepts, and Things*, edited by Angelika Malinar and Simone Müller, 91–130. Wiesbaden: Harrassowitz Verlag, 2018.

Garelick, Rhonda K. *Rising Star: Dandyism, Gender, and Performance in Fin de Siècle*. Princeton, NJ: Princeton University Press, 1998.

Gaston, Ann-Marie. *Bharatanatyam: From Temple to Theatre*. New Delhi: Manohar, 1996.

Geczy, Adam. *Transorientalism in Art, Fashion, and Film: Inventions of Identity*. London: Bloomsbury, 2019.

George, Nina C. "How Bengaluru's Opera House Came Back to Life." *Deccan Herald*, September 11, 2018. https://www.deccanherald.com/metrolife/how-it-came-back-life-692254.html.

Gerstein, Alexander, ed. *Rodin and Dance: The Essence of Movement*. London: Courtauld Gallery and the Musée Rodin, 2016.

Ghosh, Pika. *Making Kantha, Making Home: Women at Work in Colonial Bengal*. Seattle: University of Washington Press, 2021.

Goldschmidt, Hubert. "Rodin and the Dance." *Ballet Review* 47, nos. 1–2 (Spring–Summer 2019): 177–206.

Gopal, Ram. *Rhythm in the Heavens: An Autobiography*. London: Secker and Warburg, 1957.

Gopal, Ram, and Serozh Dadachanji. *Indian Dancing*. London: Phoenix House, 1951.

Greenhalgh, Paul, ed. *Art Nouveau, 1890–1914*. London: Victoria and Albert Museum, 2000.

Grossman, Wendy A. "Race and Beauty in Black and White: Robert Demachy and the Aestheticization of Blackness in Pictorialist Photography." In *Blacks and Blackness in European Art of the Long Nineteenth Century*, edited by Adrienne L. Childs and Susan H. Libby, 201–230. Farnham, UK: Ashgate, 2014.

Guha-Thakurta, Tapati. *The Making of a New "Indian" Art: Artists, Aesthetics, and Nationalism in Bengal, c. 1850–1920*. Cambridge: Cambridge University Press, 1992.

Gunning, Tom. "Colorful Metaphors: The Attraction of Color in Early Silent Cinema." In *Il colore nel cinema muto: Atti del 2. Convegno internazionale di studi sul cinema*, edited by Monica Dall'Asta and Guglielmo Pescatore, 20–31. Udine, Italy, 1995.

Gusejnova, Dina. "Jazz Anxiety and the European Fear of Cultural Change: Towards a Transnational History of a Political Emotion." *Cultural History* 5, no. 1 (2016): 26–51.

Hambourg, Morris Maria, et al. *Nadar*. New York: Metropolitan Museum of Art, 1995.

Hansen, Kathryn. "Making Women Visible: Gender and Race Cross-Dressing in the Parsi Theatre." *Theatre Journal* 40, no. 2 (May 1999): 127–147.

———. "Parsi Theatrical Networks in Southeast Asia: The Contrary Case of Burma." *Journal of Southeast Asian Studies* 49, no. 1 (February 2018): 4–33.

———. *Stages of Life: Indian Theatre Autobiographies*. Ranikhet, India: Permanent Black, 2011.

Hansen, Miriam. "Benjamin and Cinema: Not a One-Way Street." In "Angelus Novus: Perspectives on Walter Benjamin." Special issue, *Critical Inquiry* 25, no. 2 (Winter 1999): 306–343.

———. "The Mass Production of the Senses: Classical Cinema as Vernacular Modernism." *Modernism/Modernity* 6, no. 2 (1999): 59–77.

Hartman, Saidiya. *Scenes of Subjection: Terror, Slavery, and Self-Making in Nineteenth-Century America*. New York: Oxford University Press, 1997.

———. "Venus in Two Acts." *Small Axe* 12, no. 2 (June 2008): 1–14.

———. *Wayward Lives, Beautiful Experiments: Intimate Histories of Social Upheaval*. New York: Norton, 2019.

Haskell, Barbara. *Charles Demuth, 1883–1935*. New York: Whitney Museum of Art and H. N. Abrams. 1987.

Inankur, Zeynep, Reina Lewis, and Mary Roberts, eds. *The Poetics and Politics of Place: Ottoman Istanbul and British Orientalism*. Seattle: University of Washington Press, 2011.

Jackson, Travis A. "Race, Culture, Commodity, Palimpsest: Locating Jazz in the World." In *Jazz Worlds/World Jazz*, edited by Philip V. Bohlman and Goffredo Plastino, 381–401.

Chicago: University of Chicago Press, 2016.

Jafa, Navina. "Freezing Performance—Art of Avinash Pasricha." *Narthaki*, July 4, 2019. https://narthaki.com/info/articles/art460.html.

Janta, Aleksander. *Pamietnik Indyjski*. London: Officyna Poetow i Malarzy, 1970.

Jennings, Michael W., Brigid Doherty, and Thomas Y. Levin. "Editors' Introduction." In *Walter Benjamin: The Work of Art in the Age of Its Technological Reproducibility and Other Writings on Media*, 1–17. Cambridge, MA: Harvard University Press, 2008.

Jordaan, Roy E. "The Tara Temple of Kalasan in Central Java." *Bulletin de l'École française d'Extrême-Orient* 85 (1998): 163–183.

Kaimal, Padma. "Passionate Bodies: Constructions of the Self in South Indian Portraits." *Archives of Asian Art* 48 (1995): 6–16.

——. "The Problem of Portraiture in South India, circa 870–970 A.D." *Artibus Asiae* 59, nos. 1–2 (1999): 59–133.

Kale, Sunila S. "Structures of Power: Electrification in Colonial India." *Comparative Studies of South Asia, Africa and Middle East* 34, no. 3 (2014): 454–475.

Kalmus, Natalie M. "Color Consciousness." *Journal of the Society of Motion Picture Engineers* 25, no. 2 (August 1935): 139–147.

Kambon, Malaika. "The Mind That Sees: The Third Eye of Eslanda Goode Robeson." *San Francisco Bay View*, May 27, 2015. https://sfbayview.com/2015/05/the-mind-that-sees-the-third-eye-of-eslanda-goode-robeson/.

Kapur, Geeta. *When Was Modernism: Essays on Contemporary Cultural Practices in India*. New Delhi: Tulika, 2000.

Katz, Jonathan D. "Hide/Seek: Difference and Desire in American Portraiture." In *Hide/Seek: Difference and Desire in American Portraiture*, by Jonathan D. Katz and David C. Ward, 10–60. Washington, DC: National Portrait Gallery, 2010.

Kazeem-Kaminski, Belinda. "Unearthing. In Conversation: On Listening and Caring." *Critical Ethnic Studies* 4, no. 2 (Fall 2018): 75–99.

Keating, Patrick. "Artifice and Atmosphere: The Visual Culture of Hollywood Glamour Photography, 1930–1935." *Film History* 29, no. 3 (2017): 105–135.

Kellner, Bruce. *Carl Van Vechten and the Irreverent Decades*. Norman: University of Oklahoma Press, 1968.

——, ed. *The Harlem Renaissance: A Historical Dictionary of the Era*. Westport, CT: Greenwood, 1984.

——. Introduction to *The Harlem Renaissance: A Historical Dictionary of the Era*, edited by Bruce Kellner, xiii–xxvii Westport, CT: Greenwood, 1984.

Kersenboom, Saskia. "Ananda's Tandava: 'The Dance of Shiva' Reconsidered." *Marg* 62, no. 3 (March 2011): 28–43.

Kharode, Roobina, and Shukla Sawant. "City Lights, City Limits: Multiple Metaphors in Everyday Urbanism." In *Art and Visual Culture in India, 1857–2007*, edited by Gayatri Sinha, 190–205. Mumbai: Marg, 2009.

Khokhar, Ashish. "Pioneers of Indian Dance: Ram Gopal (1912–2003)." *Sahapada*, June 28, 2018. https://www.sahapedia.org/ram-gopal-1912%E2%80%932003.

——. "Ram Gopal: The King of Classical Dance." *Attendance* (Mohan Khokar Dance Foundation), 1998, 64–71.

Khullar, Sonal. "Almora Dreams: Art and Life at the Uday Shankar India Cultural Centre, 1939–1944." *Marg* 69, no. 4 (June–September 2018): 14–32.

Kirstein, Lincoln. "Carl Van Vechten: 1880–1964." *Yale University Library Gazette* 39, no. 4 (April 1965). Reprinted in *By With To & Whom: A Lincoln Kirstein Reader*, edited by Nicholas Jenkins, 31–37. New York: Farrar, Straus and Giroux, 1991.

Komroff, Manuel. "Before We Press the Button." In *The Leica Manual: A Manual for the Amateur and Professional Covering the Entire Field of Leica Photograph*, by Willard D. Morgan and Henry M. Lester, rev. ed., 7–16. New York: Morgan and Lester, 1938.

Kothari, Sunil. *Bharata Natyam: Indian Classical Dance Art*. Mumbai: Marg, 1979.

———. "Institutionalization of Classical Dances of India: Kalakshetra—The Principal Case Study." In *Traversing Tradition: Celebrating Dance in India*, edited by Urmimala Sarkar Munsi and Stephanie Burridge, 124–136. London: Routledge, 2011.

———. "Mysore School of Bharata Natyam." In *Bharata Natyam*, 136–143. Mumbai: Marg, 1997.

———. *Photo Biography of Rukmini Devi*. Chennai: Kalakshetra Foundation, 2004.

———. "Ram Gopal: At Home Abroad." *Sruti*, April 2000, 21–23.

———. "Remembering Ram Gopal." *Narthaki*, December 8, 2017. https://narthaki.com/info/gtsk/gtsk164.html.

Kramrisch, Stella. *Indian Sculpture: Ancient, Classical, and Medieval*. 1933. Revised and reprinted, New Delhi: Motilal Banarasidas, 2013.

Krauss, Rosalind. "Jump over the Bauhaus." *October* 15 (Winter 1980): 103–110.

Kreyling, Michael. "Fugitive Voices." In *The Oxford Critical and Cultural History of Modernist Magazines*, vol. 2, *North America, 1894–1960*, edited by Peter Brooker and Andrew Thacker, 508–522. Oxford: Oxford University Press, 2012.

Krishnan, Hari. *Celluloid Classicism: Early Tamil Cinema and the Making of Modern Bharatanatyam*. Middletown, CT: Wesleyan University Press, 2019.

———. "From Gynemimesis to Hypermasculinity: The Shifting Orientations of Male Performers of South Indian Court Dance." In *When Men Dance: Choreographing Masculinities across Borders*, edited by Jennifer Fisher and Anthony Shay, 378–391. New York: Oxford University Press, 2009.

Kumar, Brinda. "Of Networks and Narratives: Collecting Indian Art in America, 1907–1972." PhD diss., Cornell University, 2015.

Lacan, Jacques. *The Four Fundamental Concepts of Psychoanalysis*. Translated by Alan Sheridan. New York: Norton, 1978.

La Meri. *The Gesture Language of the Hindu Dance*. New York: Columbia University Press, 1941.

Lee, Anthony W. *The Global Flows of Early Scottish Photography: Encounters in Scotland, Canada, and China*. Montreal: McGill-Queen's University Press, 2019.

———. *A Shoemaker's Story: Being Chiefly about French Canadian Immigrants, Enterprising Photographers, Rascal Yankees, and Chinese Cobblers in a Nineteenth-Century Factory Town*. Princeton, NJ: Princeton University Press, 2008.

Légeret-Manochhaya, Katie. *Rodin and the Dance of Shiva*. New Delhi: Niyogi Books, 2016.

Lewis, George E. "Foreword: Who Is Jazz?" In *Jazz Worlds/World Jazz*, edited by Philip V. Bohlman and Goffredo Plastino, ix–xxiv. Chicago: University of Chicago Press, 2016.

Lillethun, Abbe F. "Batik in America: Javanese to Javanesque, 1893–1937." PhD diss., Ohio State University, 2002.

———. "Javanese Effects: Appropriation of Batik and its Transformations in Modern Textiles." *Textile Society of America, 9th Biennial Symposium Proceedings* 431 (2004). http://digitalcommons.unl.edu/tsaconf/431.

Littell, Robert. "Every One Likes Chocolate." *Vogue*, November 1, 1936.

Lubelsky, Isaac. *Celestial India: Madame Blavatsky and the Birth of Indian Nationalism*. Sheffield, UK: Equinox, 2012.

MacDougall, David. "Photo-Hierarchicus: Signs and Mirrors in Indian Photography." *Visual Anthropology* 5, no. 2 (1992): 103–129.

———. "Photo-Wallah: An Encounter with Photography." *Visual Anthropology Review* 8, no. 2 (1992): 96–100.

MacDougall, David, and Judith MacDougall. *Photo Wallahs: An Encounter with Photography in Mussourie, a North Indian Hill Station*. Film. Berkeley, CA: Berkeley Media, 2000.

MacLeod, Kristin. "The Library Dream-Prince: Carl Van Vechten and America's Modernist Cultural Archives Industry." *Libraries & Cultural Record* 46, no. 4 (2011): 360–387.

Maholay-Jaradi, Priya, ed. *Baroda: A Cosmopolitan Provenance in Transition*. Mumbai: Marg Foundation, 2015.

Marchesani, Robert B., and E. Mark Stern. *Frightful Stages: From the Primitive to the Therapeutic*. Hawthorne, NJ: Hawthorne, 2001.

Martin, John. "The Dance: Art of India, Shan-Kar Criticized as Departing from Canons of the Indian Classic Dance." *New York Times*, April 2, 1934.

———. "Ram Gopal Is Seen Here in Hindu Dances: Cobra Number the High Point in His New York Debut," *New York Times*, May 2, 1938.

Mathur, Saloni. *India by Design: Colonial History and Cultural Display*. Berkeley: University of California Press, 2007.

McCaulay, Elizabeth Anne. *A. A. E. Disdéri and the Carte de Visite Portrait Photograph*. New Haven, CT: Yale University Press, 1985.

McNeil, Peter. *Pretty Gentlemen: Macaroni Men and the Eighteenth Century Fashion World*. New Haven, CT: Yale University Press, 2018.

———. "'That Doubtful Gender': Macaroni Dress and Male Sexuality." *Fashion Theory* 3, no. 4 (1999): 411–448.

Meduri, Avanthi. "Bharatha Natyam—What Are You?" *Asian Theatre Journal* 5, no. 1 (Spring 1988): 1–22.

———. "Temple Stage as Historical Allegory in Bharatanatyam: Rukmini Devi as Dancer-Historian." In *Performing Pasts: Reinventing the Arts in Modern South India*, edited by Indira Viswanathan Peterson and Devesh Soneji, 133–164. New Delhi: Oxford University Press, 2008.

Mellor, David, ed. *Germany, the New Photography 1927–1933: Documents and Essays*. London: Arts Council of Great Britain, 1978.

———. "London-Berlin-London: A Cultural History. The Reception and Influence of the New German Photography in Britain 1927–33." In *Germany, The New Photography 1927–1933: Documents and Essays*, edited by David Mellor, 113–132. London: Arts Council of Great Britain, 1978.

Mijer, Pieter. *Batiks and How to Make Them*. New York, Dodd, Mead, 1925.

"Mohan Khokar Dance Archives of India, The." *Attendance: Dance Annual of India*. Accessed December 26, 2020. http://attendance-india.com/dance-archives-of-india/.

Morgan, Willard D. "Enlarging and Contact Printing." In *The Leica Manual: A Manual for the Amateur and Professional Covering the Entire Field of Leica Photography*, by Willard D. Morgan and Henry M. Lester, 145–162. New York: Morgan and Lester, 1935.

Morgan, Willard D., Henry M. Lester. *The Leica Manual: A Manual for the Amateur and Professional Covering the Entire Field of Leica Photography*. New York: Morgan and Lester, 1935.

Mumford, Kevin. *Interzones: Black/White Sex Districts in Chicago and New York in the Early Twentieth Century*. New York: Columbia University Press, 1997.

Nair, Janaki. *Mysore Modern: Rethinking the Region under Princely Rule*. Minneapolis: University of Minnesota Press, 2011.

———. "Mysore's Wembley? The Dasara Exhibition's Imagined Economies." *Modern Asian Studies* 47, no. 5 (September 2013): 1549–1587.

———. *The Promise of the Metropolis: Bangalore's Twentieth Century*. New Delhi: Oxford University Press, 2005.

National Portrait Gallery. "Carl Van Vechten." Object no. NPG.2000.36. Accessed August 19, 2021. https://npg.si.edu/object/npg_NPG.2000.36?destination=edan-search/default_search%3Fpage

%3D3%26return_all%3D1%26edan_local%3D1%26edan_q%3Dmiguel%252Bcovarrubias%252B.

Njegosh, Tatiana Petrovich. "'Africa and Broadway': Carl Van Vechten's Harlem as an American Spectacle of Color." *European Contributions to American Studies* 53 (2004): 223–242.

Okiji, Fumi. *Jazz as Critique: Adorno and Black Expression Revisited*. Stanford, CA: Stanford University Press, 2018.

O'Shea, Janet. *At Home in the World: Bharata Natyam on the Global Stage*. Middletown, CT: Wesleyan University Press, 2007.

Padgette, Paul. *The Dance Photography of Carl Van Vechten*. New York: Schirmer Books, 1981.

Pasi, Alessandro. *Leica: Witness to a Century*. New York: Norton, 2004.

Perry, Regina. Introduction to *Van Der Zee*, edited by De Lilaine Cock and Reginald McGhee, 8–17. New York: Morgan and Morgan, 1973.

Pinckney, Warren R., Jr. "Jazz in India: Perspectives on Historical Development and Musical Acculturation." *Asian Music* 21, no. 1 (Autumn 1989–Winter 1990): 35–77.

Pinney, Christopher. *Camera Indica: The Social Life of Indian Photographs*. Chicago: University of Chicago Press, 1998.

——. *The Coming of Photography in India*. London: British Library, 2008.

——. *"Photos of the Gods": The Printed Image and Political Struggle in India*. London: Reaktion, 2004.

Pinney, Christopher, and Nicholas Peterson, eds. *Photography's Other Histories*. Durham, NC: Duke University Press, 2003.

Plastino, Goffredo. "Jazz Napoletano: A Passion for Improvisation." In *Jazz Worlds/World Jazz*, edited by Philip V. Bohlman and Goffredo Plastino, 309–337. Chicago: University of Chicago Press, 2016.

Poole, Deborah. *Vision, Race, and Modernity: A Visual Economy of the Andean Image World*. Princeton, NJ: Princeton University Press, 1997.

Powell, Richard J., and Virginia M. Mecklenburg. *African American Art: Harlem Renaissance, Civil Rights Era, and Beyond*. Washington, DC: Smithsonian American Art Museum, 2012.

Purkayastha, Prarthana. "Dancing Otherness: Nationalism, Internationalism, and the Work of Uday Shankar." *Dance Research Journal* 44, no. 1 (Summer 2012): 69–92.

Raeburn, John. *A Staggering Revolution: A Cultural History of Thirties Photography*. Urbana: University of Illinois Press, 2006.

Rahman, Sukanya. *Dancing in the Family: The Extraordinary Story of the First Family of Indian Classical Dance*. New Delhi: Speaking Tiger, 2019.

Ramaswamy, Sumathi. *The Goddess and the Nation: Mapping Mother India*. Durham, NC: Duke University Press, 2010.

Rangan, Pooja. *Immediations: The Humanitarian Impulse in Documentary*. Durham, NC: Duke University Press, 2017.

——. "Transitions, Transactions: Bollywood as Signifying Practice." In *Sarai Reader: Frontiers (The Edge of Frame)*, 272–285. New Delhi: Centre for the Study of Developing Societies, 2007.

Ray, Romita. "Orientalizing the Bayadere/Fabricating Mata Hari." *Photographies* 5, no. 1 (March 2012): 87–111.

Ray, Sugata. "The 'Effeminate' Buddha, the Yogic Male Body, and the Ecology of Art History in Colonial India." *Art History* 38, no. 5 (November 2015): 916–939.

Rayner, Nicola. "Strike a Pose." *Dancing Times* 109, no. 1307 (July 2019): 23–25.

Roberts, Mary. *Intimate Outsiders: The Harem in Ottoman and Orientalist Art and Travel Literature*. Durham, NC: Duke University Press, 2007.

Roberts, Mary, and Jill Beaulieu, eds. *Orientalism's Interlocutors: Painting, Architecture, Photography*. Durham, NC: Duke University Press, 2002.

Rosen, Jeff. *Julia Margaret Cameron's "Fancy Subject": Photographic*

Allegories of Victorian Identity and Empire. Manchester, UK: Manchester University Press, 2016.

Rosenberg, Douglas, ed. *The Oxford Handbook of Screendance Studies*. New York: Oxford University Press, 2016.

———. *Screendance: Inscribing the Ephemeral Image*. Oxford: Oxford University Press, 2012.

Rutherford, Emma. *Silhouette*. New York: Rizzoli, 2009.

Ruyter, Nancy Lee Chalfa. *La Meri and Her Life in Dance: Performing the World*. Gainesville: University Press of Florida, 2019.

Ryan, James. *Picturing Empire: Photography and Visualization of the British Empire*. London: Reaktion Books, 1997.

Sancho, Vittoria A.-T. "Respect and Representation." *Third Text*, no. 44 (Autumn 1998): 55–68.

Schanke, Robert A. *"That Furious Lesbian": The Story of Mercedes de Acosta*. Carbondale: Southern Illinois University Press, 2003.

Sekula, Allan. "Photography and the Limits of National Identity." *Gray Room* 55 (Spring 2014): 28–33.

Sewell, R. "Review of Ars Asiatica, No. III by A. Rodin, A. Coomaraswamy, E. Havell, V. Goloubew." *Journal of the Royal Asiatic Society of Great Britain and Ireland*, no. 1 (January 1923): 126–128.

Shah, Purnima. "Transcending Gender in the Performance of Kathak." *Dance Research Journal* 30, no. 2 (Autumn 1998): 2–17.

Shah, Reena. *Movement in Stills: The Dance and Life of Kumudini Lakhia*. Ahmedabad, India: Mapin, 2005.

Shawn, Ted. *Gods Who Dance*. New York: Dutton, 1929.

Shilliam, Nicola J. "From Bohemian to Bourgeois: American Batik in Early Twentieth Century." *Contact, Crossover, Continuity: Proceedings of the Fourth Biennial Symposium of the Textile Society of America*, September 22–24, 1994, 253–263. http://digitalcommons.unl.edu/tsaconf/1052.

Sikand, Nandini. "Bodies and Borders: The Odissi Costume Controversy." In *Dance Matters Too: Markets, Memories, Identities*, edited by Pallabi Chakravorty and Nilanjana Gupta, 58–59. New York: Routledge, 2018.

Sinha, Ajay. "Carl Van Vechten." *Accelerate: Access & Inclusion at the Tang Teaching Museum* (Frances Young Tang Teaching Museum, Skidmore College), no. 2 (2018): 14–15.

———. "Mysore Modern across the Arts." In *K. Venkatappa and His Times*, edited by Pushpamala N. and Deeptha Achar. New Delhi: Routledge, forthcoming.

———. "Notes on a Painting of a Painted Photograph." *Trans Asia Photography Review* 3, no. 2 (Spring 2013). http://tapreview.org.

———. "Pushpamala N. and the 'Art' of Cinephilia in India." In *Transcultural Turbulences: Towards a Multi-sited Reading of Image Flows*, edited by Ronald Wenzlhumer and Christiane Brosius, 221–248. Berlin: Springer, 2011.

Sinha, Ajay, and Raminder Kaur, eds. *Bollyworld: Popular Indian Cinema through a Transnational Lens*. New Delhi: Sage, 2005.

Sinha, Mrinalini. *Colonial Masculinity: The "Manly Englishman" and the "Effeminate Bengali" in the Late Nineteenth Century*. Manchester, UK: Manchester University Press, 1995.

Smalls, James. *The Homoerotic Photography of Carl Van Vechten: Public Face, Private Thoughts*. Philadelphia: Temple University Press, 2006.

Solomon-Godeau, Abigail. "The Armed Vision Disarmed: Radical Formalism from Weapon to Style." In *The Contest of Meaning: Critical Histories of Photography*, edited by Richard Bolton, 83–107. Cambridge, MA: MIT Press, 1989.

Soneji, Devesh, ed. *Bharatanatyam: A Reader*. New Delhi: Oxford University Press, 2010.

———. *Unfinished Gestures: Devadasis, Memory, and Modernity in South India*. Chicago: University of Chicago Press, 2012.

South Asian Diaspora Arts Archive. "Ram Gopal in Javanese Costume Playing King Klana—Photograph." Accessed August 17, 2018. https://sadaa.co.uk/archive/dance/ram-gopal/ram-gopal-in-javanese-costume-playing-king-klana-photograph.

Srinivasan, Amrit. "The Hindu Temple Dancer: Prostitute or 'Nun'?" *Cambridge Anthropology* 8, no. 1 (1983): 73–99.

——. "Reform and Revival: The Devadasi and Her Dance." *Economic and Political Weekly* 20, no. 44 (1985): 1869–1876.

——. "Why Sadir?" *Seminar* 676 (December 2015): 33–37.

Stein, Gertrude, and Carl Van Vechten. *The Letters of Gertrude Stein and Carl Van Vechten, 1913–1946*. Edited by Edward Burns. New York: Columbia University Press,1986.

Stern, E. Mark. "The Awesome and the Awestruck: Bessie Smith and Carl Van Vechten." *Psychotherapy Patient* 11, nos. 3–4 (2001): 27–35.

Street, Sarah, and Joshua Yumibe. *Chromatic Modernity: Color, Cinema, and Media of the 1920s*. New York: Columbia University Press, 2019.

Stuelke, Patricia. "The Queer Optimism of Jessie Tarbox Beals' Greenwich Village Postcards." *Photography and Culture* 7, no. 3 (November 2014): 285–302.

Sundaram, Vivan, and Deepak Ananth. *Umrao Singh Sher-Gil: His Misery and His Manuscript*. New Delhi: Photoink, 2008.

Thaggert, Miriam. *Images of Black Modernism: Verbal and Visual Strategies of the Harlem Renaissance*. Amherst: University of Massachusetts Press, 2010.

Thompson, Krista. "The Evidence of Things Not Photographed: Slavery and Historical Memory in British West Indies." *Representations* 113, no. 1 (2011): 39–71.

——. *An Eye for the Tropics: Tourism, Photography, and Framing the Caribbean Picturesque*. Durham, NC: Duke University Press, 2006.

Trachtenberg, Alan. "Mirror in the Marketplace: American Responses to the Daguerreotype, 1839–51." In *Lincoln's Smile and Other Enigmas*, 3–25. New York: Hill and Wang, 2007.

Trouillot, Michel-Rolph. *Silencing the Past: Power and the Production of History*. 1995. Reprint, Boston: Beacon, 2015.

Um, Nancy. *Shipped but Not Sold: Material Culture and Social Protocols of Trade during Yemen's Age of Coffee*. Perspectives on Global Pasts. Honolulu: University of Hawai'i Press 2017.

Van Vechten, Carl. *The Blind Bow-Boy*. 1923. Edited with introduction by Kirsten MacLeod. Cambridge, UK: Modern Humanities Research Association, 2018.

——. *The Dance Writings of Carl Van Vechten*. Edited by Paul Padgette. New York: Dance Horizons, 1981.

——. "The Editor's Workbench." *Trend* 8, no. 1 (October 1914): 100–101.

——. "In Defence of Bad Taste." In *The Merry Go Round*, 11–21. New York: Knopf, 1918.

——. *The Nigger Heaven*. New York: Knopf, 1926.

——. "Pastiches et Pistaches." *Reviewer*, no. 2 (February 1922): 268–273.

——. *Peter Whiffle: His Life and Works*. New York: Knopf, 1922.

——. "Portraits of the Artists." *Esquire* 57 (December 1962): 170–174, 256–258.

——. "The Reminiscences of Carl Van Vechten." Interview by William Ingersoll. Oral History Research Office, Columbia University, New York, March 3, 1960.

——. *Spider Boy*. New York: Knopf, 1928.

——. *The Tiger in the House*. New York: Knopf, 1920.

——. "War Is Not Hell." *Trend* 8, no. 2 (November 1914): 146–152.

Venkatachalam, G. *Dance in India*. Bombay: Nalanda, n.d.

Venkateswaran, Usha. *The Life and Times of La Meri: The Queen of Ethnic Dance*. New Delhi: Indira Gandhi National Center for the Arts, 2005.

Vertinsky, Patricia, and Aishwarya Ramachandran. "Uday Shankar and the Dartington Hall Trust: Patronage,

Imperialism, and the Indian Dean of Dance." *Sport in History* 38, no. 3 (2018): 289–306.

Wall-Romana, Christoph. "Epstein's *Photogénie* as Corporeal Vision: Inner Sensation, Queer Embodiment, and Ethics." In *Jean Epstein: Critical Essays and New Translations*, edited by Sarah Keller and Jason N. Paul, 51–73. Amsterdam: Amsterdam University Press, 2012.

Ward, Janet. *Weimar Surfaces: Urban Visual Culture in the 1920s Germany*. Berkeley: University of California Press, 2001.

Warren, Vincent. "Yearning for the Spiritual Ideal: The Influence of India on Western Dance, 1626–2003." *Dance Research Journal* 38, nos. 1–2 (Summer–Winter 2006): 97–114.

Waters, Ethel, with Charles Samuels. *His Eye Is on the Sparrow: An Autobiography*. New York: Da Capo, 1992.

Waugh, Thomas. "Posing and Performance: Glamour and Desire in Homoerotic Art Photography, 1920–1945." In *The Passionate Camera: Photography and Bodies of Desire*, edited by Deborah Bright, 58–77. New York: Routledge, 1998.

Weinberg, Jonathan. "Boy Crazy: Carl Van Vechten's Queer Collection." *Yale Journal of Criticism* 7, no. 2 (1994): 25–49.

Wessels-Mevissen, Corinna. "Introducing a God and His Ideal Form: A. K. Coomaraswamy's 'Dance of Siva,' 1912/1918." *Indo-Asiatische Zeitschrift: Mitteilungen der Gesellschaft für indo-asiatische Kunst, Berlin* 16 (2012): 30–42.

Wexler, Laura. "I Am a Camera: The Photographic Process and the Reconfiguration of the Self." *Berkshire Review*, 1982, 118–131.

White, Edward. *The Tastemaker: Carl Van Vechten and the Birth of Modern America*. New York: Farrar, Straus and Giroux, 2014.

Williams, Lyneise E. *Latin Blackness in Parisian Visual Culture, 1852–1932*. New York: Bloomsbury, 2019.

Windover, Michael. *Art Deco: A Mode of Mobility*. Québec City: Presses de l'Université du Québec, 2012.

Wipplinger, Jonathan O. *The Jazz Republic: Music, Race, and American Culture in Weimar Republic*. Ann Arbor: University of Michigan Press, 2017.

Wollen, Peter. *Paris/Manhattan: Writings on Art*. London: Verso, 2004.

Youngerman, Suzanne. "Movement Notation Systems as Conceptual Frameworks: The Laban System." *Journal for the Anthropological Study of Human Movement* 19, no. 2 (Fall 2012): 33–45.

Yumibe, Joshua. "The Color Image." In *The Image in Early Cinema: Form and Material*, edited by Scott Curtis, Philippe Gauthier, Tom Gunning and Joshua Yumibe, 142–150. Bloomington: Indiana University Press, 2018.

Zabel, Gary. "Adorno on Music: A Reconsideration." *Musical Times* 130, no. 1754 (April 1989): 198–201.

Zervigón, Mario Andrés. "Photography's Weimar-Era Proliferation and Walter Benjamin's Optical Unconscious." In *Photography and the Optical Unconscious*, edited by Shawn Michelle Smith and Sharon Sliwinski, 32–47. Durham, NC: Duke University Press, 2017.

INDEX

ABOUT THE AUTHOR

Ajay J. Sinha is a professor of art history at Mount Holyoke College in South Hadley, Massachusetts. He is coeditor with Raminder Kaur of *Bollyworld: Popular Indian Cinema through a Transnational Lens* and author of *Imagining Architects: Creativity in the Religious Monuments of India*.